HANDBOOKS

GRAND CANYON

KATHLEEN BRYANT

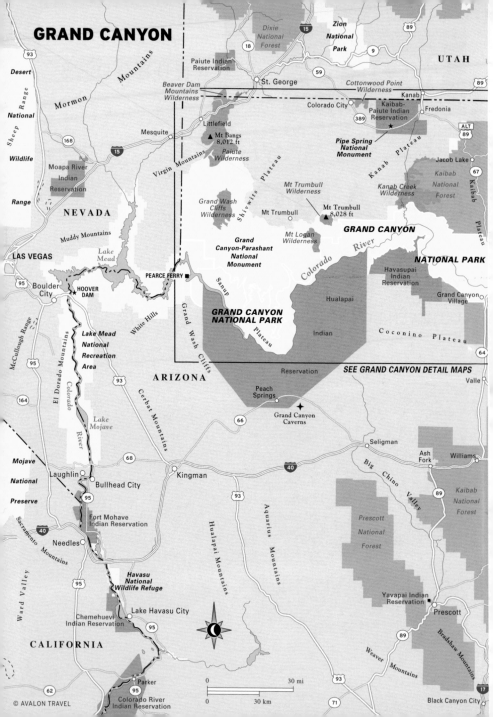

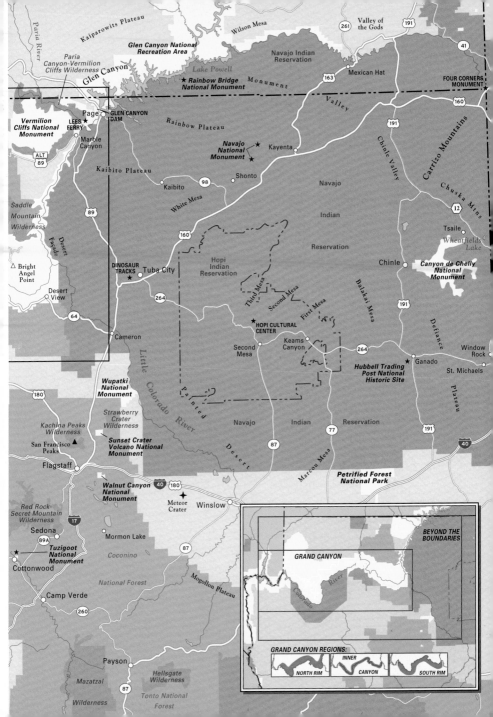

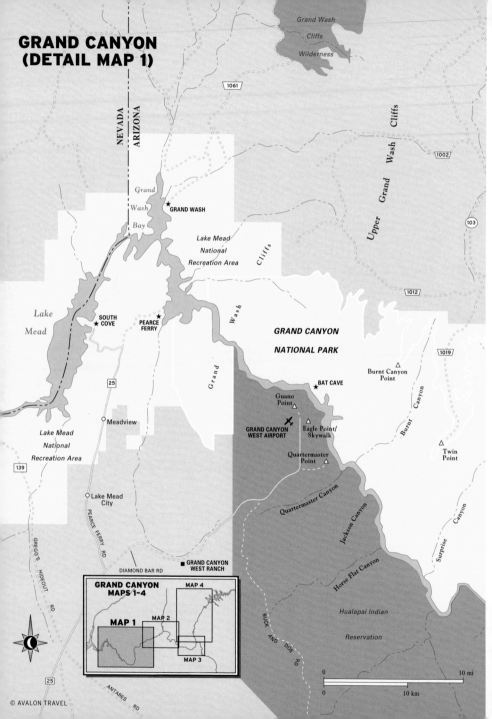

MAP SYMBOLS

Expressway	**◖**	Highlight	✕	Airfield	⚲	Golf Course
Primary Road	○	City/Town	✈	Airport	**P**	Parking Area
Secondary Road	◉	State Capital	▲	Mountain	▲	Archaeological Site
Unpaved Road	⊛	National Capital	✦	Unique Natural Feature	⚲	Church
Trail	★	Point of Interest			⛟	Gas Station
Ferry	•	Accommodation	🕊	Waterfall		Glacier
Railroad	▼	Restaurant/Bar	▲	Park		Mangrove
Pedestrian Walkway	▪	Other Location	**⊓**	Trailhead		Reef
Stairs	Λ	Campground	⛷	Skiing Area		Swamp

CONVERSION TABLES

°C = (°F - 32) / 1.8
°F = (°C x 1.8) + 32
1 inch = 2.54 centimeters (cm)
1 foot = 0.304 meters (m)
1 yard = 0.914 meters
1 mile = 1.6093 kilometers (km)
1 km = 0.6214 miles
1 fathom = 1.8288 m
1 chain = 20.1168 m
1 furlong = 201.168 m
1 acre = 0.4047 hectares
1 sq km = 100 hectares
1 sq mile = 2.59 square km
1 ounce = 28.35 grams
1 pound = 0.4536 kilograms
1 short ton = 0.90718 metric ton
1 short ton = 2,000 pounds
1 long ton = 1.016 metric tons
1 long ton = 2,240 pounds
1 metric ton = 1,000 kilograms
1 quart = 0.94635 liters
1 US gallon = 3.7854 liters
1 Imperial gallon = 4.5459 liters
1 nautical mile = 1.852 km

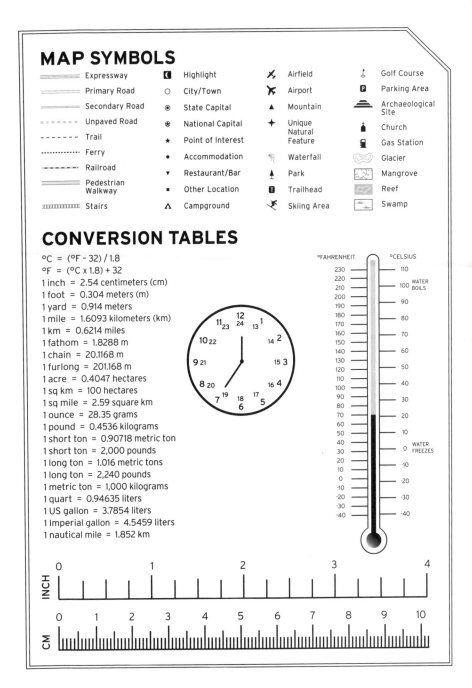

MOON GRAND CANYON

Avalon Travel
a member of the Perseus Books Group
1700 Fourth Street
Berkeley, CA 94710, USA
www.moon.com

Editor: Elizabeth Hollis Hansen
Series Manager: Sabrina Young
Copy Editor: Christopher Church
Graphics Coordinators: Sean Bellows, Elizabeth Jang
Production Coordinators: Sean Bellows,
    Elizabeth Jang
Cover Designer: Elizabeth Jang
Map Editor: Albert Angulo
Cartographers: Kat Bennett, Kaitlin Jaffe,
    Chris Hendrick
Proofreader: Danielle Miller
Indexer: Greg Jewett

ISBN-13: 978-1-59880-899-5
ISSN: 1537-1840

Printing History
1st Edition – 1999
5th Edition – October 2011
5 4 3 2 1

Front cover photo: Lightning over the Grand Canyon © designpics/123rf.com

Title Page: from Toroweap Overlook, Lava Falls below © Kathleen Bryant

Interior color photos: p. 12 Lee's Ferry at sunset © Kathleen Bryant; p. 13 (left) aspen leaves © Kathleen Bryant, (middle) Hedgehog cactus blooms © Kathleen Bryant, (right) the Desert View Watchtower © Kathleen Bryant, (bottom) South Rim view © Chee-Onn Leong/123rf.com; p. 14 (inset) wild rose along North Kaibab Trail © Kathleen Bryant, (bottom) Yaki Point looking east to Vishnu Temple © Kathleen Bryant; p. 15 (top left) Navajo weavings for sale at Hopi House © Kathleen Bryant, (top right) hiker on Cliff Spring Trail © Kathleen Bryant, (bottom left) Hopi House, designed by Mary Colter © Kathleen Bryant, (bottom right) Bighorn sheep in the Inner Gorge © Mark Lellouch, NPS; p. 16, 18, 19, 20, 21 © Kathleen Bryant; p. 22 © Richard Mayer; p. 23 © Kathleen Bryant; p. 24 Richard Mayer; p. 26, 27 © Kathleen Bryant

Printed in Canada by Friesens

KEEPING CURRENT

If you have a favorite gem you'd like to see included in the next edition, or see anything that needs updating, clarification, or correction, please drop us a line. Send your comments via email to feedback@moon.com, or use the address above.

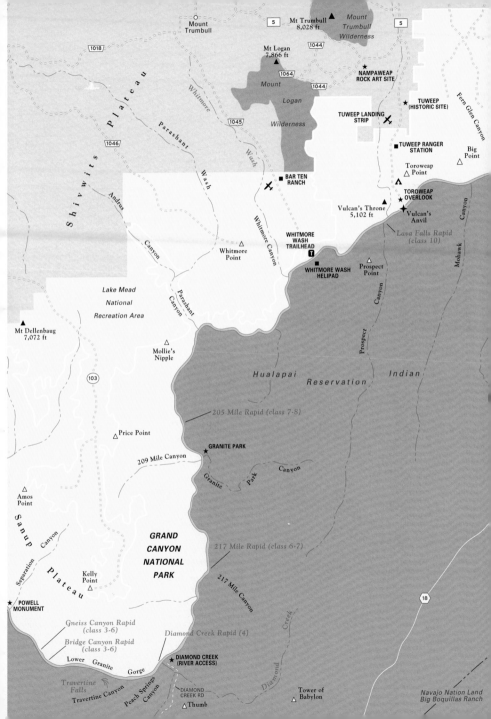

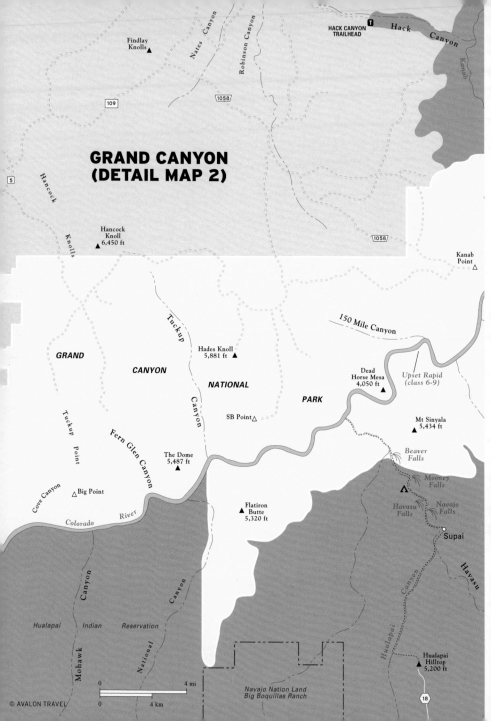

GRAND CANYON (DETAIL MAP 2)

Findlay Knolls ▲

Nates Canyon

Robinson Canyon

HACK CANYON TRAILHEAD

Hack Canyon

Kanab

109

1058

5

Hancock Knolls

Hancock Knoll ▲ 6,450 ft

1058

Kanab Point △

Tuckup Canyon

150 Mile Canyon

GRAND

CANYON

Hades Knoll 5,881 ft ▲

NATIONAL

Dead Horse Mesa 4,050 ft ▲

Upset Rapid (class 6-9)

PARK

Mt Sinyala 5,434 ft ▲

SB Point △

Tuckup Point

Fern Glen Canyon

The Dome 5,487 ft ▲

Beaver Falls

Mooney Falls

Cove Canyon

Big Point △

Flatiron Butte 5,320 ft ▲

Havasu Falls

Navajo Falls

Colorado River

Supai

Havasu

Mohawk Canyon

National Canyon

Hualapai Indian Reservation

Hualapai Canyon

Havasu

Hualapai Hilltop 5,200 ft ▲

0   4 mi

0   4 km

Navajo Nation Land Big Boquillas Ranch

18

© AVALON TRAVEL

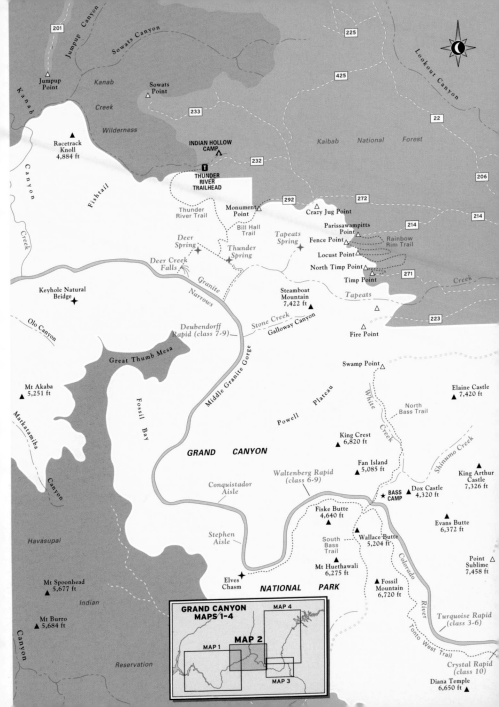

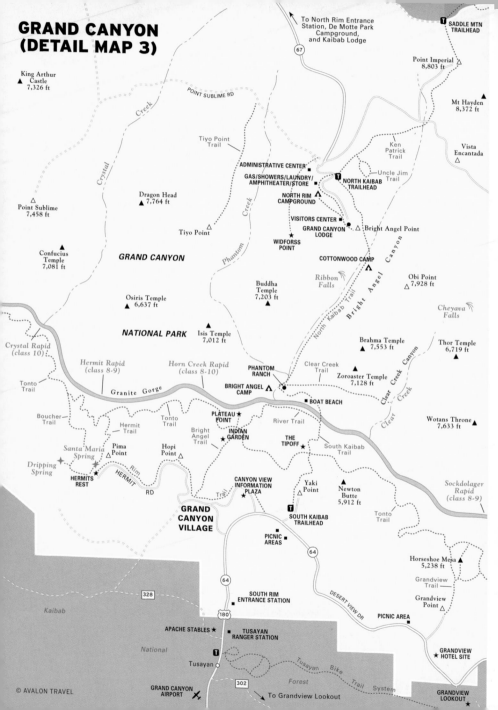

GRAND CANYON (DETAIL MAP 3)

King Arthur Castle 7,326 ft

To North Rim Entrance Station, De Motte Park Campground, and Kaibab Lodge

67

SADDLE MTN TRAILHEAD

Point Imperial 8,803 ft

POINT SUBLIME RD

Mt Hayden 8,372 ft

Tiyo Point Trail

Ken Patrick Trail

Vista Encantada

Point Sublime 7,458 ft

Dragon Head 7,764 ft

ADMINISTRATIVE CENTER

GAS/SHOWERS/LAUNDRY/ AMPHITHEATER/STORE

NORTH KAIBAB TRAILHEAD

Uncle Jim Trail

Tiyo Point

NORTH RIM CAMPGROUND

Confucius Temple 7,081 ft

GRAND CANYON

VISITORS CENTER

GRAND CANYON LODGE

Bright Angel Point

WIDFORSS POINT

COTTONWOOD CAMP

Osiris Temple 6,637 ft

Buddha Temple 7,203 ft

Ribbon Falls

Obi Point 7,928 ft

Cheyava Falls

NATIONAL PARK

Isis Temple 7,012 ft

Brahma Temple 7,553 ft

Thor Temple 6,719 ft

Crystal Rapid (class 10)

Hermit Rapid (class 8-9)

Horn Creek Rapid (class 8-10)

PHANTOM RANCH

Clear Creek Trail

Zoroaster Temple 7,128 ft

Tonto Trail

Granite Gorge

BRIGHT ANGEL CAMP

BOAT BEACH

Wotans Throne 7,633 ft

Boucher Trail

Hermit Trail

Tonto Trail

PLATEAU POINT

River Trail

Santa Maria Spring

Bright Angel Trail

INDIAN GARDEN

THE TIPOFF

South Kaibab Trail

Dripping Spring

Pima Point

Hopi Point

HERMITS REST

HERMIT RD

CANYON VIEW INFORMATION PLAZA

Yaki Point

Newton Butte 5,912 ft

Tonto Trail

Sockdolager Rapid (class 8-9)

GRAND CANYON VILLAGE

SOUTH KAIBAB TRAILHEAD

PICNIC AREAS

64

Horseshoe Mesa 5,238 ft

Grandview Trail

328

SOUTH RIM ENTRANCE STATION

DESERT VIEW DR

Grandview Point

PICNIC AREA

Kaibab

180

APACHE STABLES

TUSAYAN RANGER STATION

GRANDVIEW HOTEL SITE

National

Tusayan

302

Tusayan Bike Trail System

GRAND CANYON AIRPORT

To Grandview Lookout

Forest

GRANDVIEW LOOKOUT

© AVALON TRAVEL

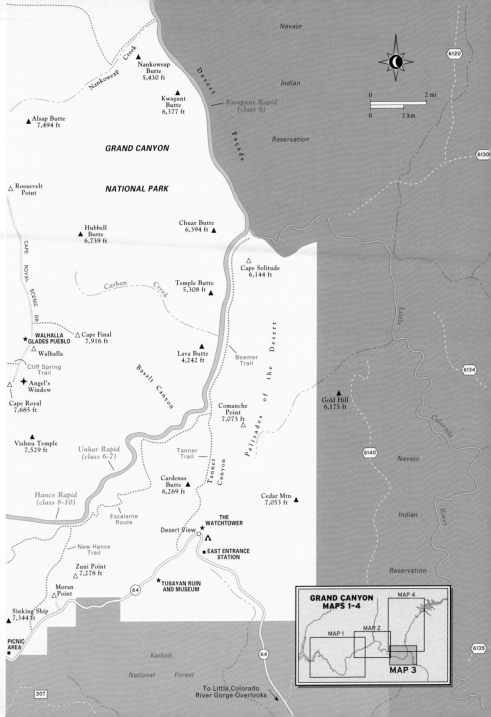

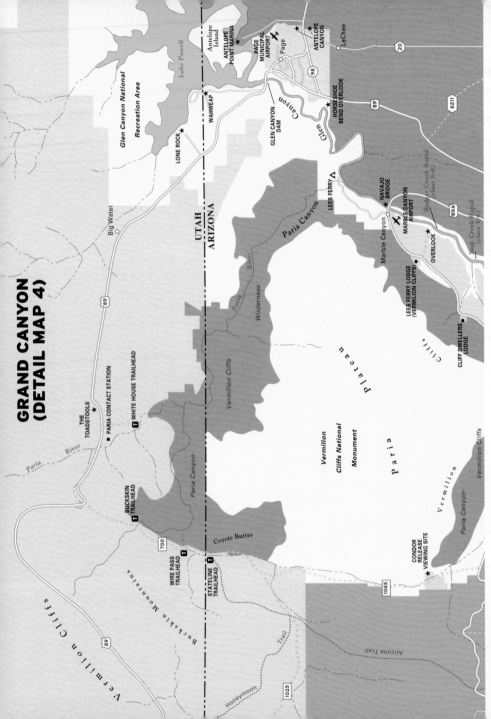

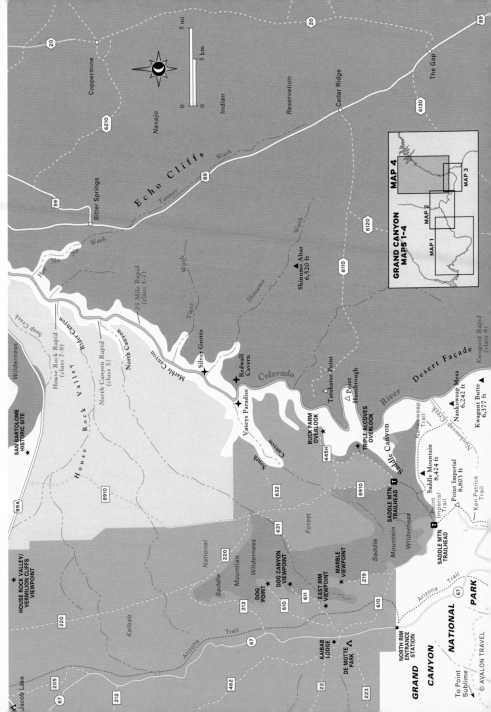

Contents

Discover
Grand Canyon

Grand Canyon is so vast and rugged that it seems completely beyond the human experience. Yet people have lived along its river and rim for 10,000 years, moving with the seasons and leaving behind signs of their passing in rock art, stone pueblos, and pottery shards. The canyon's diverse environments, from low desert to montane forest, support more than 2,000 species of plants, mammals, birds, reptiles, amphibians, and fish, including several endangered and threatened species.

The canyon's cliffs are a history book of the planet. The layered spectrum of red, orange, gray, and tan stone record three eras of geological time, with rocks along the Colorado River that are 2 billion years old. The canyon itself is "only" 5 or 6 million years old... and still changing. Wind and moisture continue to sculpt fantastical stone shapes one grain of sand at a time. But nature doesn't always work slowly – a room-sized platform of limestone at Mather Point toppled overnight after appearing in thousands of postcards and snapshots. One storm turned Crystal Rapids from a mellow ride to a feared torrent. Recent floods destroyed one waterfall in tributary Havasu Canyon and created two more. Grand Canyon is a place of grand drama and serene vistas.

Grand Canyon National Park's mile-deep abyss and 1.2 million acres hold a multitude of experiences and environments, from the North Rim's boreal forests to the desert environs along the Colorado River, from

bustling Grand Canyon Village to wild and lonesome wilderness. Visitors can tour a 1,000-year-old pueblo or step onto the Skywalk, the 70-foot-long glass-bottomed observation deck stretching over Grand Canyon West at the Hualapai Reservation.

Ever since travelers began coming to the canyon more than 100 years ago, they have struggled to describe its vastness. Although one 1892 visitor referred to Grand Canyon as a "great hole in the ground," the canyon is actually a collection of gorges and peaks. Sinuously curved side canyons, secret waterfalls, towering monuments of stone – any one of these would be a landmark attraction someplace else. Here, places like Vishnu Temple, Elves Chasm, or Matkatamiba Canyon are just small pieces of a whole that is considered one of the world's seven greatest natural wonders.

In 1903, Teddy Roosevelt urged every American to see Grand Canyon. Today, some 5 million visitors each year explore the canyon's expanses by hiking, backpacking, mule riding, or river rafting. With something here for everyone, Grand Canyon truly is America's park.

Planning Your Trip

▶ WHERE TO GO

The South Rim

The South Rim, the most visited area of Grand Canyon National Park, extends roughly 40 miles from Hermits Rest to Desert View. Scenic overlooks offer views of the canyon and its maze of tributaries, monuments, and rivers. For most visitors, Mather Point offers the stirring first glimpse of the canyon. Grand Canyon Village bustles with lodging, dining, shopping, and activities from bicycle tours to star parties. Architect Mary Colter's eccentric buildings perch along the rim, and several South Rim hiking trails lead into the canyon's depths.

Mather Point at sunrise

The North Rim

The North Rim, inaccessible in winter due to heavy snow, is 1,000 feet higher than the South Rim and more remote. Only one in 10 park visitors sees the North Rim. Most activities center on Bright Angel Point, where Grand Canyon Lodge and the park's campground offer canyon views. Scenic Cape Royal Drive leads to Point Imperial and Angel's Window, with stops for picnicking and hiking along the way. Jacob Lake is the nearest town, about 30 miles from the park's entrance station and the heart of neighboring Kaibab National Forest, where back roads wind through 1,000 square miles of evergreen and aspen to canyon overlooks, open meadows, and trails. The North Rim's mixed boreal forests include fir, spruce, and aspen.

The Inner Canyon

Accessible only on foot, by mule, or by boat, the inner canyon contains tall buttes and monuments, hidden waterfalls, and tributary canyons, all connected by the Colorado River. The river drops nearly 2,000 feet

IF YOU HAVE . . .

- **A WEEKEND OR TWO DAYS:** Go to the South Rim, stop at one of the visitors centers, see the sights at Grand Canyon Village, hike along the Rim Trail, and explore Hermit Road.

- **A WEEK:** Add Desert View Drive and, if it's summer, spend a couple of days on the North Rim, or take a mule trip to Phantom Ranch in the Inner Canyon.

- **TWO WEEKS:** Add a visit to Havasu Canyon and Supai Village, or sign up for a rafting trip through the Inner Canyon.

- **THREE WEEKS:** Raft the length of the canyon, and spend a few days exploring the North and South Rims, including scenic drives and hikes.

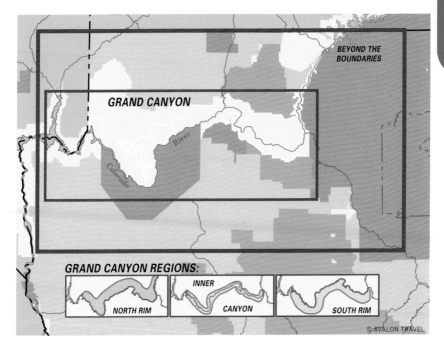

BEYOND THE BOUNDARIES

GRAND CANYON

River

Colorado

GRAND CANYON REGIONS:

INNER

NORTH RIM

CANYON

SOUTH RIM

© AVALON TRAVEL

on its 277-mile journey from Lees Ferry to Lake Mead, churning over close to 200 rapids. The dangerously hot desert environs of the Inner Gorge are relieved by springs and creeks. Historic Phantom Ranch offers the only lodging and dining in the heart of the canyon.

Beyond the Boundaries

The rims and tributaries of Grand Canyon extend beyond national park boundaries into land managed by the Forest Service and Bureau of Land Management or held by the Havasupai, Hualapai, and Navajo tribes. Havasu Canyon, the Grand Canyon Skywalk, historic Lees Ferry, and Marble Canyon overlooks all lie beyond the boundaries of the park but share the spirit of Grand Canyon. Though exploring remote areas sometimes requires a high-clearance vehicle and a permit to enter Native American lands,

those who want to escape the crowds will be rewarded by lonely vistas, rich cultural traditions, and landscapes that vary from stark desert to dense forest.

Gateways to Grand Canyon

Flagstaff, Williams, Page, Fredonia, and Kanab all promise convenient access to the canyon, but each of these gateway towns offers much more than that. The mountain town of Flagstaff combines urban pleasures with a dazzling array of outdoor activities. Williams will delight train buffs and Route 66 fans. At Page, Lake Powell's sandstone canyons lure boaters and backpackers alike. Fredonia and Kanab straddle the Arizona-Utah border and make a convenient jumping-off point not only for the North Rim but also for Zion, Bryce Canyon, and other national parks and monuments on the Grand Circle of the Southwest.

▶ WHEN TO GO

High season is April–October (with an early blip in March on the South Rim during spring break). For the North Rim, high season doesn't begin until mid-May, and summer is the only season, unless a snowy 50-mile trek sounds like fun. But don't let winter keep you from the canyon: The South Rim can be magical in winter, and the inner canyon is temperate for hikers and backpackers, though commercial river trips don't run. Winter is also an especially good time for watching wildlife. Deer and elk wander close to Grand Canyon Village, and ponderosa pines shelter juncos, nuthatches, and chickadees. Keep in mind that the higher North Rim can be inaccessible in winter months.

Autumn is a glorious time to visit Grand Canyon. Summer crowds have eased, and summer temperatures lose their grip on the South Rim and inner canyon. Warm, sunny afternoons and clear nights bring ideal hiking weather. On the North Rim, aspens begin to turn gold in September, peaking the first week of October. Summer lingers longer on the South Rim—fall doesn't arrive with a burst of color but with a musical crescendo as the annual Grand Canyon

Music Festival begins. If you're a birder, bring your binoculars, because September and October are great months to watch migrating raptors use the canyon as a flyway.

Spring is a little chancier—snow can blanket North Rim locations into May, and spring snowstorms aren't uncommon on either rim. Wildflowers begin blooming in the inner canyon deserts, moving up to the South Rim by April, adding splashes of red, yellow, and purple along rocky rim overlooks. Temperatures are usually comfortable, though the rim can be windy, especially in March.

Summer at Grand Canyon requires coping strategies. Though mornings and evenings on both rims are relatively cool, the midday sun bakes trails and overlooks, and the inner canyon becomes a shadeless furnace. Time hikes for early or late in the day, choose trails with afternoon shade, and pack plenty of water. Or head for the higher environs of the North Rim, where purple lupine lingers under a canopy of aspen and spruce, and mule deer graze in mountain meadows.

Be ready for anything. Even on the South

Aspen trees turn gold along forest roads in Kaibab National Forest.

Blue lupine blankets the forest floor in late spring and summer.

Rim, it can snow in June, and it isn't uncommon for temperatures to hit 90°F in October. Canyon roads, trails, and buildings may close temporarily for needed maintenance. Your cell phone may not get a signal, and the train could be late. But the afternoon thunderstorm that spoils your hike to Indian Garden might yield a rainbow during a sunset viewed from Yaki Point.

What to Take

No matter what season you visit, you'll want to bring an easy-to-carry water bottle and moisturizers for your skin and lips as well as protection from wind and sun. Weather conditions can change quickly. Layering is the best strategy to help you shift from chilly mornings to sunny afternoons. Pack for your activities: broken-in boots for a hike, a small flashlight for camping or for walking around Grand Canyon Village at night, a waterproof jacket if you're visiting during the summer monsoon.

What you won't need at Grand Canyon is a tie or dressy heels. As long as you lose the backpack and put on a pair of clean jeans and a nice shirt, you'll pass—even at El Tovar, the canyon's swankiest restaurant.

▶ BEFORE YOU GO

Visitors to the Grand Canyon most often fly into Phoenix or Las Vegas and then travel overland via bus, train, or car. Accommodations outside the canyon can be found in the gateway cities of Flagstaff, Williams, and Page. Reservations are a must. River trips and mule tours often fill up six months to a year in advance, and backpacking permits require careful trip planning and applications up to four months before the month of your trip. Accommodations on the South Rim often sell out during high season. North Rim rooms are especially hard to get during autumn, when aspens turn gold and leaf-peepers head for higher elevations.

If you travel the Grand Canyon area by car, gas up whenever you get the chance, especially if you plan on exploring roads in the national forest or reservation lands surrounding the park, where distances are great and service stations few. Even on the South Rim, there's only one gas station inside park boundaries, and it's 25 miles from Grand Canyon Village. And always, always keep water in the car.

To make the most of your time, do your research in advance. The National Park Service website (www.nps.gov/grca) includes helpful tools for planning a trip, including permit applications, trail closures, backpacking advice, and weather forecasts.

Explore Grand Canyon

▶ THE BEST OF GRAND CANYON

Though a week isn't nearly enough time to experience all of Grand Canyon's dimensions (length, width, and depth), it's time enough to sample some of the best the canyon has to offer: sightseeing on both the North and South Rims, plus hiking a corridor trail or taking a mule trip into the canyon's heart. For a sampling of scenery, history, and activity, tour the South Rim from Hermits Rest east to Desert View, driving through the Navajo Reservation and Marble Canyon area before winding up the Kaibab Plateau to Jacob Lake and the canyon's quiet north side.

Day 1

Begin at the South Rim's Grand Canyon Village, taking a day to get used to the elevation and acquaint yourself with the canyon. Check in at the Bright Angel Lodge Transportation Desk to confirm your mule tour reservations and schedule an orientation session that afternoon. In the meantime, take

in a ranger program or nature walk. If you plan to hike into the canyon rather than ride a mule, loosen up with a walk along the Rim Trail. The section from the village to Mather Point doubles as a sightseeing excursion. You'll intersect with the path to Mather Circle and Shrine of the Ages, where many ranger programs are held. You can even travel through time with the trailside geology displays. At Yavapai Observation Station and the Grand Canyon Visitors Center and its surrounding plaza, you can learn more about the geological layers you'll be passing through when you make your descent into the canyon. Enjoy sunset colors on the walk back to the village.

Day 2

Have a hearty breakfast before meeting your mule and the rest of the riders at the Old Stone Corral near the Bright Angel Trailhead. As you enter the first tunnel on Bright Angel Trail, look up to the left at the pictographs

Yavapai Observation Station

Mormon tea growing at Hopi Point

on the cliff wall. You're descending a route used for centuries by Havasupai Indians before it was adapted as a toll "road" by prospector and politician Ralph Cameron in the late 1800s. The trail is now on the National Register of Historic Places. Midday, you'll have a chance to dismount, stretch your legs, and eat a sack lunch at Indian Garden, where Cameron maintained a tourist camp. Bright Angel Trail gets more scenic with every hoofbeat as you follow Garden Creek deeper into the canyon, arriving at Phantom Ranch in the afternoon. You can stretch saddle-sore legs with a stroll around the historic stone-and-wood cabins designed by architect Mary Colter, or a walk to the Ancestral Puebloan ruin near the campground. If you're feeling more energetic, hike a mile or two up the Clear Creek Trail for fabulous views of Phantom Ranch and the Inner Gorge. Or spend the rest of the day drinking lemonade and writing postcards. Dinner at the canteen is steak, stew, or a veggie alternative.

Day 3

After a flapjack breakfast at Phantom Ranch, you'll saddle up for the trip out of the canyon. Mule trips ascend the South Kaibab Trail, traversing colorful Cedar Ridge before topping out on Yaki Point at midday, where a waiting bus returns you to the village. After lunch, rent a bike or take the Hermit Road shuttle to explore the West Rim. From the Trailview Overlook, you can see parts of the Bright Angel Trail you traveled the day before. Other overlooks offer distinct perspectives, from the wide panorama at Hopi Point to the sheer drop down from The Abyss. You can leave the shuttle to hike along sections of the Rim Trail, or find a perch to watch the play of light and shadow. Pick out a spot for sunset before heading back to the village for dinner, or come prepared with sandwiches from the General Store deli to eat at the best table in the house—the edge of the canyon.

Day 4

Make your last morning in Grand Canyon Village special. You could ride the early shuttle to Yaki Point and watch the sunrise, have a leisurely breakfast at historic El Tovar Lodge, or take in a ranger program. Order a box lunch from one of the lodges or pack a picnic from the deli to take with you as you explore the East Rim on Desert View Drive. Beginning just south of Mather Point, Highway 64 travels miles to Desert View. Stop at Grandview Point to gaze down at

Horseshoe Mesa, then continue to Tusayan Ruin. You can take a self-guided tour of this 800-year-old dwelling, or look around the adjacent museum and bookstore while you wait for the next ranger-guided tour. You'll want at least an hour at Desert View to enjoy the views of the eastern canyon and explore Mary Colter's fabulous Watchtower. If you haven't packed a picnic, try to save your appetite for the Cameron Trading Post, 30 miles away on the Navajo Reservation. En route, you'll follow the edge of the Little Colorado River Gorge, a major canyon tributary. You can spend the night at the trading post's comfortable motel or drive up to Page, arriving in time to watch the sun set over Lake Powell.

Day 5

Start your day in Page with a smooth-water float from Glen Canyon Dam to Lees Ferry, a scenic voyage on the Colorado River between gorgeously colored sandstone cliffs. Canyon Discoveries will shuttle you back to Page, where you can begin the three-hour drive to the North Rim. As you descend toward Marble Canyon on U.S. 89A, stop at the Glen Canyon National Recreation Area Visitors Center. Here, you can walk across the Colorado River on the historic Navajo Bridge. As you drive

Vermilion Cliffs from House Rock Valley

toward Jacob Lake, look south for glimpses of the canyon, a dark gash across the broad Marble Platform. The Vermilion Cliffs rise above you on the north. The road quickly ascends the Kaibab Plateau. From Jacob Lake, it's a scenic 50 miles to the North Rim, passing through ponderosa forest and aspen-lined meadows. Watch the sunset from the tip of Bright Angel Point or, if you've made reservations, from the expansive dining-room windows at Grand Canyon Lodge.

Day 6

Get up early for sunrise at Point Imperial. You can spend several hours exploring sights along the Cape Royal Road as it winds to the end of the Walhalla Plateau. Take time for a hike to Cape Final, about two hours, or the Cliff Spring Trail, less than an hour. Stop at Walhalla Overlook to learn more about the Ancestral Puebloans who once called the canyon home. Cape Royal, where you can gaze through Angel's Window or look down on Wotans Throne, is a lovely picnic spot. Return to the lodge for a ranger program or a stroll through the ponderosas on the Transept Trail. Toast your last canyon sunset from the lodge's veranda, watching as lights from Grand Canyon Village begin to twinkle across the canyon, 10 miles away.

Day 7

If you don't need an early start on the long return to back civilization, you could begin your last day at Grand Canyon with a hike, heading partway down the North Kaibab Trail or getting a fresh canyon perspective from the rim-side Widforss Trail. Or you could drive the back roads to Jacob Lake, exploring shady forest byways as you plan your next canyon visit. Because this is when it hits you: Even though you've toured the national park from rim to river, west to east, and north to south, there's so much more you want to see. Maybe you could call in sick?

A ROMANTIC WINTER WEEKEND

Winter is a romantic time to visit the South Rim.

The most romantic time to visit the South Rim is during the winter, when crowds are light and the possibility of being snowed-in beckons. **El Tovar** offers a special romance package from late November to mid-February. Or reserve one of the historic cabins at **Bright Angel Lodge.** Some have fireplaces or rim views. If you want to impress your sweetie with a romantic candlelight dinner, make reservations for El Tovar's elegant dining room.

After breakfast the next morning, pick up a picnic lunch at the General Store deli and spend a few hours exploring the overlooks along the West Rim's **Hermit Road.** Weather permitting, you can hike the Greenway to the Abyss (the mile-deep plunge is sure to have you snuggling closer), then warm up with some hot chocolate at **Hermits Rest.** Rumor has it that the architect of this fanciful structure, Mary Colter, liked to steal away for a few moments of solitude along the rim close by. If it's not too icy, you might try looking for her special perch or hiking a short distance down nearby Hermit Trail.

Winter sunsets arrive early, often painting the canyon walls in brilliant orange, pink, and lavender, thanks to the sun's low angle. **Hopi Point** is the most popular sunset spot; opt for **Maricopa** or **Mohave Points** if you'd prefer to avoid a crowd. After watching the show, you can return to the village and warm up by your cabin's fireplace. No fireplace of your own? There's usually a blaze going in **El Tovar's Rendezvous Room,** and the lounge is a cozy spot for a hot drink. After dinner, bundle up for a **moonlight stroll along the Rim Trail,** spend some time in the art gallery at **Kolb Studio,** or attend a program at **Shrine of the Ages.**

Sunrise or sleep in? If you decide to greet the dawn from somewhere other than your window, grab a quick bite at the **Canyon Coffee House** in Bright Angel Lodge, and hop the shuttle to **Yaki Point.** You may be the only ones to enjoy the **sunrise** from this beautiful overlook, but perhaps you'll find a fellow traveler to snap a photo of you and your sweetie. Return to the village for a hearty breakfast or early lunch.

Afterward, stroll along the rim to **Hopi House,** designed by architect Mary Colter in 1905. Inside this historic structure is the canyon's finest collection of Native American jewelry, perfect if you want to buy a memento of your special weekend. Spend the rest of the day exploring the **East Rim** by car, watching **sunset from Lipan Point** or the **Desert View Watchtower,** another Colter creation. To the west, inner canyon temples and buttes fade to blue and purple as golden light strikes the colorful hills and valleys of **Unkar Delta** and the sheer limestone walls of **Marble Canyon** – a dramatic finale for your weekend.

► FOUR DAYS OF FAMILY FUN

Day 1

If this is your family's first trip to Grand Canyon, you can learn about the canyon's geology, ecology, and human history on a one- or two-day program led by an instructor from the Grand Canyon Field Institute. The two-day program includes meals and lodging as well as a guided hike partway down Bright Angel Trail and a walking tour of historic Grand Canyon Village. Activities are suitable for adults and children aged 10 and older.

Younger children can learn about the canyon by becoming a Junior Ranger. Kids aged 4–14 earn a certificate and badge when they participate in ranger-guided hikes or activities. The Junior Ranger activity book will help keep kids focused as your family explores the canyon through a variety of programs, such as condor talks, fossil walks, or stargazing.

Day 2

If you haven't signed up for a two-day tour, arrange a mule trip or bike ride for your second day at the canyon. There's no age limit for the three-hour mule ride to the Abyss, though riders need to be at least 4 feet 7 inches tall. Children younger than 16 must be accompanied by an adult on this ride through piñon-pine forest to the most dizzying overlook on the West Rim. If you'd rather not travel here by mule, Bright Angel Bicycles rents adult- and youth-sized bikes and guides tours to the Abyss. Children younger than age eight can ride in a pull-trailer behind Mom or Dad.

Alternately, you can spend a few hours exploring the West Rim and Hermits Rest on the park's free shuttle buses. If you'd like to walk along the rim or picnic at an overlook, you can linger and wait for a later shuttle bus to continue your journey.

Day 3

After a day or two of guided explorations, you may want to strike out on your own. Though all hikes leading into the canyon are steep (with drop-offs that will terrify some parents),

sunset from Bright Angel Point

GRAND CANYON WILD

Maybe you've already visited Grand Canyon Village and the other developed areas along the South and North Rims. Or perhaps you simply prefer your vacations to be a little on the wild side. If outdoor adventure is your passion, you're in luck: There's no better way to get to know Grand Canyon than by taking the road – or trail – less traveled. And in the process, you'll probably learn a lot more about yourself too.

WHITE-WATER RAFTING

On a guided Colorado River **white-water rafting trip**, long, peaceful stretches are sharply punctuated by wild rides through the canyon's 160-plus rapids. River guides lead hikes up intriguing side canyons, such as sinuously eroded **Matkatamiba,** and stop to frolic at waterfalls and pools. Most trips put in at **Lees Ferry** and take out at **Diamond Creek,** a journey lasting up to 18 days. If your time is limited, you can hike in or out at **Phantom Ranch** for a half-canyon trip. Outfitters include meals, gear, and shuttle service, so all you need to worry about is how you're going to readjust to the real world afterward.

HIKING AND BACKPACKING

You can also explore the wild side of the canyon on foot. No permits are needed for day hikes, and you could hike every day at the canyon for a week and still have plenty of trails left to explore. If you want to spend a night in the canyon, however, you must apply for a backpacking permit. The central corridor – **Bright Angel, South Kaibab,** and **North Kaibab Trails** – is busy, but it's best to start here if you don't have canyon experience, taking two or three days to hike and camping at **Indian Garden, Bright Angel,** or **Cottonwood Campgrounds.** If you're ready to graduate to a wilderness trail, **Grandview Trail to Horseshoe Mesa** or **Hermit Trail to the Colorado River** combine views with historic sites on 2–3-day trips. If you already have a degree in canyon backpacking, you can get your post-doc by planning a multiday trip

looping two or more trails together, such as the **Grandview-Tonto-South Kaibab loop.**

CLIMBING AND CANYONEERING

Grand Canyon is a treasure trove of peaks like **Vishnu, Zoroaster,** and **Shiva Temples.** There are no official routes, but climbers have tackled 150 of the canyon's summits. You can find out more by joining a climbing forum, hiring a guide, or signing on to a chartered river trip that has a climbing focus. Scores of tributary canyons like **Rider** or **Kanab** lead to the main canyon, many of them obstacle courses of pour-overs, pools, chockstones, and boulder fields. Canyoneering combines climbing skills with rock-hopping, hiking, and wading or swimming in order to descend and ascend canyon routes.

EXPLORING BACK ROADS

If you want to get away from it all on wheels, **Kaibab National Forest** has miles of dirt roads for driving or biking, and you'll rarely meet more than half a dozen other vehicles. Many forest roads are suitable for passenger cars, though they tend to get rockier as you approach remote North Rim viewpoints like **Parissawampitts** or **Timp Points,** which overlook the **Tapeats Amphitheater.** One of loneliest spots in Grand Canyon National Park is **Toroweap,** where 10 campsites await at the end of 60 miles of dirt roads. A trail leads to a rocky ledge where, 3,000 feet below, you'll see and hear roaring **Lava Falls.**

WINTER ADVENTURES

South Rim snowfalls usually aren't enough to tempt Nordic skiers, but on the other side of the canyon, the higher elevations of the **Kaibab Plateau** can be blanketed in white. Although roads and visitor services close on the park's North Rim mid-October–mid-May, you can **ski into the park** and **snow-camp** or reserve the park's **winter yurt.** If you'd rather stay cozy and warm at Jacob Lake Inn, you can **snowmobile, ski, or snowshoe** in surrounding **Kaibab National Forest.**

Colorado River from the Desert View overlook

many day-hike destinations partway down the trail are manageable for kids, including the hike to Ooh Aah Point (less than two miles round-trip) on the South Kaibab Trail. Start in early morning as this hike is dangerously hot and exposed during summer months, and bring plenty of water.

The Rim Trail is relatively level and easy to hike a section at a time, making it an ideal place to teach younger children about nature. The mile-long section between Verkamp's Visitors Center and the Yavapai Observation Station, known as the Trail of Time, highlights touchable samples of the canyon's rock layers. Rim Trail brochures, available near the Yavapai Observation Station, can be used to identify plants or animals. Seeing a squirrel or a mule deer can stimulate a conversation about why it's important not to feed animals or to get too close while taking a photo.

If wild animals are making themselves scarce, mules are a sure thing. Take an afternoon walk to the historic barns to watch the mules eat their dinner. Or, if your youngster is crazy about trains, you can head for the depot and watch the Grand Canyon Railway arrive or depart. (Better yet, begin your trip to Grand Canyon via the train, which departs from Williams in the morning and arrives at Grand Canyon before noon.)

The South Rim in particular has so many activities and sights that it's easy for kids (and adults) to get overwhelmed. Plan to disengage from the bustle for some quiet time, whether it's a shady rest in the ponderosa pine forest around the village or a nap in your room. If all else fails, take the kids to the Grand Canyon IMAX movie in nearby Tusayan, guaranteed to mesmerize them for 34 whole minutes.

Day 4

Drive or take a motor coach tour to Desert View, the South Rim's easternmost viewpoint. Stop to explore Tusayan Ruin, an 800-year-old pueblo that can be viewed from a gentle loop trail. Your kids will love climbing the winding staircase to the top of the Desert View Watchtower, the grand finale on this 25-mile scenic journey along the East Rim. From here, you have the option of returning to Flagstaff via U.S. 89A. If you have time, make a side trip through Wupatki and Sunset Crater Volcano National Monuments, where you can explore ancient pueblos or clamber up an extinct cinder cone.

▶ NATIVE AMERICAN LEGACY

Though it appears harsh and forbidding from the rim, Grand Canyon has provided food and shelter to people for thousands of years. Descendants of the canyon's first residents live in the region today. A 5–7-day trip exploring the canyon's native cultures combines archaeology, adventure, and sightseeing. The best time to schedule this trip is mid-September through October, when the South Rim and Havasu Canyon are less crowded and the monsoon season has ended. You'll need advance reservations for all lodging and to dine at El Tovar. You can obtain permits for visiting the Hualapai reservation when you arrive, but you must reserve your permit to visit Havasu Canyon well in advance.

Day 1

Travel to Grand Canyon via the Navajo Reservation. As you drive U.S. 89 north of Flagstaff, you'll skirt the Painted Desert, passing archaeological treasures such as Wupatki National Monument and historic sites that include Cameron Trading Post. On your way to the East Entrance Station, stop for views of the Little Colorado River, an important Hopi pilgrimage route. Spend an hour or two enjoying the panoramas at Desert View and the 70-foot-tall Watchtower. Architect Mary Colter studied Ancestral Puebloan watchtowers before designing her reconstruction, which opened in 1933. The striking murals and paintings inside are a symbolic history of Southwestern Native American cultures. Along Desert View Drive, several overlooks offer dramatic canyon views.

Historians believe that somewhere near Moran or Lipan Points, Hopi guides led Spanish conquistadors to the edge of the canyon in 1540. On the way to Grand Canyon Village, stop at the Tusayan Ruins and Museum, timing your visit for a tour or ranger program. Cohonina farmers occupied this masonry pueblo 800 years ago. The adjacent museum has displays of prehistoric, historic, and contemporary Native American cultures. Spend the night at one of the lodges or campgrounds in the village. If you dine at El Tovar, note the large paintings depicting Arizona Indian tribes, part of the hotel's original 1905 decor.

Day 2

After an early breakfast, visit Hopi House, designed by Mary Colter to resemble the pueblo of Old Oraibi. The gallery upstairs has museum-quality pottery, jewelry, carvings, and Navajo rugs. If your timing is right, you may be able to watch a rug weaver at work. But try to tear yourself away by late morning, because it's a three-hour drive from Grand Canyon Village to Peach Springs on the Hualapai Reservation. (If this is your

Desert View Watchtower, designed by Mary Colter

EXPLORING THE ECOSYSTEM

Do you want more from your vacation than a bunch of snapshots from the rim? Have you always wanted to learn how to backpack and camp in the wilderness? Have you ever wondered what it would be like to work as an archaeologist or geologist? Do you prefer active vacations that end with a sense of accomplishment?

During a learning vacation or service trip, you can get to know the canyon in the company of scientists, photographers, and other experts. The following organizations offer trips that are more than just sightseeing tours.

- **Grand Canyon Field Institute:** Offers classes from basic backpacking skills to botanical surveys collecting plants for the canyon's herbarium. Geology trips are a specialty, investigating the canyon from its popular central corridor to remote reaches like **Nankoweap Creek** or **Surprise Valley.**

- **Sierra Club:** Organizes volunteer trips to stabilize canyon trails or restore native vegetation.

- **Forest Service's Passport in Time Program:** In recent years, forest volunteers have surveyed archaeological sites near Grand Canyon's South Rim and restored historic **Hull Cabin** near Grandview Point.

- **Grand Canyon Volunteers:** This conservation group associated with Grand Canyon Trust leads hands-on volunteer projects for groups and individuals, such as removing invasive plants and collecting native seeds.

You'll benefit from your experiences on trips like these, and the canyon will too.

first visit to Grand Canyon, you'll probably want to schedule an extra night or two at the South Rim before continuing your trip.) En route, you can stop for lunch in the historic Route 66 towns of Williams or Seligman.

When you arrive at Peach Springs, check for tour possibilities at the Hualapai Lodge. The Hualapai (People of the Tall Pines), historically known for their vast trade network, have translated those entrepreneurial skills into tour operations, with rafting, 4WD, helicopter, and bus tours centered around Grand Canyon West, which is home to the Skywalk. If you don't have time for a tour today, you can arrange one for the last day of your trip.

Days 3-4

Spend the night at Hualapai Lodge and get an early start for the 65-mile dirt-road drive from Peach Springs to Hualapai Hilltop, the launch point for the 8.5-mile hike into Havasu Canyon, which takes about 3–4 hours. You can also arrange to travel by horse, mule, or helicopter, giving you more time (and energy) to explore Havasu Canyon and its magical creek and waterfalls. Historically, the Havasupai (People of the Blue-Green Water) roamed the length of Grand Canyon in search of game and plants, forging many of the trails used today for hiking. If you spend two nights at the lodge or campground, you'll have more time to enjoy the canyon's waterfalls and travertine pools, although it's possible to make this an overnight trip, especially if you travel by mule or helicopter.

Day 5

You may find yourself reluctant to leave this paradise for the long hike back to the rim. If you have time, explore more of the Hualapai Reservation before heading home, or be content to end your journey with visions of blue-green water still flowing in your mind.

THE SOUTH RIM

At more than 1,900 square miles, Grand Canyon National Park is larger than the state of Rhode Island and encompasses more land than Luxembourg, Liechtenstein, Malta, and Andorra put together. If Grand Canyon National Park were a nation itself, the South Rim's Grand Canyon Village would no doubt be its capital city, complete with a historic district, modern conveniences, and cosmopolitan flair.

Ever since the Santa Fe Railroad completed a spur line here in 1901, the village has been a launching point for sightseeing and recreation: traveling to overlooks for theatrical sunrises or sunsets, venturing below the rim for a day hike, touring ancient Indian ruins, watching mule wranglers hitch up for the ride down the trail. The village boasts half a dozen lodges, a bank, a post office, numerous gift shops, and a general store that stocks everything from toothpaste to tents.

If you grab an ice cream cone or cappuccino and wander the sidewalk between Bright Angel Lodge and Lookout Studio, you're as likely to hear German or Japanese as English. You can watch a Navajo rug weaver at work or attend a program hosted by a ranger raised in one of the Hopi villages. You can hike all day, then enjoy an elegant dinner at El Tovar, see an art or photography exhibit at Kolb Studio's gallery, or even listen to a live chamber orchestra during the canyon's annual music festival.

To this cultural mix, add the local critter population: mule deer wandering through the ponderosa pines at dawn or twilight, a gang of ravens raiding a trash bin, a skunk skulking through the parking lot at night. The South

© KATHLEEN BRYANT

HIGHLIGHTS

◖ Mather Point: Most visitors' first views of the canyon are from Mather Point. Across the road, Canyon View Information Plaza offers a shuttle stop, a ranger station, a bookstore, and all-around orientation to the canyon (page 44).

◖ Yavapai Observation Station: This historic pueblo-style building features displays of Grand Canyon's geology as well as fabulous views of the central canyon (page 44).

◖ Grand Canyon Village Historic District: Meet the human side of Grand Canyon – Fred Harvey and the Harvey Girls, the Kolb brothers, sheriff and Rough Rider Buckey O'Neill, and architect Mary Elizabeth Jane Colter. All are immortalized in the village's historic buildings (page 45).

◖ Hopi Point: Hopi Point is notable for its stunning sunrise and sunset views. You can see 30 miles or more in either direction: east to the Palisades of the Desert, and west to Havasupai Point (page 52).

◖ Hermits Rest: Mary Colter, an architect for the Santa Fe Railway, designed Hermits Rest in 1914 to resemble a prospector's cavern-like lair. She based her imaginary prospector on turn-of-the-century miner Louis Boucher, who hosted tourists at his camp at nearby Dripping Springs (page 53).

◖ Grandview Point: One of the highest points on the South Rim, Grandview delivers just what its name promises. From Grandview's ponderosa pine forest, look down on Horseshoe Mesa, where the Last Chance Mine once yielded copper ore (page 53).

◖ Tusayan Ruins and Museum: The Ancestral Puebloans summered in this 800-year-old masonry complex. The adjacent museum focuses on the canyon's prehistoric, historic, and contemporary Native Americans (page 53).

◖ Desert View Watchtower: From this 70-foot-high masonry tower designed by Mary Colter, you can see the Painted Desert and Vermilion Cliffs. Murals inside the tower, painted by Fred Kabotie and other artists, are a pictorial history of the Grand Canyon region's Native American past (page 54).

◖ Bright Angel Trail: Starting just west of Bright Angel Lodge, the Bright Angel Trail is not only a popular path into the canyon but also a national historic landmark. This prehistoric Indian route has been used by mule tours since pioneer times. Walking down the trail, even for a short distance, gives the sense of entering the canyon's embrace (page 58).

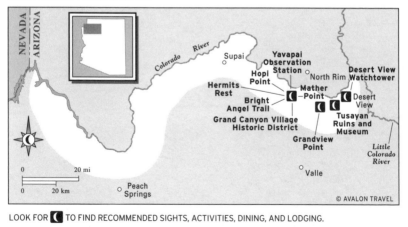

LOOK FOR ◖ TO FIND RECOMMENDED SIGHTS, ACTIVITIES, DINING, AND LODGING.

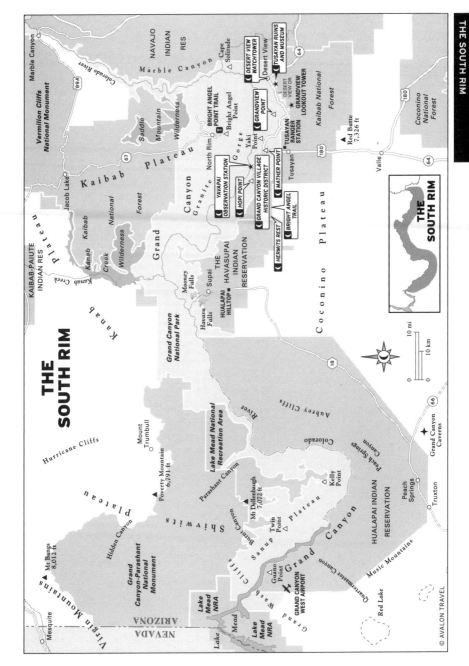

Rim offers a wide spectrum of experiences, along with spectacular views, fascinating history, comfortable lodging, and wilderness only a few steps away.

But even on a busy summer day, when the South Rim hosts upwards of 10,000 visitors, it's always possible to find a quiet spot along the edges. Minutes or even hours pass pleasantly, with limestone as your backrest and the canyon spread out at your feet as you watch cloud shadows chase each other across an infinity of cliffs.

PLANNING YOUR TIME

A quick note of orientation: The park's South Rim is further delineated into the West Rim, including the Grand Canyon Village area west to the end of Hermit Road, and the East Rim, beginning where Highway 64 turns east and ending at Desert View. The East Rim is generally higher, cooler, and less visited than the West Rim, well worth the additional 2–6 hours it takes to explore this side of the canyon.

You can sample the South Rim in two days, but a week allows time for a hike or two, a mule trip, and a leisurely exploration of the overlooks east and west of Grand Canyon Village. You can access the South Rim from either the south or the east, and it's possible to plan a loop route through Flagstaff. If you arrive from one direction and return in the other, you'll see a lot more of the Grand Canyon region, including the Navajo Reservation, Wupatki and Sunset Volcano National Monuments, the San Francisco Peaks, and the Route 66 towns of Flagstaff and Williams.

Set aside at least an hour or two during your visit to explore **Grand Canyon Village.** History and architecture buffs will want to spend even longer admiring the village's landmark structures, including El Tovar lodge, the train depot, and Lookout Studio. Buildings and sidewalks are most crowded during the afternoon, when tour buses unload and the train pulls into the station, so consider taking your village walking tour after dinner. Most of the gift shops, including historic Hopi House and Kolb Studio, are open late. Beware of slipping

into the dreaded village shuffle, though. You'll know you've succumbed when you find yourself staring zombielike at a gift-shop selection of polished rocks for the third time that day.

The remedy? Remember that the main attraction is the canyon itself. From east to west, overlooks are scattered along the rim like beads on a string, each offering a different perspective on the complex network of tributaries and temples that make up Grand Canyon. It helps to memorize a few landmarks, like Vishnu Temple, Plateau Point, or the Battleship, then watch how they seem to reshape themselves as distance or daylight changes.

You could easily spend two to four hours exploring the views west of the village, taking the Hermit Road shuttle or walking along sections of the gentle Rim Trail. For the best photos and fewest crowds, time your visit to the overlooks along Hermit Road for early morning. Sunsets are also dramatic, and crowds gather for the show like they would for an opening-night symphony performance.

East Rim overlooks are less crowded, and you have the option of touring them in your own vehicle, although you could also choose a guided motor-coach tour. (The exception is Yaki Point, closed to private vehicles year-round.) Although it's just 30 miles from the village to **Desert View,** the easternmost overlook, you'll need at least two hours to explore this section of the park. Sunrise and sunset panoramas of the eastern canyon and the river's broad Unkar Delta are especially good from Lipan Point or Desert View. Archaeology buffs will enjoy the guided walk of Tusayan Ruins, and kids will love climbing the watchtower at Desert View.

If you want to get to the bottom of the canyon, you'll need at least two days for mule riders or strong hikers, longer if you plan to explore some of the canyon's length. Corridor trails are the best choice for those new to hiking or to the canyon. Wilderness trails require backcountry skills and are best attempted in three days or more. Advance planning is essential, and backcountry permits go quickly for popular areas.

Do not attempt to hike from the rim to the river and back in one day. Park rangers rescue about 400 people a year in Grand Canyon, most of whom have overestimated their abilities. Day-hike destinations such as the **Bright Angel** rest-houses, Dripping Springs, Ooh Aah Point, Cedar Ridge, and Horseshoe Mesa are scenic, historic, and most definitely geologic. Though permits aren't required for day hikes, you still need to plan ahead to ensure you have adequate water, salty snacks, and sun protection. The myriad warnings about hiking in the canyon are meant to help you prepare, not to dissuade you. Walking below the rim, even a short distance, takes you into a different realm where your senses seem fresh and new and the world seems very, very old.

WEATHER AND SEASONS

In summer, temperatures along the rim are pleasant, topping out in the 80s. Because of low humidity and high elevation, daytime and nighttime temperatures can vary 30°F or more, so plan to wear layers and shed them by midday. On summer afternoons, temperatures below the rim can rise above 100°F, so plan your outdoor activities for early in the day. Afternoon thunderstorms are likely in July and August.

Spring and fall are usually ideal for outdoor activities, though the weather can change quickly. Hang on to your hat—sometimes literally. Sudden wind gusts can catch you by surprise, especially along overlooks.

The South Rim is open year-round, and winter hikes into the canyon might start in ice and snow, making trails treacherous, before leading into pleasant low-desert temperatures along the Colorado River.

Most winter precipitation lands on the South Rim between December and March, but snowstorms can strike anytime from November through May, occasionally making travel difficult. Closed roads usually reopen within a day or two, giving you access to a wonderland of pines embellished by snow and icicles.

Exploring the South Rim

Decisions, decisions: The South Rim offers a bounty of breath-stealing vistas, sites, trails, and tour options. When El Tovar opened in 1905, travelers would spend several weeks relaxing at the lodge and touring the rim. Today, most of us are lucky to have a few days, and it can be daunting to choose the activities and experiences that help us make the most of our visit. The South Rim comes in many flavors—peaceful, frenetic, adventurous, laid-back, historic, scenic, pristine, populated. Whether you decide to zero in on a single trail or to sample as much of the South Rim as you can, it's up to you research your options and pick your flavor. The better you plan, the more likely you'll be to get the flavor you ordered.

VISITORS CENTERS

Grand Canyon Visitors Center (8 A.M.–6 P.M. daily spring–fall, 9 A.M.–5 P.M. daily winter) is located across from Mather Point, about five miles north of the South Entrance. The visitors center complex with its adjoining plaza was designed as an all-in-one stop. Facilities include parking, picnic pavilions, shuttle stops, pay phones, restrooms, and a large store, **Books & More** (8 A.M.–8 P.M. daily spring–fall, 8 A.M.–6 P.M. daily winter). Outdoor kiosks introduce canyon geology, hiking, and other topics and are open 24 hours a day, although the plaza's lights go out at 9 P.M.

The plaza was originally designed to be the center of a light-rail system, but lack of support from Congress stalled the project, and the park has since added an enormous parking lot for vehicles. From here, you can opt to leave your vehicle behind and get on one of the park's free shuttle buses, or walk or bike the paved two-mile Greenway Trail that connects the visitors center to Grand Canyon Village.

The visitors center's main building has exhibits on natural history and news about the

Books & More, located near the Grand Canyon Visitors Center at the South Entrance

latest weather forecast, road conditions, and trail closures. Rangers are on hand to answer questions, and they love it when you ask one that tests their trail savvy or natural history knowledge, instead of just "Where are the bathrooms?" or "What time does the canyon close?" The adjoining theater, completed in spring 2011, seats 200 people for screenings of an orientation film. If you're interested in a guided tour or need to make shuttle arrangements to the North Rim, you can find out more at the transportation desk.

Ranger programs are scheduled throughout the day, and they're a good way to get to know the canyon in a short amount of time. Check the current schedule of programs in *The Guide* or posted inside the visitors center. You can also sign up the kiddos for the park's Junior Ranger Program here.

You'll find park information, copies of *The Guide,* and exhibits on the canyon's natural and cultural history at many other locations along the South Rim. Each of these smaller visitors centers has a special interpretive theme

or focus, and nearly all of them include retail areas with books and gifts:

- The **Yavapai Observation Station** (8 A.M.–8 P.M. daily spring–fall, 8 A.M.–6 P.M. daily winter) combines displays about the canyon's geology with afternoon ranger talks and the best indoor views of the canyon. A hands-on outdoor geology experience, Walk Through Time, follows the Rim Trail between the observation station and Verkamp's.

- **Verkamp's** (8 A.M.–8 P.M. daily spring–fall, 8 A.M.–6 P.M. daily winter) hosts ranger talks on its shady veranda. Indoors you'll find displays about the history of Grand Canyon Village and its pioneer residents.

- **Kolb Studio** (8 A.M.–8 P.M. daily spring–fall, 8 A.M.–6 P.M. daily winter) has displays about the Kolb Brothers, the adventurous photographers who constructed this multilevel building as their home and studio. Their downstairs movie auditorium is now an art gallery with rotating exhibits.

- **Park Headquarters** (8 A.M.–4:30 P.M. Mon.–Thurs.) houses the Grand Canyon's research library and the Shrine of the Ages Auditorium, where ranger programs and special events are held daily.

- The **Backcountry Information Center** (928/638-7875, 8 A.M.–noon and 1–5 P.M. daily), tucked behind Maswik Lodge, is the best resource for serious hikers and backpackers. You can learn more about trails and campsites, pick up a *Backcountry Trip Planner*, or apply for a backcountry permit.

- **Tusayan Museum** (9 A.M.–5 P.M. daily) exhibits and interprets the prehistory and history of the region's Native American cultures. The museum, located 22 miles east of the village on Desert View Drive, has a retail area specializing in titles on archaeology and anthropology. Ranger-guided walks of the ruins are held daily.

- The GCA-operated **Desert View Bookstore and Information Center** (9 A.M.–5 P.M. daily, if staffing permits) has an especially fine selection of children's books, games, and puzzles.

ENTRANCE STATIONS

The park's South Rim has two entrances, both located along Highway 64. Most visitors arrive via the larger **South Entrance,** accessible from Flagstaff or Williams. It seems like every couple of years the park adds more lanes to reduce waiting lines; still, traffic often backs up during summer weekends and holidays. But there are ways you can avoid idling in traffic on a sizzling summer afternoon. First, plan your arrival for the cooler, less busy morning or evening hours. Second, if you already have a Grand Canyon annual pass or an Interagency pass, you can skip the longest lines and use the special entry lane for prepaid fees. You can also use this faster lane if you prepay at the National Geographic Visitors Center (home of the *Grand Canyon* IMAX movie) in Tusayan, a mere two miles south of the entrance, or in the gateway city of Williams.

The **East Entrance Station** at Desert View is smaller than the South Entrance and receives far fewer visitors. About 30 miles east of Grand Canyon Village, the East Entrance Station is accessible via U.S. 89 and Highway 64. It adds a few miles to the drive from Flagstaff, but you can start off your visit to the canyon by exploring the East Rim overlooks on your way to Grand Canyon Village, arriving just about the time you can check into your room at the lodge.

When you enter, the ranger working the entry booth will hand you a copy of *The Guide,* the park's official newspaper. The South Rim edition is updated each spring, summer, and winter, listing current ranger programs, special events, sunrise and sunset times, and other helpful information, including the all-important map of parking areas and shuttle stops.

TOURS

You can see the Grand Canyon in many ways: on a guided tour, on foot, on a bike, on a mule or horseback, by air, by motor coach, or via a white-water adventure. In some cases, you'll need to plan ahead (four months to a year ahead for river expeditions, mule trips, or popular backpacking destinations), but even if you get the urge to take a tour after your bags are already unpacked, you'll have several options. A good place to start is at one of the **transportation desks** located around Grand Canyon Village. Think of the transportation desk as a concierge service focusing on tours. You'll find them at Grand Canyon Visitors Center and in Maswik, Bright Angel, and Yavapai Lodges. The transportation "concierge" can describe tour options and help you make reservations. Desk hours vary seasonally.

Hermit Road Driving Tour

Historic Hermit Road has seasonal restrictions on personal vehicles. Most of the year, free shuttle buses on the Hermits Rest Route leave every 15–30 minutes and stop at all the West Rim overlooks. You can get out and snap photos, catching the next shuttle bus or walking the Rim Trail to the next shuttle stop. You can also explore Hermit Road by Harveycar,

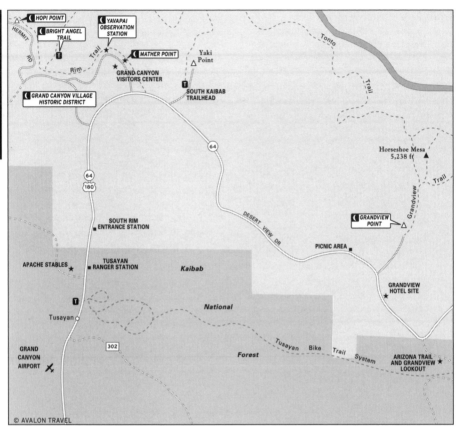

one of the guided motor coach tours operated by Xanterra Parks & Resorts. Either way, you can gawk at the views without worrying about the winding road. If you're sitting on the right-hand side of the bus, you'll be able to gaze out at the canyon during much of the ride to Hermits Rest.

From December through February, Hermit Road is open to passenger cars (weather permitting). The drive begins just west of Bright Angel Lodge, traveling between the canyon and the piñon-juniper woodland that characterizes much of the South Rim. From either of two **Trailview Overlooks,** you'll have outstanding views of the historic village and Bright Angel Trail.

Continuing on Hermit Road, about 1.5 miles from the village **Maricopa Point** is marked by the tram tower that once served the Lost Orphan Mine, which yielded copper and later uranium but ceased operations in the 1960s. Far below, the Inner Gorge reveals the oldest rocks in Grand Canyon, Zoroaster granite (pink) and Vishnu schist (gray-black). The formation below the rim to the right is known as the Battleship.

The memorial at **Powell Point,** two miles from the village, honors John Wesley Powell, the one-armed Civil War veteran who led the first expeditions down the Colorado River through Grand Canyon in 1869 and 1872.

The views from **Hopi Point,** the

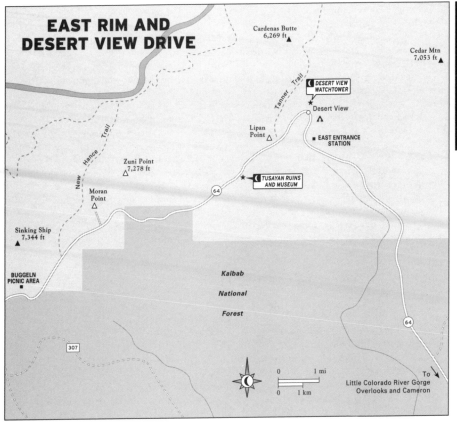

EAST RIM AND DESERT VIEW DRIVE

Cardenas Butte
6,269 ft ▲

Cedar Mtn
7,053 ft ▲

Tanner Trail

⊂ DESERT VIEW
WATCHTOWER ★

Desert View ○ △

Lipan
Point △

■ EAST ENTRANCE
STATION

New Hance Trail

Zuni Point
△ 7,278 ft

★ ⊂ TUSAYAN RUINS
AND MUSEUM

64

Moran
Point △

Sinking Ship
7,344 ft ▲

BUGGELN
PICNIC AREA ■

Kaibab

National

Forest

64

307

0   1 mi

0   1 km

To
Little Colorado River Gorge
Overlooks and Cameron

northernmost point on the South Rim, encompass the Palisades of the Desert to the east all the way to Havasupai Point on the west. It's a panorama nearly 100 miles wide, making this one of the most popular overlooks for viewing sunrise or sunset.

The Colorado River stretches in either direction far below **Mohave Point,** three miles west of the village. Three rapids—Hermit, Salt Creek, and Granite—are visible from this overlook. You might even be able to hear Hermit Rapids, the farthest west, formed by debris from Hermit Canyon.

A mile farther down Hermit Road, **The Abyss** marks one of the steepest drops from the canyon rim. The Great Mohave Wall, a sheer cliff of sandstone and limestone, plunges nearly 4,000 feet down to Monument Creek and Monument Canyon, named for the pillars found in its depth.

Pima Point is farther off the main road than the other overlooks, making it a good place to pause and enjoy the natural quiet. In addition to a sweeping panorama across the canyon, taking in the North Rim from Powell Plateau to Cape Royal, you can see the crumbling foundations of historic Hermit Camp below.

Built in 1914 as a rest stop for tourists traveling the West Rim stage, **Hermits Rest** was designed by architect Mary Colter. Inspired by Louis Boucher, a prospector who lived at Grand Canyon in the 1890s, Colter imagined the building as a cavern-like refuge carved out of the cliffs. The arched fireplace is 12 feet high and nearly 10 feet deep. It's said that Colter—who had a reputation for being a stern taskmaster—liked to relax on a natural limestone seat below the building. Just west of Hermits Rest, Hermit Trail begins its nearly 10-mile descent to the Colorado River. You'll find restrooms, a snack bar, and a gift shop at Hermits Rest, a National Historic Landmark.

Desert View Driving Tour

South of Grand Canyon Visitors Center, Highway 64 turns east for Desert View Drive, a scenic 23-mile stretch along the East Rim. This good paved road is open to personal vehicles year-round, though snow sometimes forces road closures for brief periods in the winter. From Pipe Creek Vista to Desert View, the road climbs through ponderosa forest to the South Rim's highest elevations. If you don't have a car, Xanterra Parks & Resorts offers guided bus tours along this route. The East Rim is much quieter than the Grand Canyon Village and Hermit Road areas—sweet relief from summer sun and summer crowds.

The paved turnout just past the intersection is **Pipe Creek Vista.** Stop for a good view of the central canyon, including Plateau Point and O'Neill Butte, though the views aren't as fine as from Yaki Point. Since Yaki Point is closed to private vehicles, many people make do with this easily accessed viewpoint marking the end of the Rim Trail.

Twelve miles east of the village, **Grandview Point** is one of the South Rim's highest overlooks at nearly 7,400 feet. Surrounded by quiet ponderosa pine forest, it's hard to believe this was once the hot spot at Grand Canyon and home to a hotel, tent cabins, and a mining operation centered on Horseshoe Mesa, visible below the rim. The Grandview Trail starts at the east end of the stone barrier and leads to the mesa 3,000 feet below.

About three miles past Grandview, you'll see the Buggeln picnic area, a shady and peaceful place for lunch. Although the rim is brushy here, you can walk through the forest for glimpses of the Sinking Ship, a rock formation that tilts back toward the rim.

Moran Point, overlooking Red Canyon, is one of the few rim overlooks that wasn't named for a North American Indian tribe. Moran Point honors artist Thomas Moran, who captured the canyon's dramatic vistas in drawings and paintings, including *Chasm of the Colorado,* which hung in the U.S. Capitol building in Washington, D.C., for many years. Moran was a member of explorer John Wesley Powell's third canyon expedition in 1873. His assignment was to sketch scenes that would be converted to engravings for magazine articles about the canyon.

Tusayan Ruins, 25 miles east of the village, was inhabited 800 years ago. This masonry complex of rooms sheltered about 30 people who farmed nearby in the summer, migrating to the canyon's floor in the winter. Rangers guide daily walks of the ruins. The adjacent museum highlights prehistoric and contemporary Native American cultures of the region and houses a small Grand Canyon Association bookstore. Restrooms are located just west of the building.

Lipan Point has one of the East Rim's best views, taking in the canyon from its turn west at the Palisades of the Desert to the Inner Gorge. Across the canyon is Cape Royal, and below it the rocks of the Grand Canyon Supergroup: soft, colorful layers carved into the hills and valleys above the river's Unkar Delta. Nearby, the challenging Tanner Trail leads to the river.

Navajo Point also has fine views of the colorful Supergroup layers. In 1540, Hopi guides led a detachment from Francisco Vásquez de Coronado's expedition to the rim of Grand Canyon somewhere in the vicinity of Navajo, Lipan, or Moran Points. Nearby, Hopi trails led into the canyon to sites that they still consider sacred today. We can imagine that the Hopi guides watched silently—and perhaps with some amusement—as the Spanish explorers tried to reach the river, a frustrating and failed endeavor they recorded in expedition journals.

Desert View, the easternmost overlook inside the park, offers views of the Colorado River as it exits Marble Canyon and bends west toward the Inner Gorge. Nearby is the park's East Entrance Station along with a campground, a gas station, a general store, a snack bar, and a bookstore. The highlight is Mary Colter's fabulous Watchtower, inspired by the Ancestral Puebloans (also known as the Anasazi). From the top of the 70-foot tower, you can look east to the Painted Desert.

Walking and Hiking Tours

Free **ranger-guided hikes** vary from a gentle nature stroll to a challenging four-hour hike to Cedar Ridge. Hikes focus on fossils, geology, flora and fauna, archaeology, and other topics. Walking tours include a stroll through the historic village. Tours and talks are scheduled throughout the day at various locations around the village, including Lookout Studio, Yavapai Observation Station, or the shady veranda at Verkamp's. Twice-daily tours of the Tusayan Ruins, located on the East Rim, last 30–45 minutes. Though fewer offerings are available in the winter, nature hikes and moonlight walks are usually among the year-round choices. See *The Guide* for the current program schedule.

The **Grand Canyon Field Institute** (GCFI, 800/858-2808, www.grandcanyon.org/field-institute) offers guided walking and hiking tours, some suitable for families with children as young as 10 years. GCFI is a nonprofit park partner with the goal of educating visitors and helping them enjoy the canyon.

Bicycle Tours

Bright Angel Bicycles (928/814-8704, www.bikegrandcanyon.com) rents bikes and offers a guided tour twice daily during spring and summer. The 5.6-mile West Rim ride ($40 adults, $32 children) includes all gear and lasts about 2.5 hours, traveling from Hopi Point to Hermits Rest. Guides stop at several overlooks en route. Round-trip shuttle service is included.

Air Tours

To see the canyon by helicopter or plane, you need to start outside the park. The nearest airport is in Tusayan, with airfields on the Hualapai Reservation (Grand Canyon West)

and at Marble Canyon. Air tours over Grand Canyon are strictly regulated by the Federal Aviation Administration and are confined to particular areas and routes that exclude the central canyon. (Arizona senator John McCain was among those who fought for quiet over Grand Canyon in 1987, setting a precedent for other national parks.) Even after being restricted to the western and eastern ends of the canyon, there are nearly 100,000 air tours annually—plenty of options for those who want to fly over the canyon, and plenty of irritation for those who prefer natural quiet in national parks.

Keep in mind as you shop for a tour that canyon routes are identical among companies, and your decision will probably be based on a company's customer service and the creativity of the packages it offers. Aircraft also vary in comfort, quiet, and visibility. Helicopter tours are generally more expensive but fly slower and lower. Companies listed below offer fixed-wing and helicopter tours from Grand Canyon Airport in nearby Tusayan. You can also find tours originating in Las Vegas, Phoenix, Page, and other locations. Most companies discount rates for children, and some offer discounts for tours booked online.

- **Air Grand Canyon** (928/638-2686 or 800/247-4726, www.airgrandcanyon.com) and **Grand Canyon Airlines** (928/638-2359 or 866/235-9422, www.grandcanyonairlines.com) offer options combining fixed-wing flights with helicopter flights, smooth-water rafting, and land tours. Tours are available in several languages.

- **Grand Canyon Helicopters** (928/638-2764 or 800/541-4537, www.grandcanyonhelicoptersaz.com) offers tours in several languages. Charter flights and custom itineraries are also available.

- **Papillon/Grand Canyon Helicopters** (928/638-2419 or 888/635-7272, www.papillon.com) offers a wide selection of destinations and tours, including package tours with hiking, rafting, Jeep, and bus options. Tours are offered in several languages in addition to English.

- **Maverick Helicopter Tours** (928/638-2622 or 888/261-4414, www.maverickhelicopter .com) offers custom charters and tours, including wedding packages, rafting packages, and flights to the Skywalk on the Hualapai Reservation.

Bus Tours

Following a tradition established by the Fred Harvey Company, which offered stagecoach or Harveycar tours during the early 1900s, **Xanterra South Rim** (303/297-2757 or 888/297-2757, fax 303/297-3175) offers year-round guided motor coach tours along the South Rim. Call or visit one of the transportation desks (928/638-2631) in Bright Angel Lodge, Maswik Lodge, or Yavapai Lodge for more information. Times vary according to season, but options include sunrise or sunset tours as well as scenic drives along Hermit Road and Desert View Drive. Tours are free for children age 16 and under with an accompanying adult.

The narrated **Hermits Rest Tour** ($25), more than two hours long, travels eight miles to overlooks along Hermit Road, also known as West Rim Drive. The **Desert View Tour** ($44) travels the East Rim, lasts nearly four hours, and stops at Lipan Point and the Desert View Watchtower. The highlight of the 90-minute **Sunrise Tour** ($20) is watching the sun come up over the curtain of cliffs known as the Palisades of the Desert. The **Sunset Tour,** also 90 minutes, travels either to Mohave Point or Yaki Point, introducing historic Grand Canyon Village en route. Two tours can be combined ($57) in any order or on different days.

Train Tours

The Santa Fe Railway completed a spur line to Grand Canyon in 1901. The railroad partnered with the Fred Harvey Company to build and manage El Tovar, Hopi House, and other attractions, luring tourist services away from their original center near Grandview Point. Eventually, automobiles outpaced train travel, and the last train pulled out of Grand Canyon station in 1968. For more than 20 years, the tracks were silent. They were on the verge of being torn up by a salvage company when a retired couple wound up with 20 miles of track

© KATHLEEN BRYANT

Train tours arrive daily at historic Grand Canyon Depot.

as repayment for a bad debt. Against the advice of business consultants, they determined to restore train service to the canyon.

Today, **Grand Canyon Railway** (800/843-8724, www.thetrain.com) offers four classes of passenger service from Williams to Grand Canyon's South Rim, including package tours that combine the train ride with lodging and guided rim tours. All train travel is on refurbished vintage rail cars powered by steam or diesel, depending on the season. Trains depart from Williams in the morning and leave the South Rim depot in the afternoon. The route passes through ponderosa pine forest, piñon-juniper woodland, and open prairie.

Although you won't get any canyon views from the train, you might get Western-style skits or musical entertainment to break up the two-hour-plus ride. Ticket prices ($70–190 adults, $40–110 children) vary according to the style of railcar, service, and season. Group rates are available, and the railway offers seasonal discounts and specials.

Grand Canyon Railway's **Polar Express** ($30 adults, $20 children) is a nighttime train ride through the forest complete with hot chocolate, cookies, and a visit to Santa's workshop. Advance reservations are strongly recommended for this excursion, which is wildly popular with the younger set. Polar Express package deals add dining and lodging options.

Mule Trips

The Grand Canyon tradition of mule tours began more than 100 years ago, when miners and prospectors began guiding tourists into the canyon's depths on sturdy, dependable mules. Among the riders depicted in historic photos of the Bright Angel Trail are Teddy Roosevelt, William Jennings Bryan, and Arizona's indomitable Sharlot Hall.

Spending a day on the back of a mule isn't for wimps. Riding requires good strength, especially in your back and abdominal muscles—and after several hours in the saddle, your bottom might not be the only part that's sore. But it's a great way to see a lot of the canyon in a relatively short time.

Xanterra Parks & Resorts offers a couple of options for mule rides into the canyon: a day ride to the Abyss overlook and two- or three-day rides with a layover at Phantom Ranch. The **Phantom Ranch** trip ($482 one night, $674 two nights, reduced rates for second person) begins in the morning at the corral near the Bright Angel Trail. After lunch at Indian Garden, riders continue to the bottom of the canyon and Phantom Ranch, a total of 10.5 miles (about 5.5 hours). The return trip, after breakfast on the second or third morning, is via the South Kaibab Trail, 7.3 miles (4.5 hours).

The cost includes meals and a stay at the Phantom Ranch cabins. Discounts are available for additional people in the same party. A duffle service is available for those who want to take more than the basic essentials. Those who make the wise choice to stay a second night can spend a day stretching sore muscles by hiking and exploring the inner canyon, or resting and enjoying the shady oasis of Phantom Ranch before saddling up for the return trip.

Although previous riding experience isn't necessary, height and weight restrictions are observed. Riders must be at least 4 feet 7 inches tall and weigh 200 pounds or less in full gear. Riders must speak English, must be in good health, and cannot be pregnant. Children 15 and under have to be accompanied by an adult.

Reservations for overnight rides to Phantom Ranch can be made by calling **Xanterra South Rim** (303/297-2757 or 888/297-2757) up to 13 months in advance. The tours often fill up quickly. Last-minute cancellations are possible, however, and you can add your name to the waiting list at one of the transportation desks. The waiting list is shortest in winter, when cancellations are most likely.

Confirm your reservations (928/638-3283) 2–4 days prior to your ride, not only to hold your place but also to learn about the latest weather and trail conditions. It's preferable to check in at the Bright Angel Lodge transportation desk the day before your trip so you can attend an orientation and weigh-in session. If you fail to check in by 6:15 A.M. on the day of your ride, you risk losing your reservation and deposit.

FRED HARVEY AND THE SANTA FE RAILWAY

The successful partnership between the Santa Fe Railway and the Fred Harvey Company changed the face of the West. Harvey, an Englishman, was appalled at the poor fare and service he found in train stations and at depot hotels. A restaurant owner turned freight agent, Harvey convinced the Atchison, Topeka, and Santa Fe Railway that he could do better, given the chance. The first Harvey House opened in 1876, and its success led to dozens of restaurants, hotels, and gift shops throughout the region.

Critical to the company's success was its efficient, neat, and attractive young waitresses. Thousands of Harvey Girls, hired to work in lunchrooms from Topeka to Los Angeles, brought refinement and wholesomeness to rough-and-tumble communities settled by prospectors, loggers, merchants, and train crews. Harvey Girls married ranchers and other locals, and it's said that many a boy baby was christened "Fred" or "Harvey" as the wild and woolly West was tamed.

Partnering with Fred Harvey wasn't the only way the Santa Fe endeavored to boost passenger traffic. Through a calculated campaign of image crafting, the railroad paid fares for artists to encourage them to visit locations and paint them. The Santa Fe then distributed free lithographs (such as Thomas Moran's *Chasm of the Colorado*) to popularize its destinations. The railroad banked on the romantic appeal of the West. Between 1896 and 1920, the Santa Fe built 17 hotels and more than a dozen train stations, most designed in regional styles.

At Grand Canyon, the Santa Fe Railway built a "log palace" to rival Yellowstone's Old Faithful Inn, and the Fred Harvey Company lured them in with Harvey Girls, an Italian chef from New York City, and "steak more tender than a woman's love." Then Fred Harvey Company and Santa Fe partnered again to hire brilliant architect Mary Elizabeth Jane Colter, whose fanciful constructions romanced visitors at Hopi House, Lookout Studio, Hermits Rest, the Desert View Watchtower, and Bright Angel Lodge.

Fred Harvey died in 1901 without seeing the company's marvelous Grand Canyon buildings, but several El Tovar staff members claim to have witnessed his ghost wandering about. You can see him too – his portrait hangs in the History Room at Bright Angel Lodge.

A new option for those who don't have the time (or nerve) for the long journey into the canyon is the Abyss Overlook mule tour ($119). This three-hour trip departs twice daily from the historic livery barn for a pleasant ride through the forest to the Abyss, a precipitous overlook along the West Rim. Reservations are required, and riders must check in at Bright Angel Lodge at least 90 minutes prior to departure.

Xanterra sells DVDs and videotapes of mule trips (Mule Trip Videos, Xanterra Parks & Resorts, P.O. Box 97, Grand Canyon, AZ 86023) that are useful as keepsakes or as preparation for a trip.

Horseback Tours

Apache Stables (928/638-2891, www .apachestables.com) offers the only horseback tours near the South Rim. One-hour ($49),

two-hour ($89), and campfire ($59) rides are available. Guests can pack hot dogs and fixings to cook over the campfire. Wagon rides ($26) are also available. Rates are discounted for children, who must be accompanied by an adult. None of the tours go below the rim but travel instead on National Forest lands that adjoin the park. The stables are located on Moqui Drive (Forest Rd. 328) between Tusayan and the park's south entrance.

Audio Tours

If you have a cell phone, you can listen to two-minute audio tours for selected sites from Yaki Point west to Hermits Rest. Look for the numbered "Park Ranger Audio Tour" signs, dial 928/225-2907, enter the stop number, and listen to the narration. There are 18 audio-tour locations along the South Rim, linked to prerecorded narratives by park rangers. Topics range from night skies to Native Americans. The mini tours are free, but be aware that cell coverage can be spotty along the rim, and not all service providers cover park locations. If you prefer, you can listen to the narrations online (www.nps.gov/grca) or download text versions.

Virtual Tours

It's not exactly Wii—at least not yet—but you can preview (or review) your visit to Grand Canyon through the park's online multimedia offerings (www.nps.gov/grca). Choose from among ranger lectures and interviews, hiking and river-running podcasts, or fascinating videos about the canyon's archaeology or geology. You can even go on a virtual raft trip down the Colorado River.

Learning Adventures

If this is your first visit to the canyon, you can accelerate your knowledge by signing up for an educational outing with several venerable institutions. Field trips carry on the legacy of geologists, archaeologists, and others who made careers of studying the canyon.

In 1993, the Grand Canyon Association (GCA), a longtime partner of the park, launched the **Grand Canyon Field Institute** (GCFI, 928/638-2485 or 866/471-4435, gcfi@grandcanyon.org, www.grandcanyon.org/fieldinstitute) with the goal of offering in-depth canyon knowledge and skills. The GCFI programs incorporate day-hiking, backpacking, and camping that focuses on geology, archaeology, photography, or cultural and natural history, among other topics. Experts lead the single-day and multiday programs. Classes are geared to the general public, though participants often include canyon residents and employees who want to expand their knowledge. Family classes and women-only programs are also offered. Discounts are available to groups and GCA members.

In coordination with Xanterra Parks & Resorts, the GCFI offers an introductory two-day program called **Learning & Lodging** (928/638-2525, www.grandcanyonlodges.com, $356–420). Fees include meals and two nights at Maswik or Yavapai Lodges, plus two full days of guided hiking and bus tours. Topics include photography, ecology, and pioneer history. Children must be age 10 or older to attend.

The Flagstaff-based Museum of Northern Arizona (MNA) began archiving and exhibiting examples of the cultural and natural history of the Colorado Plateau region in 1928. Among MNA's educational programs are guided excursions throughout the Grand Canyon region. **MNA Ventures** (928/774-5211, ext. 230, ventures@musnaz.org, www.mnaventures.org) feature a rim-to-rim backpacking trip, but MNA will design mild-to-wild custom trips for groups (schools, organizations, friends and family).

For teachers and students, the park's Environmental Education staff offers free curriculum-based resources designed for grades K–7. Programs include field trips on geology, ecology, and history. Distance learning using video-conferencing equipment is also an option, and rangers may occasionally be able to arrange classroom visits. Teachers can attend free workshops to learn more about the program. For information on class visits or teacher workshops, see the park's website (www.nps.gov/grca) or call the park's education staff (928/638-7931).

Northern Arizona University (www.grandcanyonsemester.nau.edu) cosponsors a Grand Canyon Semester, a challenging immersion experience for undergraduates. Up to 18 credit hours focusing on current issues in the American West can be earned in the classroom, on the river, or around a campfire.

Other Tours

Travelers who stop en route to Grand Canyon will be greeted by racks and racks of colorful brochures advertising Grand Canyon tours by Jeep, off-road vehicles, or passenger vans. Many of the companies that advertise outside of Grand Canyon National Park are not park-approved concessionaires, so inquire carefully about route locations and guide experience before making a decision. To arrange a tour with an approved concessionaire, visit one of the transportation desks in the park lodges or visitors centers.

Sights

Most South Rim sights are located along Hermit Road's eight-mile length and Desert View Drive, about 35 miles. In between these two scenic routes is Grand Canyon Village, best explored on foot. Sights are described in the order that visitors see them arriving from the South Entrance Station.

VILLAGE AND WEST RIM
◖ Mather Point

Most visitors view Grand Canyon for the first time from Mather Point, the first canyon overlook inside the South Entrance Station. Cars are now banned from the overlook, which can be reached by a paved path from the **Grand Canyon Visitors Center** and plaza. Your short walk will be rewarded with canyon views anchored by a stunning foreground of natural platforms and pillars of Kaibab limestone. A paved path descends to the top of the pillars, where you can stand and take in one of the canyon's loveliest perspectives.

Recent enhancements at Mather Point include picnic areas and an informal amphitheater. The point is named in honor of Stephen T. Mather, the first director of the National Park Service. The overlook is a beautiful introduction to Grand Canyon, well worth a return visit at sunset or sunrise.

◖ Yavapai Observation Station

Designed by architect Herbert Maier and opened in 1928, this pueblo-style structure of native limestone and wood blends into the rim. Its original purpose and function were as a museum and weather station, with the goal of helping visitors understand the canyon's outdoor environment. Broad canyon-facing windows frame panoramic views of the North Rim and Inner Gorge. Spotting scopes provide even closer views, and there's often a ranger nearby who will help you focus the lens on Phantom Ranch, tucked among bright green cottonwoods at the bottom of the canyon, or on the bridge

that leads hikers across the river to Bright Angel Campground.

If you're interested in learning more about the canyon's geology, Yavapai Observation Station is a must-stop. Recently updated displays, including a three-dimensional canyon map and geological column, explain how the canyon was formed. There are daily ranger talks, guided nature walks, and a small Grand Canyon Association bookstore. If the parking lot is full, you can return via the shuttle, but it's even more pleasant to arrive on foot along the Rim Trail. The 0.75-mile section between the heart of the village and Yavapai Observation Station is paved, relatively level, and partly shady—an easy effort rewarded by wonderful views.

Trail of Time

Between the Yavapai Observation Station and Verkamp's Visitors Center, the Rim Trail becomes a walk through the canyon's geologic past. Interpretive markers and rock samples from the canyon's depths line the paved trail, forming a geologic timeline—the Trail of Time. Each meter of the timeline equals 1 million years of history. It's your choice to travel forward or backward in time as you learn about 2 billion years of the canyon's geologic past, from the oldest rock, Elves Chasm gneiss (formed 1,840 million years ago), to the newest, Kaibab limestone (270 million years old). Viewing tubes and touchable rock samples help bring the vastness of geologic time closer to human understanding.

Park Headquarters and the Shrine of the Ages

Park Headquarters is a modern brick building that served for years as the South Rim's main visitors center. Visitor services have since been relocated to the Grand Canyon Visitors Center and its surrounding plazas. The headquarters houses administrative offices, the park's research library, and a ranger-staffed service desk where you can ask questions or sign up the kids for the park's Junior Ranger Program. But most likely you're here for one of three reasons: to park (the large lot often has open spaces), to find employment (a bulletin board lists current Park Service openings), or to attend a program in the auditorium known as the Shrine of the Ages.

Shrine of the Ages is a spacious indoor auditorium where many ranger programs, public meetings, and special events are held. Just west of the headquarters building is the Pioneer Cemetery, the final resting place for such canyon luminaries as John Hance, Ellsworth and Emery Kolb, and William Wallace Bass. There's also a memorial here for the victims of the horrific 1956 TWA-United collision over the canyon. History buffs and taphophiles (people who like tombstones) can easily while away an hour or two here. Between the HQ building and the rim is Mather Amphitheater, where rangers host outdoor talks during temperate months. This area of Grand Canyon Village is also home to Market Plaza, Yavapai Lodge, and Mather Campground.

◖ Grand Canyon Village Historic District

Perched on the rim, Grand Canyon's town site is a registered National Historic Landmark District, with 257 contributing structures. Buildings designed by architect Mary Colter, historic craftsman-style offices and residences, log cabins, and Santa Fe Railway structures are all linked by the Village Loop Road, but the best way to explore is on foot. A self-guided walking tour map is available at the transportation desks in Bright Angel Lodge, El Tovar, and Maswik Lodge.

GRAND CANYON DEPOT

You can begin the walking tour anywhere, but for Grand Canyon's early visitors, the launching point was the Grand Canyon Depot, completed in 1909. At the time, well-heeled Easterners arrived by Pullman car, having enjoyed elegant meals prepared by the Fred Harvey Company. The depot echoes the log-cabin styling of El Tovar, the Santa Fe Railway's flagship hotel. Details include custom copper and wrought iron hardware. Train service ceased in 1968, and two decades passed before trains once again whistled their way into and out of Grand Canyon Village.

EL TOVAR

Uphill from the train station, the elegant "log palace" of El Tovar looked down on the relatively uncivilized assortment of tents, shacks, and mud paths south of the tracks where livestock once wandered and open sewage ponds wafted. For visitors running the gauntlet of guides and motel operators hustling for business, the turreted roofline of El Tovar must have been a reassuring sight. The hotel was designed by Charles Whittlesey, an Illinois native who studied with Louis Sullivan (often credited as the father of modern architecture), before moving west to work for the Santa Fe.

When it opened in 1905, El Tovar was an eclectic mix of Victorian scale, European detailing, and rustic materials, from its rubble masonry foundation to its Queen Anne–style shingled turret. The first floor's log slab siding was given corner notching to create an illusion of log construction. Balustrades, indoors and out, were jigsawed in a Swiss chalet style. Murals in the Norwegian-styled dining room depicted Arizona's native peoples. The Rendezvous Room was decorated with arts and crafts furniture and hunting trophies, including a mountain lion killed by Western novelist Zane Grey.

The original floor plan included a solarium, a ladies' lounge, and a billiard room, with a kitchen garden, a poultry barn, and a dairy nearby. El Tovar set a standard, and its appeal to a growing number of visitors no doubt contributed to the establishment of Grand Canyon as a national monument in 1908. Tastefully updated and refurbished, El Tovar continues to offer the rim's finest accommodations and dining.

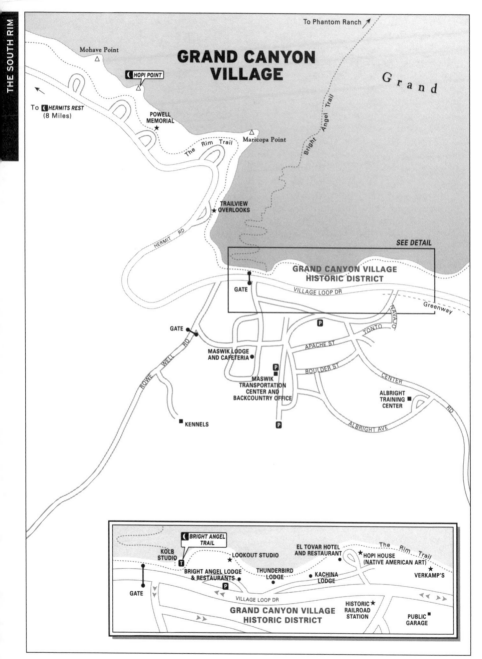

To Phantom Ranch ↗

Mohave Point △

GRAND CANYON VILLAGE

Grand

◖ HOPI POINT
△

To ◖ HERMITS REST
(8 Miles)

POWELL MEMORIAL ★

Maricopa Point △

The Rim Trail

Bright Angel Trail

TRAILVIEW OVERLOOKS ★

HERMIT RD

SEE DETAIL

GRAND CANYON VILLAGE HISTORIC DISTRICT

GATE

VILLAGE LOOP DR

NAVAJO

Greenway

GATE

ROWE WELL RD

MASWIK LODGE AND CAFETERIA ■

P

APACHE ST

TONTO

P

MASWIK TRANSPORTATION CENTER AND BACKCOUNTRY OFFICE

BOULDER ST

CENTER

ALBRIGHT TRAINING CENTER ■

RD

KENNELS ■

P

ALBRIGHT AVE

◖ BRIGHT ANGEL TRAIL

The Rim Trail

KOLB STUDIO

LOOKOUT STUDIO

EL TOVAR HOTEL AND RESTAURANT

★ HOPI HOUSE (NATIVE AMERICAN ART)

T

BRIGHT ANGEL LODGE & RESTAURANTS

THUNDERBIRD LODGE

★ VERKAMP'S

P

KACHINA LODGE

GATE

VILLAGE LOOP DR

GRAND CANYON VILLAGE HISTORIC DISTRICT

HISTORIC ★ RAILROAD STATION

PUBLIC ■ GARAGE

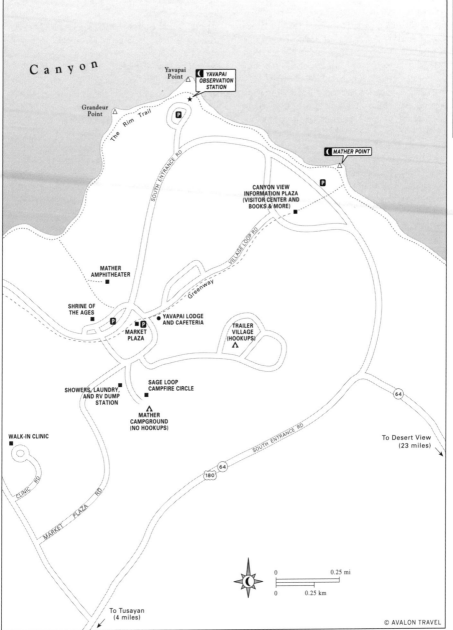

Canyon

Yavapai Point △

YAVAPAI
OBSERVATION
STATION

Grandeur
Point △

The Rim Trail

P

MATHER POINT △

P

SOUTH ENTRANCE RD

CANYON VIEW
INFORMATION PLAZA
(VISITOR CENTER AND
BOOKS & MORE)

VILLAGE LOOP RD

MATHER
AMPHITHEATER

Greenway

SHRINE OF
THE AGES

YAVAPAI LODGE
AND CAFETERIA

P

P

TRAILER
VILLAGE
(HOOKUPS)
Λ

MARKET
PLAZA

SHOWERS, LAUNDRY,
AND RV DUMP
STATION

SAGE LOOP
CAMPFIRE CIRCLE

Λ
MATHER
CAMPGROUND
(NO HOOKUPS)

64

WALK-IN CLINIC

SOUTH ENTRANCE RD

To Desert View
(23 miles)

CLINIC RD

MARKET PLAZA RD

64
180

0   0.25 mi

0   0.25 km

To Tusayan
(4 miles)

© AVALON TRAVEL

HOPI HOUSE

Across the circular drive from El Tovar's veranda stands Hopi House, architect Mary Colter's first building at Grand Canyon. It opened shortly before El Tovar in 1905. Inspired by the Hopi village of Old Oraibi, Colter designed a rectangular masonry building of three stories, terraced to provide rooftop plazas where resident families, hired by the Fred Harvey Company to demonstrate crafts, could work and play. Outdoor plazas connect to each other via stone steps and rough-hewn wooden ladders. Stacked pottery chimneys ornament the building's corners, and heavy log vigas protrude from the masonry walls.

Colter wanted visitors who stepped through the low doorway to feel as if they were entering another time and space, an effect enhanced by low lighting, log-and-brush ceilings, and roughly plastered walls. Pottery, blankets, and baskets were artfully displayed throughout the salesrooms. Although the building and displays have been modernized, Native American art remains the focus at Hopi House.

VERKAMP'S

Farther east along the rim, Verkamp's Curios operated in a large bungalow-style building, once the home of the Verkamp family. John Verkamp sold curios and Indian crafts from a tent for the Babbit Brothers before starting his own business in 1905. In 2008 Verkamp's ended its run as the longest family-owned business in the national park system. The Park Service acquired the 1906 building and reopened it as a visitors center with displays focusing on pioneer life in Grand Canyon Village.

BRIGHT ANGEL LODGE

West of El Tovar, on the other side of the mid-century Thunderbird and Kachina Lodges, is Bright Angel Lodge. Mary Colter designed the lodge buildings to reflect the village's past as a pioneer settlement, with scattered structures in log cabin, clapboard, and Spanish Colonial themes. This approach allowed her to incorporate two existing buildings with long canyon

histories: Buckey O'Neill's log cabin and the Red Horse Station.

Bright Angel Lodge, which opened in 1935 during the Great Depression, was meant to appeal to travelers on modest budgets. The main lodge has two large fireplaces designed by Colter. The inglenook fireplace in the lobby, with the Fred Harvey Company's trademark thunderbird above, warms hikers on cold winter days. The **geologic fireplace,** located in what is now the History Room, replicates canyon strata. Park naturalist Edwin McKee worked with Colter to find samples from rock layers in the canyon. The canyon's basement rocks are represented by the Vishnu schist at the base of the fireplace. Around its opening are the layers of the Grand Canyon Supergroup. Above that are narrow bands of the canyon's Paleozoic layers. The fireplace chimney is Kaibab limestone, the layer that forms the canyon's rim. The history room focuses on the Fred Harvey Company and the **Harvey Girls,** the efficient white-aproned waitresses who worked in lunchrooms, train stations, and hotels on the Santa Fe lines.

BUCKEY O'NEILL'S LOG CABIN

Buckey O'Neill, an enterprising and handsome young man, helped shape Arizona Territory's frontier communities, working as a newspaper editor, probate judge, supervisor of schools, and county sheriff. An investor in the Anita Mine, south of the village, O'Neill was garnering support for a rail line to Grand Canyon when the Spanish-American War began. He was the first to volunteer for the regiment later known as Teddy Roosevelt's Roughriders and was killed in Cuba in 1898. Buckey O'Neill's log cabin, built in the 1890s, still stands on the rim and is used today as suite accommodations.

RED HORSE STATION

Red Horse Station, also built in the 1890s, once served as a station on the stagecoach line south of the village. It is the oldest building at Grand Canyon. In 1902, Ralph Cameron moved the station to the village, added a second story and veranda, and operated it as the Cameron Hotel. The building later served as the South Rim's post office. Mary Colter saved it from demolition, and Red Horse Station was restored to its original single-story log structure as one of the lodge's guest cabins.

LOOKOUT STUDIO

Another Colter building, Lookout Studio, perches on the rim west of Buckey O'Neill's cabin. Completed in 1914, partly to compete with the Kolb brothers' successful photography business, the studio displayed photographs of the canyon and featured a telescope for viewing the canyon from its balconies. Low-roofed and with terraces constructed of the rim's Kaibab limestone, Lookout Studio blends almost seamlessly into the landscape. The building functions as a gift shop today, and it still provides a sheltered perch—for humans and condors—from which to view mule riders and hikers descending Bright Angel Trail.

KOLB STUDIO

Multistoried Kolb Studio clings precipitously to the edge of the canyon. The wood-frame building was shaped and reshaped over 23 years as Ellsworth and Emery Kolb made room for a growing business selling souvenir photos and screening the movie they made of their 1911–1912 run down the Colorado River. From one window they took pictures of tourists on mules, and from another sold the photos and tickets for the movie, shown in the studio's auditorium. Today, Kolb Studio houses a gift shop and gallery space. Peek into the projection room to see the equipment the Kolbs used in the early 1900s.

SOUTH ALONG LOOP DRIVE

Those who enjoy historic architecture or want to extend their pleasant walk through the village can continue on the south half of Loop Drive. The impressive **Powerhouse** near the railroad tracks was built in Swiss chalet style in 1926. Some of the **Maswik Lodge** cabins on the south side of the tracks date to the village's first motor lodge, circa 1927, later replaced by Maswik Lodge. Past the lodge, the road enters the village's residential area.

© RICHARD MAYER

Lookout Studio is a favorite perch for visitors . . . and condors.

Past the community building (1935), the **mule and horse barns** (circa 1907) are wood clapboard with massive rooftops broken by cupolas and small dormers. The road loops near the garage, built to maintain the Fred Harvey Company's fleet of touring cars, and the craftsman-style park operations building, constructed in 1929. At the base of the hill where El Tovar stands, another craftsman-style structure (circa 1921) served originally as the administration building, then the supervisor's residence, and now as offices for Xanterra Parks & Resorts. Although their functions have shifted with the times, many of Grand Canyon's historic buildings still stand.

Bright Angel Trail

The steep descent down Bright Angel Trail begins just west of Bright Angel Lodge. The trail, now on the National Register of Historic Places, was built by Ralph Cameron, a territorial county sheriff and supervisor who later became Arizona's U.S. senator. Cameron had mining claims in the area and charged riders $1 to use his trail. Above the trail is the old stone corral, where mule parties still saddle up every morning to make the journey to Indian Garden or Phantom Ranch. The trail passes within a few feet of Kolb Studio, where a small window allowed Emery or Ellsworth to take pictures of mule riders. The Bright Angel Trail is the South Rim's most popular route to the bottom of the canyon. Even a short walk down the trail gives the sense of being enveloped by the canyon's walls. Aim for the first trail tunnel cut into the stone. Look up to your left, where you'll be able to make out prehistoric pictographs high above, probably made by Havasupai people long ago. Like many South Rim trails, Bright Angel was once a Havasupai route.

Hermit Road

Eight-mile-long Hermit Road was once a stagecoach route linking the village with Hermits Rest, built as a tourist attraction in 1914 by the Santa Fe Railway and Fred Harvey Company. For $1.50, travelers could enjoy the dusty but scenic round-trip by horse-drawn stage. In later decades, the Fred Harvey Company's fleet of Harveycars (open touring cars) traveled the old stage route. Today, depending on the season, you can explore sights along Hermit Road by car (winter), by free shuttle bus (spring–fall), by guided bus tour (year-round), or by bicycle.

Trailview Overlooks

The two Trailview Overlooks are named for their stellar views of Bright Angel Trail. From either overlook, you can watch hikers and mule parties descending the trail's switchbacks into the canyon. Bright Angel Trail, once a toll trail named for Ralph Cameron, follows a long, straight fault line that stretches between the canyon's North and South Rims. During the summer, look for a patch of bright green roughly halfway down the canyon walls: They are the cottonwoods that mark Indian Garden. The relatively level gray-green Tonto Platform extends into the canyon, and you'll probably be able to make out the line of the trail snaking toward Plateau Point.

If you look east along the rim, you'll see the historic buildings of Grand Canyon Village. Look for El Tovar's distinctive roofline and the multiple levels of Kolb Studio perched above and below the rim. It's a pleasant walk to Trailview from the village along the Rim Trail. This mile-long section of the trail is paved and fairly level.

Maricopa Point

Maricopa Point is the site of the Lost Orphan Mine, which continued operations into the 1960s. Daniel Hogan, a prospector and deputy sheriff who served under Theodore Roosevelt in the Spanish-American War, filed his copper claim in 1893. He opened a tourist camp along the rim in 1936. For a while, the cabins and saloon were managed by Will Rogers Jr. Only after Hogan sold out did he learn that his mine contained some of the richest uranium ore in the Southwest, yielding millions of dollars of uranium for later owners and creating something of a nuisance for the National Park Service. The parcel of land became part

JOHN WESLEY POWELL

In May 1869, a group of 10 men set out from Green River in Wyoming Territory, their goal to float from the Green River to the Grand River and then onto the Colorado River through Grand Canyon. The inner canyon was terra incognita – unmapped and virtually unknown to anyone except local Native Americans. Nineteenth-century America waited for news of the expedition with the same fascination that later generations felt for the Apollo missions.

The leader of the expedition, John Wesley Powell, was a Civil War veteran who'd lost his right arm to a cannonball during the Battle of Shiloh. He returned to the war after the wound healed and was promoted to major in the Union Army. He later taught geology at Illinois Wesleyan University, having been fascinated by natural history since childhood. As a professor, he made field trips West, sparking his idea to explore the Colorado River through Grand Canyon.

When the expedition launched, the 35-year-old Powell was in charge of nine men, few with river experience, probably more than one interested in whatever gold they might find. One man left a month after they started out. When the remaining nine floated into Grand Canyon, they virtually dropped out of sight. Powell wrote in his journal, "We have an unknown distance yet to run, an unknown river to explore. What falls there are, we know not; what rocks beset the channel, we know not; what walls rise over the river, we know not."

Fierce rapids battered the expedition's four wooden dories, and the summer sun bore down on them. With food supplies dwindling and their clothing in rags, the men faced near starvation. In late August, three men left the expedition rather than face another brutal stretch of white water. Powell named it Separation Rapids, and it proved to be the last difficult rapids they would face. Two days later, the remaining six reached the Colorado's confluence with the Virgin River. From Mormon settlements nearby, they were able to send word of their survival. Their journey took 99 days and covered 1,000 miles. Powell learned that the three who'd chosen to leave were murdered on their hike to civilization. He included them in the dedication to his book about the expedition; published in 1875, it remains one of the finest adventure stories about Grand Canyon.

Powell repeated his canyon journey in 1872 and returned to the Southwest numerous times. Because of his strong interest in the native peoples of the region, Powell was named the first director of the Bureau of American Ethnology in 1880. He became the second director of the U.S. Geological Survey in 1881. He was remarkably prescient about water issues in the West and warned that communities must carefully plan growth, cooperating to conserve water. Powell died in 1902, his warnings unheeded. The vast reservoir of Lake Powell bears his name, impounded behind the dam that forever changed the nature of the river he explored.

of the park in 1987. Access is restricted for safety reasons, but along the Rim Trail you can see the headframe, shafts, cables, and other remnants of the mine, which bored deep into the earth.

Powell Memorial

At Powell Point, a memorial honors the members of John Wesley Powell's expedition down the Colorado River in 1869, when the area was still a blank spot on the national map. Four decades later, in 1920, the dedication ceremony for Grand Canyon National Park took place here. You can catch a glimpse of the river far below. If you climb the stairs to the top of the memorial, turn away from the canyon and look south for views of the San Francisco Peaks. Follow the slopes of the peaks up and imagine an even higher single peak, blown away when an extinct volcano erupted 400,000 years ago. Of the existing peaks formed when the ancient peak blew its top, Mount Humphrey marks the highest point in Arizona at 12,633 feet.

◖ Hopi Point

Hopi Point thrusts farther into the canyon than any other point on the South Rim, offering panoramic views. Across the canyon, below the North Rim, you can spot the temples of Osiris, Shiva, Isis, and Horus, named by geologist Clarence Dutton in the 1880s. Dutton, a student of world history and philosophy, named many of the canyon's peaks for mythological figures. A mile below, the Colorado River looks like a narrow blue-green band, or reddish-brown if it has been raining. Look for Granite Rapid—it helps to have binoculars—marked by flecks of white.

Mohave Point

Below Mohave Point, you can see three of the canyon's 160-plus rapids: From left to right are Hermit, Granite, and Salt Creek Rapids. Most rapids on the Colorado River through Grand Canyon were formed when boulders washed down tributary canyons after flash floods. A long, narrow formation, the Alligator, stretches from the point into the canyon below. The cliffs to the east are known as the Hopi Wall.

The Abyss

From the Abyss, you can look down one of the rim's steepest drops to the river, nearly 4,500 feet. The drainage below the Abyss leads to Monument Canyon. With binoculars or sharp eyes, you might be able to spot the Monument, a pillar found in the depths of this tributary. If you enjoy the thrill of heights, walk west along the Rim Trail for especially vertiginous views. Pima Point is three miles farther; Hermits Rest is four miles. If the shuttle is running, you can catch a later bus at either point.

Pima Point

Far below Pima Point, you can see the ruins of historic Hermit Camp. The Santa Fe Railway built Hermit Trail and established the tourist camp here in 1912 to compete with Ralph Cameron's Bright Angel Trail and Indian Garden camp. Tourists traveled to the camp

From Pima Point, the dark rocks of the Inner Gorge appear like a gash across the canyon depths.

© KATHLEEN BRYANT

on mules after taking the train to the village and the stagecoach to Hermits Rest, where the Hermit Trail began. During its glory days, Hermit Camp offered mule riders well-furnished tent cabins, a dining hall presided over by a Fred Harvey chef, stables, a blacksmith, restrooms, phones, and showers. Operating until 1930, the camp got its supplies via an aerial tramway leading 6,000 feet down from Pima Point. At the time, the tramway was the longest single-span cable system in the world.

Hermits Rest

Hermits Rest was designed by architect Mary Colter and completed in 1914 as another attraction to help the Santa Fe Railway entice tourists to the canyon. Drawing on the local history of miners guiding visitors to their inner canyon camps, she imagined the setting as a prospector's lair carved into the hillside. The interior is cave-like, with a massive fireplace set into the back wall. When Santa Fe employees kidded Colter that the rest stop looked like it needed a good cleaning, she replied, "You can't imagine what it cost to make it look this old." (The price tag, about $185,000, was an impressive investment for the Santa Fe and Fred Harvey Company, which charged $1.50 pp to take the stage to Hermits Rest.) Just west of the building is the start of Hermit Trail.

EAST RIM
Yaki Point

Yaki Point, about a mile past the turnoff on Desert View Drive, is accessible only by shuttle or tour bus. Because of this, many people often forgo visiting one of the most beautiful overlooks on the South Rim. Though Hopi and Mohave Points get raves for sunset and sunrise photo opportunities, many prefer Yaki Point. If you're a photographer, you'll appreciate the gnarled piñon pines that lend foreground and framing to canyon scenes. Below, reddish-orange Cedar Ridge rises toward O'Neill Butte. Look closely and you'll see the South Kaibab Trail stretching across Cedar Ridge before making steep switchbacks below Skeleton Point. The trail starts 0.5 miles south of the rim.

Grandview Point

Grandview offers grand views of the central canyon as well as a peek into the canyon's pioneer past. Today, it's the South Rim's most forested overlook, shady and peaceful, but 100 years ago this was the bustling center of Grand Canyon's tourist operations, with hotels and a post office that used the cancellation mark of "Tourist, Arizona." Victorian-era travelers praised the log cabin–style Grand View Hotel and Captain John Hance's tourist camp and trail. This was also the headquarters of Grand Canyon's most successful copper mine. Mining ruins can be seen on Horseshoe Mesa at the bottom of the three-mile Grandview Trail, which starts just east of the overlook's stone barrier. After the Santa Fe Railway built tracks to present-day Grand Canyon Village, 12 miles west, traveling to Tourist fell out of favor. Mary Colter used logs from the Grand View Hotel for the ceiling of her Watchtower, a few miles down the road. The Park Service removed the remaining buildings in the 1970s, and today only ghosts whisper through the pines at Grandview.

Tusayan Ruins and Museum

About 800 years ago, this small village was home to the Cohonina, one of the prehistoric cultural groups that lived in the Grand Canyon region. The people who built this multiroom pueblo tended crops nearby in addition to hunting game and gathering wild plants for food, fuel, and medicine. The masonry complex includes living spaces, a storage area, and two kivas, or circular structures. The San Francisco Peaks, sacred to many of the area's indigenous cultures, are visible through the surrounding ponderosa pines.

Rangers guide daily walks of the ruins, although you can take the self-guided loop trail if a ranger program isn't scheduled while you are here. Displays at nearby Tusayan Museum focus on prehistoric and contemporary Native American cultures. Artifacts include split-twig figurines found in Grand Canyon. The bookstore selection includes titles on archaeology and ethnology.

ARCHITECT MARY ELIZABETH JANE COLTER

By all accounts, Mary Colter was a remarkable woman, born in 1869 but meant for the new century. Her architectural partnership with the Fred Harvey Company and Santa Fe Railway set the stage for the way people experienced Grand Canyon as well as how other architects approached designing buildings for national parks, or "parkitecture."

Colter, who studied architecture in California, had a keen appreciation for North American Indian culture and for the craftsman aesthetic of designing structures that harmonized with their natural setting. She didn't simply show visitors the Southwest; she made it possible for them to experience it. Her buildings at Grand Canyon include Hopi House (1905), Lookout Studio (1914), Bright Angel Lodge (1935), Phantom Ranch (1922), and the Desert View Watchtower (1932).

When the Fred Harvey Company contacted Colter to decorate retail space in Albuquerque, New Mexico, she was 33 years old and teaching mechanical drafting at a boys school in St. Paul, Minnesota. She worked to support her widowed mother and ailing sister, also finding time to lecture on world history and architecture, review books as a newspaper literary editor, and take classes in archaeology to further her interests in Native American cultures. After the summer job in Albuquerque, she returned to Minnesota.

The public responded enthusiastically to Fred Harvey's "Indian building," and two years later, the company called on Mary Colter once more, this time to design an Indian building to complement El Tovar, then under construction on the Grand Canyon's South Rim. An impeccable researcher, Colter traveled to the Hopi village of Oraibi for inspiration for Hopi House, which opened on January 1, 1905, days before El Tovar. The design was an instant success, but it was 1910 before the Fred Harvey Company offered Colter a permanent full-time job designing the hotels, restaurants, and rail stations the company managed for the Santa Fe Railway.

When Colter studied architecture in the late 1880s, few universities taught it, few women studied it, and very few architects were licensed. Like many other would-be architects, Colter learned by apprenticing with a working architect. Because she was never licensed, she developed concepts and drew preliminary designs, floor plans, and elevations. These were sent to the Santa Fe's engineering department, and the railroad's

Lipan Point

From Lipan Point you can see Unkar Delta, a sinuous curve along the Colorado River where some of the canyon's Ancestral Puebloans had winter homes. In broad Unkar Valley, the colorful tilted layers of the Grand Canyon Supergroup have eroded into soft hills and folds. Above the valley is the North Rim's Cape Royal, surrounded by majestic temples and buttes. To the east are the Palisades of the Desert, marking the end of Marble Canyon and the river's turn westward toward the Inner Gorge. The Tanner Trail leads east of Lipan Point to the river, a 10-mile journey that was once part of a trail used by horse thieves to move stolen stock from Arizona to Utah.

◖ Desert View Watchtower

Designed by Mary Colter, Desert View Watchtower is a masterpiece of atmosphere and ethnohistory. Rising 70 feet above the rim, the Watchtower combines prehistoric masonry style overlying a hidden steel frame built by railway engineers. Colter traveled the Four Corners area by touring car and small plane to study towers built by the Ancestral Puebloans, which some archaeologists believe are observatories. Her tower, built in 1932, is a re-creation of prehistoric structures.

The tower's interior presents a visual and symbolic history of Southwestern cultures. At the base of the circular tower is a mural of Tiyo and the Hopi snake dance, painted by Fred Kabotie. Upper stories feature designs from the Mimbres culture and ancient cave paintings.

architects drew the final plans. The Santa Fe Railway owned the buildings; the Fred Harvey Company operated and furnished them. Both companies contributed to Mary Colter's salary.

Colter, who frequently traveled the Santa Fe rail lines to design new hotels and refurbish old ones, became an integral player in the railroad's image-building efforts. As for her own image, well, "eccentric" describes it best. The chain-smoking Colter often dressed in pants and a Stetson, knew how to shoot a pistol, and avidly collected books and Indian silver. Her jewelry collection numbered 1,000 pieces, and she wore rings on every finger.

She developed a reputation for bossiness with male construction workers, perhaps due to her past as a teacher. While working on the geological fireplace at Bright Angel Lodge, she scolded park naturalist Edwin McKee as though he were one of her schoolboys. Hopi artist Fred Kabotie remembered struggling to mix paint colors exactly as Colter envisioned them, and painters referred to the shade used as trim in Bright Angel Lodge as "Mary Jane Blue." Colter, who insisted Harveycar guides be precise when describing her buildings to tourists, wrote her "boys" a 75-page primer on

the Desert View Watchtower, which opened to national publicity in 1932.

Thanks largely to Colter's efforts at Grand Canyon, architecture at the West's most scenic areas began to take on a distinct aesthetic. This rustic, handcrafted style eventually fell out of favor, phased out in 1956 by the park service's Mission 66, a 10-year program designed to accommodate growing numbers of visitors with streamlined contemporary architecture. Historic structures viewed as deteriorated and dangerous were razed. Though Mary Colter's buildings at Grand Canyon were spared, some of her work elsewhere was lost.

In 1957, one of Colter's favorite buildings, La Posada Hotel in Winslow, Arizona, closed. A few months later, another of her buildings, Gallup's El Navajo Hotel, was demolished. She told an interviewer, "There's such a thing as living too long."

Mary Colter died in 1958, but her Grand Canyon creations continue to fascinate and inspire today. Eleven of her works are listed on the National Register of Historic Places, including La Posada (reopened as a hotel in 1997) and Grand Canyon's Bright Angel Lodge, Hopi House, Hermits Rest, Lookout Studio, and the Watchtower.

Construction details include a kiva-style ceiling made with logs salvaged from the former Grand View Hotel as well as petroglyphs on exterior stonework. The second-story observation deck offers views of Comanche Point, the Colorado River, and the Little Colorado River Gorge. Eastern views encompass Navajo country, including Cedar Mountain, the Echo Cliffs, and the edge of the Painted Desert.

IN TUSAYAN
IMAX Theater

Outside the national park boundaries in the town of Tusayan, the **National Geographic Visitors Center** (928/638-2206, www.explorethecanyon.com, 8:30 A.M.–8:30 P.M. Mar. 1–Oct. 31, 10:30 A.M.–6:30 P.M. Nov. 1–Feb. 28) shows

the most-watched, highest-grossing IMAX film ever made: *Grand Canyon: The Hidden Secrets.* Millions of viewers have seen this 34-minute film, which screens every hour on the half-hour. Most bus tours stop here, and for the many tourists who don't have time to do justice to the canyon itself, the movie has become almost a substitute. The white-water rafting scenes and hawk's-eye views of the river are the closest most day visitors will get to the inner canyon. Tickets are $13 for "adults" (age 11 and older), with discounts for children and groups that reserve in advance. The theater seats 500-plus, but if you have to wait for the next screening, you can spend the time browsing through the visitors center's gift shop and exhibits or grab a quick bite at the deli. Park passes can also be purchased here.

Recreation

It's easy to get caught up in the bustle of Grand Canyon Village, but the most memorable hours of your trip will be the ones you spend outdoors exploring the canyon itself or the forests along the South Rim. You can rent a bike or take a hike, enjoy a gentle stroll to soak up some rim-side views, or get your blood pumping with a trek to Grandview Mesa or Dripping Springs. Prepare for your adventure with sun protection and plenty of water.

HIKING

The National Park Service warns, "There are no easy hikes below the rim." Rim-to-river trails are steep and exposed to the sun, with sheer drop-offs and other potential hazards. If you're looking for a simple walk or stroll, try sections of the scenic Rim Trail or wander around the village area.

If you decide to enter the realm below the rim, don't let the ease of traveling downhill lure you into hiking farther than you have water, time, or energy for. As a rule of thumb, it takes twice as long for the return trip. Novice hikers should stick to the South Rim's corridor trails, Bright Angel and South Kaibab, before attempting wilderness trails. The maintained and patrolled corridor trails are easy to follow and so popular that help usually isn't far away, should you need it. Even getting to the trailheads is easy. If you're staying at Bright Angel Lodge, Bright Angel Trail is practically on your doorstep.

But hiking in Grand Canyon isn't for the spontaneous. Careful planning is important, even for an autumn or spring day hike on a corridor trail. Wilderness trails may have steep drop-offs and obstacles, and they often require route-finding skills (the ability to read both a map and the landscape to locate an obscure trail). Icy winter conditions and extreme summer heat can turn a hike into a dangerous, even life-threatening, ordeal.

South Rim trails are open year-round, though upper sections, often reaching halfway into the canyon, may be snow-packed and icy for days or weeks after a winter storm. Crampons, which you can rent or buy at the

KEEP YOUR COOL

- **Wait for shade.** During hot months, plan to hike before 10 A.M. or after 4 P.M. to avoid intense midday sun. Some people hike at night, but because of narrow trails and steep drops, this can be dangerous. Carry a flashlight or headlamp, just in case you get caught after dark.

- **Get wet.** A lot of technical gear is designed to wick away perspiration. This is helpful in cooler months or climes. But on a hot Arizona summer day, when the relative humidity is 10-15 percent, cotton keeps you cooler. A light cotton shirt, cap, or bandana can be soaked with water – the evaporative effect will keep you cool much longer than synthetics.

- **Rest often.** You'll use water more efficiently if you sip a little at a time and have a light snack every so often. Besides, a short break gives you time to enjoy your surroundings.

- **Use your nose.** Panting or breathing so hard that you can't speak are both signs that you're using more oxygen than you can take in. Besides, mouth breathing wastes moisture and doesn't filter out dust as efficiently (though it does help you get past the odiferous mule waste along the Bright Angel, North Kaibab, and South Kaibab Trails). Chewing gum or sucking on hard candy can help keep your mouth moist and remind you to keep it closed.

- **Be humble.** The canyon is bigger and older and meaner than you. Don't be stubborn about turning around if you find you're out of your depth.

© KATHLEEN BRYANT

Strolling along the Rim Trail is a scenic way to get from one site to the next.

General Store, are a must to help prevent a serious fall. The plus side to winter hiking is that there are fewer people on the trails, backcountry permits are relatively easy to get, and inner canyon temperatures are pleasant.

In the summer, heat requires an entire set of strategies encompassing timing, water, and sun protection. The South Kaibab Trail, in particular, is shadeless and dry. From July to mid-September, afternoon thunderstorms are possible, bringing the danger of lightning strikes and flash floods. Spring and fall are ideal times to hike, although the weather is unpredictable. At any time of year, trail closures are possible. Check online (www.nps .org/grca) or at the visitors centers for the latest conditions.

All warnings aside, hiking in Grand Canyon is awe-inspiring. The views, of course, are amazing, but so is the feeling of walking through the ages as you descend through rock layers and vegetation zones.

Rim hikes and corridor trails are listed first. Wilderness trails are listed west to east.

Rim Trail

- Distance: 12 miles from Hermits Rest to Pipe Creek Vista, but easily hiked in shorter sections
- Duration: 20–30 minutes per mile
- Elevation gain: 480 feet
- Effort: Easy
- Trailhead: This trail can be accessed at South Rim overlooks from Pipe Creek Vista west to Hermits Rest.

Most people will choose to hike the Rim Trail in shorter sections. The trail is paved along Grand Canyon Village. This section of the Rim Trail can be crowded in places, but it is still quite pleasant, especially if you're a history or architecture buff. The Trail of Time exhibits along the Rim Trail between Verkamp's and the Yavapai Observation Station are a highlight for those who want to learn more about the canyon's geology.

You'll find great views of the village from the west at the Trailview Overlooks and from the east en route to Yavapai Point. You can make nearby forays through the ponderosa pine forest to Mather Amphitheater or Shrine of the Ages for ranger programs, while away an hour in the Pioneer Cemetery, or visit Yavapai Observation Station.

If it's solitude you're seeking, strike out from one of the overlooks farther west along the rim. From March through November you can ride the Hermit Road shuttle to an overlook and hike the Rim Trail to another overlook, where you can catch the shuttle again. (Keep in mind the shuttle stops are limited on the return route.) The trail winds in and out of piñon-juniper woodland along the cliff edges, offering spectacular canyon views. An especially scenic four-mile section lies between the Abyss and Hermits Rest. Hermit Road is farther from the trail here, so the sound of road traffic is buffered, another plus. The paved multiuse Greenway Trail joins the Rim Trail for its final three miles.

Even on the busier sections of the Rim Trail, wildlife sightings are common. Oblivious to midsummer heat, eastern fence lizards dart over rocky outcrops. Mule deer wander along trails and through the forest, especially in the morning and evening. The ponderosa pines near the village are home to tassel-eared Abert's squirrels (cousins of the North Rim's Kaibab squirrels), who depend on the tall trees for food and shelter. Their ruder relatives, rock squirrels, may try to bully you for food; don't give in. And here and there, the heady scent of cliffrose perfumes your path.

◖ Bright Angel Trail

- Distance: 9.3 miles from Bright Angel Trailhead to Bright Angel Campground, 4.6 miles from trailhead to Indian Garden
- Duration: 2 days round-trip to Colorado River, 7–9 hours round-trip to Indian Gardens
- Elevation gain: 4,380 feet from rim to river, 3,860 feet to Indian Gardens
- Effort: Moderate to strenuous
- Trailhead: In Grand Canyon Village

The Bright Angel Trail begins just west of Bright Angel Lodge, near the start of Hermit Road. The shuttle's Village Route ends here. The nearest public parking area is the dirt lot along the railroad tracks between the lodge and the depot, but if you plan on being on the trail for a few hours or overnight, an even better choice is to park at the Backcountry Information Center and take the Village Route shuttle to the trailhead.

This corridor trail is well maintained, though you will have to share it with mule parties, who have the right of way. (Step to the inside of the trail and stand quietly while they pass. Wait until the last mule is 50 feet away before continuing your hike.) Both scenic and historic, the Bright Angel is a good choice for novice hikers. Even if you have time for only a short walk, you'll appreciate the difference once you descend below the rim. And if you go the distance, you'll experience the element that makes a desert hike magical—water, in this case the clear streams of Garden and Pipe Creeks.

One of the first highlights greets hikers about 0.5 miles down the trail. Before entering the tunnel carved through the Kaibab limestone cliff, look up to see pictographs in a reddish pigment, left by Havasupai Indians who used the trail into the 1900s. A second tunnel leads to the canyon's Coconino sandstone layer. After a steep descent through reddish Hermit shale, you arrive at Mile-and-a-Half Resthouse at, you guessed it, 1.5 miles. You'll find water (available May–Sept.), toilets, and an emergency phone.

More switchbacks and more red rocks—this time the Supai layer—lead to Three-Mile Resthouse. Another possible day-hike destination, this resthouse also has water (May–Sept.), toilets, a telephone, and great views, especially from the nearby overlook perched atop the Redwall formation.

A long series of switchbacks known as Jacob's Ladder descends through the Redwall to Indian Garden, a popular turnaround for strong day hikers. Spur trails lead to the ranger station and campground, and the westbound

Tonto Trail intersects at 4.6 miles. (The trail intersects the eastbound Tonto Trail at 4.9 miles.)

The main trail continues to a rest area shaded by cottonwoods, with benches, a water fountain, and nearby toilets. This area, on the gentle slope of the Tonto Platform, watered by the springs and a creek, was once the site of Havasupai garden plots. Ralph Cameron had a tourist camp here in the early 1900s when his Bright Angel Trail was a toll trail. Emery and Ellsworth Kolb took photos of mule parties descending the trail. One of the brothers, usually Emery, would run down the trail to develop the photographs here, where there was clear running water, then dash back up ahead of the mule riders so that they could sell them their photos, a round-trip he sometimes made twice a day (think about that when you're heading back up Jacob's Ladder gasping for breath).

Below the shady oasis of Indian Garden, the trail twists and turns and flirts with lovely Garden Creek, tempting you to continue. *Don't,* unless you're an exceptionally strong day hiker or you're prepared to spend the night in the canyon. En route to the river, you'll pass the pump house that delivers water across the canyon from Roaring Springs and, at seven miles, Columbine Spring, which forms a delicate waterfall and hanging garden of fern, monkey-flower, and columbine.

After the confluence of Pipe Creek and Garden Creek, you'll come to River Resthouse at mile 7.8. There's no potable water here, but you'll enjoy the shady riparian surroundings of cottonwoods and willows. Just past the resthouse the trail joins the River Trail, which follows the Inner Gorge above the river for 1.1 miles to the Silver Bridge. Interestingly, the scenic and easy River Trail was the canyon's most difficult trail to construct, built by the Civilian Conservation Corps in the 1930s using ropes, jackhammers, and 40,000 pounds of gunpowder. Continue to the Black Bridge, less than 0.25 miles. Just beyond this bridge are mule corrals, drinking water, toilets, a telephone, and a ranger station. Beyond the ranger

station is Phantom Ranch. To get to the Bright Angel Campground, take the North Kaibab Trail left another 0.2 miles.

An option for strong day hikers or backpackers is to take the three-mile (round-trip) section of the Tonto Trail west from Indian Garden across Plateau Point. Here you'll have stunning overlooks of the Colorado River, more than 1,000 feet below, and the Inner Gorge, where the canyon's oldest geological layers are revealed. Note that the National Park Service strongly discourages day hikers from attempting Plateau Point.

South Kaibab Trail

- Distance: 7.3 miles from South Kaibab Trailhead to Bright Angel Campground, 1.5 miles from trailhead to Cedar Ridge
- Duration: 2 days round-trip to Colorado River, 3 hours round-trip to Cedar Ridge
- Elevation gain: 4,780 feet from rim to river, 940 feet to Cedar Ridge
- Effort: Moderate to strenuous
- Trailhead: Yaki Point

The South Kaibab Trailhead shares the road that accesses beautiful Yaki Point along East Rim Drive (Hwy. 64). The area is closed to private vehicles year-round. To get to the trailhead, which is 0.5 miles south of the overlook, take the Kaibab Trail shuttle from Grand Canyon Visitors Center or the Hikers' Express from the village.

The South Kaibab Trail follows ridgelines from the rim to the river, offering wide-open views of colorful O'Neill Butte and the Inner Gorge as well as several good day-hike destinations. Because of this trail's openness, a midday ascent in summer is not recommended. There's no water along the trail, so pack plenty, even for a day hike. This is a corridor trail, well maintained but also well trafficked. Mule trains have the right of way. Step to the inside of the trail and let them pass. Wait quietly until the last mule is 50 feet away before continuing your hike.

The trail switches back and forth through

South Kaibab Trail hikers need to prepare for sun exposure.

© RICHARD MAYER

the Kaibab Formation as it starts descending into the canyon. In less than a mile, views open up to the east at Ooh Aah Point, a good turnaround for a short day hike. At Cedar Ridge (1.5 miles), the park's most popular day-hike destination, you'll begin traversing the Coconino sandstone. You'll find toilets here, but no water. The trail continues along the east side of Cedar Ridge toward prominent O'Neill Butte. At three miles is Skeleton Point, another fine day-hike destination. From here, switchbacks make a steep descent to the Tonto Platform. The trail intersects the Tonto Trail at the 4.4-mile point, where there are toilets and an emergency phone.

Just beyond the intersection, at the Tip-Off, the steep walls of the Inner Gorge descend sharply toward the river. At about five miles, you'll reach Panorama Point, with views of the Colorado River and the Black (Kaibab) and Silver (Bright Angel) Bridges. The trail continues its steep descent to the junction with the River Trail. At the six-mile point, the trail passes through a 50-yard tunnel leading to the Black Bridge, which spans more than 400 feet across the river.

After crossing the bridge, the trail heads west, passing near Bright Angel Ruins and the River Ranger Station before continuing to the smaller bridge that crosses Bright Angel Creek at the entrance to the campground. Phantom Ranch is another 0.5 miles up the trail.

South Bass Trail

- Distance: 16 miles round-trip to the Colorado River
- Duration: 2 days or more
- Elevation loss: 4,400 feet from rim to river
- Effort: Strenuous
- Trailhead: 30 miles west of Grand Canyon Village

Getting to the trailhead for this wilderness hike may require two hours or more, along with a good map. You'll be crossing the Havasupai Reservation, and you may be asked to pay a fee. From the west side of the village, head south on Rowe Well Road. Turn west, following signs for Pasture Wash or Forest Road 328, a rough dirt road that may be impassable in wet weather. Even long after a rain, ruts remain, making a high-clearance vehicle a necessity and 4WD recommended. (Whenever you're traveling forest roads in remote areas like this, it's a good idea to ask rangers about current conditions before starting out.) The rewards are scenic views that encompass the Shinumo Amphitheater monuments backed by Powell Point along with the western canyon, plus a journey along the trail used by the first nonnative man to raise a family at Grand Canyon.

Like many pioneer miners, William Bass supplemented prospecting with guiding tourists, including music teacher Ada Diefendorf, whom he married in 1895. He improved what was once an Indian trail to make it accessible by horseback. His mining camp is on the opposite side of the river, reached by the North Bass Trail. Bass built a cable crossing to complete this rim-to-rim route, the first in Grand Canyon, by 1900.

The South Bass Trail descends from the rim to a series of switchbacks leading to the Esplanade, a shelf of reddish-pink and gray sandstone topped with delicate cryptobiotic crust. Avoid treading on this miniature universe of erosion-preventing mosses, lichens, and algae. Here, the trail heads northwest before descending and turning south to the head of Bass Canyon. It follows the east side of the canyon, then drops to the dry creek bed leading toward the river. The canyon ends in a pourover; look left for a trail climbing the west side. In about 200 yards, a break in the cliffs leads to the river and Bass Rapids. En route, you'll see the *Ross Wheeler,* a rusty metal boat abandoned by a 1915 river expedition.

The beaches here and across the river are popular with boat parties, who stop to explore or camp. They often shuttle back and forth across the river, and you may be able to catch a ride to explore the other side, where the North Bass Trail leads to historic Bass Camp. If you're limited to exploring the south side of the river, you can climb back up the route you took to

the beach and walk another 0.3 miles west to a cairned scramble that leads down to Shinumo Rapids.

Hermit Trail

- Distance: 19.6 miles round-trip from the trailhead to the Colorado River
- Duration: 2 days or more
- Elevation loss: 4,240 feet from rim to river
- Effort: Strenuous
- Trailhead: At Hermits Rest

Hermit Trail begins at the end of the service road west of Hermits Rest. December–February, private vehicles can drive Hermit Road to Hermits Rest and park at the signed parking area at the end of the road. March–November, access is via the Hermits Rest Route shuttle, although backpackers can go to the Backcountry Information Center and request the gate combination to Hermit Road in order to park a private vehicle at the trailhead.

Completed by the Santa Fe Railway in 1912, scenic Hermit Trail is steep but relatively easy to follow. It's a good trail to try after you've had some experience on the corridor trails, offering beautiful views of Hermit Creek Canyon, good day-hike destinations, or an overnight not far from the lush riparian environment of year-round Hermit Creek.

The trail descends toward Hermit Creek Canyon, passing through piñon-juniper woodland and chaparral of the Kaibab, Toroweap, and Coconino Formations. The reddish slopes of Hermit shale that mark Hermit Basin, near the intersection with the Waldron Trail at 1.5 miles, make a good turnaround point for a 2–4-hour day hike.

Stronger day hikers can continue another mile down switchbacks to ledges of Supai sandstone and Santa Maria Spring. En route, at 1.75 miles, the trail intersects the Dripping Springs Trail. Take the right fork to continue on the Hermit Trail to the Santa Maria Spring Resthouse (2.5 miles). The undependable trickle of water here must be treated before drinking.

The Hermit Trail continues through the red rocks of the Supai to the top of the Redwall Formation, then descends down switchbacks known as the Cathedral Stairs before angling west and intersecting with the eastbound Tonto Trail at the seven-mile point. In less than a mile, a signed junction indicates the trail to Hermit Rapids. This trail descends to Hermit Creek and follows the dry creek bed to the Colorado River, another 1.5 miles. The left fork, signed "Hermit Creek," first passes the rarely used Hermit Ranger Station, then leads to the ruins of Hermit Creek Camp, operated by the Santa Fe Railroad from 1913 to 1930. The present-day campsites are below the ruins on a bench of Tapeats sandstone. Near camp is the westbound Tonto Trail. To get to the river, follow the Tapeats narrows downstream 1.4 miles, until it opens onto a sandy beach above Hermit Rapids, another area where backpackers can set up camp.

Boucher Trail

- Distance: 8 miles from the trailhead to the Colorado River, plus 2.75 miles on intersecting trails to reach the trailhead; 21.5 miles total round-trip
- Duration: 3 days or more
- Elevation loss: 2,520 feet from rim to river
- Effort: Very strenuous
- Trailhead: Dripping Springs junction

To reach the Boucher Trail, you'll need to start on the Hermit and Dripping Springs Trails, adding 2.75 miles to your trip. Sections of the trail are hard to follow, and route-finding experience is necessary. The trail isn't recommended for day hikers, but experienced backpackers will have expansive views of the Inner Gorge and Granite Rapids, along with the chance to explore the ruins of an old mining camp. Louis D. Boucher, the French-Canadian "hermit" who inspired so many Grand Canyon place names, built this trail to his copper mine and cabin in the 1890s. One modern-day drawback: the nearly constant drone of tour helicopters during daylight hours.

The Boucher Trail begins on a piñon- and juniper-studded Supai shelf above Hermit Creek Canyon. As the trail edges the canyon, Hermit Camp and Hermit Trail come into view below. At 2.5 miles, below Yuma Point, the Colorado River and Granite Rapids are visible. There are fine campsites along this slickrock shelf.

The trail continues west toward the head of Travertine Canyon, where a very steep and dangerous descent leads down through the Supai layers to the floor of the side canyon. From here the trail climbs north toward Whites Butte, leading toward a saddle where you'll begin the final descent through the Redwall to Boucher Creek, another 1.5 miles. En route, you'll pass the junction with eastbound Tonto Trail; bear left to continue to the creek. The side canyon is narrow but pleasant, with room for a couple of tent sites not far from the ruins of Louis Boucher's cabin. Creek water must be treated before drinking.

To reach the Colorado River, follow the creek bed another 1.5 miles. As Topaz Canyon joins Boucher Creek, cairns mark the route of the intersecting westbound Tonto Trail. Bear right, continuing down Boucher Creek. Dark gray Vishnu schist—the canyon's oldest and deepest rock layer—forms the creek bed as the side canyon approaches the river and Boucher Rapids. The beach has room for a few campsites.

Waldron Trail

- Distance: 4 miles round-trip
- Duration: 2–3 hours round-trip
- Elevation loss: 1,020 feet
- Effort: Moderate
- Trailhead: Horsethief Tank, 6 miles west of Grand Canyon Village

If you have a high-clearance vehicle, the Waldron Trail offers a shadier alternative to reaching Dripping Springs or other West Rim trails. This lightly used connector trail crosses the piñon-juniper woodland of Hermit (Waldron) Basin to intersect with the Hermit Trail.

The trailhead is located six miles west of the village on a network of dirt roads, near Horsethief Tank. (A "tank" is a natural or constructed depression for capturing runoff, usually as a livestock pond.) For the most part the grade is gentle, with a steep descent about midway as the trail climbs down the Toroweap and Coconino sandstone layers.

Hermit Basin makes a good day hike destination, or you can continue past the junction with Hermit Trail to Santa Maria Spring (another mile) or Dripping Springs (another 1.5 miles) via other trails.

Dripping Springs Trail

- Distance: 6.5 miles round-trip (via Hermit Trail)
- Duration: 5 hours round-trip
- Elevation loss: 1,600 feet
- Effort: Moderate
- Trailhead: Hermits Rest

Dripping Springs Trail skirts above the head of Hermit Gorge, west of the village. The little-used historic trailhead is remote and difficult to access via several dirt roads or a long walk from Horsethief Tank. Instead, most hikers reach Dripping Springs from the east via the Hermit Trail. This route is a good day hike, and spring hikers may see blossoming barberry, cliffrose, mock orange, and redbud on the way to the spring-fed "garden" of ferns and scarlet monkey-flowers.

The junction is 1.75 miles from the start of the Hermit Trail. It's another 1.5 miles along the Dripping Springs Trail across the Hermit Shale Formation to the spring. The intersecting Boucher Trail leads deep into the canyon, where "hermit" Louis Boucher had a cabin, orchard, and copper mine around the turn of the 20th century. Keep left to reach Dripping Springs, where Boucher had another camp.

Just past three miles, the alcove that shelters the spring is a good day-hike destination. The historic Dripping Springs Trail continues west to its remote trailhead, making a steep and rocky climb to the rim. Most hikers choose to return the way they came. Spring water must be treated before drinking; begin the hike with enough water for the return trip.

Grandview Trail

- Distance: 6 miles round-trip
- Duration: 6 hours round-trip
- Elevation loss: 2,600 feet
- Effort: Strenuous
- Trailhead: Grandview Point

Look for the trailhead at Grandview Point, 12 miles east of the village off Highway 64 (East Rim Dr.). Trailhead parking is signed, and the trail begins at the east side of the viewpoint wall. The trail follows sections of a pioneer trail built by miner Pete Berry, who managed the Last Chance, a copper mine on Horseshoe Mesa. Here and there, hikers will notice the log cribbing that supported the trail when mules carried out loads of ore. The Last Chance Mine is on the National Register of Historic Places, and strong day hikers or backpackers can explore the ruins and imagine the life of a Grand Canyon miner. Views are spectacular, but the trail is steep, bringing to mind the old hiker's saying, "Don't walk and gawk at the same time."

After dropping steeply from Grandview Point, the trail traverses the Coconino Saddle between Hance and Grapevine Canyons. The saddle, at about one mile, is a good turnaround for a shorter day hike. From here the trail descends again toward Horseshoe Mesa. As you approach the mesa, you'll pass a trail branching to the right. This branch leads to the east side of the mesa for 1.8 miles until joining the Tonto Trail, passing by a spur to Page Springs, bubbling out from the base of the Redwall. This is the only local water source.

The main trail branches left and descends to the mesa, at three miles. Here, another trail leads left, heading across the west arm of the mesa and into Cottonwood Creek Canyon. However, most day hikers will want to continue straight ahead to the ruins of Pete Berry's mining cabin, just beyond the three-mile point.

© KATHLEEN BRYANT

In winter, the top of Grandview Trail is often snow-packed.

It's a good spot to turn around, although the trail continues another two miles across the west arm of the mesa and down to an intersection with the Tonto Trail.

A spur trail leads east of the cabin to a toilet and several campsites. Backpackers can use this as a base camp to explore the remains of the historic mining camp and the edges of the mesa, enjoying great views of the Inner Gorge before returning up Grandview Trail or before continuing onto other trails for a loop trip.

New Hance Trail

- Distance: 14 miles round-trip from the trailhead to the Colorado River
- Duration: 3 days or more
- Elevation loss: 4,400 feet from rim to river
- Effort: Very strenuous
- Trailhead: Desert View Drive, between Buggeln picnic area and Moran Point

The trailhead is one mile southwest of the parking area at Moran Point, 18 miles east of Grand Canyon Village. There's no parking here, but you can cache your packs near the trailhead, then park at Moran Point and walk back, adding an extra mile to the hike each way. The trail is called the New Hance Trail because pioneer John Hance built it when his original trail washed out. It's also known as the Red Canyon Trail because it follows the bed of Red Canyon, where bright orange-red Hakatai shale, part of the Grand Canyon Supergroup, makes an appearance. Probably the most difficult South Rim trail, it gives contemporary hikers a sense of the effort pioneering miners (and their mules) expended to bring minerals out of the canyon.

The trail begins as a deceptively easy walk to the rim on an old road before dropping sharply through switchbacks in the Kaibab limestone. The Sinking Ship looms to the west, tilting up from behind Coronado Butte. The trail clambers over and around boulders and slabs on its way to a saddle at the base of the Coconino sandstone formation, just over one mile. Washouts and side trails can make route-finding difficult—just one of the reasons many backpackers consider New Hance to be the South Rim's most difficult route. Another is its steepness: allow plenty of time for the hike out; consider spending a second night in the canyon.

The trail descends from the saddle into the Supai Group, then follows the east rim of Red Canyon for about one mile, a rough up-and-down traverse across several rocky drainages. The mile-long section along the top of the Redwall formation edges a 500-foot vertical drop—step carefully. Cairns mark a break in the Redwall limestone at approximately three miles. For experienced day hikers, this makes a good turnaround point, offering views into fault-formed Red Canyon and across the main canyon to the North Rim's Cape Royal and Wotans Throne.

The trail drops from a fin of Redwall limestone down steep talus slopes, reaching the bottom of seasonally dry Red Canyon at about five miles. The winding creek bottom leads a couple of miles farther to the Colorado River, where you'll see—and hear—the "rock garden" of Hance Rapids, the most challenging rapids that river runners face in Grand Canyon's upper half.

Tanner Trail

- Distance: 20 miles round-trip from the trailhead to the Colorado River
- Duration: 2 days or more
- Elevation loss: 4,600 feet from rim to river
- Effort: Very strenuous
- Trailhead: Lipan Point

The Tanner Trail begins at Lipan Point, 23 miles east of Grand Canyon Village. Look for the trailhead east of the overlook's loop-shaped parking area. The trail, an old Indian route later improved by Seth Tanner and other prospectors, was once favored by horse thieves moving stock to and from the Arizona Strip. The trail is challenging and isn't maintained, but it offers views of the Colorado River and the broad eastern canyon, where the layers of the Grand Canyon Supergroup have been sculpted into colorfully banded hills and folds. You'll be able to see the Colorado River for much of the hike—a view you might find taunting, considering that there's no water and virtually no protection from the sun along the trail. The park service discourages hiking this trail in summer.

The trail begins in the piñon-juniper woodland of the rim, then descends steeply toward Tanner Canyon. After switching back and forth through talus slopes, the trail reaches a saddle ridge between Tanner Canyon and Seventyfive Mile Creek Canyon, just under two miles. This is a good destination for a day hike, considering the steepness of the trail.

After crossing the saddle, the trail traverses Escalante and Cardenas Buttes (named for the Spanish explorers). Once past Cardenas Butte, the trail descends the Redwall Formation to a fork at about 3.5 miles. The left spur leads to an overlook with excellent views of Tanner Rapids and broad Tanner beach, all the way upriver to the point where the canyon narrows at the Palisades of the Desert. This is another possible day-hike destination for strong hikers.

The Tanner Trail continues to the right, descending steeply toward a saddle, then down the Bright Angel Shale Formation, traversing the open slopes above the edge of Tanner Canyon. The trail drops sharply again before reaching the Colorado River near Tanner Rapids. The large sand dune at the mouth of Tanner Canyon is closed to visitors. Campsites can be found near the river on the east side of Tanner Canyon, and you may be sharing them with river runners.

BIKING

If you left your bike at home, you can rent one from **Bright Angel Bicycles** (928/814-8704, www.bikegrandcanyon.com, 8 A.M.–6 P.M. daily May–Sept., shorter hours Mar.–Apr. and Oct.–Nov.), located at the South Rim's Grand Canyon Visitors Center. Also available are child-size bikes, pull-behind trailers, and adult-size tricycles. The staff here can help you choose a route, and they offer guided tours twice daily, weather permitting. Bright Angel Bicycles also operates a shuttle service, allowing bicyclists who want to travel Hermit Road to bypass the traffic-congested village area.

Traffic throughout the park is heaviest on summer weekends. Play it safe—wear a helmet and bright colors, use hand signals, and ride single-file in the same direction as traffic. In Arizona, bikes are subject to the same traffic rules as automobiles. Biking is allowed on all paved and dirt roads on the South Rim. However, all hiking trails on the South Rim are off-limits to bicycles. The only exception is the multiuse Greenway Trail.

Hermit Road

Scenic Hermit Road is closed to passenger vehicles March–November. Shuttle buses travel Hermit Road during those months, and bicyclists need to use caution, allowing the large vehicles to pass. At the Monument Creek overlook, bikers can leave Hermit Road for the Greenway Trail, a paved, nonmotorized, multiuse route following the rim for 2.8 miles before rejoining Hermit Road the rest of the way to Hermits Rest. Much of this section of the Greenway follows the 1912 alignment of Hermit Road, when stagecoaches toured the rim.

The Greenway

The Greenway is a nonmotorized bicycle and pedestrian pathway projected to be 45 miles long when complete. Currently, only two short segments have been completed, the 2.8-mile trail along the West Rim, beginning at Monument Creek Vista, and a paved trail connecting the historic village area with Grand Canyon Visitors Center. Eventually, the Greenway will also link to other South Rim locations and the town of Tusayan, outside the park.

Forest Roads

Adjoining Kaibab National Forest (www.fs .usda.gov/kaibab) has miles of dirt roads and trails open to cyclists who want longer rides. Most are lightly traveled, so you'll have a good chance of seeing deer and elk while enjoying natural quiet, shady ponderosa forests,

historic sights, and glimpses of the canyon. One possible side trip is to take Forest Road 307 to Hull Cabin. You can start your adventure by climbing the 80-foot-tall **Grandview Lookout Tower,** built in 1936 by the Civilian Conservation Corps. The tower was used by forest rangers to spot smoke plumes or other signs of wildfire. Today, it marks the start of the Arizona Trail. Built in 1888, **Hull Cabin** is the oldest standing cabin in the Grand Canyon area, the home of sheepherders Philip and William Hull, who partnered with John Hance to bring the first tourists to Grand Canyon. The cabin is on the National Register of Historic Places. (Neighboring cabins house seasonal forest rangers and work crews. Please respect their privacy.)

Depending on winter snow depths, unpaved forest roads can be muddy through April. For current conditions, maps, or additional information about these rides, contact the Tusayan Ranger District of the **Kaibab National Forest** (928/638-2443) or stop by the ranger station, located one mile north of Tusayan on the west side of Highway 64.

Arizona Trail

The Arizona Trail offers several options for mountain bikers. This scenic nonmotorized trail, when complete, will cross the state from the Utah border to the Mexican border, 800 miles in all. To get to the Arizona Trail from inside the park, take Desert View Drive (Hwy. 64) east about nine miles, passing the Grandview Point overlook and continuing two more miles to the Arizona Trail sign, then turning right. The trail begins at the Grandview Lookout Tower, built in 1936 by the Civilian Conservation Corps. If you're starting from Highway 64 in Tusayan, turn east on Forest Road 302 and follow the signs to Grandview Lookout (16 miles). You'll be traveling over old logging roads that meander through ponderosa pine forest. (With the aid of a good map, you can loop back on different roads for the return trip.)

The 12-mile **Coconino Rim** segment of the Arizona Trail, which is open to mountain bikers, hikers, and equestrians, begins south of Grandview Point. The trail follows the edge of a 500-foot-high escarpment that curves to the southeast, offering unusual perspectives on Grand Canyon and distant views of the Painted Desert. At eight miles, a bypass route for bikes avoids a steep series of switchbacks. Just pass 10 miles, the trail crosses Forest Road 310. If you like, you can loop back to the park on Forest Road 310, another seven miles.

For a longer ride, you can continue onto the **Russell Wash** segment of the trail, which begins just south of Russell Tank and parallels a historic stagecoach route. In about three miles, the trail crosses Forest Road 313 and nears the historic Moqui Stage Station, a remnant of the route from Flagstaff to Grand Canyon, in operation from 1892 to 1901. This station was a stop on the 20-hour, $20 ride to the Grandview Point area, the center of tourist accommodations at the time. The Arizona Trail continues all the way to Flagstaff, but you'll probably want to head back to the Grandview area and the national park boundary.

For an especially picturesque side trip, you can add the **Vishnu Trail,** a 1.1-mile scenic loop that starts just north of the fire tower. The trail leads to an overlook on the Coconino Rim offering distant Grand Canyon views, then loops back to the Grandview area via the Arizona Trail.

TRAIL RIDING

Equines (horses, mules, and burros) are allowed on primitive roads and specific trails: the South Kaibab, Bright Angel, River, and Plateau Point Trails. At this writing, the South Kaibab trail was closed to equine use during reconstruction. During the reconstruction period, stock traffic will be heaviest on Bright Angel Trail, and the park service has requested that all potential stock users contact Xanterra's livery stables (928/638-2526, ext. 6095) when planning a trip. In addition, all riders should check in at the **Backcountry Information Center** (928/638-7875, 1–5 P.M. Mon.–Fri.) prior to the trip.

A backcountry permit is required for overnight use, and there are restrictions on the number of animals per group. Permit fees and additional stock fees apply. If riders plan to stay at Phantom Ranch, at least one member of the group must stay in the campground with the animals. Campgrounds can accommodate only one group of equestrians at a time. On the South Rim, there is a horse camp 0.5 miles from the Bright Angel Trailhead.

Animals must stay on specified trails. No grazing is allowed, and feed must be packed in. Hay must be weed-certified. Pack animals must be tied together and led single file. Riders accept all responsibility for their own and their animals' safety.

Trails and roads in neighboring Kaibab National Forest are open to equine use (horses, mules, or burros) unless otherwise posted, or unless the animals pose a danger to free-ranging livestock. Contact the forest's **Tusayan Ranger District** (928/638-2443) for more information.

WINTER ACTIVITIES

The South Rim is open year-round, and winter hikes into the canyon might start in ice and snow, making trails treacherous, before leading into pleasant low-desert temperatures along the Colorado River. Trails may be snow-covered down to the Redwall Formation (roughly one-third to halfway from rim to river)—but with crampons or snow cleats to negotiate icy sections, winter hiking offers solitude and quiet; clear air; beautiful sunrises and sunsets, due to the lower angle of the sun; and plenty of wildlife-watching.

The park website (www.nps.gov/grca) has current weather information as well as valuable trail-specific information about typical winter conditions. Backcountry updates are posted online, and notices about current trail conditions and closures are available as an RSS feed. For the latest information, contact the **Backcountry Information Center** (928/638-7875, 1–5 P.M. Mon.–Fri.).

Cross-country skiing and **snowshoeing** opportunities are relatively limited on the South Rim. Snowfall varies from year to year, and due to Arizona's longstanding drought,

THE KOLB BROTHERS

Ellsworth and Emery Kolb arrived at Grand Canyon in 1902. The enterprising and energetic brothers bought out a photographic studio in Williams, Arizona, and moved the equipment to Grand Canyon, setting up their new business in a canvas tent. They photographed mule riders descending the Bright Angel toll trail owned by Ralph Cameron. Nearby, Cameron had fashioned a hotel out of the Red Horse stage station, which he'd moved to the canyon's rim. The Kolbs, Ralph Cameron, and Cameron's Bright Angel Trail were stiff competition for the Fred Harvey Company and the Santa Fe Railway, which answered with Hermit Trail and Hermit Camp.

At the time, the rim's water supply was limited, so the Kolbs set up a developing lab 4.5 miles down Bright Angel Trail at Indian Garden, the nearest source of clear running water. They photographed tourists descending the trail in the morning, then ran ahead to process the glass plates. They returned to the rim in time to sell the mule riders their souvenir portraits. A dashing pair, the Kolb brothers also hiked and explored, taking photos of their cliff-dangling exploits (and off-duty Harvey Girls).

The Kolbs began building their wood-frame studio in 1904. In 1911-1912, they ran the Colorado River through Grand Canyon, filming the expedition. Very few parties had successfully navigated the Colorado since Powell's journeys, and the Kolbs were the first to make a moving picture of the trip. For decades, Grand Canyon visitors gathered to watch the film in the studio's auditorium.

Emery married a Harvey Girl, Blanche Bender, in 1905, and Ellsworth moved to Los Angeles in 1924. Construction on their studio continued through 1926 as business – and Emery's family – expanded. Blanche and Emery's daughter Edith often accompanied her father on his photographic explorations. In later years, some people considered Kolb Studio an eyesore and lobbied the Park Service to oust Emery. But feisty Emery prevailed, showing his movie until his death at age 95. The Park Service acquired the studio in 1976, after Emery's death, and decided to preserve it. The Grand Canyon Association (GCA) funded the building's restoration. The Kolbs' vast photo collection is archived at Northern Arizona University's Cline Library. The library and the GCA prepared the interactive video on display in the studio's projection room, showing clips of the Kolb brothers running the Colorado River.

the last few winters have been on the dry side. The best location for finding adequate snow cover is the Grandview Point area on the East Rim, and the best time is mid-December–early March. The ponderosa forest shelters a winter population of juncos, chickadees, nuthatches, and Steller's jays. Below the pines, deer and elk tracks trail through the snow.

Two miles east of Grandview Point, the **Arizona Trail** parking area offers access to the **Kaibab National Forest** (928/638-2443, www.fs.usda.gov/kaibab). If snow cover is adequate, and if you don't mind breaking trail, you can head off into the forest in any direction, including historic Hull Cabin or the scenic Coconino Rim.

Entertainment and Events

RANGER PROGRAMS

From June to September about two dozen ranger programs are offered each day, including guided walks and nature talks, at various locations around Grand Canyon Village, Grand Canyon Visitors Center, Tusayan Museum, and Desert View. These free programs, lasting from 20 minutes to four hours, are a great way to gain a more in-depth understanding of Grand Canyon, whether your interest is condors or constellations, birds or brachiopods. Many programs are geared toward families and children, such as storytelling, easy nature hikes, or activities leading to a Junior Ranger certificate and badge.

Offerings are fewer during the winter, but still include a variety of lectures, hikes, and other activities throughout the day. See *The Guide* for schedules. Sometimes additional programs are added at the last minute; announcements about changes or additions are posted at the Grand Canyon Visitors Center, along the rim near El Tovar or Bright Angel Lodge, and at Yavapai Observation Station.

EVENTS

Park events are distributed throughout the year, peaking in fall when the weather is at its finest. Possibilities include lectures by visiting scholars, free digital camera workshops offered by vendors, art openings at Kolb Studio, or book signings and author appearances in lodges and shops. Annual events are posted on the park's website (www.nps.gov/grca) or described in *The Guide*, which you can preview online before your visit to help you plan your time.

One of the park's most anticipated events is the **Grand Canyon Music Festival** (928/638-9215 or 800/997-8285, www.grandcanyonmusicfest.org), an annual gathering of musicians that has grown since its inaugural 1984 season to more than half a dozen concerts over a two-week period each September. Every year the festival offers a wide repertoire of classical to contemporary music, and some events are free.

Past performers have included Robert Bonfiglio (a festival cofounder), R. Carlos Nakai, the Amadeus Trio, and the Calder Quartet. Most of the concerts are held at the Shrine of the Ages, an indoor auditorium on the east side of the village at Park Headquarters.

A relatively new event—or rather, series of events—is the fall **Celebration of Art,** when landscape painters from around the United States travel to the South Rim to work *en plein air,* painting outdoors on location. A highlight is the "quick draw," when artists create paintings in two hours to be auctioned later in the day. The Celebration of Art culminates in a juried exhibit with an opening reception at Kolb Studio.

Fall is a good time for naturalists to visit the canyon. Every October, the public is welcome to participate when members of **HawkWatch International** record the annual hawk migration over Yaki Point. The park usually hosts lectures or informal talks on Grand Canyon's raptors to coincide with this event. Also in October, special programs are featured during Earth Science Week.

March is Arizona's Archaeology Awareness Month, with statewide events that include **Archaeology Day** at Grand Canyon with various family-oriented hands-on activities such as making split-twig figurines like those on display in Tusayan Museum. In June, the South Rim holds its highly popular annual **Star Party,** when amateur astronomers present a slide show at the main visitors center and set up telescopes for nighttime viewing.

Historic **Kolb Studio,** located a few yards west of Bright Angel Lodge at the head of Bright Angel Trail, hosts revolving exhibits that sometimes launch with opening-night festivities. Exhibits change three or four times a year, usually featuring paintings, photographs, or historic artifacts relating to the canyon.

Art events such as workshops, demonstrations, or performances are offered monthly by the South Rim's **artists-in-residence.** Artists specializing in a variety of media compete for the chance to live and work at Grand Canyon. Writers, photographers, visual artists, and performers have participated in past artist-in-residence programs at the South Rim. Check *The Guide* for art events scheduled during your stay. If you're an artist interested in applying for residency, visit the park's website (www.nps .gov/grca/supportyourpark/air.htm) for more information.

During the canyon's less-visited periods, rangers and staff may host impromptu events, such as an off-season, behind-the-scenes tour of Kolb Studio, a condor puppet show, or a full-moon walk through the South Rim's pioneer cemetery. Last-minute programs are posted at Grand Canyon Visitors Center and at locations around the village.

NIGHTLIFE

If your alarm isn't set for dark-thirty to get an early start on a hike or to watch the sunrise, you'll find a few things to while away the evening in Grand Canyon Village. The Village Route shuttle runs until 11 P.M. daily June–August, and until 10 P.M. daily in May and September, but many venues are within walking distance of rim lodges. It's a good idea to carry a small flashlight for getting around the village area after dark.

Nighttime ranger programs include campfire talks at Mather Amphitheater and moonlight walks near Mather Point. Shrine of the Ages, located at Park Headquarters, often hosts ranger talks or art performances.

Inside Maswik Lodge, the **Pizza Pub** (5–11 P.M. Mon.–Fri., 3–11 P.M. Sat.–Sun.) has suds and snacks, TVs tuned to current games, and pool, air hockey, and video games. **The Bright Angel Bar** (11 A.M.–close, hours vary seasonally) occasionally offers live entertainment, generally folk or acoustic country music. **El Tovar's lounge** is a comfortable, quiet place to gather for drinks and conversation or a light meal.

South of the park entrance in the town of Tusayan, hotel lounges at the **Canyon Plaza** (928/638-2673), **Grand Canyon Squire** (928/638-2681), and the **Grand Hotel** (928/638-3333) stay open late. The Canyon Star Saloon in the Grand Hotel often has live music or performances. The Grand Canyon Squire has a billiards lounge and bowling alley.

SHOPPING

You'll find roughly three shopping categories at the canyon (or four, if you count necessities like groceries and gear): inexpensive souvenirs, education-themed items, and art. Many of the canyon's shops carry some of each, so unless you're a retail maven, you can get all your shopping done in a couple of stops. If you have time to browse only two stores, make one Hopi House, notable not just for its selection but also for its landmark architecture. If you make your other shopping stop at one of the Grand Canyon Association's stores, you'll have seen the cream of the canyon's retail crop.

Grand Canyon's rich history of traders includes the Fred Harvey Company and the pioneering Verkamp and Babbitt families. The Verkamps began selling curios from a tent along the rim in 1905, and when Verkamp's Curios closed in 2008, it ended the longest family-operated concession in the national parks. The Babbitts, ranchers and Indian traders, arrived in Flagstaff, Arizona, in 1886 and operated the general stores at Grand Canyon until 1999. (Descendant Bruce Babbitt acted as Arizona's governor 1978–1987, ran for president in 1988, and served as former president Clinton's Secretary of the Interior.) The Fred Harvey Company (acquired by Xanterra Parks & Resorts in 1968) opened Hopi House in 1905 and continues to operate it and half a dozen other gift shops at the South Rim.

Fred Harvey Company stores (303/338-6070, 7 A.M.–10 P.M. daily) at Bright Angel, Maswik, and Yavapai Lodges carry similar inventories of postcards, posters, T-shirts, hats, videos, music, jewelry, and more. The broad selection ranges from inexpensive souvenirs to well-made Native American jewelry, sand paintings, and tapestries. The gift shops clearly label American-made merchandise, but if you're unsure, ask.

© ELIZABETH JANG

Hopi House features a superb selection of Native American arts and crafts.

At Maswik Lodge, you'll also find some display cases of old pawn, pieces of Indian jewelry that have gone unredeemed. Also known as "dead pawn," these vintage items are often highly collectible, especially since several of the Southwest's historic turquoise mines have been depleted, and jewelry may be set with stone types no longer available today.

El Tovar has the ritziest accommodations at the canyon, and the **lobby gift shop** (7 A.M.–10 P.M. daily) caters to tonier tastes. Look here for quality Southwestern-style clothing, lavishly illustrated cookbooks or coffee-table books, and fine Native American jewelry.

Mary Colter's imaginative architectural creations are attractions themselves, designed to entice travelers to Grand Canyon in the days when railroads competed heavily for passenger traffic. Built in 1914, **Lookout Studio** (8 A.M.–sunset daily summer, 9 A.M.–5 P.M. daily winter) offers a wide selection of rocks and fossils to please the kiddos but continues its historic focus on photography with postcards, posters, and photographic prints. Another 1914 Colter

building, **Hermits Rest** (8 A.M.–sunset daily summer, 9 A.M.–5 P.M. daily winter) has just enough room for a little bit of everything—but somehow the smaller selection, artfully arranged, looks more tempting here than in any of the lodge shops.

Mary Colter designed her first Grand Canyon building, **Hopi House** (8 A.M.–8 P.M. daily summer, 9 A.M.–5 P.M. daily winter), to showcase native cultures and their traditions. You'll find the usual T-shirts, books, and gifts downstairs, but the upstairs gallery in Hopi House boasts a selection of Native American arts and crafts that is unmatched anywhere else at Grand Canyon. A narrow staircase leads to the second level, where museum-quality work by some of the leading artisans from Hopi, Navajo, and other regional cultures is displayed. Occasionally, weavers demonstrate their craft here, just as Mary Colter had envisioned over 100 years ago.

The Desert View Trading Post and Watchtower (8 A.M.–sunset daily summer, 9 A.M.–5 P.M. daily winter) both have wide selections. In the Watchtower, which Mary Colter modeled after prehistoric structures, the gift shop emphasizes the Native American theme with musical selections by Indian performers, traditional crafts, and silver jewelry.

The Fred Harvey Company also operates two stores in Tusayan, the **Grand Canyon Trading Post** (828/638-2417, 8 A.M.–8 P.M. daily) and the Grand Canyon Airport gift shop (9 A.M.–7 P.M. daily).

The Grand Canyon Association (GCA, www.grandcanyon.org) manages stores that do double duty as information centers at Grand Canyon Visitors Center, Kolb Studio, Verkamp's, Yavapai Observation Station, Tusayan Museum, and the Desert View Visitors Center and Bookstore. Locations are staffed by canyon-savvy GCA employees and often park rangers as well.

A nonprofit organization founded in 1932, the GCA uses money from sales to support national park programs and publications. GCA members receive a 15 percent discount at the organization's shops at the canyon or online. If you're looking for maps, such as the famous "Blue Dragon" map of the canyon's geology, books on natural or cultural history, or educational items for kids, the selection at GCA stores is superb.

Books & More (8 A.M.–8 P.M. daily summer, 8 A.M.–5 P.M. daily winter), the GCA store at Grand Canyon Visitors Center, is the largest gift shop on the South Rim. GCA also stocks a small selection of books and gifts inside the General Store at Market Plaza.

Currently operated by Delaware North Companies, the **General Store at Market Plaza** (928/638-2262, 7 A.M.–9 P.M. daily summer, 9 A.M.–5 P.M. daily winter) continues to be a canyon mainstay. If you need some serious outdoor gear, such as crampons or a camp stove, you'll find it here, along with groceries, sundries, and souvenirs. The General Store rents camping and backpacking equipment, an ideal solution for those who don't feel like carrying gear on the plane. Delaware North also operates the smaller **Desert View Marketplace** (928/638-2393, 8 A.M.–6 P.M. daily summer, 9 A.M.–5 P.M. daily winter) 30 miles east of the village near the park's East Entrance.

Accommodations

It's ideal to stay at one of the lodges in Grand Canyon Village, all within walking distance of the rim and linked by the park's free shuttle system. If you're visiting the South Rim during high season, make reservations several months in advance, whether you plan to stay in a hotel or in a tent. Plan to spend $100–200 per night for a hotel room during your Grand Canyon stay, although rates go down as the distance from the canyon increases. If you stay inside the park, you'll sacrifice some amenities (like swimming pools and Internet hookups), but you'll avoid the hassle of commuting—namely, long lines at the entrance station and the search for parking.

If you're traveling with the family pet, or if you prefer resort-style accommodations, you'll find plenty of choices in the town of Tusayan, two miles south of the main entrance station.

You can also find relatively inexpensive accommodations here. During summer months, it's possible to leave your car behind at your Tusayan hotel and take one of the free shuttles to the park.

Whether it's a budget necessity or a recreation preference, camping is a fine choice. Campgrounds in the area range from rustic forest camps to RV parks with full amenities. The three campgrounds inside the park fall in the middle of that range. Wherever you're camping, arrive early. Even if you have reservations, it's a good idea to browse the available sites. During summer, you'll appreciate a site offering afternoon shade. Keep in mind that the convenience of being closer to roads or camper services may mean sacrificing quiet. Price doesn't always correspond with quality of experience. Two of the most pleasant campgrounds near Grand Canyon, the park's Desert View and the forest service's Ten-X, are among the most reasonable options. More money might translate to more amenities, but you could find yourself next to noisy Grand Canyon Airport or a busy highway.

INSIDE THE PARK
Lodges and Hotels

"You're not just close—you're there," is the mantra of **Xanterra Parks & Resorts,** and it's absolutely true. If you want to immerse yourself in the national park experience, a stay inside is a must. Xanterra (928/638-2631 for same-day reservations, 888/297-2757, www.grand-canyonlodges.com) operates six hotels at the park's South Rim, including historic El Tovar Hotel and Bright Angel Lodge, for a total of 907 rooms. In 1968, Xanterra (then known as Amfac) acquired the Fred Harvey Company, continuing to manage and operate the South Rim's lodges and many of its gift shops. If you happen to be a history or architecture buff, you'll appreciate how each lodge speaks to a different era of Grand Canyon travel.

Make reservations early; lodges are often completely booked from late spring to early autumn. In winter, some lodges may close for a few weeks, so even though there are fewer visitors, there are also fewer rooms available. Xanterra regularly renovates its lodges, and you can ask if recently refurbished rooms are available. Most lodges have some accessible guest rooms. Note that all lodges are nonsmoking, and pets aren't allowed. Promotional discounts are often available during the winter months, the canyon's off-season.

◖ **El Tovar** is the "log palace" built in 1905 by the Santa Fe Railway to lure well-heeled tourists to Grand Canyon. It is still the most elegantly appointed lodging at Grand Canyon, and its 78 guest rooms have been refurbished to satisfy contemporary tastes. With luxury suites, room service, a concierge desk, an elegant dining room, and morning coffee on the mezzanine, you might feel like you're in a major city...until you look out your window for views of the canyon or forest, or see mule deer browsing the lawn. Standard guest rooms with one double bed start at $178 ($209 queen), deluxe rooms are $273 with two queens or one king. Extra persons are $14 each. Suites ($335–426) have a bedroom and a sitting room and may include a porch or balcony.

Mary Colter designed **Bright Angel Lodge** and cabins in 1935 to look like a pioneer settlement of log, clapboard, and pueblo-style cabins. The lodge is central to rim activities, most notably the Bright Angel Trail, which begins just a few steps away. It also has a family restaurant, a steak house, a coffeehouse and bar, and a soda fountain. Accommodations range from simple "hiker rooms" with shared bath ($81) to private cabins ($113–178). The Bright Angel cabins perched along the rim are some of the nicest lodging options at the canyon. All guest rooms have phones, but only the cabins have TVs. Four of the rim cabins have their own fireplaces. Suites ($178–340) include the historic log cabin on the rim that once belonged to sheriff and Rough Rider Buckey O'Neill.

Kachina and **Thunderbird Lodges** are perched on the canyon rim between El Tovar and Bright Angel. Built as part of the Department of the Interior's Mission 66 plan for modernizing national park facilities, these lodges were slated for demolition to open up rim views and restore a more historic feel to the village. Several factors, from politics to funding, have kept park administration from proceeding with the demolition, and in the meantime, these two rim-side lodges have begun to show a certain historic appeal. Recent renovations have highlighted their midcentury style, sort of a *Jetsons*-meets-Western feel. Guest rooms ($173–184) at both of these small lodges (49 and 55 units) have two queen beds or one king, with the higher price for canyon-view rooms. Other amenities include an in-room coffeemaker and refrigerator, a telephone, and a TV. If you're staying at the Kachina, you'll check in at El Tovar. Thunderbird guests check in at Bright Angel Lodge.

Maswik Lodge is tucked into the forest about 0.25 miles from the canyon's edge. The

© KATHLEEN BRYANT

Historic Bright Angel Lodge has welcomed travelers since 1935.

lodge's north section is a few years newer than the south section, and Maswik North guest rooms have more amenities, including air-conditioning. All of Maswik's 278 guest rooms, including the cabins (summer only, $92), have private baths, phones, and TVs. Maswik North guest rooms ($173) also have in-room coffee and refrigerators and a choice of two queen beds or one king. Maswik South rooms ($92), usually a little smaller, have two queen beds. The lodge's main building includes a cafeteria, a sports pub, and a gift shop, with a transportation desk in the lobby.

With 358 guest rooms in its two wings, **Yavapai Lodge** is the South Rim's largest in-park motel. It's also the farthest from the rim, at 0.5 miles, although it is conveniently close to Market Plaza and campground services, making it a good choice for families. All guest rooms have TVs and phones, and most have two queen beds (Yavapai West, $114; Yavapai East, $163), but some Yavapai East guest rooms have one king bed. Note that Yavapai West doesn't have air-conditioning, although

ceiling fans are usually adequate for South Rim summers. Yavapai East guest rooms have air-conditioning as well as in-room refrigerators and coffeemakers.

Campgrounds

There are three campgrounds at the South Rim: two near the South Entrance Station and Grand Canyon Village, and the other at Desert View, near the park's East Entrance. **Mather Campground** (877/444-6777, www.recreation .gov) accepts reservations up to six months in advance. Although it's the park's largest campground, with more than 300 sites, Mather is usually fully booked during busy summer months. Often, however, campers leave early and spaces open up. There's no waiting list—check in person for last-minute availability.

Mather campground is located in Grand Canyon Village near Market Plaza, 0.5 miles from the rim. Sites ($18) accommodate tents and RVs up to 30 feet and have grills, picnic tables, and paved parking but no hookups. You can have up to two vehicles, three tents, and six people per site. Group sites ($50) are available for groups up to 50 people with a maximum of three vehicles. Discounts are given to Golden Age and Golden Access pass holders. Mid-November–February, fees are lower and reservations aren't accepted. The Campground Services building has coin-operated showers and laundry.

Trailer Village (888/297-2757 or 928/638-2631 for same-day reservations, www.grandcanyonlodges.com), 0.5 miles from the rim in Grand Canyon Village, has 84 paved RV sites with full hookups ($35 for 2 people) for vehicles up to 50 feet long. Sites have picnic tables, grills, and cable TV hookup. Showers and laundry are available at the Camper Services building, and a dump station is located next to Mather Campground.

◖ Desert View Campground (May–mid-Oct.), 26 miles east of Grand Canyon Village near the park's East Entrance Station, has 50 first-come, first-served campsites. During the busy summertime, the campground usually fills by afternoon. Each site ($12) has a grill but no water. Two faucets are available in the campground, and there are restroom buildings nearby with sinks and flush toilets but no showers. The campground closes for winter in mid-October.

TUSAYAN
Hotels, Motels, and Lodges

Tusayan owes its existence entirely to the park, so the town is heavy on motels and restaurants but not on charm. Hotels, motels, restaurants, shops, and other tourism businesses line Highway 64 just 1–2 miles south of the South Entrance Station. Tusayan is convenient to Grand Canyon Airport and the IMAX theater as well as numerous tour operators. Several Tusayan hotels offer the amenities of resort or business travel, and during summer months the park's free shuttle route extends here. Although the town was recently incorporated, addresses continue to read "Grand Canyon, Arizona." But don't let the address confuse you: There are no canyon views here, even though you're only a couple of miles away from the Rim.

The expansive **Best Western Grand Canyon Squire Inn** (100 Hwy. 64, 928/638-2681 or 800/622-6966, www.grandcanyonsquire.com, $90–220) has an outdoor swimming pool, an exercise room, a year-round spa, a beauty salon, and a family activity room featuring everything from billiards to video games. The Squire Inn has two full-service restaurants, and the bowling alley lounge serves drinks and snacks. Standard guest rooms, deluxe rooms, and suites are available, and rates include a continental breakfast. The 250-room inn offers vacation packages that include plane, helicopter, or raft tours, and meetings and banquets can be accommodated.

The 121-room **Grand Hotel** (149 Hwy. 64, 888/634-7263 or 928/638-3333, www.grandcanyongrandhotel.com, $99–409) was built in 1998 in an old-fashioned mountain-lodge style, with a piano lobby, a fireplace, exposed timbers, and modern amenities that include an indoor pool and hot tub, a fitness center, a lounge, a sports bar, meeting rooms, and event-planning services. Some guest rooms and suites have patios or balconies, and pets are allowed in some guest rooms. Lodging packages can be customized to include tours.

Canyon Plaza Resort (406 Canyon Plaza Lane, 928/638-2673 or 800/995-2521, www.grandcanyonplaza.com, $72–248) has guest rooms and suites. Amenities include free continental breakfast, Internet access, a dining room, a lounge, a spa, an outdoor swimming pool, and a hot tub. Meeting and banquet facilities are available, and pets can be accommodated. Packages can include air, horse, and raft tours. The hotel shares a driveway with the IMAX theater on Highway 64.

Grand Canyon Holiday Inn Express (226 Hwy. 64, 928/638-3000 or 888/465-4329, www.hiexpress.com, $71–333) has standard guest rooms and suites. Special kids' suites have bunk beds, TVs, stereos, and video games. Rates include breakfast. To make the kiddos even happier, there's an indoor pool and a spa.

The **Red Feather Lodge** (106 Hwy. 64, 928/638-2414 or 866/561-2425, www.redfeatherlodge.com, $70–163) still welcomes guests with its original neon sign that dates back to the 1960s. Guest rooms in the original motor lodge can accommodate pets and smokers. The adjacent hotel, built in 1995, has larger guest rooms and interior hallways. Together, the buildings house a total of 231 rooms. The lodge has an outdoor pool and spa, and Internet service is available.

Seven Mile Lodge (56 Powell Ave., 928/638-2291, from $62) is seven miles from Mather Point, the first canyon overlook past the park's entrance. The unpretentious motel's 20 guest rooms have queen beds, TVs, and air-conditioning, but no phones. The motel doesn't take advance reservations, but you can stop and reserve a room on your way to the park. Popular with savvy budget travelers, this motel fills up early during high season. It's located on the west side of Highway 64.

Campgrounds

Grand Canyon Camper Village (928/638-2887, www.grandcanyoncampervillage.com, Mar.–Oct.) in Tusayan, one mile south of the park's South Entrance at milepost 236, has 50 tent sites ($25) and 250 RV sites with electric ($35), water and electric ($40), or full hookups ($45–50). Off-season and group rates are available. Campground amenities include coin-operated showers and laundry, free Wi-Fi, a camp store, a playground, restrooms, and a dump site. The grocery store and many shops and restaurants are within walking distance.

Ten X Campground (877/444-6777, www.recreation.gov, May–Sept., $10), located four miles south of the park's South Entrance Station along Highway 64, is operated by the U.S. Forest Service. The campground's 70 sites are often completely booked in summer. Each site has a picnic table and a fire pit with a grill. Most are pull-through sites, and RVs up to 30 feet long can be accommodated, although there are no hookups. The campground has vault toilets but no showers. There's a nearby nature trail and an amphitheater with occasional evening ranger programs during the summer. Two group sites ($75–125) accommodating up to 100 people include covered picnic areas.

Dispersed Camping

Primitive-style camping is available in **Kaibab National Forest** (928/638-2443), which borders the national park. Stays are limited to 14 days, and no camping is allowed within 0.25 miles of water, on open meadows, within one mile of a developed campground, within 200 feet of main roadways, or within 20 feet of forest roads. Bury human and pet waste at least six inches deep and pack out all trash. Many forest roads are rugged, and depending on rainfall and winter snow cover, they can be quite muddy as well. During the summer, fire restrictions may be active. Check with the Forest Service for current conditions.

VALLE

If guest rooms near the park's South Entrance are booked, you can travel another 20 miles south to Valle, a small settlement at the intersection of Highways 180 and 64.

Motel

On the northeast corner of the intersection, the **Grand Canyon Inn** (928/635-9203 or 800/635-9203, www.grand-canyon-inn.com, $49–89 depending on the season) offers 101 guest rooms, each with two queen beds, as well as a swimming pool, a restaurant, and a gift shop. Pets are not allowed. Rooms sell out in summer, and advance reservations are recommended. The convenience store next door is a park pay station: You can purchase a National Park Pass here and use the express lane when you get to the South Entrance Station.

Campgrounds and Hostel

Bedrock City (928/635-2600, Feb.–Nov., $12 for 2 people, more for hookups), 20 miles south of the park in Valle, has tent and RV sites and a *Flintstones*-themed camper village with a grocery store, a diner, a gift shop, a game room, laundry, and showers. This campground has amenities you won't find anywhere else near the canyon: a theater showing *Flintstones* cartoons, plus tram rides in the Fredmobile. Community grills are available if you're too late for a Bronto Burger at the diner.

Red Lake Campground and Hostel (928/635-4753 or 800/581-4753, year-round) is located 43 miles south of the park between Williams and Valle. Campsites ($25) have hookups for electricity and water. Rooms in the hostel ($20 pp) are dorm style, although couples can usually be accommodated in their own room. Bathrooms and coin-operated showers are down the hall, and there's a common area with a TV, a refrigerator, and a microwave.

CAMERON AND GRAY MOUNTAIN
Motels
Cameron is 30 miles from the park's East Entrance Station, on the Navajo Reservation along U.S. 89. The **Cameron Trading Post Lodge** (928/679-2231 or 800/338-7385, $59–99 s, $69–109 d, $99–179 luxury suites), overlooking the Little Colorado River Gorge, has the lowest rates in January–February and highest May–October. Some guest rooms are wheelchair-accessible, and pets can be accommodated for an additional fee. The lodge buildings are surrounded by gardens, with a convenience store, historic and modern trading posts, and a restaurant on the property.

The **Anasazi Inn** (928/679-2214 or 800/678-2214, www.anasaziinn.com, $60–80, lower off-season) is located in Gray Mountain, 42 miles north of Flagstaff on U.S. 89 near milepost 457, which is 50 miles from the park's East Entrance Station. The motel has 112 guest rooms, an outdoor pool, and a restaurant. Because the inn is just outside the reservation, you can purchase liquor here, including off-sales.

Campground
Cameron Trading Post RV Park (928/679-2231 or 800/338-7385, $15), in Cameron 30 miles east of the park's East Entrance Station, has RV sites with full hookups; weekly and monthly rates are available. The RV park is within a short stroll of the cliffs overlooking the Little Colorado River and adjacent to historic and modern trading posts, a convenience store, and a restaurant.

Food

South Rim meal options range from hot dogs to fine dining. Leave your white tie at home, though; dinner is a casual affair at Grand Canyon, and a clean shirt and jeans will do just fine. All the lodges in the park except Thunderbird and Kachina have their own restaurants or cafeterias, and Tusayan boasts fast-food chains, steak houses, and several options in between. With the exception of El Tovar, you won't need reservations, but the wait can be long during peak hours. Room service is available at El Tovar.

INSIDE THE PARK
Restaurants and Cafeterias
Without a doubt, the 【 **El Tovar Dining Room** (dinner reservations 928/638-2631, ext. 6432, eltovar-dinner-res-gcsr@xanterra.com, breakfast 6:30–11 A.M., lunch 11:30 A.M.–2 P.M., dinner 5–10 P.M. daily) is the finest dining inside the park. Dinner reservations fill up quickly and can be made up to six months in advance by hotel guests with a reservation or 30 days in advance without room reservations.

Breakfast can be as simple as a pastry ($5) or as hearty as one of the chef's Southwestern egg specialties ($12). Lunch selections include soups, salads, sandwiches ($6–12), and entrées ($10–15). The dinner menu includes appetizers, soups, and salads ($6–14) as well as entrées ($18–31) highlighting organic and sustainable items. A perennial favorite is the Wild Alaskan Salmon Tostada ($25). Half-portions are offered for children at discounted prices. The wine list has a wide range of choices by the glass or bottle, with many sustainable selections.

The adjoining **El Tovar Lounge** (11 A.M.–11 P.M. daily) offers light fare indoors or on the veranda. No reservations are necessary, but you might have to wait for a table. It's not only one of the best spots in the village to sit back and people-watch with the canyon as backdrop, it's also the kind of place travel writers think twice about divulging.

Bright Angel Lodge offers several dining options. The **Bright Angel Restaurant** (928/638-2631, 6:30 A.M.–10 P.M. daily, breakfast $2–11, lunch $4–9, dinner $4–15) celebrates Harvey Girl history on its menu, where you'll find traditional comfort food along with regional specialties. If you want atmosphere, try to get a table in the narrow ell with mullioned windows overlooking the canyon. Next door, but with its own outdoor entrance, **Bright Angel Fountain** (hours vary, spring–fall) tempts people off the Rim Trail for ice cream cones, hot dogs, and other light fare (under $5).

The **Bright Angel Bar** (from 11 A.M. daily, closing time varies by season) serves up refreshing beverages and salty snacks in a casual atmosphere. Canyon murals cover the walls, and on summer evenings you might catch some live Western or folk music. If you overindulge and fall asleep at your table, you're in luck: The bar transforms into the Canyon Coffee House in the morning (hours vary, open seasonally), serving coffee and pastries.

The **Arizona Room** (928/638-2631, lunch 11:30 A.M.–3 P.M. daily Mar.–Oct., dinner 4:30–10 P.M. daily Mar.–Dec.), also located in Bright Angel Lodge, is a classic Western-style steak house. Lunch offerings ($5–13) range from soup and salad options to burgers and barbecue. Dinner highlights steaks, chops, and ribs ($12–26), but vegetarians can opt for the roasted vegetable–and–black bean enchiladas ($15). Beer, wine, and cocktails are available; margaritas are a specialty. Reservations aren't accepted, and sometimes the wait list is lengthy, but you can spend the time browsing the lodge's history room or gift shop.

Maswik Cafeteria (928/638-2631, 6 A.M.–10 P.M. daily, under $10) has five food stations to help lines move quickly. Selections include hot and cold breakfast items, burgers and sandwiches, pasta, and Mexican cuisine. The adjoining **pizzeria** (noon–11 P.M. Mon.–Fri., 3–11 P.M. Sat.–Sun.) sells pies ($17–23) and slices ($2) to eat in or take out. A pub atmosphere takes over in the evening, with beer, wine, and TVs tuned to sports events.

The **Canyon Café** (928/638-2631, usually 6 A.M.–10 P.M. daily, hours vary by season, under $10) at Yavapai Lodge serves up family favorites like pizza, burgers, fried chicken, and a salad bar. The cafeteria-style restaurant and lodge close for a few weeks each winter, usually in January.

In Market Plaza at Grand Canyon Village, the General Store's **❰ Canyon Village Deli** (928/638-2262) serves up salads, sandwiches, fried chicken, and more at a counter at the front of the store. You can sit and eat at the tables or order something to go. Most entrées are less than $10, and it's cash only. You'll note a lot of locals eating here, including park rangers. Check the store aisles for ready-to-eat picnic fare and smoothies.

The **Hermits Rest snack bar** (9 A.M.–sunset daily), located at the end of Hermit Road (West Rim Dr.), is convenient when the overlooks and Rim Trail have tempted you into lingering longer than you planned. For a couple of bucks, you can get a cold or hot drink and a snack to sustain you until you get back to the village.

Frankly, most of us would choose the **Desert View Trading Post Snackbar** (928/638-2360, usually 8 A.M.–6 P.M. daily, hours vary by season) only out of convenience, but for those camping at Desert View, this counter-style deli is a blessing. Sandwiches, pizza, and hot breakfasts are available for a few bucks.

Groceries

The **General Store** (928/638-2262, 8 A.M.–8 P.M. daily summer, 8 A.M.–7 P.M. daily winter), located in Market Plaza at Grand Canyon Village, sells groceries, picnic supplies, and everything you need to cook at your campsite, from stoves to firewood to fully loaded s'mores kits.

Desert View Market (928/638-2393, 8 A.M.–7 P.M. daily summer, 9 A.M.–5 P.M. daily winter), near the East Entrance Station of the park at Desert View, is a bit smaller, but if you've forgotten something for your cooler or campsite, you'll probably find it here.

TUSAYAN

Tusayan exists merely to serve Grand Canyon travelers, and you'll find numerous dining choices here. For quick meals on a budget, **Wendy's** (928/638-6484), **Pizza Hut Express** (928/638-4629), and **McDonald's** (928/638-2208) are all represented in Tusayan, along with local options like a couple of Internet cafés and **Carvel Ice Cream and Bakery** (125 E. Hwy. 64, 928/638-0101).

If you crave something spicy, **Sophie's Mexican Kitchen** (Hwy. 64 across from IMAX, 928/638-4679, 11 A.M.–9 P.M. daily, $5–17) serves favorites like burritos and quesadillas.

Three local hotels offer buffet or off-the-menu breakfasts, lunches, and dinners, including **JJK's** (406 Canyon Plaza Lane, 928/638-2673, $8–26) inside the Canyon Plaza and the Western-themed **Canyon Star** (149 Hwy. 64, 928/638-3333, $8–28) at the Grand Hotel. The best bet and a longtime local favorite is the **Coronado Room** (100 Hwy. 64, 928/638-2681, $20–30) at the Best Western Squire Inn.

Tusayan's midsize grocery, the **General Store** (928/638-2854), also sells souvenirs, RV supplies, camping gear, and firewood. Look for it on the east side of Highway 64.

VALLE

In Valle, 20 miles south of the South Rim at the junction of Highways 180 and 64, the **Grand Canyon Inn** (928/635-9203) has a reasonably priced full-service restaurant, serving American-style food for breakfast, lunch, and dinner. The adjacent gas station and convenience store has snacks and sandwiches to go. **Fred's Diner** (928/635-2600, 6 A.M.–8:30 P.M. daily summer, shorter winter hours), located

across the highway in the *Flintstones*-themed campground, has sandwiches and burgers.

CAMERON AND GRAY MOUNTAIN

If you're traveling to the canyon from the east, the **◖ Cameron Trading Post** (1 mile north of the junction of U.S. 89 and Hwy. 64, 928/679-2231 or 800/338-7385) is a must-stop. It's more than 50 miles from here to Grand Canyon Village, with only the Desert View Snackbar standing between you and hunger pangs. If you want to fill up before a long stretch of sightseeing, the trading post restaurant serves breakfast, lunch, and dinner—mostly traditional American selections, along with some tasty Southwestern fare. What you won't find on the menu is alcohol: The trading post is on the Navajo Reservation. Breakfast and lunch are inexpensive to moderate, but you can go the whole hog at dinner ($8–23) with steak, shrimp, or prime rib. The enormous Navajo taco ($10) is made with fry bread, a favorite of regional-food junkies. A children's menu is available.

If you're in a hurry to get to the park, the convenience market inside the trading post has snacks and sandwiches to go as well as a decent selection of groceries and supplies for locals and campers.

Simpson's Market (928/679-2340, 6 A.M.–9 P.M. daily summer, 7 A.M.–8 P.M. daily winter), located in Cameron at the junction of U.S. 89 and Highway 64, is a full-service grocery with a deli serving up sandwiches and other items.

The **Anasazi Inn** at Gray Mountain (42 miles north of Flagstaff on U.S. 89 near milepost 457, 928/679-2214 or 800/678-2214) has a restaurant that serves breakfast ($5–8), lunch ($7–13), and dinner ($15–25) either buffet-style or from a limited menu. Beer, wine, cocktails, and package liquor sales are available. Hours vary by season. Box lunches can be arranged, which you can enjoy at one of the East Rim's viewpoints, an hour or two away.

Information and Services

A major metropolis it's not, but you can find most everything you need here in the Grand Canyon region's most populous area. And anyway, isn't the whole idea of a vacation to get away from everyday life?

NEWSSTANDS, POST OFFICE, AND ATMS

A variety of daily national newspapers are sold in coin-operated vending machines in front of most lodges, and El Tovar has a newsstand inside the lobby. The weekly *Grand Canyon News* covers Grand Canyon Village and the towns of Williams and Valle. You can also find newspapers (and nearly anything else you need) at Market Plaza.

Market Plaza acts as a village within a village, with a general store, a post office, a bank, and public restrooms. If you're looking for picnic or camping supplies, the **General Store** (928/638-2262, 7 A.M.–9 P.M. daily summer, 8 A.M.–7 P.M. daily winter) sells everything from souvenirs to groceries and fishing licenses. You can buy or rent camping and hiking equipment, including some pretty serious gear like water-filtering systems, sleeping bags, and camp stoves. If camp cooking isn't your idea of a vacation, the deli has ready-to-go sandwiches, pizza, fried chicken, and other hot items.

Chase Bank (928/638-2437, 9 A.M.–5 P.M. Mon.–Thurs., 9 A.M.–6 P.M. Fri.) has an office nearby, along with an ATM in the lobby, open 24 hours. There's also an ATM in the lobby of Maswik Lodge and one at the IMAX theater in Tusayan, outside the park.

The **post office** (928/638-2512, 9 A.M.–4:30 P.M. Mon.–Fri., 11 A.M.–1 P.M. Sat.) has window service, and stamps are also available in the lobby (5 A.M.–10 P.M. daily).

CELL PHONES, WI-FI, AND GPS

Don't count on your cell phone if you're hiking below the rim: It's unlikely that you'll get a signal inside the canyon. Service may also be spotty on the rim and as you travel around the Grand Canyon region.

Some of the lodges have Wi-Fi service in their lobbies and cafeterias, and there's a Wi-Fi hot spot on the patio at Park Headquarters. Computers with Internet access are available for public use at the village's community library (928/638-2718) and in the research library at park headquarters. If you can't bear feeling disconnected, you may be happier lodging in Tusayan, where several motels and a couple of cafés offer Internet hookups.

The park has made a number of infrastructure changes over the past few years, and the GPS mapping features of some vehicles haven't caught up. Don't rely on your vehicle's GPS to navigate. The maps in *The Guide* and the park's brochure—a ranger will hand both of these to you at the entrance station—are up-to-date and accurate.

LAUNDRY AND SHOWERS

A coin-operated laundry and showers are available at the Camper Services building near the entrance of Mather Campground. Hours vary by season, and the current hours are posted on-site.

DAY CARE

The **Kaibab Learning Center** (928/638-6333, 7:30 A.M.–5:30 P.M. Mon.–Fri.) offers day care services for infants and children up to 12 years old, when space is available. Immunization records must be provided.

PETS

Pets are not permitted in lodges, on shuttle buses, or on hiking trails below the rim. The only exception is for service animals, and if you want to take a service animal below the rim, you must first check with the Backcountry Information Center. Pets are permitted in the village and campgrounds but must be leashed at all times.

You can board your dog or cat for the day or overnight at the **kennel** (928/638-0534,

7:30 A.M.–5 P.M. daily), located off Rowe Well Road, west of Maswik Lodge. Reservations are recommended, and proof of vaccination is required. To pick up your pet later than 5 P.M., make arrangements with Xanterra Fire and Safety (928/638-2631).

An alternative to boarding your pet at the canyon is to leave Spot or Fluffy in Williams, 60 miles south of the canyon, or Flagstaff, 90 miles away. **Canyon Pet Resort** (928/214-9324, www.canyonpetresort.com) in Flagstaff offers day care and overnight boarding, with optional extras such as walks, treats, or a cage-free executive suite. In Williams, Grand Canyon Railway's air-conditioned **Pet Resort** (800/843-8724) services are available to the general public as well as to visitors staying at the adjacent RV park or riding the train.

RELIGIOUS SERVICES

The National Park Service doesn't endorse any particular religious group or message, but a number of local congregations offer services inside the park and in nearby communities. Schedules of services are posted at Grand Canyon Visitors Center, Verkamp's Visitors Center, Mather Campground, Shrine of the Ages, and at the information kiosk near the post office.

LOST AND FOUND

If you leave something behind in a guest room or lodge, contact Xanterra's offices (928/638-2631). For all other lost items, call park administration or complete a lost property report online or in writing (Lost and Found Office, Grand Canyon National Park, P.O. Box 129, Grand Canyon, AZ 86023, 928/638-7798, www.nps.gov/grca/planyourvisit/lost-found.htm). Take found items to any of the park's visitors centers.

EMERGENCIES

Dial 911 for emergency care (9-911 from lodge rooms). Hikers can find emergency phones at ranger stations and along corridor trails: on Bright Angel Trail at Mile-and-a-Half Resthouse, Three-Mile Resthouse, and River Resthouse, and on the South Kaibab Trail at its junction with the Tonto Trail. Inner canyon ranger stations are located at Cottonwood Campground (summer only), Indian Garden, and Phantom Ranch. Emergency phones are connected to a 24-hour dispatch center and do not require coins. If your situation requires search-and-rescue services, you will be charged expenses.

For urgent medical or dental care, contact the **North Country Grand Canyon Clinic Community Health Center** (928/638-2551, fax 928/638-2598, 8 A.M.–6 P.M. daily mid-May–mid-Oct., reduced hours mid-Oct.–mid-May). The clinic, located south of the village on Clinic Road, can be reached from Center Road or from Highway 64.

Getting There and Around

Most people arrive to the South Rim in their own vehicle or a rental, but with so many transportation and tour options available, it's possible to get here by bus, plane, or train and be blissfully car-free, as long as you plan to focus your visit on the park's most developed areas. During summer months, you can even arrange for a shuttle to the North Rim.

The nearest major airports to Grand Canyon are in Las Vegas (278 miles) and Phoenix (231 miles). US Airways has continuing service from Phoenix to Pulliam Airport in Flagstaff.

A dizzying variety of Grand Canyon tours and charters—plane, helicopter, bus, van—originate in Las Vegas or Boulder City, Nevada, just outside of Las Vegas. Charter flights to Grand Canyon Airport are available from Phoenix, Sedona, and Page.

Greyhound has bus service to Flagstaff and Williams, but not to the canyon itself. Amtrak provides train service to Flagstaff or Williams, where you can board the Grand Canyon Railway and travel to the historic depot in Grand Canyon village, mere steps away from park lodges.

If you're driving, note that the road to Hermits Rest is closed to private vehicles from March through November. Road closures due to construction are possible any time of year, and winter storms occasionally result in the closure of Highway 64 between the South Rim's main entrance and Desert View. The windswept section of Highway 64 around Valle, 20 miles south of the park entrance, can also be troublesome. The park service website (www .nps.gov/grca) provides construction updates and current weather reports.

Traffic can be beastly during the high season, with street-parked cars hiding driveways, "deer jams" bringing vehicles to a standstill, pedestrians wandering everywhere, and tempers growing as heated as an Arizona summer afternoon. The best solution is to liberate yourself from your car as quickly as possible.

PARKING

There's no getting around it: The South Rim is crowded during the summer, and village-area parking is at a premium. You'll find it a relief to park your car and rely on the shuttle, which stops near all major parking areas. The good news is that the National Park Service has recently added hundreds of parking spaces near the Grand Canyon Visitors Center and plaza, including spaces large enough to accommodate RVs. It's possible to leave a vehicle here and avoid entering the traffic swarming around Grand Canyon Village.

If you decide to continue to the village in your vehicle, you'll find several smaller parking lots—though you may not find a parking space. Lot A is near Shrine of the Ages and Park Headquarters; this lot often has open spots. Lot B is in Market Plaza, where the bank and general store are located. Lot C is a small lot near the intersection of Center and Village Loop Roads. Lot E is a large paved lot near the Backcountry Information Center. At

NPS PHOTO BY MICHAEL QUINN

This parking lot near the South Rim Visitors Center is patrolled by rangers on horseback who keep traffic moving and answer visitors' questions.

the south end of this lot, you'll find spaces big enough to park an RV, but not for camping. Canyon veterans take note: You'll no longer find parking areas near the railroad tracks or at Mather Point.

Village Loop Road is mostly one-way and runs counterclockwise, which means turning right is the correct choice when you reach the stop sign at the start of the loop. For El Tovar guests, there's a small lot east of the hotel, but even if you circle like one of the canyon's turkey vultures, you may not find a parking place here. If you're driving an RV or pulling a trailer, don't even try. Thankfully, El Tovar has a baggage-handling service. The other lodges also have guest parking areas, short-term loading zones, and bell services.

GAS AND GARAGE SERVICES

Need gas? Your last chance to fill up is in Tusayan, seven miles south of the village, or at Desert View, just inside the park's East Entrance, about 30 miles from the village. The pumps at the park's **Desert View Chevron** (9 A.M.–5 P.M. daily) have 24-hour credit-card service.

Garage services (926/638-2631, 8 A.M.–noon and 1–5 P.M. daily, emergency service after hours) are available in Grand Canyon Village east of the train depot. The garage can provide basic repairs, including tires, belts, batteries, and hoses. If more serious repairs are needed, tow service is available to Williams or Flagstaff.

PARK SHUTTLE BUSES

The South Rim's **free shuttle system** offers three main routes, encompassing Hermit Road (the West Rim), Grand Canyon Village, and the Kaibab Trailhead (Yaki Point). Buses arrive at each shuttle stop every 15–30 minutes. Have faith—the wait is shorter than the time it would take to drive around in search of a parking place. During peak months (June–Aug.), shuttle buses operate from 4:30 A.M. until an hour after sunset.

Route maps are available online or in *The Guide,* the park's newspaper. Color-coding makes finding the right route relatively simple.

Look for a colored square by the shuttle's door or the route name displayed on the front. Routes intersect near the Bright Angel Trailhead and at Grand Canyon Visitors Center.

The Village Route (blue) stops at lodges, restaurants, shops, campgrounds, and Market Plaza, and also travels to Grand Canyon Visitors Center. The round-trip takes an hour, but riders can get on or off at any stop to dine, shop, or stroll in the historic district. The Backcountry Information Center is on the Village Route.

The Hermits Rest Route (red) travels back and forth between the village and Hermits Rest, eight miles away. You can ride the loop, which takes 75 minutes and stops at eight overlooks, or leave the shuttle to spend some time photographing or hiking the Rim Trail, then board another bus. After leaving Hermits Rest, the return (eastbound) route stops only at Pima, Mohave, and Powell Points. The Hermits Rest route is not in service December–February. During these three months only, passenger cars can travel Hermit Road, weather permitting.

The Kaibab Trail Route (green) travels between Grand Canyon Visitors Center and Yaki Point. The bus stops en route at the South Kaibab Trailhead and Pipe Creek Vista. This scenic round-trip takes 30 minutes.

The **Hikers' Express** is an early-morning shuttle that stops at Bright Angel Lodge, the Backcountry Information Center, and Grand Canyon Visitors Center before traveling directly to the South Kaibab Trailhead. In May and September, the Hikers' Express leaves at 5 A.M., 6 A.M., and 7 A.M. daily. June–August it departs at 4 A.M., 5 A.M., and 6 A.M. In October, express shuttles leave at 6 A.M., 7 A.M., and 8 A.M., and in November, 7 A.M., 8 A.M., and 9 A.M. December–February, the Hikers' Express leaves at 8 A.M. and 9 A.M.

Pets are not allowed on shuttle buses, except trained service animals. All park shuttle buses are accessible to wheelchairs, and all park shuttles are now equipped with bicycle racks.

Mid-May–mid-September, free shuttle buses travel outside the park to the town of Tusayan. Travelers can leave their cars in Tusayan and shuttle to the park, a trip

Park visitors board the free shuttle bus at the Hermits Rest stop on the scenic and historic Hermit Road.

of about 20 minutes. The shuttles make four stops in Tusayan, including the Grand Canyon Airport. Passengers must present valid park passes to enter the park. This park-and-ride shuttle operates at 15-minute intervals 8 A.M.–9:30 P.M.

TAXIS AND SHUTTLES

Taxi services (928/638-2822 or 928/638-2631, ext. 6563) are available 24 hours daily year-round. Destinations include Grand Canyon Airport. Taxis will even deliver hikers and backpackers to South Rim trailheads.

The **Trans Canyon Shuttle** (928/638-2820, www.trans-canyonshuttle.com) offers daily round-trip van service ($80 one-way, $150 round-trip) between the South Rim and the North Rim May 15–October 15. You can also take the shuttle to the Marble Canyon area ($65 one-way). The shuttle leaves the South Rim at 1:30 P.M., arriving at the North Rim at 6 P.M.; reservations are required. Charter shuttle services can be arranged.

Bright Angel Bicycles (928/814-8704, www.bikegrandcanyon.com) provides an hourly bicyclists' shuttle ($6 one-way, $9 round-trip) from the visitors center to Hopi Point, giving pedalers an option for avoiding the congestion around Grand Canyon Village and the first few miles of Hermit Road.

THE NORTH RIM

Only 10 miles away as the raven flies, Grand Canyon's North Rim is a world apart from the bustling South Rim. Before Navajo Bridge spanned the Colorado River in 1929, this part of the state—the Arizona Strip—was isolated from the rest. Even today, the North Rim's remoteness means far fewer visitors: about 500,000 annually. Getting here from the South Rim's Grand Canyon Village takes five hours by car or shuttle or 2–3 days on foot. Although getting here requires a bit more planning and longer travel time, if you crave peace and solitude along with stunning views, the North Rim's slower pace and outdoorsy focus will enchant you.

Higher than the South Rim by 1,400 feet and shaded by boreal forests of spruce, fir, and aspen, the North Rim is cooler in the summer—and often buried in snow during winter months. On average, the North Rim receives 142 inches of snow each year. Officially, the park service closes the North Rim on October 15, but adventurous travelers do visit during the winter to camp and cross-country ski. Beware of sudden storms: At least one apocryphal tale describes a backpacker hiking up from the inner canyon's desert reaches, unable to find his car, which has vanished under drifts of snow.

Several hiking trails follow the rim or descend into the canyon, and miles of back roads invite exploration of adjacent Kaibab National Forest. From Bright Angel Point, where the historic Grand Canyon Lodge is located, it takes nearly six hours of driving to reach Toroweap, a remote overlook with jaw-dropping views of Lava Falls.

HIGHLIGHTS

◖ Grand Canyon Lodge: The original Grand Canyon Lodge burned to the ground in 1932 and was reconstructed in 1936. The lodge's wide-open terraces overlook the canyon, and you can peer all the way across to the South Rim's Grand Canyon Village (page 91).

◖ Point Imperial and Mount Hayden: From the highest point on either rim at 8,800 feet, you can see Mount Hayden, Saddle Mountain, the Painted Desert, and the eastern end of Grand Canyon (page 95).

◖ Cape Royal: A 23-mile drive leads to Cape Royal Point, a rim overlook offering one of the finest views of the canyon. Take the short trail to the North Rim's southernmost point, pausing to gaze through Angel's Window, a natural stone arch (page 97).

◖ Toroweap: If you have a high-clearance vehicle and a taste for adventure, this lonely spot beckons. Sheer cliffs drop away to Lava Falls, one of the canyon's gnarliest rapids, 3,000 feet below (page 98).

◖ Bright Angel Point Trail: Most park services at the North Rim are located on Bright Angel Point, the rocky peninsula between Roaring Springs Canyon and Transept Canyon. You can walk along a paved trail to the very tip of Bright Angel Point. The trail is a mere half mile, but the views alone will take your breath away (page 100).

◖ North Kaibab Trail: Beginning two miles north of the lodge, this trail leads hikers and mule riders into the canyon's depths. Descend even a short distance down the trail and you will see how the canyon's vegetation and rock layers change with elevation (page 101).

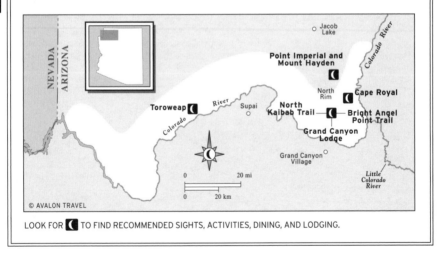

LOOK FOR ◖ TO FIND RECOMMENDED SIGHTS, ACTIVITIES, DINING, AND LODGING.

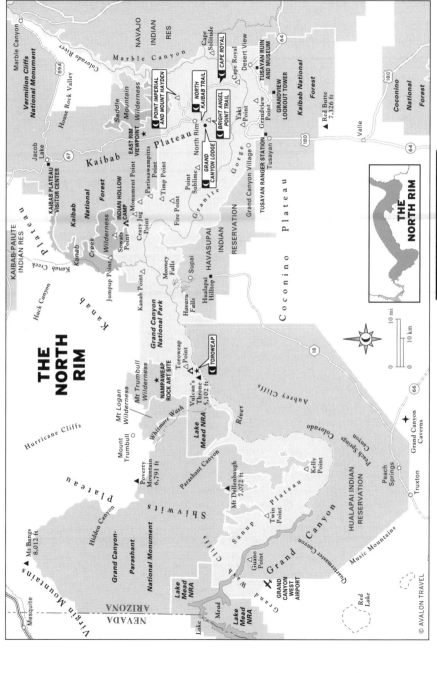

THE NORTH RIM

THE
NORTH RIM

Grand Canyon's vastness seems even more pronounced here on the North Rim, where it's obvious that "the canyon" is not simply a single grand gorge but a complex collection of intriguing side canyons. River views are rare from overlooks on the North Rim's higher elevations, where tributary canyons stretch a long distance before reaching the Colorado River. On the other hand, the North Rim's mixed forests, similar to those of northern Canada, provide stunning fall color and ample wildlife-viewing.

You can stay close to the lodge and its amenities, but if you prefer your parks a little on the wild side, bring a high-clearance vehicle, a good map, and a sense of adventure. The North Rim offers more for those who love to explore.

PLANNING YOUR TIME

Once you've found your way to the North Rim—the more remote, less visited side of Grand Canyon—you'll want to spend at least three days exploring its trails, forests, and overlooks. Highway 67 is the only road to Bright Angel Point, the heart of the North Rim, and it is open to travelers from after the snow melts in spring until the first major winter snowfall, which can occur anytime from October through December. Officially, the North Rim section of Grand Canyon National Park is open **May 15-October 15,** but it's Mother Nature, not the Park Service, who really calls the shots. Although the Park Service closes the lodge and other facilities at the North Rim on October 15, you can visit or camp until the first snowfall closes Highway 67.

In fall, aspens and maples put on a colorful show, with bursts of gold and red among the North Rim's mixed boreal forests. In late spring and summer, carpets of blue lupine and other wildflowers scent the forest with heady perfume. Even in midsummer, nights can be cool, so bring some warmer clothes as well as a jacket for afternoon showers. The Arizona monsoon rolls north in early July and lingers until mid-September, bringing brief, localized thunderstorms with possible lightning and heavy rain.

Summer is the busiest season in Grand Canyon, and lodging on the North Rim is limited, but this side of the canyon is never as crowded (or hot) as the South Rim. Plan early and make reservations for Grand Canyon Lodge or the North Rim Campground several months in advance.

Plan on a day at **Bright Angel Point** for touring the historic lodge, hiking nearby rim trails, shopping, and taking in a ranger program. Drink plenty of water and get used to the high elevation and low humidity. Set aside at least half a day for **Cape Royal,** with a side excursion to **Point Imperial,** the highest point on both rims. Along this paved, winding road, several signs direct hikers to trails, from the short, easy Roosevelt Point Trail to the more ambitious Ken Patrick Trail.

Descending even a short way into the canyon will reward you with a more intimate perspective on the North Rim's geological layers and life zones. You can travel the **North Kaibab Trail,** the only maintained North Rim trail that leads into the canyon, either on foot or by mule. Shadier rim hikes like the Transept Trail are better options for afternoons.

Alternatively, you might want to spend a day exploring beyond Bright Angel Point, traveling to **Toroweap** or Point Sublime, or into neighboring Kaibab National Forest. Many dirt forest roads are suitable for passenger cars, while some are best explored in a high-clearance 4WD vehicle. Stop at the park's visitors center at the rim or at the national forest visitors center in Jacob Lake for maps and information about road conditions before venturing off the highway.

Exploring the North Rim

At the canyon's North Rim, you'll find fewer tour options and no shuttle buses to whisk you between overlooks and sites. This side of Grand Canyon is most easily explored by car. Many of the North Rim's scenic highlights lie along the Cape Royal Road, which travels more than twenty miles across the Walhalla Plateau to Cape Royal and Wotans Throne. Shopping, dining, and entertainment choices are more limited here too, allowing Mother Nature to take center stage. The focus of your explorations will be the North Rim's exquisite natural setting. Hiking, trail riding, and scenic drives take you through lush forests and meadows sprinkled with wildflowers to overlooks with sweeping canyon vistas. Pack a picnic, wear comfortable shoes, and plan to enjoy the fresh pine-scented air and natural quiet.

VISITORS CENTERS
North Rim Visitors Center
The North Rim Visitors Center (928/638-2481, 8 A.M.–6 P.M. daily) is located at Bright Angel Point, at the end of Highway 67. The large parking area on the left at road's end is convenient to the visitors center, which is the building nearest the parking lot's south edge. You can hang out on the shady veranda and watch an informational slide show, or go inside to talk with rangers and browse through displays on flora, fauna, and history.

In the visitors center, a large three-dimensional map of the canyon—showing major viewpoints, landforms, and trailheads as well as park, forest, and reservation boundaries—helps travelers get their bearings. Weather forecasts for the North Rim, South Rim, and nearby areas are posted here daily.

Housed within the visitors center is the **Grand Canyon Association** (GCA) bookstore, with an excellent selection of books, maps, videos, and other items. Proceeds benefit the association, which partners with the park to create interpretive materials. Restrooms are located around the back of the building, where there's also a shady ramada with public phones and vending machines.

Kaibab Plateau Visitors Center
You can preview your visit to the rim with a stop at the Kaibab Plateau Visitors Center (928/643-7298, 8 A.M.–5 P.M. daily mid-May–mid-Oct., shorter hours later in the season), operated by the U.S. Forest Service in Jacob Lake. This visitors center is outside the park, 45 miles north of Bright Angel Point. Displays emphasize the Kaibab Plateau and Kaibab National Forest, although information on Grand Canyon National Park is also available here. A three-dimensional map of the plateau and canyon rim indicates forest roads, and you can purchase forest maps here if you plan to make any back-road excursions. The GCA stocks the visitors center with books about the canyon.

ENTRANCE STATION
The North Rim's sole entrance station is 12 miles from Bright Angel Point on scenic **Highway 67,** at the boundary between Kaibab National Forest and Grand Canyon National Park. The highway is usually open to travel mid-May–mid-October. In winter, deep snows often cover the high meadows between Jacob Lake and the entrance station, closing the highway, which is then gated and locked at either end. When the entrance station is staffed, you can pick up a copy of *The Guide,* the park newspaper. The North Rim edition is updated each May.

TOURS
Driving Tour
Cape Royal Drive, a 23-mile (one-way) paved road with views of the eastern Grand Canyon area, may be the highlight of your visit to the North Rim. With spectacular overlooks and fascinating sights along the way, you'll want to set aside at least half a day to explore this winding, paved road, longer if you plan to hike or picnic, or if you enjoy a slower pace. The canyon's colors are outrageous in early

FIRE!

First-time visitors to the North Rim may be surprised to see fire's great influence on surrounding forests. Over the years, wildfires have left snags, blackened logs, and silver "ghost forests" like the one along the road leading to Point Imperial. Fire is part of nature's cycle, returning nutrients to soil, reducing fuel buildup, and encouraging new growth and greater diversity among plant and animal species. But it hasn't always been viewed so benevolently. A long history of fire suppression, combined with hot, dry summers and recent drought, has created dangerous conditions in areas where forest-floor debris has accumulated.

These days, forest managers strive to find the balance between suppressing wildland fires and allowing fire's natural process to continue when conditions are favorable. Fire used as a management tool includes prescribed burns – fires planned, ignited, and monitored to achieve specific goals, such as creating defensible space around populated areas or reducing fuel burden to prevent catastrophic fires. The **Outlook Fire** of 2000 began as a prescribed burn, but it jumped over control lines during unexpectedly high winds, burning 13,000 acres on the Walhalla Plateau.

Lightning caused one of the North Rim's largest fires to date, the 2006 **Warm Fire,** which burned nearly 50,000 acres between Jacob Lake and the park and stranded 800 travelers at the North Rim. Humans also cause fires, such as the LeFevre Fire between Jacob Lake and Fredonia, which burned 300 acres in 2004. Thankfully, the number of human-caused fires has decreased lately, thanks to public education and occasional forest closures when fire risk is especially high. This most often occurs in June, when travel is at its peak and the forest is at its driest. Some years, Arizona's monsoon season begins with dry thunderstorms – when lightning strikes, but no rain reaches the earth. Everyone breathes a sigh of relief when the rains do arrive, usually by mid-July.

morning or late afternoon, and shadows add texture and depth to panoramas of the Marble Platform, Saddle Mountain Wilderness, and Unkar Delta.

To reach Cape Royal from Grand Canyon Lodge, travel north on Highway 67 for three miles, turning right on Cape Royal Road (also known as Fuller Canyon Road). The road forks at about five miles, with the left fork leading another three miles to Point Imperial, the right to Cape Royal. You won't want to miss either. You can flip a coin to decide which direction to head first, but Point Imperial is especially lovely in early morning.

To continue to Cape Royal, 16 miles away, take the right fork. The paved road is narrow and winding—watch for oncoming traffic, and take your time. A number of worthwhile sights are en route, and it's nearly impossible to backtrack if you've zipped past an enticing overlook.

Nature Walk

At least once a day, ranger-guided activities include a nature walk, usually a relaxed morning or evening stroll through the forest lasting about an hour. Rangers introduce participants to the North Rim's forest ecosystem and answer questions about the canyon. Check *The Guide* for departure times, or stop by the North Rim Visitors Center to see if additional tours have been scheduled.

Walhalla Overlook

On summer afternoons, rangers lead tours at Walhalla Overlook along Cape Royal Drive. If you correctly time your driving tour to Cape Royal, you can stop at the overlook for a 30–40 minute presentation about the Ancestral Puebloan culture, who lived in a masonry pueblo at nearby Walhalla Glades and tended fields scattered over the Walhalla Plateau.

Mule Trips

Head for Grand Canyon Lodge if you're interested in a mule tour. Staffers at the transportation desk near the lodge's main entrance can help you choose a trail ride, make arrangements for shuttle services, or sign you up for the lodge's evening cookout. **Grand Canyon Trail Rides** (P.O. Box 128, Tropic, UT 84776, 435/679-8665, www.canyonrides.com) offers one-hour rim-side mule rides ($40 pp) and half-day trips ($75 pp) along the rim to Uncle Jim's Point or partway down the North Kaibab Trail. Children as young as seven can take the one-hour rim tour.

Full-day mule trips ($125 pp, including lunch) head into the canyon via the North Kaibab Trail and travel to Roaring Springs, the water source for both rims. For this 10-mile round-trip, children must be 12 or older. The weight limit for mule tours is 200 lbs. Prices include shuttle transportation from the lodge to the trailhead.

Audio Tours

If you have a cell phone, you can listen to two-minute audio tours describing three locations on the North Rim. Look for the numbered "Park Ranger Audio Tour" signs, dial 928/225-2907, enter the stop number, and listen to park rangers talk about Grand Canyon Lodge, Bright Angel Point geology, or Roaring Springs. The prerecorded mini-tours are free, but be aware that cell coverage is particularly sketchy at the North Rim, and not all service providers cover park locations. If you prefer, you can listen to the narrations online (www.nps.gov/grca) or download text versions.

Learning Adventures

If you're interested in a guided trip or a learning vacation, research your options and plan ahead. **Grand Canyon Field Institute** (P.O. Box 399, Grand Canyon, AZ 86023, 928/638-2485 or 866/471-4435, http://grandcanyon.org/fieldinstitute) offers a wide variety of classes, including photography, art, archaeology, wilderness studies, and geology. Difficulty ranges from single-day introductory classes to multiday white-water rafting and backpacking trips. Some sessions are designed for women only, and several family-friendly trips are offered.

The **Museum of Northern Arizona** (3101 N. Fort Valley Rd., Flagstaff, AZ 86001, 928/774-5213, www.musnaz.org) offers expertly guided adventures with a natural or cultural history focus through its Ventures program. **MNA Ventures** (928/774-5211, ext. 230, ventures@musnaz.org, www.mnaventures.org) features a rim-to-rim backpacking trip, but MNA can arrange a custom trip based on your group's interest.

Sights

BRIGHT ANGEL POINT

Bright Angel Point, a peninsula extending between the Transept and Roaring Springs Canyon, is the heart of the North Rim and where nearly all services are located, including the lodge, visitors center, and campground. Past the lodge, the peninsula narrows and descends to jut out over the canyon like a diving board. You can walk to the very tip on the Bright Angel Point Trail, which hugs the side of a ridge so thin it offers stunning views on both sides. The Kaibab limestone along the trail bears fossilized remains of marine life. Rocky outcroppings and gnarled pine trees provide interesting foreground elements for photo buffs. Near the end of the peninsula, you may be able to hear Roaring Springs, the source of the canyon's drinking water, 3,100 feet below.

◀ GRAND CANYON LODGE

The original Grand Canyon Lodge was designed in 1928 by Gilbert Stanley Underwood, considered the creator of "parkitecture." He set

THE NORTH RIM

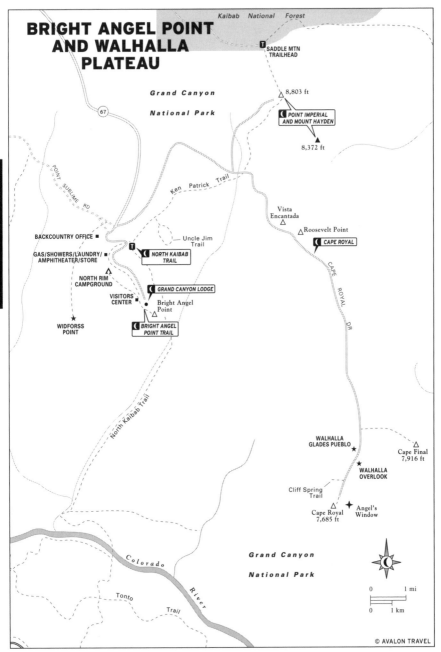

BRIGHT ANGEL POINT
AND WALHALLA
PLATEAU

Kaibab National Forest

SADDLE MTN
TRAILHEAD

Grand Canyon

67

National Park

△ 8,803 ft

POINT IMPERIAL
AND MOUNT HAYDEN

▲ 8,372 ft

Ken Patrick Trail

POINT SUBLIME RD

Vista
Encantada △

△ Roosevelt Point

CAPE ROYAL

BACKCOUNTRY OFFICE ■

GAS/SHOWERS/LAUNDRY/ ■
AMPHITHEATER/STORE

Uncle Jim
Trail

NORTH KAIBAB
TRAIL

△ NORTH RIM
CAMPGROUND

CAPE ROYAL DR

GRAND CANYON LODGE

VISITORS
CENTER ■

Bright Angel
Point

★ WIDFORSS
POINT

BRIGHT ANGEL
POINT TRAIL

North Kaibab Trail

WALHALLA
GLADES PUEBLO
★

△ Cape Final
7,916 ft

★ WALHALLA
OVERLOOK

Cliff Spring
Trail

△ Cape Royal
7,685 ft

✦ Angel's
Window

Colorado

Grand Canyon

National Park

River

Tonto

Trail

0   1 mi

0   1 km

© AVALON TRAVEL

© RICHARD MAYER

Bright Angel Point Trail follows a narrow ridge with stunning views.

the lodge right on the rim, with its foundations rising up out of the limestone cliffs, so visitors' first view of the canyon was framed by the large windows across the lobby. It's a grand entrance for a grand lodge. Guest accommodations, then and now, are outside the main lodge building in cabins scattered among the ponderosa pines.

The lodge was a jewel on the Union Pacific Railroad's Loop Tour, which included Bryce Canyon, Zion National Park, and Cedar Breaks National Monument. In early September 1932, a fire that started in the lodge kitchen spread quickly, burning the main building and two nearby cabins to rubble. In June 1937, the lodge was rebuilt using the same floor plan but with steeply sloped roofs to shed heavy North Rim snows, and hidden steel beams to replace the original pine logs.

Grand Canyon Lodge, operated by concessionaire Forever Resorts, is a National Historic Landmark. It is the center of visitor activities on the North Rim, with an air of Western hospitality that extends not just to the lodge's guests but also to the canyon's guests. Even if you're not staying in one of the lodge's cabins, you can enjoy a meal in the dining room, attend a program in the auditorium or on the veranda, or find a cozy spot for your morning coffee and paper in one of the sunroom's deep leather chairs.

KAIBAB PLATEAU

Scenic **Highway 67** crosses the Kaibab Plateau on its way from Jacob Lake to Bright Angel Point, the heart of the North Rim. The drive, almost 50 miles, is a lovely trip through grassy meadows edged by forests of pine and aspen. If you're traveling this route in the early morning or evening, you might see deer or elk grazing in the meadows, or a pack of coyotes wandering near the edge of a pond. Even bison have been spotted on these grassy expanses. Paved turnouts are a good place to stop and watch the action with a pair of binoculars. The developed

GRAND CANYON LODGE

© RICHARD MAYER

Grand Canyon Lodge was designed by Gilbert Stanley Underwood.

The Union Pacific Railroad wanted a grand finish for its Grand Circle Tour that included Zion National Park, Bryce National Monument, Cedar Breaks National Monument, and the North Rim. Grand Canyon Lodge would be the finale, and Gilbert Stanley Underwood was to be its architect. It was 1927, and Underwood had just completed the fabulous Ahwahnee Hotel in Yosemite. His lodge on the North Rim promised to be as successful.

The building site was on the very edge of Bright Angel Point. Limestone was quarried two miles away. Timber came from the Kaibab Forest, about 10 miles north. Because the mill required water and power, a hydroelectric plant was built on the Colorado River, more than 3,000 feet below the construction site.

Underwood banked the stonework foundation into the rim, and parts of the building looked like rocky outcroppings rising up out of the canyon's cliffs, a style used across the canyon by Mary Colter for Lookout Studio. Underwood designed multiple levels of open terraces that overlooked the canyon, inviting interaction with nature. He sited the lodge's 120 cabins according to the forested, hilly topography.

The Union Pacific altered Underwood's design in one key respect: Underwood's original plan called for a structural core of concrete and steel. Perhaps in an effort to save money,

company officials made the fateful decision to use a timber frame instead.

On June 1, 1928, the lodge opened its doors. For four years, the lodge charmed Union Pacific tourists with its rustic accommodations and traditional sing-aways from lodge employees. Then, early on the morning of September 1, 1932, sparks from a fireplace in the main lodge started the largest structural fire in the history of Grand Canyon National Park. The fire destroyed the lodge and two cabins. All that remained was the stone foundation and chimneys.

The lodge was rebuilt and reopened in 1936, with a steeper roof pitch helpful for shedding North Rim snows. The alteration shifted the flavor of Underwood's original design from a low-roofed craftsman or Spanish Revival style to a design that is more purely rustic. The reconstruction retains Underwood's influence, evident in the lodge's sense of scale and drama. The roofline varies with broken pitches and dormers. Large windows and open terraces overlook the canyon. The east terrace boasts a huge fireplace – large enough to stand in and a popular location to gather for ranger talks.

Massive wrought-iron chandeliers and sconces hang throughout large public spaces, and painted and carved Indian symbols contribute to the building's sense of style and place. Exposed roof trusses (steel covered by logs) soar above the lodge's public areas – the lobby, the recreation room, and the dining room, which is located several steps down from the lobby. Sunset dinner reservations are prized. From the room's tall windows, diners can watch the canyon's colors and shadows shift, until the curtain of darkness ends the spectacular nature show.

Today, Gilbert Stanley Underwood is regarded as the father of "parkitecture." He excelled at creating a deeper experience of nature from within his designs, a standard that other architects strived to follow as they built lodges and visitors centers throughout the national parks of the West.

area of Bright Angel Point is perched on the plateau's southern edge.

Outside park boundaries, the plateau is crisscrossed by forest roads, many of them suitable for passenger cars. Pine- and aspen-shaded glens make inviting picnic spots or primitive campsites. On the east side of the plateau, forest overlooks like **Dog Point** and **East Rim Viewpoint** provide access to the Arizona Trail and panoramas of the Saddle Mountain Wilderness and Marble Platform. On the west, Timp, Parissawampitts, and other points overlook the rocky platform known as the Tapeats Amphitheater.

◖ POINT IMPERIAL AND MOUNT HAYDEN

Point Imperial extends into the canyon at the southeastern edge of the Kaibab Plateau. To reach Point Imperial, the highest point on both rims at 8,800 feet, take Highway 67 to the Cape Royal Road. Turn left at the fork to Point Imperial and drive another three miles to the end of the road, where you'll find a large parking area and picnic tables beneath the shade of a ponderosa-pine forest.

For the best views, descend the short path to the overlook. Mount Hayden's spire (8,372 feet) rises above Nankoweap Canyon. Late-afternoon or early-morning sunlight turns this Coconino sandstone peak from buff-colored to a rosy gold. The 40,000-acre Saddle Mountain Wilderness, part of the Kaibab National Forest, sprawls to the north.

Restrooms are located at the north end of the parking lot, and trailheads can be found at either end of the parking area: the Point Imperial Trail to the east and the Ken Patrick Trail to the west.

WALHALLA PLATEAU

Cape Royal Road cuts across Walhalla Plateau, a peninsula of rock extending south into Grand Canyon. The 23-mile drive winds past several scenic overlooks, picnic areas, trailheads, and other sights on the way to Cape Royal. This forested plateau was a seasonal home for Ancestral Puebloans who hunted game and

grew crops here in the summer, then moved to inner canyon villages during winter months. The road begins three miles north of Grand Canyon Lodge, forking at about five miles. Turn right to proceed across the plateau to Cape Royal.

At the **Vista Encantada** overlook, six miles south of the fork, tables shaded by ponderosa pines make a great spot for a picnic. Carpets of pinecones and lavender-blue lupine spread out at your feet, and the woodsy picnic area is often visited by Kaibab squirrels and mule deer. From here, you have stunning views of Indian Country, from the Marble Platform across the Painted Desert to Navajo and Hopi lands.

Stop at **Roosevelt Point,** eight miles from the fork, to stretch your legs on the short, easy Roosevelt Point Trail, which leads through a recent burn. The overlook is named for Theodore Roosevelt, who enjoyed hunting trips to the North Rim during the early 1900s. Below, you'll see the confluence of the Colorado and Little Colorado Rivers. The curtain of cliffs forming the South Rim is known as the Palisades of the Desert.

A dirt parking area on the left, about 12 miles south of the fork to Cape Royal, marks the trailhead for **Cape Final.** The four-mile Cape Final Trail, one of the North Rim's most satisfying day hikes, leads across the Walhalla Plateau to views of Unkar Delta, a large sandy bend along the Colorado River.

You can learn more about the Ancestral Puebloans (also known as the Anasazi) at **Walhalla Overlook.** This viewpoint, 13 miles from the fork, has views of Unkar Delta, where the Ancestral Puebloans wintered in the inner canyon's warmer climes.

WALHALLA GLADES

About 13 miles up the road from its fork with Point Imperial Road, across the road from the Walhalla Overlook parking area, is one of the North Rim's most interesting prehistoric sites, Walhalla Glades. This village was occupied by the Ancestral Puebloans approximately A.D. 1050–1150. Archaeologists have studied their 10-room dwelling, learning about Puebloan

JACOB HAMBLIN, MAN WITH A MISSION

Many who visit the Kaibab Plateau community of Jacob Lake ask how the small settlement got its name. There is a lake named Jacob, though it's really more of an alpine pool, ringed by meadow grasses and filled by rain and snowmelt. Such water sources on the dry plateau have long been valued, and this one is named for Jacob Hamblin, a Mormon missionary and scout who is credited with being a peacemaker for local Native Americans.

Perhaps no nonnative has known the Grand Canyon region as well as Jacob Hamblin. He was born in Ohio in 1816 and converted to Mormonism in 1842, at a time when followers of the Church of Latter-Day Saints (LDS) were being persecuted in Midwestern communities. LDS members migrated to Utah shortly after the United States took control of Mexican territories, and Jacob Hamblin relocated near Salt Lake City. He proved himself adept at negotiating between would-be settlers and the Native Americans already living in the area.

In 1854, church leader Brigham Young asked Hamblin to serve a mission to the Southern Paiutes near St. George. Later, Hamblin established trails and guided Mormon colonists to settlements near the Little Colorado River in Arizona Territory, blazing what became known as the Honeymoon Trail. He followed the trail of the Spanish friars Domínguez and Escalante, fording the historic Crossing of the Fathers and establishing two more crossings downriver at Lees Ferry and Pearce Ferry. He founded the town of Kanab, Utah, in 1865. In 1870 he assisted Major John Wesley Powell's second canyon voyage by negotiating with local Native Americans for the expedition's safe passage. Of Hamblin, Powell said: "He is a silent, reserved man, and when he speaks it is in a slow, quiet way that inspires great awe."

In his decades of travel, Jacob Hamblin circumnavigated Grand Canyon. He crossed the high Kaibab Plateau and is said to have visited the depths of Havasu Canyon, where he promised Havasupai elders that he would never reveal the location of their idyllic village. (He never did, though others would.)

In his role as trailblazer and guide through Indian country, he acted as a diplomat and peacekeeper, following an ethic of being honest, calm, and reasonable, listening to others' concerns and dealing with people fairly. Many noted that he often didn't carry a gun.

Hamblin wasn't prone to superlatives, and most of his diaries and letters focus on his mission and his dedication to resolving differences through scripture and friendship. Albeit unspoken, his connection to the lands he explored appears to have been strong. Jacob Hamblin had a house near St. George, another in Kanab, and ranch in House Rock Valley, on the Marble Platform below the Vermilion Cliffs. He once wrote, however: "I have spent more nights under cedar and pine boughs than in a house."

After 1882, when the Edmunds Act outlawed plural marriages, Hamblin moved his families out of Utah and spent most of his remaining years evading federal authorities. He died of malaria in New Mexico in 1886.

---

daily life from pottery shards, chipped stone, and architecture.

Scattered over the Walhalla Plateau are more than 100 farming sites where the Puebloans grew corn, beans, and squash during summer months. Because the plateau is lower than surrounding elevations, warm updrafts melted winter snow and made earlier planting possible. During winters, some of the pueblo's residents migrated into the canyon, where they could farm in the desert climes of **Unkar Delta,** visible from the overlook. At Unkar Delta, a two-day journey from the rim, they built a pueblo of more than 50 rooms, the inner canyon's largest archaeological site.

During the summer months, rangers lead guided tours from Walhalla Overlook to the ruins of Walhalla Glades, discussing how people subsisted here on the North Rim 1,000 years ago.

A granary, evidence of the Ancestral Puebloans' farming activities, can be seen along the **Cliff Spring Trail,** which begins a mile farther up the road. Access to the trail is across from the paved **Angel's Window** overlook (about 14 miles south of the fork to Cape Royal).

◖ CAPE ROYAL

The road continues almost all the way to the southern edge of the Walhalla Plateau. The rocky peninsula extending into the canyon here is called Cape Royal. The road ends at a large parking area, where an easy paved trail leads 0.5 miles to the rim through cliffrose and other high-desert vegetation. Stop along the way to view the natural limestone arch that forms **Angel's Window,** which frames a view of the Colorado River and Unkar Delta. The best views of the arch are from the paved pull-out on the left side of the road, less than a mile before reaching the parking lot for Cape Royal, and also along the trail to Cape Royal Point. A spur trail leads 150 yards to the top of the arch itself, where you can stand and enjoy precipitous views of the canyon below.

Continuing on the main trail takes you to the end of Cape Royal, the southernmost point on the North Rim. See if you can make out Desert View Watchtower, sticking up like a thimble far across the canyon on the South Rim. Pause for a heady inhalation of cliffrose before taking in equally intoxicating views of Wotans Throne, Vishnu Temple, and Freya Castle. All three rise past 7,200 feet, taller than any mountain in the eastern United States, but all three peaks are below you, enveloped in the creases and folds of Grand Canyon. Sunsets are awe-inspiring close to these Grand Canyon temples, which form a dramatic backdrop for a nearby outdoor "wedding chapel" where brides and grooms can tie the knot. There's plenty of room for a picnic here, and restrooms are located at the north end of the parking lot.

POINT SUBLIME

If you're looking for a rugged mountain-bike journey or have a sturdy high-clearance 4WD vehicle, consider traveling the 17-mile route

(calling it a road would be overly generous) to Point Sublime. You'll pass through deep ponderosa forest carpeted with purple lupine and yellow butterweed, mostly over a rocky two-track. About halfway along, an overlook offers up-close views of the Dragon, a mythically shaped rock formation extending south from the rim. The end of the road, Point Sublime, is an isolated peninsula utterly surrounded by the canyon and monuments.

Before you head out, it's a good idea to check with the **North Rim Backcountry Office** (8 a.m.–noon and 1–5 p.m. daily) to find out the latest road conditions. The office is housed in a small trailer located off Highway 67, just north of the campground road.

Be sure to travel with a good spare tire and plenty of water—this infrequently traveled route presents plenty of hazards, including deep sand, high crowns, and tire-eating rocks. Allow at least five hours of daylight to drive to the point and return, and more if you plan to picnic along the way.

To get there, drive 2.5 miles north of the lodge on Highway 67. Turn left onto the gravel road that leads to the Widforss Trail parking area. Just past the parking area, the road begins to change to a rocky two-track, and it will change character several more times as it heads west to Point Sublime. En route, you'll come across a small parking area near the rock formation known as **The Dragon.** This might look like a peaceful corner of canyon for a lingering picnic, but on most summer days, helicopter tours will thunder over it at regular and frequent intervals.

As you near Point Sublime, you'll pass over a narrow causeway of dirt and stone lined with half a dozen picnic tables, cliffrose, and beavertail cactus. The rocky causeway leads to what feels like very the ends of the earth (you can't help but wonder how the picnic tables got here). A short footpath leads still farther, until you are standing on a narrow spit of limestone, the canyon dropping away on all sides. It's like being on a diving board high over the ocean, but instead of water, you are surrounded by stone.

With a backcountry permit, you can spend the night at this primitive overlook, which has fewer than a dozen campsites. The wisest course is to apply for an overnight permit well in advance. The **Backcountry Information Center** (P.O. Box 129, Grand Canyon, AZ 86023, www.nps.gov/grca) accepts permit applications up to four months prior to the month of your trip. Applications are available online, but they must be submitted by mail, by fax, or in person. If you arrive at the North Rim without a permit, however, you can check at the North Rim Backcountry office to see if a last-minute permit is available.

◖ TOROWEAP

To get to Toroweap (a Paiute word meaning "dry or barren valley"), you'll have to travel nearly 150 miles from Bright Angel Point before you're back inside park boundaries. You may decide not to visit this lonely spot overlooking Lava Falls the first, second, or even 10th time you travel to Grand Canyon, but it's one to add to your Grand Canyon bucket list.

The journey spans some 60 miles of dirt roads through Bureau of Land Management (BLM) holdings on the Arizona Strip, including a small stretch of the Grand Canyon–Parashant National Monument, established in January 2000 by President Bill Clinton. You'll need a high-clearance vehicle and a good spare tire (or two). The reward for this trip through the Strip is a perspective of Grand Canyon that few people see outside of book covers, an impressive drop to the river with no crowds or barricades, and a clear view of the ancient lava flows that captured John Wesley Powell's imagination in 1869, when he wrote: "What a conflict of water and fire there must have been here!"

It's possible to travel to Toroweap and back in a day (about six hours round-trip), but consider spending the night at Toroweap Campground, a cluster of 10 sites one mile from the rim overlook. There are no entry or camping fees—and no services except for composting toilets—but campsites may fill by midday.

To travel to Toroweap (also known as Tuweep) from Jacob Lake, take U.S. 89A to

Toroweap, a remote North Rim overlook, has stunning views.

Fredonia, turning left on Highway 387. About seven miles west of Fredonia, look for a dirt road with a sign reading "Mt. Trumbull." At 46 miles, the road forks. Continue straight to Toroweap, following the signs. Once you cross the park boundary, the road becomes rockier. Check in at the Tuweep Ranger Station on your way to the overlook, another six miles.

At 4,550 feet, Toroweap is the lowest rim overlook in the park, but one of the most precipitous: Sheer cliffs fall away 3,000 feet below to the Colorado River. You can see—and hear—Lava Falls by walking to the rim, a few hundred feet beyond the overlook parking area. The Class 10 rapids are one of the toughest on the river. There are no guardrails or fences at this primitive overlook, and peering over the edge to look at tiny rafts floating past on the Colorado River far below can stir up a strong sensation of acrophobia, even in the fearless. Views up- and downriver are stunning,

especially at sunrise and sunset. Photographers can spend hours here, looking for the perfect rocky outcropping to use as the foreground.

If you plan to do any backpacking in the area, you'll need a permit. Often you can get a last-minute permit at the ranger station here. Day-hiking possibilities include meandering along the rim near the campground and overlook, taking nearby Tuckup Trail a short way, or bushwhacking up Vulcan's Throne, a 700-foot-high cinder cone west of the overlook. Volcanic activity along the Toroweap fault began about 7 million years ago. Lava flowed into the canyon several times, damming the Colorado River. Though it wasn't the steaming conflict that Powell imagined, the reality is no less impressive: About 1.2 million years ago, lava flows created dams over 1,000 feet high, forming a lake that extended for hundreds of miles. Basalt remnants of the lava dams are visible today.

THE NORTH RIM

Recreation

Officially, the North Rim section of Grand Canyon National Park is open May 15–October 15, but it's Mother Nature, not the Park Service, who really calls the shots. The Park Service closes the lodge and other facilities at the North Rim on October 15, but you can visit or camp until the first snowfall closes Highway 67. Hardy Nordic skiers can get backcountry permits for winter camping or reserve the North Rim yurt, but for most of us, the time for outdoor recreation on the North Rim is limited to the sweet, brief summer and early fall.

Even in midsummer, nights can be cool, so bring some warmer clothes as well as a jacket for afternoon showers. Drink plenty of water and take some time to get used to the high elevation and low humidity before setting out on a challenging hike or ride.

You don't need a permit for a day hike or bike ride. The park's website (www.nps.gov/grca) and *The Guide* offer many tips and

suggestions for short meanders and full-day adventures. For overnight trips or winter camping, backcountry permits are required.

The North Rim may lack some of the creature comforts offered by Grand Canyon Village and the South Rim, but it offers a wider variety of recreational activities. If you like exploring the great outdoors, you'll be glad you made the extra effort to get to this side of the canyon.

HIKING

The North Rim's unspoiled beauty and natural quiet is best enjoyed on foot. North Rim trails offer amazing contrasts, from gentle rimside strolls to demanding descents leading from high boreal forests (similar to those in northern Canada) into the desert heart of the canyon. Because of its remoteness, your chances for solitude are much greater here. The flip side is that if you get into trouble, help can be farther away and slower in coming.

Rim-to-river trails on the North Rim tend

to be longer because they start at a higher elevation and descend into tributary canyons before reaching the Colorado River. Only one maintained trail, North Kaibab, leads into the canyon. The North Rim's other rim-to-river trails are wilderness trails—no water, faint routes, steep descents. Do not attempt to hike from rim to river and back in one day, a journey that's feasible (for a few) on the South Rim but suicidal on the North Rim.

Inexperienced canyon hikers should stick to rim trails or hike on North Kaibab Trail before attempting other descents. Though no permit is needed for a day hike, planning is important. Be prepared, pace yourself, and be sure to allow enough time for the return trip. It takes twice as long to hike the same distance coming out of the canyon as it does going in, and the North Rim's higher elevations can make even the best-conditioned hikers gasp for breath.

Temperatures rise quickly, and the sun is intense at this elevation, so you'll want to start early in the morning to hike the North Kaibab Trail. Descending even a short way into the canyon will reward you with a more intimate perspective on the North Rim's geological layers and life zones. On summer afternoons, shadier rim hikes like the Widforss Point Trail are better options.

The hikes below are listed in rough geographical order, starting with those beginning at Bright Angel Point, east to Walhalla Plateau, then west.

Bridle Path

- Distance: 3 miles round-trip
- Duration: 1 hour or less
- Elevation change: Negligible
- Effort: Easy
- Trailheads: Grand Canyon Lodge or the North Kaibab Trail parking lot

More of a stroll than a hike, this easy trail allows visitors to leave their cars behind in order to get from one place to another on Bright Angel Point. The path connects the lodge and campground and leads through a forest of ponderosa pines to the North Kaibab Trailhead. It's the only trail on the North Rim where you can bicycle or walk your pet (on a leash). Like a small-town sidewalk, this path has a friendly, social feel. You might see mule deer wandering nearby or catch a glimpse of a Kaibab squirrel leaping from branch to branch in the tall ponderosas. If no one's watching, take time out to stop and sniff a tree—the ponderosa's bark smells like butterscotch or vanilla.

◖ Bright Angel Point Trail

- Distance: 0.5 miles round-trip
- Duration: 30 minutes
- Elevation change: 200 feet
- Effort: Easy
- Trailheads: Log shelter near the easternmost cabins, or at the corner of the Grand Canyon Lodge's back porch

This paved trail leads to spectacular canyon views along a narrow ridge. At either trailhead, look for a box containing brochures for a self-guided nature tour highlighting canyon geology. Though the Bright Angel Point Trail is short, the elevation (8,148 feet) and narrowness of the trail—not to mention the views—can take your breath away. This is a popular trail, and you may need to make way for other hikers, especially the ones hugging the inside of the trail because of the heights.

En route, you can see fossils embedded in the Kaibab limestone that forms the canyon's rim. Peer over the edges into Transept or Roaring Springs Canyons or across the horizon to the South Rim, 10 miles away as the raven flies. On a clear day, the San Francisco Peaks near Flagstaff stand out on the southern horizon. Landmarks nearer the point include Brahma, Deva, and Zoroaster Temples. Any of these stone monuments would be major attractions if they were located elsewhere—but here at the canyon, they are among hundreds of stony sentinels, many named by geologist Clarence Dutton in the late 1800s to reflect their lofty and inspiring forms.

Transept Trail

- Distance: 3 miles round-trip
- Duration: 1.5 hours
- Elevation change: 100 feet
- Effort: Easy to moderate
- Trailhead: Grand Canyon Lodge or the North Rim Campground

The Transept Trail is an up-and-down meander through a ponderosa pine forest that gives way to Gambel oaks along the rim of Transept Canyon. Even though it leads along busy Bright Angel Point, the trail offers many spots to enjoy the forest solitude and rim views. If you hike in the early morning, you have a good chance of seeing mule deer, Kaibab squirrels, and several bird species. Stop midway, where a couple of rows of benches offer views of Zoroaster, Brahma, and Deva Temples—fabulous at sunset. Nearby, small Native American ruins, approximately 1,000 years old, stand next to the trail. Residents probably spent summers here on the rim, hunting and gathering wild plants in the nearby forest. Return the same way, or make a loop by taking the Bridle Path that parallels Highway 67 between the lodge and the campground.

Uncle Jim Trail

- Distance: 5 miles round-trip
- Duration: 3 hours
- Elevation change: 200 feet
- Effort: Easy to moderate
- Trailhead: At the Ken Patrick Trailhead on the east side of the North Kaibab Trail parking lot

This trail makes a loop through the forest between two side canyons, Roaring Springs Canyon and Bright Angel Canyon. Because it's shaded, it's a good choice on hot summer days. You'll be sharing the trail with mule parties, who have the right-of-way. For the first 0.5 miles, the Uncle Jim and Ken Patrick trails are a single path, skirting the rim before heading into a dense fir forest. At the signed junction,

the Uncle Jim Trail veers to the right, descending toward the head of Roaring Springs Canyon.

After about one mile, you'll come to another junction, this one unsigned, marking the beginning of the loop to Uncle Jim Point. Whether you go right or left, it's another mile to the point. The left fork continues east toward the rim of Bright Angel Canyon before looping back toward Uncle Jim Point, named for the Grand Canyon's first game warden.

From the rim, you can look down into Roaring Springs Canyon. Three thousand feet below, Roaring Springs is the source of Grand Canyon's drinking water, piped to both rims. Looking at the opposite side of the canyon, you can see the North Kaibab Trail switchbacks. On the southern horizon, 12 miles away, is the South Rim, and beyond that the San Francisco Peaks. Return the same way, or take the other half of the loop on your way back to the parking lot.

◖ North Kaibab Trail

- Distance: 28 miles round-trip to the river; 10 miles round-trip to Roaring Springs
- Duration: 3–4 days to the river; 6–8 hours to Roaring Springs and back
- Elevation change: 5,770 feet to the river
- Effort: Strenuous
- Trailhead: 1.5 miles north of Grand Canyon Lodge at a large parking lot

The good thing about North Kaibab is that it's a popular corridor trail—patrolled, wide, and well-maintained, with piped water available seasonally. The bad thing about North Kaibab is that it's a popular corridor trail—to the point of being congested with backpackers, day hikers, mule trips, and the occasional ranger on foot or mule. Because this trail offers so many hiking options, from a short excursion below the rim to a multiday backpack trip to the river, it's possible for nearly everyone to experience the magic of being drawn into the canyon's stony embrace. The trailhead parking lot often fills up by late morning, but you can

© KATHLEEN BRYANT

Mule riders and hikers descend North Kaibab Trail.

arrange for a shuttle from the lodge or walk to the trailhead via the Bridle Path.

North Kaibab Trail descends into Roaring Springs Canyon, which joins Bright Angel Canyon at approximately five miles. If you plan to hike to the river, make reservations well in advance for Phantom Ranch, or get a permit for Bright Angel or Cottonwood Campgrounds. With an early morning start, day hiking to Roaring Springs is possible though strenuous. Less experienced hikers can make a shorter descent, perhaps to Coconino Overlook (1.5 miles round-trip) or the Supai Tunnel (4 miles round-trip).

Even a short hike below the rim will give you a different perspective of the canyon as you pass through different geological layers and life zones. From the rim to the Supai Tunnel, high-country vegetation is predominant, with ponderosa pine, firs, and aspen giving way to Gambel oak, New Mexican locust, and wild rose. Past the tunnel, vegetation shifts to piñon pine, juniper, manzanita, and cliffrose.

At the Redwall limestone layer, the trail crosses a bridge over Roaring Springs Canyon before heading deeper. Listen for the sound of Roaring Springs—you'll hear it about a mile before you reach it (at 4.7 miles). The spring-water needs to be treated, but if you hike another mile to the pump house, you'll find piped water and a picnic table. This is the point of last return if you are day hiking.

At seven miles, Cottonwood Campground has water and a ranger station. Backpackers will spend the night here or at Bright Angel Campground (mile 14). Past Cottonwood Campground, desert vegetation predominates—yucca, cactus, and catclaw. At 8.5 miles, a short spur leads to not-to-be-missed Ribbon Falls, an oasis shrouded in ferns, columbine, and monkeyflower. The waterfall drops 100 feet onto a mound of travertine, creating a refreshing spray.

The main trail continues down Bright Angel Canyon, which narrows at the Box, becoming a maze of schist. After zigzagging across the creek several times, the canyon opens up again. The Clear Creek Trail junction is at

13 miles, signaling your approach to Phantom Ranch and, 0.5 miles beyond, Bright Angel Campground.

Roosevelt Point Trail

- Distance: 0.2 miles round-trip
- Duration: 20 minutes
- Elevation change: Negligible
- Effort: Easy
- Trailhead: Roosevelt Point overlook, 12 miles up Cape Royal Road

This short, easy trail passes through forest burned by the Outlook Fire in 2000, offering beautiful views of the eastern canyon as well as an up-close look at how the forest responds to wildfires. Young aspen, grasses, and wildflowers grow among blackened stumps. Snags (dead trees that still stand) shelter birds and chipmunks. A bench in this mini-Eden offers quiet respite from the road and parking area. Before returning to your vehicle, soak in the views, scanning the southern horizon for Comanche Point, which rises above the confluence of the Colorado and Little Colorado Rivers.

Cape Final Trail

- Distance: 4 miles round-trip
- Duration: 2 hours
- Elevation change: 150 feet
- Effort: Easy
- Trailhead: A dirt parking area 17 miles up Cape Royal Road, 2.5 miles from road's end

This wide, pleasant trail passes through a forest of ponderosa pine on its way across Cape Final (a thumb-like extension of the Walhalla Plateau) to rim overlooks with views of Unkar Creek, Chuar Valley, and the Painted Desert.

From the dirt parking area on the left (east) of the road, the trail climbs a forested ridge before meandering toward a rim clearing, about 1.25 miles. Here, a dramatic drop reveals views of the Chuar Valley, with Gunther's Castle rising above its soft folds. The trail narrows as the cape, a peninsula of land, becomes narrower. The trail turns south and west to cross the cape, and the vegetation changes to piñon and cactus. An intersecting path heads east through scrubby vegetation to the very tip of Cape Final. Far below, Unkar Delta, a wide, sandy curve in the Colorado River, marks the site of a large Ancestral Puebloan village, occupied seasonally until A.D. 1150.

The main trail continues to the southern edge of Cape Final, where Freya Castle rises above Unkar Creek Canyon. With a backcountry permit, it's possible to camp overnight on Cape Final, and you might find yourself envying those who chose to spend the night in this beautiful area.

Cliff Spring Trail

- Distance: 2 miles round-trip
- Duration: 1 hour
- Elevation change: 150 feet
- Effort: Easy
- Trailhead: Across the road from Angel's Window Overlook, a paved pullout 19 miles up Cape Royal Road

Although it's short, this trail offers lots of variety. From the paved overlook 0.5 miles north of the Cape Royal parking area, cross the road to find the trail marker. The well-defined dirt trail descends through ponderosa pine forest to an Ancestral Puebloan granary tucked beneath a large chunk of Kaibab limestone. The trail curves around this boulder, then continues to descend through mixed forest into a rugged wash. You'll leave behind the road noise and enter a magical world where the past feels near, as though you could look down and follow sandal prints left behind by the ancient ones who used this path. Here the trail hugs the limestone cliffs, sheltered by a stony overhang high above. Water seeps from the base of the Kaibab limestone walls, converging at Cliff Spring's shallow pools at the 0.5-mile point.

You can linger here for awhile, enjoying the sound of dripping water and watching quietly as birds visit the spring. This is the end of the maintained section of the trail, but you can continue farther along the cliff to a rugged path that descends toward Clear Creek Canyon, offering views of Cape Royal and Vishnu Temple.

Ken Patrick Trail

- Distance: 20 miles round-trip
- Duration: 5 hours one-way
- Elevation change: 300 feet, with 1,090 feet of up-and-down
- Effort: Moderate
- Trailheads: Point Imperial overlook and the North Kaibab Trail parking lot

Most of this trail's 10 miles lead through the mixed forest of the Kaibab Plateau, a shady alternative on hot days. Day hikers can walk part of the trail, or leave a car at the North Kaibab parking lot to hike the trail one-way. The section of the trail nearest Point Imperial has the most dramatic panoramas. At three miles from Point Imperial, the trail crosses the Cape Royal Road, a good turnaround point for a day hike.

The trail starts at the west end of the Point Imperial parking lot, edging the rim and offering views of Mount Hayden and the eastern canyon to the Painted Desert. As the trail continues in a generally southwest direction, you'll go up and down gently rolling terrain with occasional views into Nankoweap Canyon. At three miles, the trail ascends a rocky stair to the Cape Royal Road, and then continues through the forest seven miles to the North Kaibab parking lot.

Point Imperial Trail

- Distance: 4.4 miles round-trip
- Duration: 2 hours
- Elevation change: Negligible
- Effort: Easy
- Trailhead: North end of the parking area for the Point Imperial overlook

This trail leads through areas burned by the 2000 Outlet Fire to Saddle Mountain, just across the park boundary. The trail starts out

© KATHLEEN BRYANT

Two North Rim trails begin at Point Imperial.

paved but soon turns to dirt. Pine and fir yield to the area scorched by fire, and soon the trail is surrounded by ghostly white aspen snags and blackened pine stumps. Once-hidden views of Saddle Mountain, Marble Canyon, and—on the horizon—Navajo Mountain are visible through the burned areas. The surrounding landscape is a good example of how the natural environment recovers from fire. Wildflowers and young aspens mark the first stage in a forest's rebirth. At 2.2 miles, you'll reach the gate that marks the park's northern boundary.

You can turn around here or continue into Kaibab Forest for more views. Pass the gate and walk to the dirt road (Forest Road 610), continuing a short distance until you come to the signed trail for Saddle Mountain. A spur to the right heads up a rocky outcrop with a view across Marble Platform to the Vermilion Cliffs, worth the extra few minutes of hiking. Experienced canyon hikers use the Saddle Mountain Trail to access the precipitous Nankoweap route to the Colorado River, a challenging 4–5-day trip.

Nankoweap Trail

- Distance: 28–29 miles round-trip
- Duration: 4–6 days
- Elevation change: 4,800 feet
- Effort: Very strenuous
- Trailhead: Saddle Mountain Wilderness

There are two possible routes to this trailhead: from House Rock Valley and Forest Road 445, or south of Jacob Lake on Forest Road 610. The latter may be snowy or muddy into June. You will start outside park boundaries on the Saddle Mountain Trail for three miles (from Forest Rd. 445) or 3.5 miles (from Forest Rd. 610).

Nankoweap Trail is considered one of Grand Canyon's most strenuous hikes, with downclimbs, dangerous drop-offs, and no water along most of its length. Only experienced canyon backpackers should attempt it. Those who do will gain close-up looks at the colorful Grand Canyon Supergroup rocks along with Marble Canyon panoramas.

From the trail junction, the Nankoweap Trail drops from the rim through the Esplanade, narrowing to an inches-wide ledge at times. From Tilted Mesa, the trail descends gradually eastward. A couple of steep descents require hands and feet to reach Nankoweap Creek, about eight miles from the junction. Follow the creek bed to the Colorado River, just over three miles. The shrubby Low Sonoran Desert along the river offers good campsites.

Widforss Trail

- Distance: 10 miles round-trip
- Duration: 5 hours
- Elevation change: Moderate ups and downs totaling 1,100 feet
- Effort: Easy to moderate
- Trailhead: About 1 mile past the North Kaibab Trail parking lot, turn left onto a dirt road and drive another mile to the trailhead

This rim trail is a good choice on a hot day: It's shaded much of the way, and you won't have to climb out of the canyon in midday heat. The first 2.1 miles of trail are a scenic ramble from Harvey Meadow up to the rim of Transept Canyon, with peekaboo views of Bright Angel Point and Zoroaster Temple. Pick up a brochure near the trailhead for a self-guided tour describing highlights along this section of the trail, which makes a fine day hike. The trail continues around the head of Transept Canyon to its west rim before heading into the forest.

Shaded by fir and aspen, the trail climbs to a ridge west of the Transept. As you traverse the ridge, the forest changes to ponderosa pine and gradually opens. Just beyond a picnic table and campsite (a backcountry permit is required to camp here), the trail drops toward the rim for a splendid view of the South Rim's Coconino Plateau. See if you can spot Grand Canyon Village by pinpointing El Tovar Lodge. Below you is Haunted Canyon, and before you are several of the canyon's monumental peaks, including Buddha and Isis Temples.

THE NORTH RIM

To the southeast, a limestone spire marks Widforss Point, named for Gunnar Widforss, who painted strikingly detailed watercolors of the canyon in the early 1900s.

Tiyo Point Trail

- Distance: 12.6 miles round-trip
- Duration: 6–7 hours
- Elevation change: 400 feet
- Effort: Moderate
- Trailhead: Look for the trail, an old road leading south across a meadow, 4 miles along the Point Sublime Trail

The Tiyo Point Trail starts along the rugged 4WD road to Point Sublime, so just getting to the trailhead can be quite an adventure. From the lodge, drive one mile past the North Kaibab Trail parking lot, turn left onto the dirt road for the Widforss Trail, and then continue on the Point Sublime Trail. At approximately four miles, you'll reach a large meadow called the Basin. A dirt road, now closed to all but foot traffic, leads south across the meadow. You won't find a trailhead marker, only a sign indicating that the road is closed to vehicles.

After crossing the meadow, the trail enters a mixed forest of pine, fir, and aspen, descending gradually toward the canyon. Ignore the faint side trails and continue on the main trail, an old Jeep road. About a mile from the rim, you'll begin to catch glimpses of the canyon through the trees. The rim is brushy and sloping, and the trail turns toward a picnic table. For better views, take the short side trail to an open area, where you can see Osiris and Isis Temples rising from the canyon.

TIYO: FIRST THROUGH GRAND CANYON

John Wesley Powell is generally hailed as the first to negotiate the Colorado River through Grand Canyon. He made the voyage twice, in 1869 and 1871. A few holdouts still argue the case for James White, a Colorado prospector who claimed to have floated the length of the canyon in 1867 on a makeshift raft in order to escape a band of hostile Indians. According to stories handed down for generations of Hopi clans, however, neither man was the first to float through the canyon.

The Hopi's long oral tradition tells of Tiyo, a youth who was fascinated by the great river flowing through the canyon. He spent hours watching the river and daydreaming about its course. Tiyo determined to find out for himself where the river led. His father, a village chief, helped him make a vessel by hollowing out the trunk of a large cottonwood.

Tiyo traveled many days in his boat, until one day it ran aground on a riverbank. Here he met Spider Woman, who showed him many wonderful places and guided him to a village populated by snake people.

To enter the kiva of the snake people and learn the ceremony for making rain, Tiyo had to perform acts of courage, including capturing and taming the most frightful of the serpents. The hideous creature turned into a beautiful maiden, and he won the approval of the snake people to marry the lovely maiden, taking her back to his own village. Their offspring, however, were young snakes that bit the village children, and the snake clan was cast out.

Tiyo and his family journeyed to Walpi, a village on First Mesa, where the people had been suffering from drought. The villagers agreed to accept Tiyo's clan, and in exchange he performed the first Snake Dance. The ceremony was blessed by rain, and ever since that time, the Snake Clan and Antelope Clan have performed the multiday ceremony at the Hopi Mesas.

Artist Fred Kabotie depicted Tiyo's story on the wall of the Desert View Watchtower, a fascinating South Rim structure designed by architect Mary Colter. Kabotie's mural shows Tiyo's journey and the origins of the Hopi Snake Clan. A point on the North Rim, accessible by a six-mile hiking trail, is named for Tiyo.

Thunder River Trail

- Distance: 15 miles to the Colorado River
- Duration: 4 days or more
- Elevation change: 4,400 feet
- Effort: Strenuous
- Trailhead: Indian Hollow Campground in Kaibab National Forest

In several locations along the North Rim, access to trailheads is on U.S. Forest Service land. Trails enter the national park as they descend from the rim, as is the case here. The Thunder River Trail is a challenging multiday trip to see one of the world's shortest rivers and the impressive waterfall near its start.

The trail descends to the Esplanade, turning east to intersect with the Bill Hall Trail (an alternate start to this hike). The Bill Hall Trail shaves three miles off the hike to Thunder River—but the trailhead is higher, requiring a steep descent with downclimbs before reaching the intersection with the main trail.

From this intersection, the Thunder River Trail heads south across the Esplanade for about three miles. At the Redwall formation, the trail drops sharply to Surprise Valley, hot and shadeless in summer. In Surprise Valley, the Deer Creek Trail intersects the Thunder River Trail from the right. Turn left (east) to continue to Thunder River. You'll hear the river before you see it tumbling 100 feet from the cliffs. Thunder River ends at the confluence with Tapeats Creek, only 0.5 miles from its spring-fed origins. The Upper Tapeats campsites are near the confluence. The trail crosses the creek and continues toward the Colorado River, where the Lower Tapeats campsites are located.

Lava Falls Route

- Distance: 3 miles round-trip
- Duration: 8 hours
- Elevation change: 2,500 feet
- Effort: Very strenuous
- Trailhead: 3.5 miles south of the Tuweep Ranger Station, a 4WD road leads another

2.5 miles to the trailhead. During or after wet weather, the road may be impassable.

Although this route is the shortest rim-to-river trail in the park, it is extremely difficult, passing down a steep slope of loose basalt cobbles and boulders to Lava Falls. This Class 10 rapids, formed by debris from Prospect Canyon, drops 13 feet, making it one of the most challenging for river runners. In 1869, John Wesley Powell's expedition chose to portage the rapids, an arduous three-hour effort.

Temperatures along the Lava Falls route can reach dangerous highs, and there's no shade or water along the way. The route, indiscernible in loose scree, is marked by cairns. Even the most experienced hikers should not attempt to hike this trail during summer months.

Tuckup Trail

- Distance: 70 miles one-way
- Duration: Multiple days
- Elevation change: Mostly level
- Effort: Easy to strenuous
- Trailhead: 5 miles south of the Tuweep Ranger Station

The Tuckup Trail leads across the Esplanade shelf to 150-Mile Canyon, starting as an old road that soon fades to a barely discernible route. The old road is closed to vehicles, so hikers must squeeze their cars into a parking place along the narrow dirt road to Toroweap campground and overlook, or start from the campground, about one mile farther. Day hikers can walk a couple of miles down the trail, enjoying rim views of the western canyon before returning the same way. The trail follows the old roadway for the first three miles, but past that it's little more than a faint route that winds around finger canyons. The route is relatively level to Tuckup Canyon, the halfway point. Experienced backpackers can use the Tuckup Trail to access other routes, creating multiday loop trips into remote stretches of Grand Canyon. Popular destinations include Big Cove Point, Cottonwood Canyon, and the

Dome. The Tuckup is very exposed, having few water sources, some of which may be contaminated by livestock. Careful advance planning is a must.

BIKING

Biking is allowed on all paved and dirt roads on the North Rim. You can bring your own bike or rent one at Grand Canyon Lodge's hike and bike outfitters. In Arizona, bicycles are subject to the same traffic rules as automobiles. Traffic through the park on Highway 67 can be heavy on summer weekends, and Cape Royal Road is narrow and curving—treacherous on a bike.

Hiking trails are off-limits to bicycles, except for the Bridle Path that travels between the lodge and the campground. One option for mountain bikers is to take the **Point Sublime Trail,** a rugged two-track that begins near the Widforss Trail parking area, and travel part or all the way to Point Sublime: 17 miles, nearly a day's journey.

You must obtain a backcountry permit if you plan to camp overnight at Point Sublime. To apply, fax or mail an application to the Backcountry Information Center (P.O. Box 129, Grand Canyon, AZ 86023, fax 928/638-2125). Applications are available on the park's website (www.nps.gov/grca). However, if you arrived at the North Rim without a permit, you can check in at the North Rim Backcountry Office (8 A.M.–noon and 1–5 P.M. daily) to see if last-minute permits are available. The office is housed in a small trailer, located off Highway 67 just north of the campground road.

Neighboring **Kaibab National Forest** offers bicyclists miles of trails, dirt tracks, and gravel roads, many bordering the canyon rim. Note that bicycles are not allowed within the forest's Kanab Creek or Saddle Mountain wilderness areas. For more information, contact the **North Kaibab Plateau Visitors Center** (928/643-7298) at Jacob Lake.

TRAIL RIDING

Outside the park, **Allen's Guided Tours** (Jacob Lake, 435/644-8150 or 435/689-1370, $15–75) offers horseback trips in Kaibab National Forest. A 1–2-hour trip over gentle forest terrain to a rim overlook is suitable for children. Tours leave several times a day, and no reservations are needed. Longer horseback trips along the Arizona Trail must be booked at least a day in advance and must include four or more people.

Private stock (horses, mules, burros, or donkeys) are allowed on certain trails, including North Kaibab Trail, Uncle Jim Trail, and Tiyo Point. Overnight trips require a backcountry permit. Grazing is not allowed within the park, so riders must bring feed for their stock. Call 928/638-7809 for more information about stock use in the park. Neighboring Kaibab National Forest (928/643-7298 or 928/643-7395) offers additional trail-riding opportunities for equestrians.

WINTER ACTIVITIES

Park facilities and services are closed mid-October–mid-May, when the only way into the park is on foot, skis, or snowshoes. But for experienced and prepared winter campers, an off-season visit to the North Rim can be peaceful and rewarding. Winter conditions on the Kaibab Plateau vary. Deep snowpack, extreme cold, and blizzard conditions are possible. Some years, snows may arrive late, but travelers should be prepared and stay aware of changing conditions. The meadows and forests north of the park's boundaries often get heavier snowfalls than along the rim, where updrafts from the canyon create warmer microclimates.

Though the park's entrance road is closed after Thanksgiving, winter at-large camping is allowed from the park's northern boundary to the North Kaibab trailhead (though not at the trailhead itself). Between the North Kaibab trailhead and Bright Angel Point, camping is permitted only at the North Rim Campground's group site. After Thanksgiving, reservations can be made for the winter yurt, located about 200 feet from the North Kaibab trailhead in an administrative area of the park. The yurt accommodates up to six people, with a table, chairs, wood-burning stove, and nearby portable toilet. Groups reserving the yurt are

NORTH RIM LEGENDS: UNCLE JIM AND BRIGHTY

In 1906, President Theodore Roosevelt, an avid sportsman and canyon proponent, created the Grand Canyon Game Preserve. Earlier that same year, Congress authorized the protection of the canyon's deer herds, and in response, the U.S. Forest Service banned deer hunting and went to war on predators. Game warden James T. "Uncle Jim" Owens became the North Rim's most famous varmint hunter, leading other hunters and trappers to kill 800 mountain lions, 500 bobcats, 30 wolves, and almost 500 coyotes over the next three decades. The tactic backfired: Herds of deer in the forest grew to such overwhelming numbers that thousands starved to death during the winter of 1924-1925.

Owens, born in Texas, began to work as a cowboy for famed cattleman Charles Goodnight at 11 years of age. Thirty years later, after living in Wyoming, Montana, and then Yellowstone National Park, Owens led two bison drives of nearly 90 animals in all from Utah to House Rock Valley. The enterprise – breeding bison with cattle – proved unprofitable, and Owens's business partners sold their interests, leaving him with sole ownership of the herd. Fortunately, he had a second job: as guard, game warden, and guide on the forest preserve. His clients over the years included novelist Zane Grey, Arizona historian Sharlot Hall, and Teddy Roosevelt, whom he took on a cougar hunt in 1913. All three recounted their adventures, and Owens' skill as a lion hunter became legendary.

Near his cabin in Harvey Meadow (along the road to Point Sublime), Owens posted a sign advertising his services: "Cougars Caught to Order. Rates Reasonable." Owens gave up hunting as he grew older, no longer able to hear his hunting dogs bay, but he still watched over his horse and buffalo herds, which grazed to the overlook bearing his name today and farther east across the Walhalla Plateau. In the late 1920s, he sold his buffalo herd to the state of Arizona for $10,000 and moved to New Mexico, where he died in 1936 at age 79. Occasionally, today's park visitors spot de-

© KATHLEEN BRYANT

A statue of Brighty sits in the solarium at Grand Canyon Lodge.

scendents of Owens' herd, bison or "cattalo" (a bison-cattle hybrid) that have strayed from their usual home in House Rock Valley.

Another legendary North Rim resident, also a member of Theodore Roosevelt's hunting party, was Brighty, a burro named for Bright Angel Creek. A working animal, Brighty hauled water from a spring below the rim up to a tourist camp. He lived at the warmer canyon bottom in the winter and in the cooler rim forests in the summer, much beloved by the camp's children, who would ride him for hours on end.

Years later, author Marguerite Henry read about Brighty in an old *Sunset* magazine, and his real-life adventures became the basis for her award-winning children's book and later a movie, both titled *Brighty of Grand Canyon*. Uncle Jim and Teddy Roosevelt appear in Henry's tale, which she researched by interviewing rangers and other canyon residents.

The film company commissioned artist Peter Jepson to create a bronze statue commemorating Brighty. Today, Brighty's likeness – nose shiny from "petting" – sits in a corner of the sunroom at Grand Canyon Lodge, where he can gaze through the enormous windows to Bright Angel Canyon, his namesake and stomping grounds.

THE NORTH RIM

limited to four nights. During winter, all overnights at the North Rim require a backcountry permit.

Water is turned off seasonally at the North Kaibab trailhead and below the rim at Supai Tunnel, Roaring Springs day use area, and Cottonwood Campground. Water is available at the North Rim's Backcountry Information Center (near the campground) during winter months. However, bring extra water in case of a pipeline break.

Jacob Lake Inn (928/643-7232) stays open year-round, becoming a hub for winter activities. Kaibab National Forest roads and meadows offer snowmobiling and cross-country skiing. Forest roads east of Highway 67 and south of U.S. 89A are closed to vehicular use, making this area ideal for cross-country skiers and snowshoers in search of silence and solitude.

During the winter months, Highway 67 is gated at the entrance to the park. North of the park entrance, the highway often closes due to snow, with little or no advance warning. Check with the **Arizona Department of Transportation** (dial 511 or 888/411-7623, www.az511.gov) for road conditions. If the highway is closed, it's a snowy 50-mile trek to the rim.

Entertainment and Events

Generally speaking, North Rim night owls are the feathered kind. After a day of hiking and touring in the great outdoors, most people are happy to hit the sack early and rest up for another full day of adventure. But if you're searching for something to do past dark, you'll have a handful of options.

RANGER PROGRAMS

Free ranger programs are scheduled throughout the day and evening at various locations, including the terrace and auditorium of Grand Canyon Lodge, the North Rim Campground amphitheater, and Walhalla Overlook. Topics include geology, natural history, and archaeology. Ranger talks are entertaining and educational, and they provide a great opportunity to ask questions. Most are family-friendly too—during the condor talk, kids hold out measuring tape and don a condor costume to show off the bird's size. For more information, see *The Guide* or check the schedules posted in the North Rim Visitors Center, lodge, and campground.

STAGE SHOW

Forever Resorts, the concessionaire operating Grand Canyon Lodge, has brought a taste of Western tradition to the North Rim with their nightly **Grand Canyon Cookout Experience.** Guests are shuttled by tram to an outdoor location for a chuckwagon-style meal, followed by a live music and stage show. Reservations are recommended.

LIVE MUSIC

Coffee shop by day and lounge by night, the **Roughrider Saloon** (11:30 A.M.–10:30 P.M. daily) occasionally hosts live acoustic music in the evenings. Located next to the lodge, the saloon is a relaxed spot to unwind over a hot coffee drink or a beer.

EVENTS

In addition to regular evening ranger programs held at the campground and auditorium, in late June the North Rim hosts a weeklong **Star Party** (the celestial kind, not the Hollywood variety). Miles and miles from city lights, the skies here are velvety black, and the stars are breathtaking. During the annual star party, a nightly slide show takes center stage at the Grand Canyon Lodge auditorium. Amateur astronomers volunteer their expertise and set up their telescopes outdoors on the lodge's terrace, where park visitors can view planets, constellations, nebulae, and galaxies. The festivities spill beyond park boundaries to Kaibab Lodge,

THE NORTH RIM

© KATHLEEN BRYANT

Rangers lead tours of Walhalla Glade, an Ancestral Puebloan village.

a few miles north of the park entrance, where guests can eye the starry skies from telescopes provided by astronomers.

In August, the North Rim celebrates **Heritage Days.** For many years this event focused on the Kaibab Paiute tribe, but it has been expanded to include other regional Native American cultures. Past events have featured cedar flute music and traditional dances. For more information, contact the **North Rim Visitors Center** (928/638-2481).

Also in August, the annual **Symphony of the Canyon** brings together musicians from southern Utah and northern Arizona. The symphony performs a sunset concert on the lodge's terrace, usually for a standing room–only audience. Contact Grand Canyon Lodge (888/386-4383) for information.

Each month during the summer season, artists visit the North Rim as part of the park's **artist-in-residence program.** In exchange for their time at the canyon, artists present their work to the public through informal discussions and demonstrations, classes, lectures, or performances. Programs vary from month to month; for information about events taking place during your stay, check at the North Rim Visitors Center.

SHOPPING

Shopping choices are limited on the North Rim, but if you run out of toothpaste or want to pick up a few souvenirs to take home, you'll find what you need. The Grand Canyon Association operates a small but superb **bookstore** at the North Rim Visitors Center, stocking nature guides, posters, videos, and coffee-table books as well as learning-themed items for kids of all ages.

Forget to bring a hat or sunscreen? The **gift shop** (8 A.M.–9 P.M. daily) in the lodge complex has a wide selection of items, including hiking hats, T-shirts, jewelry, native art, books, and plenty of souvenirs for the kiddies. Additional camping gear can be found at the campground's **General Store** (928/638-2611, ext. 270, 7 A.M.–8 P.M. daily) along with sundries, snacks, and picnic supplies.

Outside the park, **Kaibab Lodge** (Hwy. 67, 5 miles north of the park entrance, 928/638-2389) has a selection of gifts and souvenirs, from cutesy country-themed items to flint knives and arrowheads knapped by a local artisan.

If you're interested in **Native American art,** be sure to stop at the Jacob Lake Inn (928/643-7232), 45 miles north of the rim, near the junction of Highways 67 and 89A. The Navajo rugs decorating the walls of the dining room are for sale, as are silver and turquoise jewelry, sand paintings, pottery, kachinas, baskets, and other traditional crafts made by Navajo, Hopi, Zuni, and Paiute Indians. The inn also has a wide selection of books, maps, and gifts.

Accommodations

Summer is the North Rim's busiest season, and although there are fewer visitors to this side of the canyon, lodging availability is limited. Plan early and make reservations, or you may find yourself anxiously awaiting cancellations or commuting from far outside the park. Be sure you understand cancellation policies; many lodges on this side of the canyon require advance notice of cancellations to avoid forfeiting a deposit. The nearest lodgings outside the park are Kaibab Lodge, 18 miles from the rim, and the Jacob Lake Inn, 45 miles away. Both these lodges fill up quickly, although cancellations are possible. If you hope to visit in early October, when aspens turn gold, make your reservations several months in advance. Campgrounds fill up quickly all season long.

INSIDE THE PARK
Grand Canyon Lodge

Grand Canyon Lodge (888/386-4383, www.foreverlodging.com) has more than 200 guest rooms, but they fill up quickly, so make reservations well in advance, up to 13 months ahead of your arrival. Last-minute rooms due to cancellations are possible—check at the lobby desk. Rooms range from historic cabins to motel-style accommodations. All have private baths, and all are nonsmoking. A few of the cabins meet ADA-accessibility standards. No pets are allowed in the lodge buildings, including the guest cabins. Rates listed below do not include tax. Rollaway cots can be delivered to some guest rooms for an additional charge.

The nicest lodging option on the North Rim is definitely the stone-and-wood Western cabins ($172, $182 with rim view) east of the lodge, boasting shady porches complete with rocking chairs. The craftsman-inspired cabins have two queen beds and a full bath. Note that the rim-view cabins, overlooking Bright Angel Canyon, book up to two years in advance.

On the west side of the lodge, some of the Frontier and Pioneer cabins overlook Transept Canyon. Ask when you check in and you might be able to get a view cabin. Frontier cabins ($118), with a double and single bed and a shower, can accommodate up to three people. The larger Pioneer cabins ($152, $162 with rim view) can accommodate up to six and have two rooms, one with a queen bed, mini fridge, and coffeepot, the other with a single bed and a full-size futon along with a shared shower.

Motel-style guest rooms ($113) may lack the atmosphere of the cabins, but they have all the basics, including a queen bed and a shower.

Camping

Because North Rim elevations range 6,300–8,000 feet, campers should be prepared for cool evenings, even in the summer. Inside the park, camping is permitted only in designated campsites, and violators may be cited and fined. If you plan on spending the night in the backcountry (including Point Sublime or Cape Final), fax or mail a completed permit application to the Backcountry Information Center (P.O. Box 129, Grand Canyon, AZ

86023, fax 928/635-2125). Permit applications are available on the park's website (www.nps.gov/grca). Dispersed no-fee camping is allowed in neighboring Kaibab National Forest, which also offers reasonably priced developed campgrounds.

North Rim Campground (928/638-7814, May 15–Oct. 15, $18) has 83 campsites. A maximum of two vehicles, three tents, and six people are allowed per site, with trailers, pop-ups, and campers counting as a second vehicle. Some sites accommodate RVs. There are no hookups, but there is a dump station. Sites with a view along the rim of Transept Canyon are $25. Senior and Access pass holders qualify for a 50 percent discount.

Reservations can be made in advance through the **National Recreation Service** (877/444-6777, www.recreation.gov). The campground fills up quickly, and it's best to make reservations as far ahead as possible—up to six months in advance, or a year for group campsites. However, if you can't resist gambling, especially against long odds, you can add your name to a waiting list after 8 A.M., then return at 3 P.M. to see if you landed a spot.

The campground is shaded by ponderosa pines, and the General Store, laundry, and showers are a short walk away. Both the Transept Trail and the Bridle Path connect the campground to the lodge, about a mile away. Pets are allowed in the campground but must be leashed and cannot be left unattended. Charcoal or wood fires are permitted in campsite grills. Wood-gathering is not permitted; wood can be purchased at the General Store.

After the park officially closes in mid-October, a few sites and limited services may be available on a first-come, first-served basis until snow closes Highway 67. Group campsites are available throughout the winter to hikers, snowshoers, and skiers with a backcountry permit. A permit is also needed to reserve the North Rim yurt, available after Thanksgiving through April 15.

Toroweap Campground (free) is also operated by the National Park Service, but it is

150 miles and a world away from Bright Angel Point. Ten primitive sites are situated around a stone amphitheater less than two miles from the rim overlook. There are fire grates, picnic tables, and composting toilets but no water, and you'll need to pack out your trash. The single group site can be reserved (928/638-7870), but others are first-come, first-served. Arrive by mid-afternoon, as the campground may fill up during the spring, especially on weekends. If the campground is full, stop at the Tuweep Ranger Station, about six miles from the rim, for information about camping on nearby Bureau of Land Management land. Because of the lower elevation (4,500 feet) and little shade, expect warmer temperatures in the summer. In winter, roads may be impassable due to mud or snow.

OUTSIDE THE PARK
Motels and Lodges
Eighteen miles north of Bright Angel Point and seven miles north of the Entrance Station, **Kaibab Lodge** (928/638-2389, www.kaibablodge.com, $85–180) sits at the edge of DeMotte Park, a meadow along Highway 67. The historic main building, constructed in the 1920s, includes a pleasant dining room with meadow views, a gift shop, and a comfortable lounge anchored by a stone fireplace on one side and a TV on the other. An alcove serves as a family area with games, an upright piano, and a pay phone.

Behind the main building, an eclectic collection of cabins offers a variety of accommodations, including rustic duplexes with a double bed and shower, a historic log cabin for up to six people, and a larger cabin with two bedrooms and a loft that can accommodate up to eight. All guest rooms have private baths and heaters but no TVs or phones. Some allow pets; all are nonsmoking. Special rates are available for groups (10 rooms or more).

The lodge, a former cattle ranch, is open mid-May–November, depending on snowfall and road closures. If you're looking for a home-away-from-home atmosphere, the friendly folks here will treat you like part of the family.

They'll even shuttle you to the rim if you prefer to leave your vehicle behind.

About 45 miles north of Bright Angel Point, at the intersection of Highway 67 and U.S. 89A, the historic **Jacob Lake Inn** (928/643-7232, www.jacoblake.com) has welcomed North Rim visitors for more than 80 years. The inn has 61 beds in cabins, a motel, and a hotel. Pets are allowed in some guest rooms. Rates quoted are average; actual rates vary according to season and the type of room.

Cabins ($89–111) have 1–2 rooms with double, queen, or king beds and can accommodate 2–4 people. Family cabins ($137) have two rooms and can accommodate up to six people. All cabins are nonsmoking and have showers, heaters, and small decks for enjoying the numerous birds that frequent the woodsy setting—but they have no air-conditioning, TV, phones, or Internet access. Motel rooms ($119) have air-conditioning, and some allow smoking; they come with double or queen beds and accommodate up to four people. Family motel units can be arranged with adjoining rooms. Hotel rooms ($138), the inn's newest accommodations, have two queens or a king bed for 2–4 people and include Internet access, TVs, and phones.

Unlike most North Rim spots, the inn is open year-round, making it a center for snowmobilers, cross-country skiers, and snowshoers. Call to inquire about snow conditions.

Camping

DeMotte Campground (928/643-7395, www.fs.usda.gov/kaibab, late May–Oct. 15, depending on snowfall, $17) is located 17 miles north of the rim and six miles north of the entrance station on the edge of a meadow just off Highway 67. Operated by the U.S. Forest Service, the campground has 38 sites for up to six people with tables and grills, drinking water, and vault toilets. Tents, trailers, and small motor homes are allowed, but there are no hookups. Sites are available on a first-come, first-served basis. The campground doesn't take reservations, and it does fill up, so arrive early. During summer months, the DeMotte

Campground Amphitheater hosts naturalist programs. Campers can dine at nearby Kaibab Lodge and shop for supplies at the North Rim Country Store, both less than a mile away.

The Forest Service also operates **Jacob Lake Campground** (928/643-7395, www.fs.usda.gov/kaibab, May 15–Nov. 1, depending on snowfall, $17) 45 miles north of the rim at the intersection of U.S. 89A and Highway 67. The campground has 53 sites for up to six people available on a first-come, first-served basis. Only the group site can be reserved (877/444-6777, www.recreation.gov). Sites can accommodate tents, trailers, or small motor homes, but there are no hookups. Amenities include tables and grills, drinking water, and toilets. Naturalist programs are offered during summer months. Nearby, campers will find horseback and nature trails as well as the amenities of Jacob Lake Inn.

Kaibab Camper Village (928/643-7804 or 800/525-0924, off-season 928/526-0924, http://kaibabcampervillage.com, May 15–Oct. 15) is located just south of Jacob Lake, less than one mile off Highway 67 on Forest Road 461. The campground offers sites with full hookups for RVs ($35), dry sites and tent sites ($17), and a small cabin with two queen beds ($85), with additional charges ($4–11 per night) for extra people. Amenities include fire pits, picnic tables, toilets, outdoor sinks, laundry, and showers. The camp store has groceries and supplies. At the nearby ranger cabin, the forest service offers interpretive programs. As a bonus, park hosts can hook you up with guided horseback tours or river-rafting trips.

No-fee dispersed camping is allowed in **Kaibab National Forest** (928/643-7395, www.fs.usda.gov/kaibab). Restrictions include stays no longer than 14 days, and no camping within 100 yards of the highway or near the East Rim Day Use Area along Forest Road 611. Practice "leave no trace" ethics. Campsites are accessible by dirt roads, many of them suitable for passenger cars. For road conditions and maps, visit the Kaibab Plateau Visitors Center (928/643-7298, 8 A.M.–5 P.M. daily mid-May–mid-Oct., shorter hours later in the season) in Jacob Lake.

Food

When dining at the North Rim, expect traditional American fare with an occasional Southwestern twist—green chilis, salsa, and tortillas. Because this side of the canyon is more remote, dining options are fewer, and most venues close during the winter. Jacob Lake Inn stays open year-round, serving hearty meals to winter travelers. Leave your suit or little black dress at home: Even at Grand Canyon Lodge, the North Rim's most elegant dining option, casual dress is the norm.

INSIDE THE PARK
Restaurants
The **Grand Canyon Lodge Dining Room** (928/638-2611, ext. 760, breakfast 6:30–10 A.M., lunch 11:30 A.M.–2:30 P.M., dinner 4:45–9:45 P.M. daily) is impressive: The high ceiling is supported by exposed log trusses (with hidden steel beams for support), and expansive windows overlook the Transept. The dining room is green-certified, with all-natural, hormone- and antibiotic-free meats, organic vegetable selections, and fair-trade coffee and tea. Children's menus and a gluten-free menu are available.

The breakfast buffet ($11 adults) includes something for everyone, from homemade granola to hot items. From the menu, you can choose a hearty breakfast of eggs, pancakes, or French toast ($5–11), or order lighter fare (under $5).

Lunch choices in the lodge's dining room include a pasta, bread, and salad bar ($12 adults). You can also order à la carte, from a selection of appetizers, salads, and lodge specialties that include the Roosevelt Burger, Uncle Jim's Beef Stew, and Navajo tacos. You can make arrangements the previous day for a box lunch ($10) to take on a picnic or hike, ready for pickup at 6:30 A.M.

Dinner choices include salads ($10–12) and sandwiches ($15–20) for lighter appetites, or elegant dishes ($16–35) such as Margarita Blackened Salmon, Sunset Mushroom Pasta, or Teddy's Bison Flank Steak. Dinner reservations (928/645-6865 Jan.–Apr., 928/638-2611 May–Oct.) are required. If you arrive without a reservation, check with the dining room host or hostess. You may be able to get a table, especially if you're willing to wait for a later seating.

An alternative to eating in the dining room (which is often fully booked, especially around sunset) is the nightly cookout ($35 adults, $22 children), where visitors can eat alfresco a short distance from the lodge. Beef brisket, roast chicken, and sides are served chuckwagon style at 6:15 P.M. nightly, and reservations can be made until 4 P.M. the same day. Transportation and entertainment are included.

West of the lodge's main entrance you'll find the **Deli in the Pines** (7 A.M.–9 P.M. daily). Selections range from ready-made salads and sandwiches to scrambled-egg breakfast burritos, pizza, and soft-serve ice cream. Most items are under $10. The deli lacks atmosphere, but you can take your sandwich and head for a quiet spot under the trees.

Just east of the lodge entrance, the **coffee shop** (5:30–10:30 A.M.) serves the rim's earliest—and best—cup of joe along with an assortment of pastries. Later in the day, it magically transforms into the **Roughrider Saloon** (11:30 A.M.–10:30 P.M.), offering appetizers and snacks to accompany soft drinks, beer, wine, and cocktails.

Groceries
Inside the park at the North Rim Campground, the **General Store** (928/638-2611, 7 A.M.–8 P.M. May 15–Sept. 30, 7 A.M.–7 P.M. Oct. 1–14) sells camping and picnic supplies, snacks, groceries, and sundries from insect dope to bars of soap. You can take your sandwich or ice cream bar outside to the shady veranda, where a couple of small tables offer a comfortable spot to watch campground comings and goings.

OUTSIDE THE PARK
Restaurants

Kaibab Lodge (928/638-2389, www.kaibab lodge.com), seven miles north of the park entrance, cooks up full breakfasts ($4–8), lunches, and casual dinners ($7–25) daily. If you're planning an early hike or an afternoon picnic, you can get lunches and breakfasts to go, and sack lunches are prepared on request. Children's menus are available. From the dining room's large windows, you can watch deer grazing in the meadows morning and evening. Watch for the daily dinner specials, listed on the board next to the registration desk.

Jacob Lake Inn (928/643-7232, www.jacob lake.com, 6:30 A.M.–9:30 P.M. summer–fall, 8 A.M.–8 P.M. winter–spring, $6–25) serves breakfast, lunch, and dinner year-round to grateful guests and travelers. Breakfast highlights are the buttermilk pancakes and French toast made from home-baked bread. The lunch and dinner menus include the popular Grand Bull Sandwich, ground beef with all the trimmings—including mushrooms and green chilis—on the inn's grilled bread. Service is friendly, but if you arrive at the same time as a bus tour, consider skipping the dining room experience and head instead for the inn's deli and bakery, where you'll find tasty baked goods.

Groceries

Seven miles north of the park entrance, across the highway from the Kaibab Lodge, the **North Rim Country Store** (928/638-2383) has a limited selection of snacks and camping supplies as well as souvenirs, newspapers, and fuel.

In addition to its restaurant, the **Jacob Lake Inn** (928/643-7232) has a small deli where you can pick up a loaf of freshly baked bread and a bottle of wine for a picnic. But if you lack willpower, avert your eyes when you pass by the bakery counter's glass cases: The giant homemade cookies are irresistible.

Information and Services

Before you schedule a tour or make dinner reservations at the lodge, check your watch. Except for the Navajo Reservation, Arizona stays on mountain standard time year-round. If you're traveling from Utah or another neighboring state, you'll need to reset your watch to the local time.

NEWSPAPERS

If you didn't get a copy of the North Rim edition of *The Guide* when you entered the park, you can pick one up at the **North Rim Visitors Center** (928/638-2481, 8 A.M.–6 P.M. daily). This is the park's free informational newspaper that lists services, events, schedules, and more.

POST OFFICE

Down the sidewalk from the gift shop, you'll find a post office window (8 A.M.–noon and 1–5 P.M. Mon.–Fri.), where you can mail all those postcards you just purchased.

PHONES

Cell phone service can be iffy on the North Rim, but there's a bank of pay phones behind the visitors center.

PUBLIC RESTROOMS

Public restrooms can be found behind the visitors center, in the lodge complex just outside the deli, and at the General Store in the North Rim Campground. All are wheelchair accessible.

ATMS

You'll find ATMs in the Roughrider Saloon (just east of the lodge's main entrance) and at the General Store, adjacent to the campground.

LAUNDRY AND SHOWERS

A public coin-operated laundry (7 A.M.–10 P.M. daily) is located along the entrance road to the

North Rim Campground. In the same building are restrooms and showers where—after a long, hot hike—you can get five minutes of blissful hydrotherapy for six quarters.

EMERGENCIES

For emergencies, dial 911, adding an extra 9 (9–911) if you're calling from a lodge phone. Cell phone reception is spotty, even along the rim. If you're closer to the river, you may be able to flag down a rafting party. River guides use satellite phones (emergencies only, 928/638-7911). Helicopter evacuations are very expensive, so it's best to avoid hiking emergencies by planning thoroughly.

EMT-trained rangers can respond 24 hours a day to medical emergencies. The nearest clinic is more than 80 miles away in Kanab, Utah. Hospitals are even farther, located in Page, Flagstaff, and St. George, Utah.

If you are hiking the North Kaibab Trail, the only emergency phone is located at the Cottonwood Campground, seven miles below the rim. The Tuweep Ranger Station has an emergency phone.

PETS

Pets (other than service animals) are not allowed on trails or inside the lodge buildings. To take a service animal below the rim, contact the Backcountry Information Center (928/638-2125). Pets can be walked on a leash along the Bridle Path between Grand Canyon Lodge and the campground, and they are also allowed in North Rim Campground, but must be leashed at all times. Unlike the South Rim, there is no kennel service available here. If Rover loves to go hiking with you, inquire about trails in nearby Kaibab National Forest.

RELIGIOUS SERVICES

Check the bulletin board inside the Grand Canyon Lodge for a schedule of religious services.

WEATHER

People who live in Northern Arizona have a saying about the weather: If you don't like it,

wait 15 minutes. Temperatures can rise dramatically from early morning to midday, and brief afternoon thunderstorms are typical July–September. The current forecast for the North and South Rims and surrounding areas is posted daily in the **North Rim Visitors Center** (928/638-2481, 8 A.M.–6 P.M. daily). You can also access a recorded weather message, updated at 7 A.M. daily, by calling the park's information line (928/638-7888).

ROAD CONDITIONS

For information about highway conditions, contact the **Arizona Department of Transportation** (dial 511 or 888/411-7623, www.az511.gov). For local road conditions, check with the **North Rim Visitors Center** (928/638-2481, 8 A.M.–6 P.M. daily) or the **Kaibab Plateau Visitors Center** (928/643-7298, 8 A.M.–5 P.M. daily mid-May–mid-Oct., fall–winter hours vary).

LOST AND FOUND

If you find an item another visitor has left behind, you can turn it in at the North Rim Visitors Center. If you've lost something, you can inquire about the missing item at the Visitors Center (928/638-2481) or at the front desk of Grand Canyon Lodge (480/998-1981 or 888/386-4383).

WHEELCHAIR ACCESSIBILITY

Lodge buildings predate accessibility requirements, and some cabins are minimally accessible. Lifts and ramps provide access to the main lodge. Wheelchairs for temporary day use are available at the North Rim Visitors Center and Grand Canyon Lodge. You can pick up an accessibility permit, which acts as a parking permit for designated spaces, at the North Rim Entrance Station when you arrive or at the North Rim Visitors Center. The park's *Accessibility Guide* can be downloaded before your trip (www.nps.gov/grca), or you can request a copy at the Visitors Center. A number of ranger programs are wheelchair-accessible; check the listings in the park newspaper, *The Guide,* for more information.

Getting There and Around

Getting around the park's North Rim in your own vehicle is a breeze. With the exception of the large public parking lot shared by the lodge and visitors center, and the occasional wait at the entrance gate, you've left traffic congestion far behind you on the canyon's other rim. The flip side is that you won't find the South Rim's guided motor coach tours or free shuttle bus service here. But if you like back-road drives and outdoor recreation, you'll wonder why more people don't visit the canyon's wilder side.

The ideal jumping-off point for exploration is Bright Angel Point, with accommodations at the lodge or the campground. Most activities and services are centered here, including food, ranger programs, and hiking trailheads. The nearest lodging and campground outside the park are 18 miles away, a manageable drive if Grand Canyon Lodge and North Rim Campground are full. In that case, look for lodging at Kaibab Lodge (18 miles), Jacob Lake (45 miles), Fredonia (75 miles), or Kanab (82 miles). You may find yourself commuting to Bright Angel Point, but what a commute—Highway 67 passes through meadows surrounded by forest, where deer graze morning and evening and dark skies are studded with stars at night.

Highway 67, which originates at Jacob Lake, is the only paved route to the rim. U.S. 89A intersects Highway 67 from the east (Marble Canyon area) and northwest (Fredonia and Kanab).

The nearest sizable city is St. George, Utah (156 miles). United and Delta fly into the St. George airport from Los Angeles and Salt Lake City. Many North Rim visitors begin their trip to the North Rim from Las Vegas (275 miles), where it's easy to sign up for a tour or rent a car. There is no public transportation to the North Rim other than the Trans Canyon Shuttle, which travels the 212 miles from the South Rim daily during summer months.

SHUTTLES

The **hiker shuttle** to the North Kaibab Trail (1.5 miles away) is available twice daily in the morning (5:45 and 7:10 A.M.), with reservations required 24 hours in advance. The cost is $7 pp, payable at the lodge's front desk.

The **Trans Canyon Shuttle** (928/638-2820, www.trans-canyonshuttle.com) offers daily round-trip van service between the North Rim and South Rim ($80 one way, $150 round-trip). The shuttle leaves the North Rim at 7 A.M., arriving at the South Rim at 11:30 A.M. Reservations are required.

Kaibab Lodge (928/638-2389), located outside the park, 18 miles north of the rim, plans to offer shuttle services to Bright Angel Point.

GAS AND GARAGE SERVICES

It's smart to keep your gas tank full if you plan on back-road explorations. You can fuel up at the **Chevron station** (7 A.M.–7 P.M. daily mid-May–mid-Oct.) along the entrance road to the North Rim Campground. Pumps are accessible 24 hours a day with a credit card. Minor car repairs are also available here.

The nearest fuel available outside the park is at the **North Rim Country Store** (928/638-2383), across the highway from Kaibab Lodge, about seven miles from the park entrance station. Basic mechanic services and propane can also be found at the service station next to Jacob Lake Inn.

THE INNER CANYON

The only way to explore the inner canyon is by foot, mule, or boat. The slower pace encourages visitors to match the rhythms of nature—the steady beat of your footsteps, the colors shifting with the angle of the sun, juniper giving way to chaparral, then cactus, as you descend in elevation.

For those new to canyon hiking or backpacking, it's best to stick to well-traveled corridors or guided trips. The inner canyon wilderness is a place of exquisite beauty but also extreme danger. Summer temperatures soar into the hundreds, with little or no water available on many trails. The Colorado River's peaceful greenish blue hides dangerous currents and bone-chilling waters impounded by Glen Canyon Dam. Fierce summer thunderstorms erode cliffs and sweep down side canyons, briefly turning the Colorado red, a reminder that the river hasn't been completely tamed.

But for the 15,000–20,000 people who float through the canyon each year on commercial or private trips, time is almost forgotten as the rhythm of the river takes over. Cliffs rise up from the water's edge, enclosing you in an embrace of colorful stone. Cell phones don't work down here, and watches become unimportant. You've entered a desert wilderness punctuated by 160-plus white-water rapids, more than a dozen waterfalls, and countless side canyons, seeps, and springs.

Hiking choices include official trails as well as casual meanders up magical side canyons like Matkatamiba or Elves Chasm. Climbers can try their skills on inner canyon peaks and monuments, while anglers can test theirs

NPS PHOTO BY MICHAEL QUINN

HIGHLIGHTS

◖ **Marble Canyon:** The first section of Grand Canyon, cutting north-south through an open valley known as the Marble Platform, is sheer-walled Marble Canyon. The first sizable rapids river runners encounter, House Rock Rapids, lies at the mouth of Rider Canyon, about 17 miles downriver from Lees Ferry (page 128).

◖ **Redwall Cavern:** About 33 miles downriver, the Colorado River carved this large cave from the Redwall limestone formation. Explorer John Wesley Powell, clearly impressed at its vast size, wrote that it could hold 50,000 people. Doubtful – but it is big. River runners often stop here for lunch on the beach or a game of Frisbee inside the cavern's sandy expanse (page 130).

◖ **Nankoweap Ruins Route:** High above the Colorado River near Nankoweap Canyon, around river mile 53, the Ancient Puebloans, also known as the Anasazi, constructed masonry granaries to protect their food stores. The steep route up to the ruins, which are about 1,000 years old, offers striking downriver views (page 131).

◖ **Little Colorado River Confluence:** Just past mile 61, the Little Colorado River

(LCR) joins the Colorado. The warmer turquoise waters of the LCR harbor several endangered fish species, while the cliffs shelter prospector Ben Beamer's historic cabin (page 131).

◖ **The Inner Gorge:** Past its confluence with the Little Colorado, the Colorado River swings west, entering the darker, harder rocks of the Inner Gorge (also known as Granite Gorge) carved below the Tonto Platform. This section is the heart of Grand Canyon, sometimes referred to as "the canyon within the canyon," with rock layers 2 billion years old (page 132).

◖ **Phantom Ranch:** Designed by architect Mary Colter, these stone-and-wood cabins are the only accommodations in the inner canyon. Shaded by cottonwoods, lying between Bright Angel Creek and the Colorado River, Phantom Ranch is a riparian oasis in the inner canyon's harsh desert environment (page 133).

◖ **Deer Creek Falls:** This 100-foot-high waterfall tumbles out of a sinuous Tapeats sandstone narrows on the lower river – an awe-inspiring sight and a popular spot for water play (page 134).

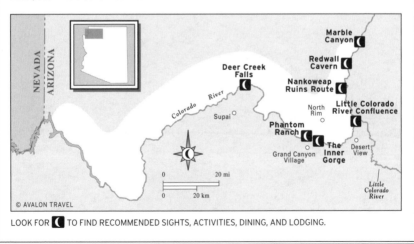

LOOK FOR ◖ TO FIND RECOMMENDED SIGHTS, ACTIVITIES, DINING, AND LODGING.

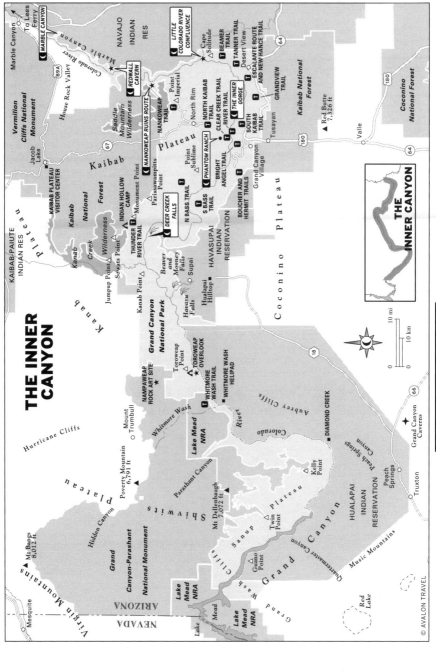

THE INNER CANYON

on rainbow trout. Between Lees Ferry and Diamond Creek, 225 miles downstream, the only outpost of civilization is historic Phantom Ranch, a cluster of log-and-stone cabins offering cold beer, hot showers, and mail service by mule train.

Very few who come to Grand Canyon experience its inner reaches because, frankly, it's not an easy journey. You'll pay for it with time, effort, and sweat—but you'll treasure it all the more because you've earned your place in the canyon's heart. You can see and hear the immense power and grace of the Colorado River, touch rocks that are 2 billion years old, and walk on trails that have been used for centuries. At night, the narrow ribbon of sky is bright with stars, and stone surrounds you. No matter how hard it is to get here, you'll be grateful that you did.

PLANNING YOUR TIME

If you want to spend a few hours or a day exploring below the rims, you can hike partway into the canyon on a number of popular trails, or travel by mule from the North Rim. But if your goal is to reach the Colorado River, take note: The National Park Service strongly

discourages anyone from attempting to hike from rim to river and back in a day. Unless you are an exceptionally strong hiker, you'll need to spend at least one night in the canyon, and that means preparing ahead.

Mule tours from the South Rim generally spend one night in the canyon, but you can arrange for a second night. A simple backpacking trip might require three days and two nights in the canyon, but you'll need several days if you take wilderness trails from rim to river, and 1–3 weeks if you plan to explore the length of the inner canyon by raft. An overnight canyon trip isn't something to do on impulse: Careful planning and preparation are essential. You may need weeks or months of lead time to apply for backcountry permits or to make tour reservations. You may also need time to improve your personal fitness.

Because of the myriad challenges (heat, wilderness, remoteness, topography), the inner canyon is an area best experienced with companions. If you haven't been to Grand Canyon before, or if you and your companions don't have a lot of hiking experience, it's a good idea to sign on to a guided tour for your first inner canyon adventure.

Exploring the Inner Canyon

Of the 5 million people who travel to Grand Canyon each year, fewer than 2 percent spend a night in the inner canyon's backcountry. Those who do automatically join the ranks of the elite. Time and money, though not absolute prerequisites, help you get there. If you make it here, you're most likely one of those admirable sorts with the ability to plan ahead. You need to be relatively physically fit to handle the terrain and temperatures, even if you ride on a raft or mule. Mental attitude is even more important: Determination, focus, and a sense of adventure can make the difference between a positive experience and an ordeal. You may be here to learn about the canyon, but in the process you'll learn more about yourself. Exploring

the inner canyon may not be for everyone, but for many, it's an epiphany.

VISITOR INFORMATION

There are no visitors centers, per se, in the Inner Canyon. Even ranger stations are few and far between, some open only seasonally.

Lees Ferry

All white-water rafting trips through Grand Canyon put in at Lees Ferry, outside Grand Canyon National Park in Glen Canyon National Recreation Area, 15 river miles below Glen Canyon Dam. Lees Ferry is the last developed area river runners will see until Phantom Ranch, nearly 90 river miles away.

It has a campground, parking (with a 14-day limit), public phones, a ranger station, toilets, and water.

The nearest visitors center is **Navajo Bridge Interpretive Center** (9 A.M.–5 P.M. daily mid-Apr.–Oct., 10 A.M.–4 P.M. Sat.–Sun. early Apr. and Nov.), located just south of the intersection of Lees Ferry Road and U.S. 89A, six miles from the campground.

Phantom Ranch and Bright Angel Campground

At the confluence of the Colorado River and Bright Angel Creek, accessible by North Kaibab Trail, South Kaibab Trail, and Bright Angel Trail, Phantom Ranch and Bright Angel Campground offer the widest range of services inside the canyon, including pay phones, an emergency phone, a ranger station, toilets, water, showers, and mail service. The Phantom Ranch Canteen sells snacks and a few sundries.

Cottonwood Campground

Situated along North Kaibab Trail, halfway between the river and the rim, Cottonwood Campground has an emergency phone and toilets. The campground is open year-round, but the ranger station is staffed only seasonally, and drinking water is available May–mid-October.

Indian Garden

Located midway down Bright Angel Trail, Indian Garden has year-round services, including a campground, emergency phone, ranger station, toilets, and water.

TOURS

Guided trips to the inner canyon include mule tours, backpacking trips, and commercial river trips. Mule trips to Phantom Ranch are scheduled year-round. The commercial rafting season runs April–October. The best times for backpacking are spring and fall, although during winter, when both rims may be covered with snow, inner canyon temperatures average 50–60°F—great hiking weather.

Mule Trips

Mule trips to the inner canyon originate from either rim. The **Phantom Ranch Mule Tour** (303/297-2757 or 888/297-2757, daily year-round, $482 pp one night, $674 two nights, reduced rates for a second person), departing from the South Rim, is the only mule trip with an overnight in the canyon. Reservations can be made up to 13 months in advance. Tours fill up quickly, but last-minute cancellations are possible, and you can add your name to the waiting list at one of the transportation desks, located in the South Rim lodges or at the Grand Canyon Visitors Center. The waiting list is shortest in winter, when cancellations are most likely.

The Phantom Ranch mule tour includes one night in the canyon, but you can arrange for a second night, which gives you more time to explore the lovely environs of Phantom Ranch. Even if you only spend a single night at Phantom Ranch, you can experience a lot of the canyon on a mule trip: history, scenery, camaraderie, and dramatic vistas from the canyon's two most popular trails, Bright Angel and South Kaibab.

On the North Rim, full-day mule trips are run by **Grand Canyon Trail Rides** (P.O. Box 128, Tropic, UT 84776, 435/679-8665, www .canyonrides.com, mid-May–mid-Oct., $125 pp includes lunch) and head into the canyon via the North Kaibab Trail. They go as far as Roaring Springs but not to the river.

Commercial River Trips
HISTORY

Commercial river running in Grand Canyon launched in 1938 with Norman Nevills, who guided a pair of botanists interested in the canyon's flora. Nevills designed a broad, flat-bottomed wooden boat called a cataract boat, and in all his river trips, he never "swam" (river-speak for capsizing). By midcentury, fewer than 100 people had run the Colorado through Grand Canyon, but commercial guiding was beginning to catch on. Among the best-known early guides was Georgie White, who lashed together trios of World War II surplus rafts and

THE INNER CANYON

COMMERCIAL WHITE-WATER OUTFITTERS

A number of commercial outfitters have concessionaire agreements with Grand Canyon National Park to lead trips on the Colorado River through the canyon. Many are based in Flagstaff or Utah but offer travel options from Las Vegas. When comparing outfitters, consider the number of days, trip dates, types of rafts, trip origination and end, and if shuttle services to and from the canyon are included. Additional charges may include park entry fees. Upper- or lower-canyon trips may require a hike in or out of the canyon; some trip packages include an overnight at Phantom Ranch. Prices are for adults. Lower rates may be available for youth, and age restrictions vary. Deposits are typically required at the time of reservations, and discounts may be offered for early payment. Trip cancellation insurance – strongly recommended – is available from a few outfitters; more likely, you will shop around for your own.

- **Aramark-Wilderness River Adventures** (P.O. Box 717, Page, AZ 86040, 928/645-3296 or 800/992-8022, www.riveradventures.com): upper and/or lower canyon trips, motorized, 3.5–8 days ($1,210–2,680); oar rafts, 5.5–16 days ($1,815–4,940), hybrid trips with oar and paddle rafts, 5.5–12 days ($1,815–3,895). Wilderness River Adventures offers family trips and flight packages from Las Vegas.

- **Arizona Raft Adventures** (4050F E. Huntington Dr., Flagstaff, AZ 86004, 928/526-8200 or 800/786-7238, www.azraft.com): upper-, lower-, and full-length canyon trips, motorized, 8–10 days ($2,420–2,830); paddle rafts ($2,040–3,600); hybrid trips with oar and paddle rafts, 6–16 days ($1,940–3,930). Some AzRA hybrid trips include a dory. Specialized trips focus on hiking, yoga, natural history, and kayaking skills.

- **Arizona River Runners** (P.O. Box 47788, Phoenix, AZ 85068-7788, 602/867-4866 or 800/477-7238, www.raftarizona.com): upper-, lower-, and full-length canyon trips; motorized, 3–12 days ($1,175–2,695); oar rafts, 6–13 days ($1,795–3,295). Supported kayak trips and hike-focused trips are available. Arizona River Runners offers family discounts for three-day trips.

- **Canyon Explorations/Canyon Expeditions** (P.O. Box 310, Flagstaff, AZ 86002, 928/774-4559 or 800/654-0723, www.canyonx.com): upper-, lower-, and full-length non-motorized canyon trips, oar rafts, paddle rafts, kayak options, 6–17 days ($1,790–4,135). They stress their experience at accommodating guests with disabilities.

- **Canyoneers** (P.O. Box 2997, Flagstaff, AZ 86003, 928/526-0924 or 800/525-0924, www.canyoneers.com): upper-, lower-, and full-length canyon trips, motorized, 3–7 days ($995–2,195); oar rafts and historic wooden cataract boat, 6–14 days ($1,795–3,250). Kayak support is available. Special trips have a geology focus.

- **Colorado River & Trail Expeditions** (P.O. Box 57575, Salt Lake City, UT 84157-0575, 801/261-1789 or 800/253-7328, www.crateinc.com): upper-, lower-, and full-length canyon trips; motorized, 4–11 days ($1,400–2,450); paddle rafts, 5–11 days ($1,800–3,450); oar rafts, 10–14 days ($2,800–3,450). Some oar trips include a paddle-raft option. Special trips focusing on natural history or hiking are available; so are kayak support trips.

- **Grand Canyon Dories/O.A.R.S.** (P.O. Box 67, Angles Camp, CA 95222, 209/736-2924 or 800/346-6277, www.oars.com): upper-, lower-, and full-length canyon trips; oar rafts, 4–18 days ($1,796–5,022); dories, 4–18 days ($1,847–5,628). Sister companies Grand Canyon Dories and O.A.R.S. specialize in nonmotorized trips with long itineraries and low guest-to-guide ratios.

- **Grand Canyon Expeditions Company** (P.O. Box O, Kanab, UT 84741, 435/644-2691 or 800/544-2691, www.gcex.com): full-length canyon trips; motorized, eight days

© KATHLEEN BRYANT

Commercial river outfitters launch from Lees Ferry.

($2,550); dories, 14 or 16 days ($3,700–3,900). Group charters can be arranged and tailored to special interests, often at a discount. Kayak support is available.

- **Grand Canyon Whitewater** (P.O. Box 1300, Page, AZ 86040, 928/645-8866 or 800/343-3121, www.grandcanyonwhitewater.com): upper-, lower-, and full-length canyon trips; motorized, 4–8 days ($990–2,355); oar rafts, 6–12 days ($1,500–3,300).

- **Hatch River Expeditions** (HC 67-35 Marble Canyon, AZ 86036, 928/355-2241 or 800/856-8966, www.hatchriverexpeditions.com): upper-, lower-, and full-length canyon trips; motorized, 4–8 days ($1,231–2,600); oar rafts, 6–12 days ($1,907–3,625). Hike-focused trips are available. Hatch also offers charter trips as well as kayak support for 16 or more people, 10 days minimum.

- **Moki Mac River Expeditions** (P.O. Box 71242, Salt Lake City, UT 84171-0242, 801/268-6667 or 800/284-7280, www.mokimac.com): upper-, lower-, and full-length canyon trips; motorized, eight days ($2,585); oar rafts, 6–14 days ($1,937–3,799).

Oar trips include dories and occasionally inflatable kayaks ("duckies"); paddle-rafts are also available.

- **Outdoors Unlimited** (6900 Townsend Winona Rd., Flagstaff, AZ 86004, 928/526-4546 or 800/637-7238, www.outdoorsunlimited.com): upper-, lower-, and full-length nonmotorized canyon trips, 5–15 days ($1,665–3,655); oar rafts, paddle rafts.

- **Tour West** (P.O. Box 333, Orem, UT 84059, 801/225-0755 or 800/453-9107, www.twriver.com): upper-, lower-, and full-length canyon trips; paddle rafts, 5–13 days ($1,715–3,415); oar rafts, 5–13 days ($1,665–3,295). A paddle-raft option is available on all oar trips. Special extended trips are offered in spring and fall. Pretrip lodging and post-trip transportation options are offered.

- **Western River Expeditions** (7258 Racquet Club Dr., Salt Lake City, UT 84121, 801/942-6669 or 800/453-7450, www.westernriver.com): full-length or lower canyon trips, motorized, 3–7 days ($1,145–2,695). Western River is the only outfitter using multipontoon J-rig rafts.

added outboard motors to create rubberized people-movers that safely slipped over rapids. She called them G-rigs; others dubbed them baloney boats. Her share-the-expense tours often featured mystery meals—a mishmash of canned food with the labels worn away by the river.

Other guides followed Georgie White's example, creating rigs that carried large groups, and by the early 1970s river traffic swelled from a few dozen to more than 16,000 people a year. The increase was also due in part to the completion of Glen Canyon Dam: Timed releases from the dam made river flows more predictable, and river running became more accessible. The higher traffic impacted the river's beaches and water quality, and in 1973 the National Park Service responded by issuing a limited number of river permits in an effort to preserve a sense of wildness within the inner canyon.

Commercial outfitting has come a long way since baloney boats and makeshift meals. A guided river trip through the canyon is the experience of a lifetime, combining jaw-dropping scenery with camaraderie and relaxation. Typically, you'll spend 4–8 hours on the river each day, with the rest of the time for hiking and exploring, or relaxing along the water's edge. All the clichés you've heard are true: It *is* like entering another world, and time *does* lose its meaning. Ten days will feel like 10 hours—you won't believe the trip is over so quickly. Luckily, 10 days will also feel like 10 months because you've packed each one with so many experiences: great hikes, good food, gorgeous views, lots of white-water thrills, and plenty of peaceful moments. Be kind and give yourself at least a day or two to transition back to civilization.

PLANNING A RIVER TRIP

Many commercial outfitters include a few focused trips each season. Some trips feature more hiking; some showcase professional geologists, photographers, historians, or other experts who share their knowledge and skills. And if you can get together a large enough group to charter a trip, you may be able to suggest your own theme, such as rock-climbing or archaeology.

One of the first choices you'll need to make when planning a trip is—to paraphrase Shakespeare—whether to motor or not to motor. Nonmotorized trips on paddle rafts, oar rafts, and wooden dories are slower and quieter—because there are no motors—and more exciting, because you sit closer to the water and may be one of the paddlers. On the other hand, motorized trips on large rafts demand less effort from passengers, offer a greater sense of safety, and allow you cover more canyon miles in a shorter period of time.

Some commercial outfitters have age limits, particularly on longer, more challenging trips. River trips are physically active, and you need to consider any health issues or limitations. You'll find a host of helpful information on outfitters' websites, and they are happy to discuss any particular concerns you might have. Being in good physical condition will help make your experience more enjoyable, but most outfitters are willing to work with people whose abilities are limited. The crew isn't there to act as personal valets, but they will do their utmost to make sure you are safe and having a great time. Crew members are professional, caring, experienced, and well-versed in canyon geology and natural history. (But don't fall for the story about the rock beavers.)

Reservations are required for trips, which can fill up to a year in advance. It's possible to get on a trip on fairly short notice, however, as cancellations do occur. Prices start around $300 per day. This may seem like a lot of money, even for a guided trip, but it's actually quite a bargain when you consider that meals and gear are included, and the experience you'll have is priceless.

If time or money are issues, you can sign on for a half-length trip. Upper-canyon trips from Lees Ferry to Phantom Ranch (about 90 miles) feature stunning scenery and milder rapids. They are generally a day shorter than lower-canyon trips (about 130 miles), which navigate the river's biggest rapids. If you leave a river trip at Phantom Ranch, you'll have to hike out of the canyon—more than nine miles and 8,000 feet of elevation. Conversely, if you join a river trip halfway, you'll have to hike down to Phantom Ranch to meet the rest of your group. Either way, you can arrange ahead of time for a mule duffel service to transport your gear.

Commercial trips are scheduled April–October, with peak months being June–August. Discounts are sometimes available for early spring or late fall trips, when storms or cold spells are more likely: Bring fleece and rain gear. During the summer, when temperatures in the canyon soar past 100°F, the Colorado River remains a chilly 45–55°F, and splashing through rapids is welcome refreshment. Another way to beat the heat and relentless sun is to soak a cotton hat, shirt, bandana, or sarong in the Colorado's cool water, then covering exposed skin. Camp shoes—a pair of flip-flops or clogs—feel great after a long day of hiking. If you bring your lucky Bears cap or wear your favorite prescription sunglasses, be sure they're attached with a clip or retainer before you go bouncing through the rapids. And no matter what type or length of trip you choose, bring plenty of sunscreen and moisturizing lotion, especially if you plan to paddle.

Backpacking Tours

If you've never backpacked before, it's a good idea to make your first overnight hike to the inner canyon with a guide and other travelers. Not only will you be safer, you'll also learn much more about the canyon's flora, fauna, and geology, enriching your experience as you gain new skills.

The wide array of offerings from **Grand Canyon Field Institute** (GCFI, 928/638-2485 or 866/471-4435, gcfi@grandcanyon.org, www.grandcanyon.org/fieldinstitute) includes guided backpacking expeditions. Backpacking

trips range 2–5 nights and cover a variety of topics such as basic wilderness skills, photography, or geology. Participants must be age 18 or older and able to carry a pack weighing 30–50 pounds, although occasional mule-assisted trips are offered. As a nonprofit organization and park partner, GCFI also leads service trips, such as archaeological surveys or an inventory of water sources in a particular section of the canyon.

Another nonprofit organization with a long history of promoting lifetime learning, though now with a new name, is **Road Scholar** (11 Ave. de Layfayette, Boston, MA, 02111, 800/454-5798, www.elderhostel.org). Formerly known as Elderhostel, Road Scholar features a number of Grand Canyon trips, including a six-day rim-to-rim backpack with a layover in the Phantom Ranch area and a couple of whitewater expeditions.

More than 20 concessionaires hold permits to lead backpacking trips within the canyon, from nationally known, focused organizations such as National Outdoor Leadership School (NOLS) to regional guide services such as **Discovery Treks** (480/247-9266 or 888/256-8731, www.discoverytreks.com) and local companies like **Grand Canyon Hikes** (928/779-1614 or 877/506-6233, www.grandcanyonhikes.com). Look for guides with Grand Canyon experience, wilderness first aid certification, and wilderness first responder (WFR) training, and don't be afraid to ask for testimonials from past clients.

Audiovisual Tours

If you're impatiently waiting for a river trip or trying to learn more about backpacking, check out the park's wealth of online multimedia offerings (www.nps.gov/grca). You can go on a virtual raft trip down the Colorado River, explore inner canyon sites on an interactive map, or listen to podcasts about current backcountry conditions.

THE INNER CANYON

Sights

The Colorado River runs 277 miles through the canyon from Lees Ferry to the Grand Wash Cliffs, dropping 2,220 vertical feet. Inner Canyon highlights are described in downriver order.

LEES FERRY AND NAVAJO BRIDGE

Leaving the Navajo sandstone cliffs of Glen Canyon behind at Lees Ferry, the river quickly begins to cut through the rock layers associated with Grand Canyon. Less than a mile downstream from Lees Ferry, the Paria River's entry creates a riffle that's choppy but too mild to call rapids. When the waters of the Paria carry sediment after a rain or flood, they form swirling patterns as they enter the clear green-blue of the Colorado River waters that have been impounded by Glen Canyon Dam.

About four miles from Lees Ferry, high above the river, Navajo Bridge links the Arizona Strip country to the rest of the state. The historic bridge, completed in 1929, is closed to vehicles, though people can walk across it for great views of rafts passing below. The newer highway bridge was built a few feet to the west. Navajo Bridge is considered by many river runners to be the gateway to Grand Canyon.

◀ MARBLE CANYON

The easternmost section of Grand Canyon cuts north–south through the Marble Platform of Paleozoic rocks for more than 60 miles. Early canyon explorer John Wesley Powell thought the smoothly polished, almost vertical walls looked like marble, so he named this section Marble Canyon. In 1969, the area became Marble Canyon National Monument to protect the river from proposed dam sites. In 1975, Marble Canyon was added to Grand Canyon National Park. Geologically speaking, it is part of Grand Canyon, though its historic appellation remains.

The rocks of Marble Canyon introduce the highest layers found throughout the rest of the canyon: the Kaibab, Toroweap, and Coconino Formations. In about five miles, past 467-foot high Navajo Bridge, reddish slope-forming Hermit Shale makes its appearance. Formed by an ancient swamp, Hermit Shale bears insect and plant fossils, especially ferns. (Hermit Shale becomes a predominant layer farther west, where it erodes to form sloped shoulders on buttes and canyon rims.)

The first sizable rapids that river runners encounter, House Rock Rapids, lies at the mouth of the tributary Rider Canyon, about 17 miles downriver from Lees Ferry. Like most rapids, House Rock Rapids was formed when flash floods through this tributary canyon pushed debris into the Colorado, creating a spillover. In 1890, when engineer Robert Brewster Stanton attempted a second survey to find a railroad route through the canyon, the expedition's photographer, Franklin Nims, was nearly killed in a fall. Stanton and his crew halted their journey to evacuate Nims via Rider Canyon.

THE ROARING TWENTIES

A series of small rapids, known collectively as the Roaring Twenties, give river runners a fast and fun run: North Canyon, Indian Dick (don't ask), 23-Mile, 23.5-Mile, 24-Mile, 24.5-Mile Rapids, and so on, are a mild roller-coaster ride and a mere preview of things to come. Harmless as it seems today, this section of canyon plagued Stanton's ill-prepared first attempt at running the canyon in 1889, and 25-Mile Rapids is also known as Hansbrough-Richards Rapids for the second and third men drowned on that fateful expedition.

The Supai Group of rocks, which begin to appear about 11 miles downstream from Lees Ferry, form the bedrock of beautiful North Canyon, entering from the west at mile 20. Shortly after that, cliff-forming Redwall limestone appears. This limestone, left by a shallow sea 320–360 million years ago, is actually off-white but stained reddish by the overlying layers. Throughout the canyon, Redwall cliffs

IDENTIFYING FLOATING OBJECTS

In the decades before equipment was regulated by the park service, river runners pitted their skills against the Colorado River's rapids in some rather unusual floating objects, including inner tubes, Sportyaks, a Chris-Craft motorboat, and the first and only legal upriver run on jet boats. (However, if you fall in with the camp of diehard believers who consider prospector James White the first through the canyon, you can add a driftwood raft to that list.)

Dories are the classic canyon conveyance, rigid oar boats with a pointed bow, in the tradition of the all-wood dories used by John Wesley Powell, Emery and Ellsworth Kolb, and other early canyon explorers. Today's dories are usually less than twenty feet long and made of wood, fiberglass, or aluminum, holding the oarsman, 3-4 passengers, and gear. Elegant and lively, dories are considered the ultimate Grand Canyon craft.

Most commercial outfitters on the Colorado River use inflatable rafts made of coated nylon or polyester. **Oar rafts** are typically 18 feet long, rigged with a metal frame that doubles as storage compartments for the field kitchen and other equipment. Relatively stable, they hold 3-5 passengers and sit low to the water. Oar rafts are guided by an oarsman – or woman – who expertly studies the river and uses a pair of long oars to maneuver through rapids. **Paddle rafts,** usually 14-18 feet long, hold up to 10 passengers who work as a team to power and steer using paddles. They may be rigged with a metal frame. **Motorized rafts** are big – nearly 40 feet long in some cases – and passengers sit high above the water on a metal deck. Side floats can be pontoon-style or some other arrangement. Engines are relatively quiet, operated by a boatwoman or boatman, who is assisted by a swamper.

Private river trips in particular may include quite a variety of craft: hard-shell kayaks, duckies (inflatable kayaks), hand-built wooden boats, and government-surplus rafts, in addition to the more typical paddle rafts and oar rafts.

If you're not one of the lucky few to participate in a river trip, the best place to get an up-close look at canyon conveyances is at Lees Ferry, especially in the morning, when most trips launch. Another good viewing spot is at Phantom Ranch. If you have a pair of good binoculars, it's fun to stand at overlooks with river views, such as Pima Point or Desert View, to see if you can spot a colorful flotilla of rafts as it passes far below.

are streaked with tapestries of desert varnish—dark manganese oxide stains.

Tributaries like Rider Canyon, South Canyon, and Buck Farm Canyon not only make fascinating day-hike opportunities for river runners but also offer backpacking adventures for people entering from the House Rock Valley area. Some tributaries have obstacles barring further progress from river or rim, so canyoneers often carry technical climbing gear to rappel down pour-overs (dry waterfalls) or small inflatable rafts to float packs across long, deep pools.

SOUTH CANYON

Now that you're traveling in the Redwall, repetitive neck strain is a real possibility. From river level, it's fascinating to gaze up and examine the cliffs right and left for natural features like pockets, caves, arches, and alcoves, formed where water has dissolved softer deposits in the limestone. Some alcoves harbor Ancestral Puebloan dwellings built a millennium ago, such as the ruins at the mouth of South Canyon, which enters Marble Canyon at mile 31. River runners often stop to explore South Canyon's polished limestone narrows. Stanton and the remainder of his crew abandoned their first attempt to run the Colorado and used South Canyon to return to the rim, stashing their gear in a dry limestone cave nearby. Just downstream, **Stanton's Cave** is a veritable treasure trove where scientists have found the bones of a Pleistocene-era giant sloth

THE HONEYMOON OF GLEN AND BESSIE HYDE

Grand Canyon has served as a dramatic backdrop for legends and tall tales, heroic feats and terrible tragedies. But probably no canyon tale haunts more than the story of Glen and Bessie Hyde, a pair of newlyweds who set out on an adventurous honeymoon trip on October 20, 1928. The Hydes would have joined a very elite group of expeditions to run the Colorado River successfully through Grand Canyon, and Bessie Hyde would be the first woman to accomplish the feat. But the fame and fortune they hoped for was not to be.

Glen, an Idaho native, spent a couple of summers on the Snake and Salmon Rivers. Based on his experience, he built a wooden scow, flat-bottomed and heavy, steered by a long wooden sweep. He hoped to complete the Grand Canyon journey in seven weeks, setting a new record for the shortest running time for the trip. Because Lees Ferry was still remote and isolated, the Hydes, like most early canyon explorers, began their trip in Green River, Utah.

After nearly a month of guiding the heavy scow in windy and rainy conditions, with Bessie going overboard at least once, the couple reached Grand Canyon's Inner Gorge. On November 15, they hiked up to the South Rim to resupply. Emery Kolb photographed the couple, and behind her smile, he thought that 22-year-old Bessie appeared tired and nervous. The Hydes hiked back to the river to continue their journey. When they didn't return to Idaho in December as planned, Glen's father launched a search. The scow was discovered at river mile 237 in Lower Granite Gorge. Its towline was caught, but the scow was upright, the couple's supplies still intact. Their camera was recovered from the boat, and the film was developed. The last frame appeared to be taken somewhere around river mile 165.

The couple's disappearance fueled imaginations, and rumors eddied. Many speculated the Hydes were swept from the boat on rapids downstream, but no definitive evidence was found. Did Glen or Bessie fall from the boat and the other drown in a failed rescue attempt? Did they abandon the scow and attempt to hike out, perishing in a remote tributary canyon? Was it murder? Decades later, a woman came forward claiming that she was Bessie, and that she had killed her abusive husband and escaped the canyon on foot. Her tale proved to be false, but the truth still eludes canyon historians. Author and boatman Brad Dimock reconstructed their fateful voyage in his book, *Sunk Without a Sound: The Tragic Colorado River Honeymoon of Glen and Bessie Hyde*. The Hydes' disappearance is one of Grand Canyon's most enduring mysteries.

and split-twig figurines from the Archaic period, as well as the gear left by Stanton's expedition. (The cave is closed to visitors.)

A little farther downriver, **Vaseys Paradise**, a lush green spring-fed oasis, decorates the canyon's west wall (river right). Powell named this beautiful feature for a botanist who accompanied him on earlier expeditions. Crimson and yellow monkey-flower, ferns, watercress, and other species thrive in this natural garden. River parties often stop here, but unless you know what poison ivy looks like, be careful where you frolic. The Park Service would prefer you didn't frolic here at all because human activity may impact one of Grand Canyon's endangered species, the Kanab ambersnail, a tiny land snail with only two native habitats, Vaseys Paradise and a meadow near Kanab, Utah, where it is threatened by commercial development.

◖ REDWALL CAVERN

On river left, Redwall Cavern gapes at mile 33. The Colorado River carved this large cave from the Redwall limestone formation at river level. Explorer John Wesley Powell, clearly impressed at its vast size, wrote that it could hold 50,000 people (unlikely, but it is big). River runners often stop here for lunch on the beach or a game of Frisbee inside the cavern's sandy expanse, but no camping is allowed.

Grayish Mauv limestone, the oldest of the Paleozoic rocks (formed about 500 million years ago), begins to appear at mile 34. Five miles downstream is the Marble Canyon dam site, proposed and test-drilled in 1963. (Imagine, for a moment, if all the natural beauty you'd just floated through had been drowned by water impounded behind the proposed dam.) The river continues to meander gently until mile 41, when it bends sharply east around Point Hansbrough, toward President Harding Rapids, before turning west toward Saddle Canyon. This hairpin is an entrenched meander, a river bend deepened by downcutting. Above is Eminence Break, a northwest-facing escarpment formed along a fault line. A challenging route leads to the rim from the camp below President Harding Rapids.

On his second attempt at running the canyon, six months after hiking out of South Canyon, Robert Brewster Stanton discovered the body of Peter Hansbrough near this rapids. He buried Hansbrough here, leaving an inscription on the cliff as an epitaph. The rapids were named by a later expedition, a U.S. Geological Survey mapping trip led by Claude Birdseye, with Emery Kolb as chief boatman. The 1923 expedition carried a radio, and when they heard that President Harding had died, they camped here for a day and named the rapids in remembrance.

At mile 50, Bright Angel Shale appears, a late-Paleozoic series of mudstone, sandstone, and limestone in shades of green, tan, and lavender. Easily eroded, it forms fantastic shapes farther downriver. In the central canyon, it is found on top of the Tonto Platform, where it has mostly eroded away from the underlying Tapeats sandstone, creating the rim of the inner canyon.

◖ NANKOWEAP RUINS ROUTE

High above the Colorado River near Nankoweap Canyon, at river mile 53, the Ancestral Puebloans constructed masonry granaries to protect their food stores. The steep route up to the Nankoweap ruins, which are about 1,000 years old, offers striking views of Marble Canyon, the river a gently undulating silver ribbon below. It is one of the finest river views in the inner canyon. This area is also accessible from the North Rim and Saddle Mountain Wilderness via the **Nankoweap Trail,** a 15-mile route that many consider to be the canyon's most difficult. In past winters, bald eagles have been known to gather to fish for spawning rainbow trout at the mouth of Nankoweap Canyon.

◖ LITTLE COLORADO RIVER CONFLUENCE

A couple of miles before the confluence of the Colorado and Little Colorado Rivers, Tapeats sandstone makes its first appearance, forming dark grayish-brown stratified cliffs and ledges that intermingle in places with Bright Angel shale. On river right at mile 61 the turquoise waters of the Little Colorado River (LCR) join the deep green Colorado. Because there are several sites significant to the Hopi Indians as well as the historic cabin of Ben Beamer, no camping is allowed near the confluence except by rangers and others who have special research permits. Fishing is also restricted here because the warmer waters of the Little Colorado host several endangered fish species, including the humpback chub.

River runners often ferry across the Colorado to explore **Beamer Cabin,** Ancestral Pueblo ruins that the prospector "remodeled" after coming to the canyon in 1889, and to play in the warmer waters of the LCR. Sometimes, the LCR's flow is just right for a waterslide. It's also fun to hike a mile or so along the Tapeats ledges that form the LCR's banks, trying out mud pools for beauty packs or foot soaks.

Just past the confluence, the **Great Unconformity** appears. Think of an unconformity as pages missing from the geological record. In this case, between Tapeats sandstone and an underlying layer of Vishnu schist, the unconformity is a gap of hundreds of millions of years. The missing pages of the Grand Canyon Supergroup have all but eroded away, still visible in this section of the canyon as colorful strata that have been uplifted and tilted, forming the soft, low hills of Unkar Valley.

On June 30, 1956, about a mile southwest of the confluence, a TWA Super Constellation and a United DC–7 collided at 21,000 feet, killing 128 people and scattering debris on both sides of the river. The Park Service had most of the wreckage removed in the 1970s, but river runners may see remnants of the horrific crash reflecting in the sun on the slopes of Chuar Butte, near mile 65. (A memorial for the crash victims stands in the pioneer cemetery on the South Rim. This incident was one of a series of crashes that prompted Congress to pass the Federal Aviation Act of 1958, creating the Federal Aviation Agency and giving it control of U.S. airspace.)

Below the great curtain of rock known as the **Palisades of the Desert,** the river begins to swing west toward Unkar Valley. At Unkar Delta, the ancestors of today's Hopi Indians, known as Ancestral Puebloans, or Anasazi, established a village and raised corn, beans, and squash in nearby plots. The warmer inner canyon temperatures meant a longer growing season, and the villagers moved between rim and river according to the season. In the summer, villagers would return to the Walhalla Plateau on the North Rim. (To protect the delta's fragile archeological resources, camping is prohibited here. If you are exploring on foot, please stay on the trails.)

Below Comanche Point, the highest point along the Palisades, Tanner Rapids marks the mouth of the tributary Tanner Canyon. The Tanner Trail leads 10 miles from here to the rim at Lipan Point, one of many prehistoric Indian trails later adapted by miners and pioneers. Before the Colorado River was dammed, it was possible to cross to the other side during seasons of low water, climbing up to the opposite rim via what is now the Nankoweap Trail. In the late 1800s, this route was a favorite of horse thieves who traveled back and forth between Arizona and Utah.

◖ THE INNER GORGE

Hance Rapids is the first challenging white water that river runners encounter—a preview of things to come as the river enters the narrower confines of the Inner Gorge, or, as explorer John Wesley Powell called it, the Granite Gorge:

> *Heretofore hard rocks have given us bad river; soft rocks, smooth water; and a serious of rocks harder than any we have experienced sets in. The river enters the gneiss! We can see but a little way into the granite gorge, but it looks threatening.*

Just past Hance Rapids, the oldest rock in the canyon, pink and red Zoroaster granite and dark gray Vishnu schist, appears. These harder rocks form steep cliffs below the Tonto Platform, creating a canyon within a canyon. In the Lower Sonoran Desert climate zone, summer temperatures can push toward 120°F, and even lizards take cover in midday. Cremation Camp, a popular overnight for river runners at mile 87, appears stark and rocky at midday, but when late-afternoon sun hits the Zoroaster granite, the rocks seem to smolder with inner fire.

BRIGHT ANGEL CREEK

Bright Angel Creek, flowing down the longest tributary canyon, joins the Colorado River at about 88 miles, a welcome oasis. Powell and his crew rested here for several days in 1869, and Powell named the creek Bright Angel for its clear and gentle waters. (The predam Colorado River was so laden with silt that pioneers joked it was "too thin to plow, too thick to drink.")

Powell's men weren't the first—or the last—to appreciate this peaceful spot. The Ancestral Puebloans settled near the confluence, building a small L-shaped pueblo. Trail builder David Rust established a camp here in the early 1900s, connecting his North Rim trail to trails from the South Rim via a cableway. He planted cottonwood trees and rented tents to guests, including Theodore Roosevelt. After Grand Canyon became a national park in 1919, visitation increased, and the Santa Fe Railway decided to build a lodge on the site.

◖ PHANTOM RANCH

Architect Mary Colter expanded and modernized Rust's simple inner canyon camp, adding conveniences and touches of elegance while maintaining the flavor of a rustic, family-run guest ranch. Phantom Ranch opened in 1922, though construction continued until 1930. Designed to resemble a working ranch, the cluster of guest cabins and a canteen are the only accommodations in the inner canyon. Shaded by cottonwoods, lying between Bright Angel Creek and the Colorado River, Phantom Ranch is a riparian oasis. In addition to native seep willow and coyote willow, peach, pomegranate, and fig trees grow around the ranch. During the 1930s, the Civilian Conservation Corps (CCC) set up a winter camp here and made several improvements.

For hikers, river runners, and mule riders who spend a night or two, there's plenty to explore. The CCC-built **River Trail** follows the south side of the river, leading to Pipe Creek. On the opposite side of the river, the CCC also built the **Clear Creek Trail,** which climbs the cliffs for excellent views of Phantom Ranch and the Inner Gorge. Ribbon Falls, another possible day-hike destination, lies six miles north of Phantom Ranch along the North Kaibab Trail.

For some river runners, the trip ends here at Phantom Ranch or about a mile downriver at lovely Pipe Creek, followed by the long, steep hike up Bright Angel Trail. For those who've booked lower-canyon trips, this is where the adventure begins. (Whether you're hiking up or down, Bright Angel Trail is challenging—there's no shame in arranging ahead of time for a mule to carry your gear, or you.)

THE GEM SERIES

For passengers who continue downriver, serious white water lies ahead. On most rivers, rapids are rated on the International Scale of River Difficulty, from Class I to Class VI. In Grand Canyon, rapids are ranked on a scale of 1 to 10, with 1 being a small riffle and 10 the

THE INNER CANYON

NPS PHOTO

Phantom Ranch hosts mule riders, river runners, and hikers.

highest difficulty that is still navigable. The severity of rapids can fluctuate with changes in river flows (releases from Glen Canyon Dam, runoff from rainstorms), and many rapids have more than one possible run or route, with differences in difficulty. Granite and Hermit Rapids, at mile 93 and mile 95, respectively, are both ranked 9.

At mile 98, notorious Crystal Rapids was a mere riffle until the river channel filled with flash-flood debris in 1966. Crystal changed again in 1983 when another flood swept downriver, moving boulders and creating a 10-plus rapids with a notorious hole. Boaters have their own lexicon to discuss the river's white water: "washing machine," "cheese grater," "haystack," and other colorful terms. A hole is the boat-sucking hydraulic on the downstream side of a large rock, and the hole in Crystal is said to be the canyon's biggest, capable of trapping and recirculating even very large rafts. Past Crystal, boaters encounter the rapids known as the Gem Series—Agate, Sapphire, Turquoise, Jasper, Jade, Ruby, and Serpentine Rapids.

BASS CANYON TO GRANITE NARROWS

At mile 107, Bass Canyon enters from the southwest. The area near William Bass's historic camp is a popular layover for river runners and backpackers. Bass built a cable crossing here to connect his two trails, the first rim-to-rim route in Grand Canyon. The Tapeats sandstone bench on river right makes a great campsite, with historic Bass Camp a couple of miles up the **North Bass Trail.** On river left is the abandoned *Ross Wheeler,* a metal boat left behind during a 1915 expedition. The site can also be reached by the **South Bass Trail.**

Just past mile 116, Royal Arch Creek enters the main canyon from the south. Elves Chasm, a magical grotto of maidenhair ferns and trickling water, is a short walk from the river, near the mouth of Royal Arch Canyon. Two straight river passages—Stephens Aisle, which runs north–south from mile 117 to mile 119, and Conquistador Aisle, heading east–west from mile 120 to mile 123—lead to Middle Granite Gorge. Ask river runners to identify their favorite rock layer in Grand Canyon and most of them will probably answer "Tapeats sandstone." There's a lot of it in this section of the canyon.

Blacktail Canyon, at mile 120, and Tapeats Canyon, at mile 134, are both carved from the Tapeats. This dark brown sandstone, formed about 545 million years ago, erodes into interesting platforms and ledges and often bears fossilized brachiopods, trilobites, or "worm tracks." The **Thunder River Trail** leads up Tapeats Canyon to 0.5-mile-long Thunder River, also accessible from the North Rim. The dark mile-long section of the canyon from Helicopter Eddy to Deer Creek is known as Granite Narrows, where the canyon pinches to a width of 76 feet.

【 DEER CREEK FALLS

At Deer Creek, a 100-foot-high waterfall tumbles out of a sinuous Tapeats sandstone tributary, creating a welcome oasis on the lower

Deer Creek Falls is a popular stop for river runners.

river at mile 136. River runners often stop at Deer Creek Falls to frolic in the water and hike around the falls to the high slot canyon of Deer Creek Narrows. The route is not for acrophobes, as it requires carefully stepping along a trail barely wider than a boot and suspended high above the rushing creek waters. From the falls, it's possible to hike to Thunder River or all the way to the rim. It's a strenuous 15 miles from Deer Creek Falls to the Thunder River trailhead, located west of park boundaries in Kaibab National Forest along the North Rim.

Matkatamiba Canyon, at mile 148, is another sinuously carved side canyon and a favorite with photographers and hikers. Its walls, ledges, and pools are formed from Muav limestone, shaped into linear ridges that make scrambling and climbing relatively easy.

HAVASU CANYON

Havasu Creek enters the Colorado River at mile 157. From the mouth of Havasu Canyon (formerly known as Cataract Canyon), it's 5.5 miles to Mooney Falls, one of several waterfalls in the Havasu Canyon area. Supai Village is approximately halfway between the rim and river, about eight miles. The Havasupai people lived at Grand Canyon for centuries, widely roaming the rims and tributaries in search of game and plants until the government established their small reservation in 1882.

Today, the Havasupai support themselves with tourism. People come from all over the world to see the waters of Havasu Creek, spilling into travertine-lined pools that reflect the sky. Sadly, two major floods in 2008 and 2010 seriously damaged village residences and destroyed one of the canyon's most-photographed waterfalls. The tribe has requested disaster funding to help rebuild. Havasu Canyon's campground and trails may reopen sometime in 2011.

LAVA FALLS TO WHITMORE WASH

Just past Tuckup Canyon, at mile 165, the south edge of the Colorado River forms the boundary of the Hualapai Reservation. A few miles downstream on the right, 3,000-foot high cliffs loom above the river. On top is **Toroweap,** a remote overlook on the North Rim's western reaches. Below, at mile 179, is Lava Falls. Some consider these falls, a class 10 rapids, the fiercest white water in Grand Canyon. The Colorado River drops 37 feet in just a couple of hundred yards. In 1869, Powell's men chose to make an arduous three-hour portage rather than risk their wooden boats and remaining food stores against the churning rapids.

Powell recognized the signs of past volcanic activity along this section of the river. Upriver from the rapids, a volcanic neck, the black monolith Vulcans Forge, juts out of the water. Downriver, cascades of basalt rock mark the canyon walls, the flow of a volcano that erupted 1.2 million years ago. The flows created a dam about 1,400 feet high. An even higher dam formed near Prospect Canyon, creating a lake that extended all the way to present-day Moab. Over time, the sediment-laden Colorado River ground its way through these natural dams.

Lava flows are also evident at Whitmore Wash, at mile 188. The canyon walls are lower here, and the trail that leads up to the rim is less than a mile long, the shortest rim-to-river route in Grand Canyon. (The Lava Falls Route, at 1.5 miles, is the shortest entirely within the bounds of the park.) Because of its proximity to the rim, some outfitters use the beach at Whitmore Wash as a passenger-exchange point. The Bar-10, a family-operated ranch, offers lodging and an airstrip on the north side of the canyon, and on the south side, the Hualapai tribe operates a helipad.

DIAMOND DOWN

At mile 226, Diamond Creek enters the canyon, marking the takeout point for most whitewater trips. The wide beach at the edge of the river is also used as a put-in for rafting trips managed by the Hualapai tribe as well as for private groups that have reserved a "Diamond Down" trip to raft the canyon's remaining 54 miles through Lower Granite Gorge. The

THE INNER CANYON

An oar raft plunges through Lava Falls, one of the river's most powerful rapids.

NPS PHOTO BY MARK LELLOUCH

Diamond Creek Road climbs 16 miles from the river to Peach Springs on the Hualapai Reservation, a rugged scenic route.

Powell's party camped above the rapids at mile 239 in late August 1869. Weary, tattered, and disheartened, the men had opened their last sack of flour two days earlier. Several believed the rapids would be impassible. The next morning, three crew members left the expedition, and Powell named the roiling water Separation Rapids. Below it, the canyon widened, and the river became quieter. Two days later, the six remaining expedition members reached the mouth of the Virgin River and nearby Mormon settlements. Only later did they learn that the three men who left were murdered. (The exact fate of the men is still unknown. Though Shivwits Indians have long been blamed for their deaths, canyon historians have also made convincing arguments that the murderers were Mormon settlers.)

At mile 276, the Grand Wash Cliffs mark the geographical end of Grand Canyon and the start of the basin-and-range topography of the Mojave Desert. The boundary between Grand Canyon National Park and Lake Mead National Monument lies just beyond. The waters of Lake Mead, impounded by Hoover Dam, slow the river's current after Separation Rapids.

Long-term drought in the Southwest has severely impacted Lake Mead's water levels, evident by the white "bathtub ring" that rises high above the surface of the lake. Sustained drought left the takeout point at Pearce Ferry high and dry, and for several years river runners had to continue on to busy South Cove beach to de-rig. In 2010 the Pearce Ferry Road was extended another two miles to the changed waterline, a $1 million project that once again allows river takeouts.

Not far from Pearce Ferry, the Colorado's currents scoured—or superimposed—a new channel through the lake's sediment deposits, resulting in new rapids with a nasty hole that has been known to flip rafts. Pearce Ferry Rapids, also known as Superimposition Rapids, is yet another example of how the canyon and river are constantly changing over time.

Recreation

Grand Canyon, judged by early explorers as an obstacle, is a vast collection of rugged tributary canyons. For backpackers, hikers, river runners, climbers, and canyoneers, this maze-like landscape offers a dizzying range of possibilities for exploration. Viewed from above, Grand Canyon is an unknowable, remote macrocosm of ridges and buttes that fade into each other in the harsh light of midday. But those who venture inside the canyon's walls gradually become aware of the almost infinite number of microcosms held within: fossils and wildflowers and lizards, ancient sites, historic camps, slot canyons, exquisite waterfalls and grottoes, challenging climbing routes, pristine beaches, and more. To explore all these worlds within worlds would take longer than a lifetime, and that tantalizing mystery of the still-unseen is what keeps so many canyon adventurers coming back for more.

HIKING AND BACKPACKING

Inner canyon trails range from rigorous multiday backpacking adventures to short explorations from river camps. Backpackers often make the Colorado River their goal, but "halfway hikes" can also be very rewarding, offering beautiful river panoramas from viewpoints on the Tonto Trail or along the Esplanade. Inner canyon trails lend a sense of intimacy to your explorations, revealing details that are hidden from perspectives on the rim: historic mining camps, springs and seeps, clear-flowing creeks, waterfalls, sandy beaches, and beautifully eroded schist and granite. Many sites are readily accessible only from the river, and chances are you'll get a wider range of sightseeing in a two-week river trip than you could in years of hiking from the rim.

At river elevations of 1,200–3,200 feet, the inner canyon's Sonoran Desert climate is like being in Tucson or Phoenix. Expect a 20–30°F difference between rims and river, choosing gear—and food—accordingly. Sun protection is crucial: appropriate clothing, a hat, sunglasses, and sunblock. Many trails have exposed sections, and at midday even the river is in full sun. A light, long-sleeved shirt can help shield you from the intense desert rays.

For summer hikes, thin cotton is best. The rest of the year, polyester fleece and quick-drying fabrics work well for hiking. Be prepared for afternoon showers during Arizona's monsoon season, mid-July–mid-September.

Bring boots that are broken in, plenty of socks, and an emergency kit. Pack adequate water (including iodine tablets for emergencies and a filtering system for backpacking trips) and salty snacks. If you are hiking near the rims during winter months, you may need crampons, for sale or rent at the General Store.

A good trail map is a must for wilderness backpackers, along with an understanding of desert hiking and route-finding. For example, "Creek" on a map might refer to a dry wash, a year-round stream, or a stream that flows seasonally during spring melt or briefly after a rainstorm. Before attempting a multiday backpacking trip, research potential water sources. Hiking guidebooks are good resources, as is the online bulletin board managed by the **Grand Canyon Hikers and Backpackers Association** (www.gchba.org).

No permit is necessary to day hike in Grand Canyon National Park, but in order to camp anywhere other than the developed rim campgrounds, a backcountry permit is required. The Park Service strongly discourages anyone from attempting to hike from rim to river and back in a day. Unless you are an exceptionally strong hiker, you'll need to spend at least one night in the canyon, and that means preparing months ahead by applying for a backcountry permit.

Backcountry Permits

In 2009, the Park Service received nearly 19,000 applications and issued 13,616 permits. You can increase your chances of landing a permit by being thorough on your application and paying attention to timing.

THE INNER CANYON

WATER: TOO MUCH OR TOO LITTLE?

The Park Service recommends that hikers carry at least a gallon of water per person per day in warm months. Ideally, you should drink a quart of water for every hour that you're hiking. Because sweat evaporates rapidly in the canyon's high elevation and low humidity, you might not realize how much moisture you're losing. The earliest signs of dehydration can be very subtle: crankiness and mild headache.

If you're hiking the Bright Angel or North Kaibab Trails, you can usually refill your water bottles at trailside resthouses. But if you're planning a long hike in warmer weather, it's important to research water availability before you set out. Water from springs, creeks, and the Colorado River must be filtered or treated before drinking.

Even day hikers should be prepared with a few iodine pills in case water equipment is under repair. Although iodine pills aren't recommended for several days' use, they are handy for emergencies, such as a broken pipeline or a failed water filter.

Just as dangerous as dehydration is water intoxication, or hyponatremia. This happens when hikers drink water without replacing electrolytes – the minerals that nerves and muscles need to function. Pack salty snacks, eating a little each time you take a water break, or mix an electrolyte-replacement (powder or concentrate) with your water.

Rangers treat up to 20 cases of heat exhaustion (serious dehydration) each summer day, but water intoxication is also common. Some symptoms of hyponatremia are very similar to heat stroke: altered judgment, nausea, and arrhythmia.

In order to complete an application, you'll first need to establish an itinerary. Take advantage of the park's Trip Planner—available online, in person, or by mail (Backcountry Information Center/GCNP, P.O. Box 129, Grand Canyon AZ, 86023, www.nps.gov/grca), as well as the information available on the park's website detailing use areas, camp types, and stay limits. Permit requests must include the trip leader's contact information and credit-card information, group size, license plate numbers of cars to be left at the trailhead, and a proposed itinerary. The itinerary must show dates and use areas for each night of the trip. If your application is complete and accurate, you'll increase your chances of getting a permit.

Popular hikes book quickly, as do popular seasons. Summer, despite deadly temperatures, is the most popular time to hike the canyon. Late spring and early fall are next. Although few people apply for winter permits, inner canyon temperatures are moderate at that time of year. Being flexible about starting and ending dates, or about locations, helps increase your permit chances.

The sooner you apply for a permit, the more likely you are to get your chosen dates and location. Permit requests can be made on the first of the initial month, that is, the month that is four months prior your trip's start date. For example, if you want to start your backpacking trip on May 15, you can send or fax your permit request on January 1.

Memorize this phrase: *initial month permit request*. For years, canyon insiders knew their best shot at getting a permit was by bringing an application in person to the backcountry office the first day of the initial month (a.k.a. "fourth-month-out") or, if they were unable to travel to the canyon, to fax the application first thing that morning. But when first-of-the-month crowds at the doors of the backcountry office began to resemble the scene at a rock concert ticket booth and the fax line was relentlessly busy, the policy was adjusted.

Walk-in applicants are no longer given immediate assistance during the initial month. You can still personally deliver an application on the first day of the initial month, but it will be ordered randomly by computer with all other applications received by 5 P.M. that day. In other words, during the initial month, all applications have an equal shot at the end of the day, no matter how or when they came in.

The preferred method for submitting a permit application is by fax. You can fax (928/638-2125) your application anytime day or night. You can also mail your request—but since mail-in requests must be postmarked no earlier than the first day of the initial month, you'll be late to the gate. The gate remains closed for applications by phone or email—don't even try it. (However, the park does plan to work with online requests at some future date.)

In case you aren't confused yet, note that the updated policy applies only to initial month permit requests. If you walk into the backcountry office with an application for a date three months hence (or less), your application will be considered immediately, before any mailed or faxed applications received that day.

No matter how you applied for a permit, if you land one, you'll be notified by U.S. mail. Allow a minimum of three weeks for the response. Your credit card will be charged up to the amount you specified on your application. Fees are $10 per permit plus $5 pp per night if you are camping below the rim, or $5 per group if you are camping above the rim.

If your application is denied, you can try to get a permit for one of the corridor campgrounds (Indian Garden, Bright Angel, or Cottonwood Camp) by placing your name on a waiting list when you arrive at the canyon. You must be present at the Backcountry Information Center at 8 A.M. to obtain a last-minute permit for that day. If none are available by the time your number is called, you can add your name to the next day's waiting list (and repeat as necessary). Even during popular seasons, last-minute permits are possible.

Trails described below include routes that start and end inside the canyon as well as day trips from the river. Even if you're only venturing a few hundred yards from camp, it's safest to travel with companions. Also remember that the Navajo, Hualapai, and Havasupai tribes hold land surrounding the park. Be sure to apply for permits from tribal offices if you will be hiking into or across Indian land.

Tonto Trail

- Distance: 93 miles from Garnet Canyon to Red Canyon
- Duration: Multiple days
- Elevation gain: 1,200 feet
- Effort: Moderate to strenuous
- Trailhead: This inner canyon trail is accessed by a number of connecting trails.

The Tonto Trail crosses the Tonto Platform, a shelf of Tapeats sandstone above the steeper-walled Inner Gorge. The Tapeats sits on top of Vishnu schist and Zoroaster granite, with the intervening Grand Canyon Supergroup entirely eroded away, creating a visible unconformity. Most backpackers use the Tonto Trail as a connector to make a loop with two or more rim-to-river trails, such as the Bright Angel and South Kaibab Trails, or the Boucher and Hermit Trails. In *The Man Who Walked Through Time,* Colin Fletcher described his two-month-long journey through the length of the inner canyon, much of it over the Tonto.

The Tonto Platform is a broad east–west shelf averaging 3,000 feet below the rim. Although the platform appears relatively level in places, the trail climbs up and down numerous drainages across the shadeless and dry Upper Sonoran Zone, making it challenging to find routes. The most traveled segments are the four-mile section closing the loop between the Bright Angel and South Kaibab Trails, and the 12-mile link between the Bright Angel and Hermit Trails. If you're planning a loop route anywhere in the canyon, be sure to research water sources in advance.

Beamer Trail

- Distance: 19 miles round-trip
- Duration: 2 days
- Elevation gain: 960 feet
- Effort: Moderate
- Trailhead: Tanner Beach or Little Colorado River confluence

More route than trail, this path paralleling the Colorado River leads to the ruins of Ben Beamer's cabin. Beamer, a prospector who arrived at the canyon around 1890, remodeled an Ancestral Puebloan (Anasazi) dwelling to fashion a cabin at the mouth of the Little Colorado River. His trail followed part of the salt trail, a pilgrimage route used for centuries by Ancestral Puebloans and their descendants, the Hopi Indians. The route is rich in cultural history, but the real reward is at the Little Colorado River (LCR): The turquoise-blue waters are warm enough to soak in and edged with mud pools that are more fun than any spa treatment.

Backpackers can start the Beamer Trail at either end, but because of camping restrictions at the Little Colorado River, most will begin at Tanner Beach (accessible by the Tanner Trail from the South Rim), following bright red Dox sandstone cliffs that line the beach. At mile 4, the trail reaches Palisades Creek, the site of an old copper mine worked by Seth Tanner, where there's a small campsite. From here, the trail makes a series of steep switchbacks, topping out on a bench of Tapeats sandstone. The cliffs are narrow in places, and the trail crosses several drainages, making it difficult to find routes.

Beamer's cabin is on the west side of the LCR. Depending on the flow, you may be able to ford the LCR to the other side. Camping and fishing are prohibited near the confluence due to the archaeological resources and endangered native fish species found here.

Clear Creek Trail

- Distance: 18 miles round-trip
- Duration: 2 days
- Elevation gain: 1,520 feet
- Effort: Moderate to strenuous
- Trailhead: At the North Kaibab Trail, 0.3 miles north of Phantom Ranch

The Clear Creek Trail climbs up to the Tonto Platform before descending again to Clear Creek. For backpackers or mule riders staying

The Kaibab suspension bridge crosses the Colorado River.

NPS PHOTO BY MICHAEL ANDERSON

THE INNER CANYON

a few days at Bright Angel Campground or Phantom Ranch, the Clear Creek Trail is a scenic side trip, though dangerously hot and dry in the summer. There are campsites and a pit toilet at flowing Clear Creek, the trail's only water source. Spring backpackers may see seasonal Cheyava Falls, while day hikers at any time of year can enjoy aerial views of Phantom Ranch and the Silver and Black Bridges.

From its junction with the North Kaibab Trail, the Clear Creek Trail ascends 0.75 miles to Phantom Overlook, a good day-hike destination with views of Bright Angel Canyon and the oasis of Phantom Ranch, 550 feet below. When the Civilian Conservation Corps constructed the Clear Creek Trail, they made a bench of Vishnu schist so hikers could rest and enjoy the view. The trail continues up to the rim of Granite Gorge, offering stunning views up and down the river. Another good turnaround point for a day hike is Sumner Wash, about 2.5 miles from the trailhead, where the trail turns north, away from the gorge, to reach the Tonto Platform.

The trail rises gradually through the Tonto's scrubby desert terrain, with wide-open views of the eastern canyon's cliffs and buttes, before reaching the edge of Clear Creek Canyon. From here, it's a steep descent to the creek and its cottonwood-shaded campsites. Depending on the season, adventurous hikers may want to explore farther: It's another five miles north to Cheyava Falls, tumbling 800 feet from the Redwall during spring snowmelt. The rough route crosses the streambed several times. For those with rock-climbing skills, it's the same distance south to the Colorado River.

North Canyon

- Distance: 1.2 miles round-trip
- Duration: 1–2 hours
- Elevation gain: 800 feet
- Effort: Easy
- Trailhead: River right, mile 20

Several tributaries in Marble Canyon's 60-mile stretch make beautiful from-the-river hikes, and a few can be accessed from the Marble Platform for rugged canyoneering adventures. North Canyon is notable for its sinuously eroded reddish Supai Group sandstones, carved by centuries of flooding into narrows and pools. As you make your way up this side canyon, you'll encounter boulders and a couple of pour-overs that you can climb around. Depending on the season and rainfall, you may encounter pools that you'll need to wade across to continue upcanyon. If there's enough water, the deepest pools may form waterslides for those who like getting wet. Unless you have technical climbing gear and plenty of time, the end of the hike will be a little over 0.5 miles from the river, when you encounter a pour-over too high to scramble.

Silver Grotto

- Distance: 0.5 miles round-trip
- Duration: 1–2 hours
- Elevation gain: 1,000 feet
- Effort: Difficult
- Trailhead: River right, mile 31

This tributary is also known as Shinumo Wash or Twenty-Nine Mile Canyon, although river runners usually refer to the lower portion, inaccessible from the upper wash, as Silver Grotto, named for its smooth limestone walls. It's less than one mile before progress from the river is halted by a high pour-over, but this is not an easy hike. In fact, it's not a really a hike at all—it is more of a scrambling, swimming, climbing, canyoneering adventure. A boat ferry might be necessary to get across the first pool, and other obstacles await. This series of slickrock scrambles and swims through a lovely limestone narrows is for those who have some climbing and canyoneering experience. It's also for hot afternoons when no rain threatens: The pools are cold, and the canyon is prone to flash flooding.

For hikers and backpackers, the upper canyon is accessible from the Navajo Reservation near Cedar Ridge. Unless you have technical gear and experience, you won't be able to make

THE INNER CANYON

it into the grotto. However, you can bypass the lower part of the wash, forking either right (to the river's edge) or left (continuing on top of the Redwall), where you'll have views of Vaseys Paradise, a splash of brilliant green on the opposite cliffs.

South Canyon

- Distance: 0.5 miles round-trip
- Duration: 30 minutes
- Elevation gain: 800 feet
- Effort: Easy
- Trailhead: River right, mile 31

Redwall limestone makes its appearance about five miles upriver, and by the time you reach the mouth of South Canyon, just past mile 31, you are floating between Redwall cliffs along one of the most fascinating stretches of the Colorado River. Like North Canyon, South Canyon can be explored from river or rim. Even a short hike from the river is awe-inspiring, leading through narrows of Redwall limestone. More determined canyoneers can clamber up through boulders and around pour-overs to the confluence with Bedrock Canyon, where Supai narrows await.

Those who don't have climbing skills can explore along the Colorado River, up- or downstream from South Canyon. Just upstream from the mouth of South Canyon is an Ancestral Puebloan ruin, occupied about 900 years ago. From the back of the river camp, a short hike up to the Redwall Formation leads to Stanton's Cave, where engineer Robert Stanton stored his expedition's gear in 1889 after three men drowned. If Stanton had explored deeper into the cave, he might have discovered a cache of split-twig figurines approximately 3,000–4,000 years old, left here by Archaic-period hunter gatherers. Inside the dry limestone cave, paleontologists have also found the bones of a giant sloth, a mammal that lived during the Pleistocene era. Because of past looting, the cave is now off-limits, although you can peer inside.

A little farther downstream, reached most safely by boat, is Vaseys Paradise, a lush oasis created by a spring erupting from the Redwall. Powell named it in honor of a botanist colleague because it supports a number of species, including redbud, willow, monkey-flowers, watercress, and—beware—poison ivy. Also be careful of the endangered Kanab ambersnail, which might be crawling underfoot.

Eminence Break

- Distance: 4 miles round-trip
- Duration: 8–9 hours
- Elevation gain: 2,600 feet
- Effort: Difficult
- Trailhead: River left, mile 44

This rugged route starts at the lower campsite near President Harding Rapids. The trail follows an old Indian route, crossing the Eminence Break Fault and leading up to the rim, where your efforts will be rewarded with sweeping views. Scrambling and climbing skills are needed to make the last couple of hundred feet, and the shadeless route shouldn't be attempted during summer.

To find the trail, walk below the rapids, looking at the Redwall slope to the left. Getting to the top of the Redwall takes a little under an hour, so it's a good destination if you aren't planning a layover at Harding camp. From here, you'll have good views of the river and the entrenched meander made by the Colorado River, carving out Point Hansbrough (named for Peter Hansbrough, one of the men who drowned during Robert Stanton's ill-fated 1889 expedition).

If you continue, cairns lead the way through Supai cliffs and slopes, requiring scrambling past the upper Supai. The slope is very steep, with a lot of loose rock. From the Kaibab limestone rim, you'll have views of the Echo and Vermilion Cliffs to the north, the forested Kaibab Plateau to the west, and flat-topped Shinumo Altar directly east. The trail tops out near Tatahatso Point, an overlook on the western Navajo Reservation.

NPS PHOTO BY MARK LELLOUCH

The Nankoweap Granaries overlook the river in Marble Canyon.

Nankoweap Granaries

- Distance: 1.5 miles round-trip
- Duration: 1.5–2 hours
- Elevation gain: 1,500 feet
- Effort: Moderate
- Trailhead: River left, mile 52

This short but steep route starts just downstream (south) of Nankoweap Creek. The camps in this area are overgrown with tamarisk, and there's a network of unofficial trails. Look for the well-traveled trail paralleling the base of the cliffs, then locate the spur leading uphill toward the ruins. It's a rocky climb through broken Muav limestone, but the view at the top is one of the finest along the river. Plan to spend some time hanging out here and enjoying the views. In late afternoon, the walls of Marble Canyon turn shades of peach and rose, reflecting in the waters of the Colorado River. The delta of Nankoweap Creek must have provided the Ancestral Puebloans with good garden plots, and they stored surplus grains in this high, dry alcove. This area is also accessible from the North Rim via the difficult Nankoweap Trail.

Monument Creek

- Distance: 2 miles round-trip
- Duration: 1 hour
- Elevation gain: 500 feet
- Effort: Easy
- Trailhead: River left, mile 93

The trail begins at the mouth of Monument Canyon, above Granite Rapids, where many river trips camp or pull out to scout the challenging rapids. This hike's highlight is the tall spire that gives Monument Canyon its name. From the river, it's 0.75 miles to the narrows that loop around the monument to the left. You can rejoin the main canyon by climbing out of the narrows, then following a small drainage to complete the loop around this pinnacle and back down to the creek bed before hiking out.

TRAILBLAZERS: PIONEERS AND LEGENDARY HIKERS

Many Grand Canyon trails are named for pioneers who came to the canyon in the late 1800s. **William Wallace Bass** headed west in 1880 because of his failing health. By the time he took the newly completed A&P line to Williams in 1883, he was fit enough to tackle a number of jobs, including town constable, but the canyon lured him northward. He began prospecting and trail building, and within a couple of years, he had a tent camp on the rim near Havasupai Point, linking it by road to Williams and by trail to the river. He improved several old Indian trails, often with the help of Havasupai Indians he'd befriended, added a road to Ash Fork, and guided tourists during the summer.

In 1894, music teacher Ada Diebendorf and her aunt stayed for a few days at the rim-side camp. Five months later, Ada became Mrs. Bass. She and Bill raised four children at the canyon, dividing their time between tent camps and two houses that offered visitor accommodations. By the turn of the century, Bass had completed the first rim-to-rim trail, which crossed the river via a cable system at Bass Camp. The park service acquired his enterprise in 1927, and Bass died in 1933. His ashes were scattered over Holy Grail Temple, known for years as Bass Tomb.

Seth Tanner, a scout and guide for Mormon colonists, began exploring and prospecting in eastern Grand Canyon in the 1870s. He lo-cated several claims along the Colorado River downstream from its confluence with the Little Colorado, and improved an Indian trail that was later extended by another prospector to Lipan Point. Before Glen Canyon Dam, seasonal river crossings were possible in this area. Fording the river linked the Tanner Trail to the Nankoweap Trail, built by John Wesley Powell in 1882. Horse thieves used the route to drive stolen stock down the Tanner Trail, altered their brands, then used the Nankoweap Trail to take the horses north for sale, repeating the process in reverse.

Brothers **Philip and William Hull** came to Grand Canyon in the early 1880s with a herd of sheep and a part-time employee and hopeful prospector by the name of **John Hance.** In 1884 the trio hosted Mr. and Mrs. Edward E. Ayer of Flagstaff, arguably the canyon's first tourists. Hance's Red Canyon Trail, now known as the New Hance Trail, was his second route to his asbestos and copper mines along the river. His first, an old Havasupai trail along Hance Creek, was buried under rock slides. By all accounts, Hance was an accomplished guide who thoroughly enjoyed entertaining guests with his fantastic canyon fables. He gave up mining for tourism and remained a fixture at the canyon until his death in 1919, a few weeks before President Woodrow Wilson signed Grand Canyon National Park into being.

Those who want a longer hike can continue on the Monument Trail, which joins the Tonto Trail 1.5 miles from the river. From the junction, you'll have a raven's-eye view of the monument.

Shinumo Creek Falls

- Distance: 0.2 miles round-trip
- Duration: 1 hour
- Elevation gain: 300 feet
- Effort: Easy
- Trailhead: River right, mile 108

There's lots to explore around Bass Camp, at the foot of the North Bass and South Bass Trails, including historic artifacts and a refreshing 15-foot waterfall on Shinumo Creek. For river runners, it's an easy walk about 200 feet up the creek bed to reach the falls. Depending on the season, the pool at the base of the falls may be a couple of feet deep, a comfortable swimming hole, or Shinumo Canyon may be flooded, making the waterfall inaccessible.

For backpackers who aren't intimidated by a little rock climbing, or who have been assured

French-Canadian miner **Louis D. Boucher,** who arrived at the canyon around 1890 and became known as "the Hermit," built trails between the rim, Dripping Springs, and his mine in Long Canyon (now known as Boucher Canyon). Like Hance and Bass, he learned that it was more profitable to take tourists into the canyon than to pack minerals out. Boucher guided visitors over his trails and hosted them at his camps. Though hardly a hermit, he may have looked the part with his white hat and beard, riding a white mule named Calamity Jane. Hermit or not, he is honored with more Grand Canyon place names than any other individual, from Eremita Mesa (*eremita* is Spanish for "hermit") to Hermits Rest.

The dashing and daring Kolb brothers set up a tent photo business in Grand Canyon Village in 1902. They ran the river and traveled trails, photographing scenic views and thrilling exploits. In 1937, **Emery Kolb** climbed Shiva Temple ahead of a highly publicized "first ascent" backed by the American Museum of Natural History. The museum's team hoped to find isolated species and other marvels, but their most embarrassing discovery (not divulged in any of the scientific reports) was an empty Kodak box. Emery, perhaps miffed that he hadn't been asked to guide the expedition, had beaten the scientists to their goal and left his calling card.

Harvey Butchart (1907-2002), a Northern Arizona University (NAU) math professor, hiked some 15,000 miles in Grand Canyon, making daring loops, bushwhacks, and first ascents – including some escapades today's park rangers would beg you not to try, such as crossing the Colorado River on an air mattress. Butchart's map, complete with notes, hangs in the map room at the Backcountry Information Center. NAU's Cline Library has a copy of his personal hiking log, 1,000 pages long. Butchart, who published several guidebooks describing his routes, continued to hike Grand Canyon until he turned 80.

Colin Fletcher (1922-2007) made the first recorded hike through the length of the inner canyon. He backpacked across the Esplanade and Tonto Platform for two months in 1963, describing his trip in *The Man Who Walked Through Time*, a book as much about the inner journey of canyon hiking as the external journey.

Though many canyon trails are named for pioneers, most routes existed long before settlers or Spanish explorers arrived. The Hopi, Hualapai, and Havasupai people have traveled the canyon for centuries, seeking plants, game, and salt and leaving behind rock art and legends. Ancestral Puebloan farmers migrated between the rims and the river to raise corn, and archaic hunters secreted split-twig figurines inside the canyon's caves. As you hike in their footsteps, think about those who have passed before you – and consider those who will pass after you.

beyond doubt by swimmers that the pool is deep enough to dive that day, the falls are accessible from Bass Camp along the North Bass Trail. Weather permitting, it's possible to head up the creek for a longer hike. Shinumo Creek has the potential for flash flooding during late summer thunderstorms.

Deer Creek Trail

- Distance: 10 miles round-trip
- Duration: 4–6 hours
- Elevation gain: 1,700

- Effort: Strenuous
- Trailhead: River right, mile 136

Most river trips stop to enjoy Deer Creek Falls and hike the Deer Creek Trail to the head of Tapeats Narrows, a challenging 0.5-mile hike, or to Deer Spring, 1.5 miles; the trail continues to Surprise Valley, connecting to the Thunder River Trail at five miles. The waterfall is a refreshing sight after floating through the dark confines of Granite Narrows, bursting from the cliffs 100 feet above the beach.

Starting from the river, the trail climbs around Deer Creek Falls and enters a labyrinthine narrows of Tapeats sandstone. With the creek flowing below, the trail hugs the cliff inside the narrows, a serious challenge for any hiker with acrophobia or claustrophobia. The trail exits the narrows at Deer Creek Valley, where cottonwoods shade a few campsites.

From here, the trail climbs toward a spur trail that leads to a smaller waterfall created by Deer Spring. The main trail ascends through Muav limestone to shadeless Surprise Valley, where it joins the Thunder River Trail at five miles. Most hikers starting from the river will turn around long before this point. From here, it's another 10 miles to the North Rim and the forest service campground at Indian Hollow, though backpackers can shorten the hike by taking the Bill Hall Trail to Monument Point. Connections to Thunder Spring and Tapeats Creek are possible for multiday backpacking loops from the rim or a pleasant daylong loop from the river.

Elves Chasm

- Distance: 0.5 miles round-trip
- Duration: 1 hour or less
- Elevation gain: 200 feet
- Effort: Easy
- Trailhead: River left, mile 116

The charming grotto of Elves Chasm is less than 0.25 miles from the river. A delicate waterfall trickles around huge boulders into a pool in this shady canyon of ferns and mosses. It's possible—but dangerous—to swim across the pool and climb the water-slick rocks to the cave behind the waterfall. It's also possible to make the risky climb up-canyon, where another waterfall and Royal Arch await. A few hardy backpackers have accessed Elves Chasm from rim trails that involve route finding, rock scrambling, and rappelling—it's hard to believe that with only a short walk, river runners achieve the same reward.

Kanab Creek

- Distance: 8 miles round-trip
- Duration: 3–5 hours
- Elevation gain: 400 feet
- Effort: Moderate
- Trailhead: River right, mile 143

Whether you have time for a couple of miles or double that, Kanab Creek and its side canyons are fun to explore. Kanab is Paiute for "willow," and desert willows grow in the lower canyon along with cottonwood, Apache plume, Mormon tea, agave, and cactus. There's no trail, and following the creek bed means going around or over cobbles and boulders, with easier going across ledges of Muav limestone on the east side of the creek.

The mouth of the canyon isn't very interesting, but the farther you travel from the river, the more intriguing the canyon becomes. It's negotiable all the way to Kanab, Utah, 50 miles away. On his second expedition through Grand Canyon in 1872, John Wesley Powell and his crew left the river at Kanab Creek, deciding their boats were too worn to continue down the main canyon. It took them four days to hike to Kanab.

A little more than halfway between the Colorado River and the mouth of Jumpup Canyon, springs emerge from the Redwall Formation, giving lower Kanab Creek its perennial flow. To explore that far, you'll need about two days; sometimes backpackers spend a week or more in this network of canyons, Grand Canyon's largest tributary system on the north side.

A good destination for a long day hike is Whispering Falls Canyon, which enters from the east at about four miles. A short way up this canyon is the waterfall that gives the canyon its name, sliding down bedrock into a plunge pool surrounded by a grotto of stone.

Matkatamiba Canyon

- Distance: 0.5 miles round-trip
- Duration: 1 hour

- Elevation gain: 400 feet
- Effort: Easy
- Trailhead: River left, mile 148

"Matkat," as it's affectionately known to river runners, is a popular stop on river trips. The canyon's layered and curved Muav limestone walls are a delight for photographers. If you like rock scrambling and wading, it's a pleasant 0.25 miles to the patio, where the narrows open up into an amphitheater of ledges and platforms decorated with ferns and mosses. The distance is short, but most hikers will linger to practice Spider-Man moves in the narrows or to play in the small waterfalls. Stronger hikers have the option of continuing up Matkatamiba Canyon to where it forks. The left fork continues another mile or so before reaching impassable cliffs. The right fork leads to Mount Akaba, a difficult canyoneering adventure.

Havasu Creek

- Distance: 19 miles
- Duration: 8 hours
- Elevation gain: 4,400 feet
- Effort: Strenuous
- Trailhead: River left, mile 156

The Havasupai ("People of the Blue-Green Water") have lived for centuries along Havasu Creek's Edenic waterfalls and travertine-lined pools that reflect the sky. A permit is required to enter reservation land. Backpackers and equestrians can make the trip from Hualapai Hilltop down to Supai Village, where there's a campground and a motel, at eight miles. From the river, the village is 8.5 miles. Most river runners only go as far as Beaver Falls, but even a short hike up Havasu Creek leads to shady pools, perfect on a hot summer day.

From the river, the trail up Havasu Canyon crosses the creek several times and can be difficult to follow as it washes out frequently. At about three miles you'll reach Beaver Falls, a pretty series of travertine cascades. The trail climbs around Beaver Falls to a ledge before dropping back down to the creek. At about six miles, Mooney Falls plummets nearly 200 feet into the turquoise-colored pool below. The trail to the village, another 2.5 miles, tunnels through the travertine at Mooney Falls, a slippery route with ladders and chains for handholds. En route to the village the trail passes Havasu Falls, twin plumes of water falling 100 feet, as well as 75-foot Navajo Falls.

Although you'll be wading and swimming a lot on this trail, you should pack plenty of water. The water in Havasu Creek water isn't drinkable, and most day hikers from the river won't make it to the campground or village, where water is available.

Fern Glen

- Distance: 1 mile round-trip
- Duration: 1 hour
- Elevation gain: 300 feet
- Effort: Moderate
- Trailhead: River right, mile 168

Allow time to linger on this short hike leading to a fern-draped grotto and pool. Redwall and Muav limestone walls have been carved into shelves and chutes. The canyon walls narrow a short way from the beach, creating welcome shade. There's no trail, but scrambling up limestone staircases is only moderately challenging. Springs, like the one in Fern Glen Canyon, are formed when rain and snowmelt percolate down through the relatively porous limestone and sandstone layers above until more resistant Bright Angel shale blocks its progress. The water pools on top of the shale, forming an aquifer in the Redwall formation that is easily dissolved into caves and chambers. Where Redwall is exposed in canyon walls, water issues forth as springs, relatively common in the tributaries along this section of Grand Canyon. Cliff walls block further progress up Fern Glen Canyon, but it's pleasant to pause by one of the pools and listen to the trickling water before returning to the river.

Whitmore Wash

- Distance: 2 miles round-trip
- Duration: Less than 1 hour
- Elevation gain: 800 feet
- Effort: Moderate
- Trailhead: River right, mile 188

The shortest river-to-rim hike in Grand Canyon, this trail starts at prehistoric ruins, passes through an ancient lava flow, and ends at a historic line cabin—an interesting time-line, especially if you add the modern helipad across the river on the Hualapai Reservation, used for passenger exchanges.

A short walk across the beach leads to masonry ruins, protected by cliffs and a retaining wall built by the Park Service. To the left of the ruins are some pictographs. To the right a trail leads up to the rim, where local ranchers built a line shack. At this point, the walls of the canyon rise less than 1,000 feet from the river, and a Bureau of Land Management road leading from St. George, Utah, crosses through ranch land to the edge of the canyon. With a good map and a high-clearance vehicle, it's possible to access Whitmore Wash from above.

Travertine Canyon

- Distance: 4 miles round-trip
- Duration: 2–3 hours
- Elevation gain: 900 feet
- Effort: Difficult
- Trailhead: River left, mile 229

Depending on how much time you have (and how hot it is), you can make the short, mildly challenging scramble to Travertine Falls, a lovely 35-foot plunge, or attempt the difficult scramble to the source of the canyon's water, a spring surrounded by dense vegetation. To get to Travertine Falls, follow the creek bed up a steep and slippery slope of Vishnu schist. The waterfall is at the back of a narrows of travertine-covered cliffs. Hiking to the falls and back takes less than an hour.

If you want a longer, more challenging hike, and your climbing skills are sharp, return to

the river and walk past the creek (upriver), heading up the ridge to go up and around the falls. Look for cairns to guide you back into the creek bed. You'll encounter three smaller waterfalls on your way up the creek, requiring some hand-and-foot climbing to get around. The springs are marked by thick vegetation, and you can turn back or go a bit farther to the top of the Tonto Platform for good views.

NONCOMMERCIAL RIVER RUNNING

Experienced river runners wait eagerly for a chance to challenge the canyon's rapids themselves, choosing their own pace and campsites. If you have your own gear, a private (noncommercial) trip costs a fraction of the price of a guided commercial trip. The hallmark of a private trip is that all participants (maximum 16) contribute, and no one gets paid a fee. But private trips have been hard to score on a river with strict limits on the number of annual visitors. In order to keep a sense of the wild in this wilderness and protect the canyon's fragile environments, the National Park Service doles out a certain number of private-trip permits each year. The most coveted are for 12–25-day trips from Lees Ferry to Diamond Creek. In 2008, more than 2,000 people applied.

It's easier to get a permit for 2–5-day trips through the Lower Granite Gorge, launching from Diamond Creek. "Diamond Down" trips navigate about 15 miles of white water on a 54-mile length to Lake Mead's South Cove. The Park Service issues permits for two trips per day of up to 16 people each. Applications are available online or from the **River Permits Office** (P.O. Box 129, Grand Canyon, AZ 86023, 800/959-9164, fax 928/638-7844, grca_riv@ nps.gov) and can be submitted up to a year in advance. The Park Service doesn't charge for permits, but arrangements and fees must be handled with the **Hualapai River Running Department** (P.O. Box 246, Peach Springs, AZ 86434, 928/769-2210 or 800/622-4409) prior to the trip's launch date.

PRIVATE TRIP SUPPORT

For those who need help with trip logistics or equipment, a number of companies specialize in outfitting noncommercial Grand Canyon trips. Most offer all-inclusive packages or allow you to select what you need from a lengthy list of possibilities, including dry bags, toilet boxes, and satellite phones. Rental boats and rafts all meet National Park Service regulations, but you'll find some differences between companies in regard to the sizes and types of watercraft they offer.

- **Cañon Outfitters** (8585 Arroyo Tr., Flagstaff, AZ 86004, 928/660-1711, www.canonoutfitters.com): oar and motorized rafts, hard-shell and inflatable kayaks, equipment, shuttle services, food options

- **Canyon REO** (1619 N. East St., Flagstaff, AZ 86004, 928/774-3343 or 800/637-4604, www.canyonreo.com): oar and paddle rafts, hard-shell and inflatable kayaks, equipment, shuttle services, food options

- **Ceiba Adventures** (P.O. Box 2274, Flagstaff, AZ, 86003, 928/527-0171 or 800/217-1060, www.ceibaadventures.com): oar, paddle, and motorized rafts, inflatable kayaks, equipment, shuttle services, food options

- **Moenkopi Riverworks** (2206 E. Chisholm Tr., Flagstaff, AZ 86001, 928/856-0012, www.moenkopiriverworks.com): oar, paddle, and motorized rafts, inflatable kayaks, equipment, shuttle services, food options

- **Professional River Outfitters** (2800 W. Rte. 66, Flagstaff, AZ 86001, 928/779-1512 or 800/648-3236, www.proriver.com): oar and paddle rafts, inflatable kayaks, equipment, shuttle services, food options

Other companies provide vehicle and/or person shuttle services only:

- **Lake Mead Air** (P.O. Box 60035, Boulder City, NV 89006, 702/293-1848 or 702/293-9906)

- **River Runners Shuttle Service** (P.O. Box 61, Meadview, AZ 86444, 928/564-2194, www.rrshuttleservice.com)

- **Scenic Airlines:** (P.O. Box 1385, Page, AZ 86040, 928/645-2494 or 800/245-8668, www.scenic.com)

THE INNER CANYON

Due to an ever-growing waiting list for permits (upward of 20 years out), the Park Service switched to a weighted lottery system for granting permits to noncommercial 12–25-day river trips launching from Lees Ferry. The weighted system increases the odds for those who haven't been on a river trip during the past five years. During the transition to the new system, a percentage of applications from the existing waiting list were included in each annual lottery. By 2011, the former waiting list will be depleted, and all of the 500 available permits will be allocated through the lottery system.

Lottery applications can be submitted a year in advance. Unlike commercial trips, which have a limited season, private river trips launch all year. Winter months are less popular, and you may increase your lottery chances if you apply for a winter launch date. The main lottery is held in February, with smaller lotteries throughout the year to fill cancellations or leftover trips. The application fee is $25, and you can be listed on only one application per year. If you win the lottery, a $400 deposit holds your reservation. Applications are available on the park's website (https://npspermits.us). You must complete an online profile to apply for the lottery. The Park Service has compiled a helpful list of Frequently Asked Questions (FAQs) about the permit lottery system, available on the park's main website (www.nps.gov/grca).

Before applying, it's a good idea to familiarize yourself with the regulations and issues surrounding a private trip. Grand Canyon National Park has published a 28-page booklet called *Noncommercial River Trip Regulations,* available on the park's website as a PDF file. The booklet addresses everything from watercraft requirements to waste management. The website will also link you to a free podcast of the park's River Orientation Video.

Even if you decide that you aren't ready to apply for a trip permit, you can set up a profile and register online. There's no charge, and you'll receive periodic announcements via email regarding future launch dates and other river news.

Another option for getting on a private trip is to fill an opening on an existing reservation. The **Grand Canyon Private Boaters Association** (www.gcpba.org), a group of experienced river runners, shares information on its website, including occasional announcements about trip openings.

The biggest drawback of planning a private trip is, well, the planning—about 300 hours' worth. It takes a lot of river savvy not only to navigate the canyon's rapids but also to keep groceries fresh down to the last ice block. Private trip leaders must have experience. If you're leading a trip, you'll want your passengers to have experience too. On a private trip, everybody works.

You can turn over a lot of the pretrip logistics to a pro. Several companies specialize in outfitting private Grand Canyon trips, offering everything from equipment rental to menu planning and shopping. Most private-trip outfitters are based in Flagstaff, and shuttles to and from the river are available.

Among the rewards of putting together a private trip are being able to gear the experience to the interests of you and your companions, perhaps planning layovers around longer hikes or technical climbs, stopping for photography or filming, or bringing old photos and journal entries to retrace the footsteps of a historic expedition. You can camp somewhere new and interesting every night, or spend more time on a single beach, pretending that you're castaways living off the land (or off that enormous cooler stocked with everything from apples to zin). Whatever the theme, your journey will be memorable.

CLIMBING

In 1958, climbers Dave Ganci and Rick Tidrick made the first technical ascent (using ropes and other mountain-climbing equipment) in Grand Canyon, reaching the top of Zoroaster Temple. During the decades since, climbers have made technical and nontechnical ascents of some 150 of the canyon's peaks, including Vishnu and Shiva Temples. Famed canyon hiker Harvey Butchart is said to have climbed 83 summits, making 50 first ascents. Even more daring are routes scaling walls, faces, and features like the pinnacle in Monument Creek.

Many of the Grand Canyon's rock layers are limestone and sandstone, notoriously "rotten" surfaces, and researching routes is essential for a safe climb. There are no official climbing routes, but you can learn about Grand Canyon climbs by connecting with enthusiasts via climbing blogs or by networking in nearby Flagstaff, home to a popular indoor climbing center, **Vertical Relief** (205 S. San Francisco St., Flagstaff, 928/556-9909, www.verticalrelief.com). Flagstaff climbers Aaron and Pernell Tomasi wrote *Grand Canyon Summits Select: A Compilation of Obscure Ascents in the Grand Canyon Backcountry,* which details dozens of their canyon routes. The 2001 edition is out of print, but the authors sell an updated version on their website (http://pseudalpine.com).

CANYONEERING

Canyoneering, an increasingly popular pursuit in the Southwest, combines climbing, boulder hopping, hiking, and wading or swimming in order to descend and ascend canyon routes. Scores of tributary canyons lead to the Colorado River, many of them originating on the Navajo Reservation to the east, Kaibab National Forest to the north, and the Hualapai Reservation to the west. (Permits are required on reservation lands.)

In wild tributaries like Rider Canyon, South Canyon, Kanab Canyon, and Diamond Creek, canyoneers will encounter obstacle courses of pour-overs, pools, chockstones, and boulder fields. Some canyoneering routes are on official trails while others are explorations requiring route-finding skills and a lot of trial and error. The rugged terrain presents many dangers, foremost among them the possibility of catastrophic flash floods. But if you are experienced and prepared, canyoneering can take you to wild and enchanting places seldom seen.

FISHING

After Glen Canyon Dam impounded the waters of the Colorado River, cooler downstream temperatures changed the river's environment. Today, the chilly waters of the Colorado River below the dam provide a good habitat for rainbow trout. Introduced species commonly found in the river include rainbow, brown, and brook trout as well as carp. Channel catfish and striped bass are seen occasionally, although they prefer the warmer downstream waters of Lake Mead. Of the native species, only speckled dace are common, with several others, including bonytail chub, considered extinct in Grand Canyon.

The best time for trout fishing is in the fall or winter. Popular spots include Bright Angel Creek, accessible from the Bright Angel, South Kaibab, or North Kaibab Trails; Tapeats Creek; and Nankoweap Creek. No fishing is allowed near the confluence of the Little Colorado River and the Colorado. The warmer waters of the LCR are a refuge for several threatened and endangered species of native fish such as the humpback chub. If you should catch a protected fish, it must be immediately released unharmed.

To fish in the canyon, you'll need an Arizona state fishing license (unless you're under age 14) and a trout stamp. Bag limits vary, depending on which area of the canyon you're fishing. For most of the canyon, from 21-Mile Rapids to Separation Canyon, trout, striped bass, and catfish are unlimited. No live baitfish may be used. Licenses are sold at the General Store on the South Rim, Lees Ferry, or Jacob Lake. Currently, licenses can't be purchased over the phone or online; you'll need to pick one up at an authorized dealer or an Arizona Game & Fish office. For more information about fishing regulations, contact the **Arizona Game & Fish Department** (602/942-3000, www.azgfd.gov).

Accommodations and Food

The only lodging and dining establishment in the inner canyon is Phantom Ranch. But don't worry: Whether you're cooking up a package of instant noodles on your backpacking stove or enjoying sunset while a handy boat crew fixes you steak and strawberry shortcake, it all tastes better when every table has a view and you've worked up a good appetite exploring. If you're backpacking, be sure not to attract unwanted dinner guests: Use an ammo can or a high-tech food sack to keep ringtails and rodents out of your food supply.

Competition for river camps can be fierce during the high season, and if you're on a commercial trip, you'll notice that guides often pause to confer with each other about where their group plans to spend the night. Some beaches are large enough to offer space for two or three parties of 10 or more. Other camps have space for only a few boaters and backpackers, so it's important to plan ahead, have a backup, and be courteous to everyone you encounter, since you just might be sharing camp with them downriver.

Commercial rafting companies usually provide tents, sleeping bags, and pads. During the summer rainy season, most thundershowers pass before sunset. Unless the weather is threatening, you'll probably find yourself forgoing a tent and sleeping under the stars.

PHANTOM RANCH

◀ Phantom Ranch (888/297-2757, www.grandcanyonlodges.com), the only place inside the canyon where you'll find sheets and showers, consists of a cluster of historic wood-and-stone buildings along Bright Angel Creek, near its confluence with the Colorado River. Phantom

THE INNER CANYON

Ranch has dormitory-style rooms for men and women, 11 rustic cabins, and a canteen serving breakfast, lunch, and dinner. The canteen also acts as post office and grocery. Room reservations (not available online) are accepted up to 13 months in advance, and rooms sell out quickly. Men's and women's dorms ($42 pp) with 10 bunks each are available for hikers and river runners, with a shared shower and restroom. The cabins are reserved for mule riders and are included in tour fees. Cabins and dorms have heat and evaporative cooling (referred to affectionately by Arizonans as "swamp coolers").

The ⟨ **Phantom Ranch Canteen** sells snacks and serves up a simple but hearty breakfast ($20), sack lunch ($12), and dinner ($26–42). Dinner options include steak, stew, or a veggie meal. Meals are part of the package for mule-tour guests, but hikers and river runners need to make meal reservations well in advance of their trips.

CAMPGROUNDS

Other than the costs of a backcountry permit, no additional fees are charged to stay in the Inner Canyon's three developed campgrounds. Do note that "developed" is a relative term. Don't expect showers—let alone cable hookups—if you're spending the night in the canyon. Stays are limited to two nights per hike (four nights Nov. 15–Feb. 28), and your site is reserved when you apply for a backcountry use permit. Permit fees ($10 per permit plus $5 pp per night) include camping, whether you're staying at an established corridor campground or sleeping on a patch of sandstone in a primitive area. To cut pack weight, some backpackers forgo tents during summer, but be aware that afternoon thunderstorms are likely in July–August.

⟨ **Bright Angel Campground,** along Bright Angel Creek near its confluence with the Colorado River, has 31 campsites (including two group sites), year-round drinking water, food storage boxes, picnic tables, an emergency phone, and toilets. The campground is accessible from the Bright Angel, South Kaibab, and North Kaibab Trails. You'll need a backcountry permit to stay here, and sites do fill up quickly

in spring and summer. The ranger station is nearby, and during summer months, rangers host evening programs. Phantom Ranch is 0.5 miles north.

Cottonwood Campground, 6.8 miles from the North Rim via the North Kaibab Trail, has 11 campsites with picnic tables and food storage boxes. The campground also offers toilets, an emergency phone, and a ranger station (staffed May–Oct.). Although its name might suggest the whispering shelter of grand old cottonwoods, Cottonwood Campground actually has very little shade. Water is available seasonally, May–mid-October. Always check the park service website (www.nps.gov/grca) for announcements about seasonal water shut-offs, and be prepared to purify or filter water in case of a pipe break.

Indian Garden Campground is a shady oasis of grapevines and cottonwoods midway down the Bright Angel Trail, 4.5 miles from the South Rim. A backcountry permit is required to reserve one of the 15 campsites. Amenities include potable water year-round, pack hangers, food storage boxes, and composting toilets. Indian Garden also has a ranger station and an emergency phone.

BACKCOUNTRY AND RIVER CAMPS

The backcountry is divided into zones and use areas that may be hundreds or thousands of acres in size depending on ecology, terrain, and popularity. Backcountry camping is limited to campgrounds or designated campsites in the Corridor and Threshold zones, where amenities range from developed campgrounds with piped water and flush toilets to dry sites with pit toilets. In the Primitive and Wild zones, at-large camping is allowed, with certain restrictions.

The **Corridor zone** includes Bright Angel, Cottonwood, and Indian Garden campgrounds. The **Threshold zone** includes Clear Creek, Horn Creek, Salt Creek, Cedar Spring, Monument Creek, Granite Rapids, Hermit Creek, Hermit Rapids, Horseshoe Mesa, Widforss, Point Sublime, and Eremita Mesa use areas. Stays in campsites in these areas are limited to two nights, except during the off-season (Nov. 15–Feb. 28), when stays of up to four nights are possible.

Backcountry permits must be displayed while you are in camp, either attached to a pack or tent or elsewhere in plain view. Backcountry campsites must be a minimum of 100 feet from water sources. This protects water quality for other campers and wildlife (and helps protect you and your food supply from thirsty nighttime critters). Don't try to improve on Mother Nature with trenching or other earth moving—the site should look undisturbed when you leave. Pack out all trash, used toilet paper, and food scraps. Even the tiniest crumb attracts ants, mice, and other unwelcome visitors.

When you make camp, secure your food first, using the park's food storage boxes where available. Bringing 20–30 feet of rope to hang packs is oft-recommended, but be warned that inner-canyon ringtails can outwit the most elaborate pack defenses in search of food. Pack edibles inside storage containers, such as an ammo can or sacks made with lightweight polymer, steel mesh, or some other material strong enough to thwart sharp little teeth. In riparian areas, particularly around Phantom Ranch, skunks and raccoons also make unwelcome nighttime visits.

Don't feed animals—deliberately or inadvertently. It is not only illegal (with fines for violators) but also unethical and even dangerous. Human food can damage animals' digestive systems. Wild creatures can become dependent on handouts, lose their ability to fend for themselves, and lose their caution around humans. Many cases of animals becoming aggressive toward people have been documented at Grand Canyon. On some popular trails, squirrels and other rodents have become outright bandits, ripping into your pack if you set it down even for a few seconds. This may seem relatively harmless, but a damaged pack is a hassle, and losing part of your well-planned food supply is worse. Rabies and bubonic plague outbreaks aren't uncommon in Arizona. Hantavirus, while less common, is deadly. If you think food has been contaminated, wrap it up and pack it out.

If you're hiking to the river, be aware that you may be sharing camps with boating parties. You might enjoy the company (and they may even feed you or let you cadge a beer), but if you prefer privacy, choose a tent site far away from the most likely boat landing.

Information and Services

Visitor services are limited inside the canyon, with Phantom Ranch the only purveyor of such creature comforts as lemonade and postcards. Cell phone service is unlikely, and only a few emergency phones are available at ranger stations and resthouses. River guides carry satellite phones. The biggest concern for hikers and backpackers, however, is water. Inner canyon water pipes are shut off in the off-season, and verifying water sources before you hike is essential.

LEES FERRY

All white-water rafting trips through Grand Canyon put in at Lees Ferry, outside Grand Canyon National Park in Glen Canyon National Recreation Area, 15 river miles below Glen Canyon Dam. Lees Ferry is the last developed area river runners will see until Phantom Ranch, nearly 90 river miles away. It has a campground, parking (with a 14-day limit), public phones, a ranger station, toilets, and water.

RESTHOUSES

Many of the wood or stone resthouses along the canyon's corridor trails were built by the Civilian Conservation Corps (CCC) in the 1930s. The CCC was a Great Depression–era program that provided jobs for young men at parks and forests throughout the United States, including firefighting, tree planting, trail and road building, and other construction projects.

Several CCC companies created much-needed infrastructure at Grand Canyon.

On the Bright Angel Trail, Mile-and-a-Half Resthouse has toilets, an emergency phone, and seasonal drinking water (May–Sept.). Three-Mile Resthouse has an emergency phone and seasonal drinking water (May–Sept.). River Resthouse, at mile 7.7, where Pipe Creek joins the Colorado River, has an emergency phone.

On the South Kaibab Trail, Cedar Ridge Resthouse, 1.5 miles below the rim, has toilet facilities. At 4.4 miles, the Tonto Trail Junction Resthouse has an emergency phone. The Tip-Off, a few steps farther along, has toilet facilities. No water is available along the South Kaibab Trail.

On the North Kaibab Trail, there are toilet facilities and occasional seasonal water at Supai Tunnel, two miles from the rim. Roaring Springs, at 4.7 miles, has toilet facilities and seasonal drinking water (May–Sept.).

MULE DUFFEL SERVICE

Xanterra, the park's South Rim lodging concessionaire, offers daily pack-mule services year-round for backpackers and river runners who need assistance shuttling their gear between Phantom Ranch and Grand Canyon Village. There's a weight limit of 30 pounds, and fees run about $70 one-way. Advance reservations are necessary, and items must be properly packed and delivered to the drop-off points by a specified time. For details or reservations, contact Xanterra (303/297-3175 or 800/297-2757, www.grandcanyonlodges.com). If you don't have your own duffel bag, you will be provided (no kidding) with a repurposed grain sack.

EMERGENCIES

It's highly unlikely that your cell phone will pick up a signal inside the canyon. Consider leaving the phone at home or at the rim; electronic devices can be downright irritating to

You can hire a pack-mule to carry your gear.

backpackers and river runners who cherish natural quiet.

The **emergency phones** available at some resthouses and campgrounds are connected to a 24-hour dispatch center and do not require coins. Rangers patrol the trails and river, and ranger stations are located at Indian Garden, Bright Angel Campground, and Cottonwood Campground (unstaffed in the off-season). River guides carry satellite phones, and they are trained to assist with emergencies.

Stay on established trails: On numerous occasions, hikers have been rescued only yards away from a trail. The National Park Service rescues about 400 visitors each year, and most are first-time canyon hikers. If you require rescue, you will be responsible for the cost. Exhaustion doesn't constitute an emergency.

You can leave the park administration telephone number (928/638-2477) with someone who is aware of your itinerary. If you've told your contact you will call after hiking out of the canyon, be sure to do so to avoid unnecessary search-and-rescue efforts on your behalf.

Getting There and Around

Foot, mule, or boat—those are your choices for exploring the Inner Canyon. Backpacking and hiking excursions will originate from river or rims. Mule trips begin from the South Rim year-round, and from the North Rim during summer months. Most white-water raft trips put in at Lees Ferry on Grand Canyon's eastern end. If these options seem limited, well, that's what makes a trip inside Grand Canyon rare and special.

SHUTTLES

For those planning rim-to-rim hikes, the **Trans Canyon Shuttle** (928/638-2820, www.trans-canyonshuttle.com) offers daily round-trip van service between the North Rim and South Rim ($80 one way, $150 round-trip), making a stop in the Marble Canyon area near Lees Ferry.

River shuttles from Flagstaff and other locations are usually provided by commercial outfitters. Those planning a private river trip have a number of options for shuttling vehicles or people with the help of companies offering private trip support. Most private trip support companies are located in Flagstaff.

MULE SUPPORT

Backpackers and river runners can arrange for a mule duffel to move their gear between Phantom Ranch and Grand Canyon Village. There's a weight limit of 30 pounds, and fees run about $70 one-way. For details or reservations, contact Xanterra (303/297-3175 or 800/297-2757, www.grandcanyonlodges .com).

THE INNER CANYON

BEYOND THE BOUNDARIES

Beyond the national park boundaries, Grand Canyon is bordered by miles of national forest, a vast national recreation area, thousands of acres of Bureau of Land Management (BLM) land, and three Indian reservations, the Navajo, Hualapai, and Havasupai nations. The lands outside the park offer different flavors of the Grand Canyon experience, from wild, empty places to locations rich with cultural traditions.

The Pai tribes occupy the west side of Grand Canyon, south of the Colorado River. The Havasupai live in Havasu Canyon, a hidden jewel where Havasu Creek flows over ledges to form breathtaking waterfalls. The creek's turquoise waters empty into the Colorado River 35 miles west of Grand Canyon Village as the raven flies. Supai Village, 5,000 feet below the rim, can be reached only by foot, horseback, or helicopter.

The Hualapai Reservation borders over 100 miles of Grand Canyon west of the park's South Rim, all the way to the Grand Wash Cliffs, the canyon's geophysical western boundary. The main reservation covers parts of three counties and includes grasslands, ponderosa pine forest, and the rugged canyon rim. The tribe hosts thousands of river runners annually, with many trips putting in or taking out on Hualapai land at Diamond Creek. Most tourism activities, including the glass-bottomed Skywalk, are centered at Grand Canyon West.

Navajo, forest, and BLM land rim the 60-mile stretch of the steep-sided eastern end of Grand Canyon that explorer John Wesley Powell described in 1869 as "beautifully

HIGHLIGHTS

Cameron Trading Post: Step into Arizona's past at this historic post, which has operated on the Navajo Reservation for nearly a century. The post serves travelers and locals, offering meals, groceries, supplies, and a dazzling array of jewelry, pottery, kachina dolls, sand paintings, and other treasures made by Southwestern Native American artisans (page 167).

Little Colorado River Gorge: Don't skip the chance to peer into the steep-walled canyon carved by one of the Colorado River's major tributaries, the "Little C." The Little Colorado River makes its final run to Grand Canyon across the Navajo Nation near Cameron (page 168).

Lees Ferry: At Lees Ferry, you can drive to the edge of the Colorado River to fish, watch river runners, or explore this area where Glen Canyon ends and Grand Canyon begins (page 169).

Vermilion Cliffs: Part of the Southwest's Grand Staircase of cliffs, these colorful walls

of stone rise high above the Marble Platform. California condors, an endangered species returning from the brink, were reintroduced to the Grand Canyon from the top of the Vermilion Cliffs, and the big birds continue to soar in the skies above Marble Canyon (page 171).

Kaibab Plateau: Few people see Grand Canyon's North Rim, and fewer still take the time to stop and explore the Kaibab Plateau en route. Ah well, that means even more solitude for those who hike, bike, or ride the plateau's forest roads and trails, which meander through aspen, pines, and wildflowers on the way to remote canyon overlooks (page 172).

Havasu Canyon Trail: The inner-canyon home of the Havasupai Indians is an oasis of breathtaking waterfalls and turquoise pools. The only way into the canyon is by descending this eight-mile trail on foot, horse, or mule, or by riding a helicopter from the canyon rim (page 173).

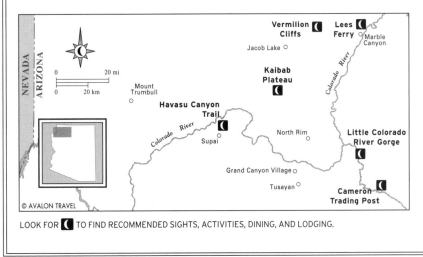

LOOK FOR **(** TO FIND RECOMMENDED SIGHTS, ACTIVITIES, DINING, AND LODGING.

colored marble." The sheer cliff walls are actually Redwall limestone, but this section of Grand Canyon still bears the name Marble Canyon. Navajo horse, cattle, and sheep herds graze on their lands on the canyon's east side. Lees Ferry, 14 miles below Glen Canyon Dam, is the geophysical dividing point between Glen Canyon and Marble Canyon, and between the Navajo Reservation and public lands. Lees Ferry is also the launch point for Grand Canyon boat trips as well as a popular spot for camping, hiking, picnics, and fishing. West of Lees Ferry, en route to the North Rim, the Vermilion Cliffs rise above desolate House Rock Valley, where California condors were reintroduced to the Grand Canyon region in 1996.

From House Rock Valley, U.S. 89A climbs more than 3,000 feet to the Kaibab Plateau, where the national forest provides over 1,000 square miles of backcountry hiking and driving for travelers interested in getting away from it all. This lonely stretch north of the North Rim, part of the Arizona Strip, is one step in the series of rocky plateaus known as the Grand Staircase. Here, there's less of everything: fewer people, less development, not as many restrictions. On several trails, you can ride a mountain bike or bring your dog. You can camp nearly anywhere, and on trails and overlooks you'll find solitude and views unobstructed by guardrails, buildings, or tour buses.

PLANNING YOUR TIME

The Big Ditch is surrounded by fascinating cultural and natural history, and no matter what roads you take to travel here, spending a couple of days or more exploring beyond park boundaries will literally and metaphorically broaden your horizons.

Travelers interested in history or Native American culture can add 1–3 days to a Grand Canyon itinerary to visit Hualapai and Havasupai lands on the west end of the canyon or the Navajo Nation on the east. Most Native American governments require permits to hike or camp on reservation land. Reservations for Havasu Canyon fill up in advance, especially during the busy summer season. On Hualapai lands, however, tour choices abound, and you can often get a reservation with only a day's notice, even for the Skywalk.

Outdoor enthusiasts and adventure travelers won't need reservations or permits to explore national forest and BLM lands on the Kaibab Plateau or House Rock Valley, but advance planning is essential. The driving time to these remote areas is substantial. Set aside at least two days, longer for backpacking trips. If you're hiking in the Saddle Mountain or Kanab Creek Wilderness Areas, a Forest Service map is a must. Plan routes carefully, researching water availability and trail conditions in advance. Let someone know your itinerary before you set out, and share your wilderness experience with hiking companions.

Spring and fall are the best times to explore the greater Grand Canyon region, though if you can get a reservation, Havasu Canyon is a summer delight for swimmers. On the Kaibab Plateau, heavy snows close roads November–mid-May, and muddy roads can persist into June. If you're exploring tributary canyons, especially on the Marble Platform or Vermilion Cliffs, avoid the summer monsoon season, from July–mid-September. A storm cell miles away can create flash-flood conditions. No matter what the season, check the forecast before you leave. Elevation changes can mean sudden shifts in the weather, so be prepared.

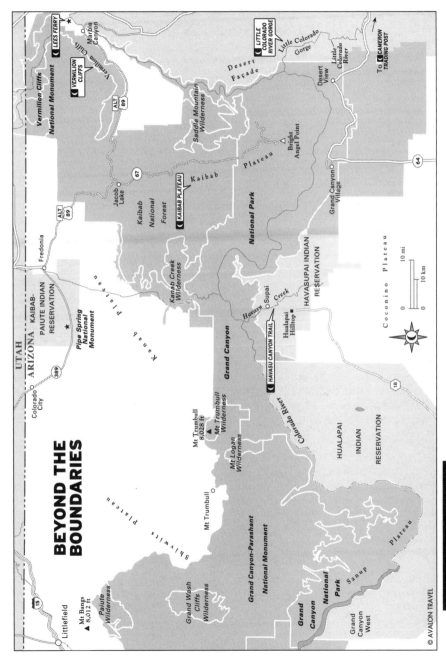

BEYOND THE BOUNDARIES

LEES FERRY ★

Marble Canyon

Vermilion Cliffs

Vermilion Cliffs National Monument

VERMILION CLIFFS

LITTLE COLORADO RIVER GORGE

Little Colorado Gorge

Little Colorado River

To CAMERON TRADING POST

Desert Façade

Desert View

ALT 89

UTAH

ARIZONA

KAIBAB-PAIUTE INDIAN RESERVATION

Fredonia

ALT 89

Jacob Lake

67

Kaibab KAIBAB PLATEAU

Kaibab National Forest

Saddle Mountain Wilderness

Plateau

Bright Angel Point

National Park

Grand Canyon Village

64

Colorado City

389

Pipe Spring National Monument

Kanab Plateau

Kanab Creek Wilderness

Grand Canyon

Supai

Havasu Creek

HAVASUPAI INDIAN RESERVATION

Hualapai Hilltop

HAVASU CANYON TRAIL

Coconino Plateau

10 mi

0

10 km

0

15

Littlefield

Mt Bangs 8,012 ft

Paiute Wilderness

Grand Wash Cliffs Wilderness

Shivwits Plateau

Mt Trumbull

Mt Logan Wilderness

Mt Trumbull Wilderness

Mt Trumbull 8,028 ft

Colorado River

18

Grand Canyon-Parashant National Monument

HUALAPAI INDIAN RESERVATION

Sanup Plateau

Grand Canyon National Park

Grand Canyon West

© AVALON TRAVEL

Exploring Beyond the Boundaries

Generally speaking, long drives are required to get to sites and trailheads located in the vast spaces around Grand Canyon. The Hualapai Nation welcomes commercial ground or air tours to Grand Canyon West, but nearly everywhere else in this big country, you're on your own. Settlements are small, few, and far between, dominated by rocky cliffs or sweeping sage flats. You might feel as though you've traveled back in time. Cell phone service is spotty, and you may drive for miles before seeing another car. But for independent-minded travelers willing to trade modern conveniences for new horizons, the landscape around Grand Canyon is rich with possibilities.

VISITORS CENTERS
West of GCNP

The **Hualapai Office of Tourism** (928/769-2636 or 888/868-9378, www.grandcanyonwest.com) is inside Hualapai Lodge in Peach Springs, about three hours west of Grand Canyon Village. You'll find information about tour possibilities, and you can obtain permits for driving, hiking, or camping on reservation land.

The **Havasupai Lodge** (928/448-2111 or 928/448-2201, 8 A.M.–5 P.M. daily) and **tourist office** (928/448-2121, 928/448-2141, or 928/448-2174) act as visitors centers at Supai Village, eight miles by foot trail below **Hualapai Hilltop.** After suffering two devastating floods in 2008 and 2010, the Havasupai Nation closed Havasu Canyon to visitation. The campground and trails sustained heavy damage, but they hope to reopen the canyon to visitation sometime in 2011. Contact the tourist office for updates.

Reservations must be made well in advance of a Havasu Canyon trip, and you'll also need to make a down payment for your entry fees and camping and lodging costs in order to hold your reservation. The tourist office takes cash and credit cards, but not traveler's checks. Because of Havasu Canyon's size, the annual number of visitors is limited to 12,000, so plan ahead. The village has a café, a general store, and a post office, one of the few in the U.S. that sends and receives mail via mule. On arrival, all visitors must check in at one or the other office.

East of GCNP

Cameron Visitors Center (P.O. Box 459, Cameron, AZ 86020, 928/679-2303), located at the junction of U.S. 89 and Highway 64 in Cameron, serves the western Navajo Nation, including the Little Colorado River Tribal Park. You can inquire about current conditions and obtain permits for nearby hiking trails on Navajo land.

Navajo Bridge Interpretive Center (928/355-2319, 9 A.M.–5 P.M. daily mid-Apr.–Oct., 10 A.M.–4 P.M. Sat.–Sun. early Apr. and Nov.) is one of several visitors centers for the 1.2-million-acre Glen Canyon National Recreation Area. Inside the visitors center, an excellent bookstore sells hard-to-find regional titles as well as posters, videos, and souvenirs. At Lees Ferry, six miles from the bridge, there's also a ranger station, where you can get information about hikes in Glen Canyon National Recreation Area and the eastern end of Grand Canyon. Occasionally, you can pick up a last-minute backcountry permit here for the Marble Canyon area.

North of GCNP

Visitors to Grand Canyon's North Rim often stop at the **Kaibab Plateau Visitors Center** (928/643-7298, 8 A.M.–5 P.M. mid-May–mid-Oct., shorter hours later in the season), operated by the Forest Service in Jacob Lake. The helpful staff at the visitors center can field questions about the national park as well as provide information for current conditions, camping, hiking, biking, and driving in the North Kaibab district of the Kaibab National Forest (www.fs.usda.gov/kaibab).

North Kaibab **district headquarters** (430 S. Main St., Fredonia, 928/643-7395) can also provide maps and information. Though

PUBLIC LAND AND RESERVATION LAND

Close to 60 percent of land in Arizona is public, and more than a quarter of the state is owned by 21 Indian tribes, leaving less than 18 percent of Arizona's land in private hands. Grand Canyon National Park is administered by the National Park Service, a division of the U.S. Department of the Interior. The Park Service's mission is to preserve and protect.

The U.S. Department of Agriculture presides over national forest lands, mandated to manage timber, game, grazing, minerals, and other resources, which may include scenery and historic structures or artifacts. Kaibab National Forest neighbors Grand Canyon National Park on the north and south.

The Bureau of Land Management (BLM), another agency within the Department of the Interior, is charged with sustaining the health, diversity, and productivity of public land in its jurisdiction. In Arizona, the BLM administers 12.2 million acres, including Grand Canyon-Parashant National Monument and Paria Canyon-Vermilion Cliffs Wilderness Area west and north of Grand Canyon.

Wilderness areas have even higher levels of protection. Motorized and mechanized uses, including mountain bikes, are prohibited. Several wilderness areas surround the national park, including the Saddle Mountain and Kanab Creek Wilderness Areas that straddle the Kaibab Plateau.

VISITING RESERVATION LANDS

Reservations are not public land but sovereign nations. Permission is required to hike, camp, or film on Indian reservations, such as the Havasupai, Hualapai, or Navajo Nations bordering Grand Canyon. Each reservation has its own government and establishes its own rules for visitation.

Photography, recording, and sketching are usually prohibited within villages, although rules vary among reservations. You may be asked to purchase a photography permit to take photos for personal noncommercial use. Do not take photos of individuals without their permission.

Reservations may have a cultural center. Trading posts or stores sometimes act as unofficial cultural centers, offering directions, sightseeing suggestions, and information about schedules or permits. Most reservations require permits for hiking, camping, hunting, fishing, and other backcountry uses, as well as for commercial purposes like professional filming.

There is a distinct difference between performances and ceremonies. It is a privilege to be invited to a ceremony, and your good behavior is important to its purpose and outcome. Behave as if you were in a church or temple – dress modestly and neatly and maintain a quiet, respectful attitude. Do not address the dancers during a ceremony, and don't applaud following a ceremony. Performances, such as those held at Hopi House or the Museum of Northern Arizona, are reenactments, and the atmosphere may be more relaxed.

Visitors must remember that villages are peoples' homes, not museums or sets. Unless you are invited to enter a private home, perhaps to see baskets or pottery, you should remain in public places like shops and restaurants. Cemeteries, shrines, and other sacred areas are generally off-limits to visitors.

Alcohol and drugs are prohibited on reservations.

Toroweap overlook is located inside the boundaries of Grand Canyon National Park, most of the route is over remote forest and Bureau of Land Management land. Forest rangers in Fredonia and at Jacob Lake are especially knowledgeable about road conditions to Toroweap and can share travel tips.

Just north of Fredonia in neighboring Kanab, Utah, the **Bureau of Land Management** (BLM) operates a district field office (435/644-4600) and the Kanab Visitors Center (435/644-4680, www.blm.gov) for Grand Staircase–Escalante National Monument. Contact the BLM if you plan to spend time exploring Paria Canyon, Buckskin Gulch, or the Vermilion Cliffs.

TOURS
West of GCNP

Havasu Canyon is a delight for swimmers, if you can get a reservation. The canyon's lodge and campgrounds fill up far in advance, especially during the busy summer season. If the eight-mile trail from Hualapai Hilltop to Supai Village sounds intimidating, you have a couple of tour options. First, you can travel on horseback one or both ways ($75–150). Havasupai packers provide saddle and pack horses through the **Tourist Office** (928/448-2121, 928/448-2141, or 928/448-2174). Reservations must be made in advance for one-way or round-trip (overnight) rides. Tribe members also lead horseback tours of the waterfalls ($60), departing from the lodge.

Riders must have some experience, be able to mount and dismount, know how to guide their horses, and be dressed appropriately (jeans, a long-sleeved shirt, and a brimmed hat or cap). Small fanny packs (less than 25 pounds) can be carried, along with a canteen and camera. Arrangements must be made for a pack mule or horse to carry backpacks or larger packs. Riders must weigh 250 pounds or less and be at least four feet, seven inches tall. Children younger than age five can ride with an adult if their combined weight doesn't exceed 250 pounds.

Airwest Helicopters (623/516-2790, 10 A.M.–1 P.M. Thurs.–Fri. and Sun.–Mon. summer, 10 A.M.–1 P.M. Fri. and Sun. winter, from $85 one way) provides transportation from Hualapai Hilltop to Supai Village. Reservations for the helicopter ride aren't necessary, but tribe members have first priority, and wait times can be long during busy periods. Schedules are subject to change depending on the weather and federal or tribe holidays, so it's a good idea to call ahead. (Because of daily use limitations, you'll still need to make a reservation with the tribe to enter the canyon.)

If you'd rather turn over the work of obtaining the various permits and reservations involved in visiting Havasu Canyon to someone else, the **Wildland Trekking Company** (800/715-4453, www.wildlandtrekking.com)

leads 3–4-day mule-assisted trips to Havasu Canyon May–September. Guides are well-versed in natural and cultural history. Some tour packages include a train ride and hike at Grand Canyon National Park's South Rim.

A wide range of tour packages are available for exploring the Hualapai Reservation's rimside **Grand Canyon West** (928/769-2636 or 888/868-9378, www.grandcanyonwest.com). Lodging and meals can be added to any tour. You can book tours directly with the Hualapai Tribe, although several companies in Las Vegas include a visit to Grand Canyon West as part of their tour packages. You can also drive to Grand Canyon West yourself or take a park-and-ride shuttle from Meadview (702/260-6506, $15) to avoid the last 10 miles of bumpy dirt road.

À la carte tours include trail rides on horseback ($35–75) and helicopter tours from the rim to the river ($129–159). Another option is the Skywalk, the glass-bottomed bridge that extends 70 feet from Eagle Point and overhangs the canyon. Prices start at $30 for the Skywalk (not including transportation and reservation entry fee). Advance reservations aren't required for the Skywalk, but it's a good idea to call ahead and have tickets waiting to reduce time spent waiting in line.

Hualapai River Runners (928/769-2636 or 888/868-9378, May–Oct.) guides white-water raft tours that launch from Diamond Creek, the only one-day white-water trip in Grand Canyon. Guides are knowledgeable about Hualapai history and canyon lore. The trip includes a moderate hike to Travertine Falls, snacks, lunch, and a waterproof storage container to hold minimal gear, although if you want to bring a video camera, you should supply your own dry bag. Children must be at least eight years old to participate.

East of GCNP

The Navajo Nation is vast, and most tour companies focus on a specific area, such as Monument Valley or Canyon de Chelly. For a journey with a broader scope, **Navajo Trails** (P.O. Box 1190, Pinon, AZ 86510, 888/862-

9534, http://gonavajotrails.com) offers 1–2-week tours across the reservation, exploring the sacred mountains of the Diné (Navajo), staying with Navajo families and working on community projects, or camping, horseback riding, and hiking in wild areas.

Lees Ferry marks the southern end of 1.2-million-acre **Glen Canyon National Recreation Area** (www.nps.gov/glca). The recreation area's main attraction is Lake Powell and its many waterways. Numerous tours of the lake are available in Page, Arizona, including a six-hour boat trip to Rainbow Bridge National Monument (www.nps.gov/rabr).

One company, **Colorado River Discovery** (130 6th Ave., Page, 888/522-6244, www.raftthecanyon.com) leads smooth-water rafting tours through the 15-mile section of Glen Canyon that hasn't been inundated by the lake. Year-round motorized rafting tours start at Glen Canyon Dam and end at Lees Ferry, a pleasant trip lasting half a day, suitable for children as young as age four. Oar raft tours, available during summer months, spend a day floating between the Glen's beautiful Navajo sandstone cliffs.

North of GCNP

Allen's Guided Tours (Jacob Lake, 435/644-8150 or 435/689-1370, $15–75) leads horseback trips on the Kaibab Plateau, which rises above Grand Canyon. A 1–2-hour trip over gentle forest terrain to a rim overlook is suitable for children. Tours leave several times a day, and no reservations are needed. Longer horseback trips along the Arizona Trail must be booked at least a day in advance and must include four people or more.

DRIVING TOUR
Diamond Creek Road

You can drive to the inner canyon on Indian Road 6, also known as Diamond Creek Road or Peach Springs Canyon Road. The only road from the rim to the river between Lees Ferry and Pearce Ferry, Diamond Creek Road starts at 4,950 feet and leads 20 miles to the river at 1,550 feet, about a two-hour round-trip drive.

Stop at the tourism office at Hualapai Lodge in Peach Springs to get a permit and inquire about current conditions. Most of the route is gravel, which is fine for passenger cars, with some washboard sections. The last mile, however, is another story. From here to the river, the road runs the creek bed. Flash floods are possible, and after a heavy rain, the road can close for days. If you are in a sedan, you can turn around and head back up the canyon or park and hike the last mile to the river. But even if you're in a high-clearance or 4WD vehicle, do not attempt to drive or hike the creek bed if the creek has flooded (i.e., if the water is muddy), or if there is any danger of rain in the vicinity.

Diamond Creek Road starts on the north end of Peach Springs, the Hualapai Nation's capital. After you leave the residential area behind, the road heads across open piñon-juniper woodland. Once you've descended about halfway, the walls of Peach Springs Canyon surround you, desert vegetation takes over, and the scenery becomes more dramatic. You may see feral burros wandering the canyon. As you approach the river, pyramid-shaped Diamond Peak rises up in front of you. Just before the creek crosses the road, you'll come to a small rest area. Park here, or turn around if you're driving a passenger car.

For the last mile, you'll be driving the bed of Diamond Creek to the Colorado River. This is a major takeout point for river runners, who may be unloading from a trip through the canyon. It's also the put-in point for "Diamond Down" trips, so the beach might be bustling with activity. The inner canyon's oldest rocks, Vishnu schist and Zoroaster granite, form the rugged cliffs here in the Lower Granite Gorge. There's a small campground, and a few ramadas offer respite from the desert sun. It's hard to believe today, but the first hotel at Grand Canyon, the Farlee Hotel, was built here in 1884, a few years and a few yards from where explorer Joseph Christmas Ives camped, declaring that his group would "doubtless be the last party of whites to visit this profitless locality."

Sights

The lands beyond the boundaries of Grand Canyon National Park share the park's scenic qualities but offer very different perspectives on the canyon. At Lees Ferry to the east and Lower Granite Gorge to the west, the canyon is a narrow chasm, and you can drive to the Colorado River to fish or watch river runners launching or leaving.

While visiting the reservation lands east and west of the park, you may come to see the canyon in a new light—not just as an awesome sight but also as shelter or touchstone. And a journey through the remote Arizona Strip and Kaibab Plateau can take you back to a time when road travel was truly an adventure. When driving through reservations or in the wide-open spaces north of the park, bring everything you need and fill your car up with gas when you can.

WEST OF GCNP
Havasu Canyon

The Havasupai (People of the Blue-Green Water) live in the heart of Grand Canyon, eight miles below the rim. Their home in Havasu Canyon is inaccessible to vehicles, so visitors must leave cars at the rim. Devastating floods have forced the tribe to close the canyon twice in recent years; check with the tourist office before you begin planning your trip. If you plan to hike in, make reservations for at least two nights at the lodge or campground so you have time to enjoy the idyllic setting. Other options are riding in on horseback or taking a helicopter to the bottom of the canyon.

Spring-fed Havasu Creek contains high amounts of minerals that precipitate, forming travertine basins or pools that reflect the sky. Gorgeous waterfalls tumble over the reddish cliffs into turquoise pools, where the water remains about 70°F year-round. The series of waterfalls begins at the campground and continues four miles along Havasu Creek: **Havasu Falls, Mooney Falls,** and **Beaver Falls.** (Navajo Falls was destroyed by a 2008 flood,

but two new falls were created.) The creek joins the Colorado River about six miles below the campground.

The village of Supai, population 450, is the center of the tribe's historic reservation at the bottom of the canyon. Centuries ago, Havasupai hunters and gatherers roamed vast distances in the canyon and along its rims. (Congress restored some of those traditional lands to the Havasupai in 1975.) Today, tribe members rely on tourism, farming, or wage jobs outside the canyon. All supplies and mail are brought into the canyon by pack animals, by helicopter, or on foot. The village has a clinic, a school, a church, a police station, and a post office as well as the lodge, a general store, and a café. The tourist office houses a small museum.

Trips into Havasu Canyon begin at Hualapai Hilltop, a 61-mile drive from Peach Springs on Indian Road 18. It's about four hours to the trailhead from Grand Canyon Village, so most people spend the night in Peach Springs or camp on Bureau of Land Management land near Hualapai Hilltop in order to get an early start.

Grand Canyon West (Hualapai Reservation)

The Hualapai (People of the Tall Pines) live on the rim of western Grand Canyon on a reservation of about 1 million acres, bordering the canyon for 108 miles. The tribe has developed Grand Canyon West, a tourist area near the Grand Wash Cliffs, which mark the end of Grand Canyon and beginning of Lake Mead. If you like wide-open spaces, this is for you: The population includes only 2,300 people on more than 1 million acres, encompassing grassland, desert, piñon-juniper woodland, tall pine forest, and rugged tributary canyons of the Colorado River. Historically known for their trading skills, the Hualapai today focus on tourism, cattle-ranching, and timber sales.

Many people prefer the canyon views offered

CONDORS AT THE CANYON

Imagine Grand Canyon during the last ice age, 50,000 years ago. The climate was cooler and moister. The rim forests extended deep into the canyon. Mammoths and ground sloths grazed on grassy plateaus. California condors flew overhead, scanning the area for a meal, the carcasses of fallen Pleistocene megafauna.

As northern glaciers receded, the continent warmed up and dried out. Climate change, as well as a new species, the Paleo-Indian hunters who entered North America toward the end of the last ice age, decimated the populations of mammoths and other megafauna. With the loss of their food source, condor numbers also dwindled. Once condors ranged across North America from Mexico to Canada, but by the time of the Spanish Entrada, they lived only along the Pacific Coast.

As California was settled by gold miners and pioneers, condors were hunted for their feathers or for sport. The last reported nesting site in Arizona was near Lees Ferry in the 1890s, and the last sighting was in 1924. In California, the condor population continued to plummet. The large ranges condors need for scavenging were broken by power lines and other hazards. Use of the pesticide DDT weakened eggshells, and new fledglings became increasingly rare. A common cause of death continues to be lead poisoning, which occurs when condors eat carcasses riddled with lead shot. By 1985, only nine birds remained in the wild.

In 1987, biologists decided to capture the remaining condor population and focus on captive breeding programs, a task that required patience. Condors don't reach breeding age until they're six years old, and a pair may produce only one egg every year or two.

Biologists released breeding pairs back into the wild in sanctuaries in Central California in 1992, where about 20 condors fly today. In 1996, six juvenile condors were outfitted with radio transmitters and identification tags and transported to an acclimation pen on top of the Vermilion Cliffs near Lees Ferry. When released, they became the first condors to fly over Arizona in 70 years.

The condors adjusted to life in the wild, learning its hazards, but eagles have killed at least three. One died when it flew into a power line, and another was shot and killed. Several have died after ingesting lead shot. (The Arizona Game and Fish Department now offers hunters coupons for nonlead ammunition.) The first successful nesting occurred in 2003, when a young condor hatched and fledged. Sadly, the young bird died in Grand Canyon in 2006, probably from starvation. Condors continue to be released into the wild, and two more young hatched and fledged in 2004 and 2005.

The condor population has now climbed to 300 captive and wild birds, with around 60 plying the skies over Northern Arizona. A condor can fly more than 100 miles in a single day in search of food. The birds are curious, often spotted investigating a campsite or gazing into the windows of Hermits Rest and Lookout Studio. They sometimes perch or soar near overlooks. Much larger than ravens, condors have a wingspan of up to nine feet, and when flying, their leading edge is white. If you see a condor during your canyon visit, make note of the tag number and report the sighting to a ranger.

NPS PHOTO BY MARK LELLOUCH

by the overlooks at Grand Canyon West to those in the national park. Although this section of the canyon doesn't have the temples and monuments of central Grand Canyon, the sheer walls and steep drops to the river are impressive. No protective barriers separate you from the views, and you won't have to share them with as many people. Grand Canyon West hosts about 3,000 visitors a month, while the South Rim's Grand Canyon Village handles about 10,000 a day.

If you're traveling to Grand Canyon West from Las Vegas, you'll be driving on the paved **Pearce Ferry Road,** a scenic trip through the Mojave Desert, where you'll see plenty of the iconic Joshua Trees. The last 14 miles of the journey are over the rough and dusty Diamond Bar Road. If you prefer not to drive your own vehicle, you can take a shuttle the rest of the way. If you're driving from Peach Springs, the partially paved Buck and Doe Road (IR 1) leads 50 miles to Grand Canyon West. Traveling unpaved reservation roads requires a permit ($16 per day).

Grand Canyon West is lightly developed, with three main overlooks. During the 1950s, **Guano Point** was part of a fertilizer operation. A short hike leads down to the site of a cable crossing, where dung from the "bat cave" across the canyon was delivered. From the point, you can see a long stretch of the Colorado River. The tribe serves meals at the very rim, usually as part of a bus tour. The bus tour doesn't include **Quartermaster Point,** but if you're visiting in your own vehicle, you can drive the short road that leads to the overlook. Another overlook, **Eagle Point,** is home to the Grand Canyon Skywalk. From here you can see the cliff walls that suggested the point's name: a ridge that resembles a large bird with its wings spread wide.

Grand Canyon Skywalk

From Eagle Point, the 70-foot-long Skywalk juts 25 feet beyond the rim, more than 3,000 feet above the canyon floor. Construction of this ambitious—and controversial—project was completed in 2007 at a cost of $30 million.

A Las Vegas architectural firm designed the cantilevered Skywalk. It looks graceful, even delicate, from the side, but it's built to withstand the weight of 71 loaded Boeing 747 jets, or the force of a magnitude 8.0 earthquake within 50 miles. Even so, many visitors feel compelled to hold onto the Skywalk's railings as they make the dizzying walk over the chasm below. The floor's crystal-clear surface is made from five layers of glass that provide support; the topmost layer can be replaced if it becomes clouded from scuffmarks or scratches.

To protect the glass surface of the floor from scratches, you'll be asked to rent protective booties and check all personal items, including cameras, before you proceed onto the Skywalk. Admission is $30 (in addition to travel permits and entry fees), though you can view the Skywalk from the side and photograph it without paying the admission fee. The tribe offers tour packages that include the Skywalk. If you travel on your own, be aware that by the time you pay all permit and entry fees, a walk on the Skywalk will cost close to $100.

Near the Skywalk, an Indian Village attraction replicates traditional dwellings of various tribes. The amphitheater here hosts demonstrations and performances. Also nearby is Hualapai Ranch, where you can sign up for a trail ride or watch a gunfight reenactment. Future plans for Eagle Point include a large visitors center.

Peach Springs

Once a bustling Route 66 tourist hub, Peach Springs is the Hualapai Nation capital and home to about 600 people. Though well past its glory days, tiny Peach Springs is a convenient staging area for a trip to Grand Canyon West or Havasu Canyon. The tribe owns and operates Hualapai Lodge, where tour information is readily available. The tourism bureau inside the lodge also sells the permits required for driving on reservation roads. If you're looking for adventure, you can get a permit to drive the **Diamond Creek Road,** a 20-mile journey to the bottom of Grand Canyon.

A trip to Peach Springs means an opportunity

to get your kicks on **Route 66,** the American West's most celebrated highway. If you're traveling from Flagstaff or Williams, take I-40 west to Seligman, turning north on Route 66 for 28 miles. If you're arriving from the west, you can exit I-40 in Kingman and take Route 66 to Peach Springs, traveling over 45 miles of the longest remaining stretch of the Mother Road. The only gas station in Peach Springs is a derelict leftover from the heyday of Route 66, so be sure to fill up your tank en route.

EAST OF GCNP
Cameron Trading Post

Between Flagstaff and Page, the Navajo Reservation town of Cameron acts as a gateway to the East Rim of Grand Canyon, 30 miles away. The historic trading post is a convenient stop for travelers heading for the canyon, Lake Powell, the Painted Desert, or the Hopi Reservation. If you have only a day or a few hours to add to your canyon visit, and you want to experience regional Indian cultures, plan to enter the canyon via the East Entrance and spend some time on the Navajo Reservation in the Cameron area.

Hubert and C. D. Richardson established a trading post near this crossing along the Little Colorado River in 1916. In the 1930s, the Grand Canyon Hotel welcomed visitors here. A new motel was built nearby, and now the old hotel houses the trading post's gallery, where you'll find museum-quality artifacts and items crafted by artisans from various U.S. tribes.

Cameron Suspension Bridge

Next to the trading post, a historic suspension bridge crosses the Little Colorado River at the Navajo Nation town of Cameron. The bridge was named for Ralph Cameron, Arizona's territorial senator, the same man who became a thorn in the side of the Santa Fe Railway at Grand Canyon. Navajo government is organized around "chapters," or settlements, and the name for the Cameron chapter is *Na ni' ah' hasani,* which translates as "old structure across," in reference to the bridge. Built in 1911, the Cameron bridge is now listed on the

© KATHLEEN BRYANT

Historic Cameron Trading Post sits along the Little Colorado River.

National Register of Historic Places. Once used by automobiles and herds of sheep, the 660-foot bridge closed to all traffic in 1958. On a summer evening, it's pleasant to walk along the edge of the gorge for different perspectives of the bridge.

◖ Little Colorado River Gorge

Steep walls of Kaibab limestone and Coconino sandstone confine the Little Colorado River, dubbed the LCR or "Little C," to a narrow gorge on its final run to the Grand Canyon, where it joins the Colorado River. The LCR starts in Arizona's White Mountains and travels 315 miles to the Grand Canyon, reaching the Colorado River 61 miles downstream from Lees Ferry. During the LCR's final 30 miles to Grand Canyon, it drops 2,000 feet before joining the Colorado River. The LCR drains the Painted Desert area to the northeast but dwindles to a trickle during dry periods. Mineralized springs farther downstream create travertine, giving the Little C its turquoise hue before it reaches the confluence. About 10 miles west of the Cameron junction, Highway 64 passes two overlooks into the gorge. The Little Colorado River Gorge is a Navajo Nation Tribal Park, and the tribe charges a small entry fee to stop at the overlooks. Ramadas provide shade during summer, and there are picnic tables and toilets. A couple of rugged trails explore this area, prone to flash flooding and recommended for experienced canyon hikers only. For more information about current conditions and a permit (necessary for hiking on Navajo land), stop at the Cameron Visitors Center.

The Painted Desert

Those who head for Grand Canyon National Park's East Entrance via U.S. 89 will get a peek of the Painted Desert's southwestern edge near Cameron. Erosion gently rounds the colorful Chinle Formation into soft hills of purples and browns, and turns the dark red Moenkopi sandstone into strange shapes. For a short but scenic side trip, continue north past Cameron to the junction with Highway 160, about 15 miles. Turn right and follow the highway northeast. As the highway climbs toward Tuba City, you'll gain a fine overlook of the Painted Desert, which stretches eastward more than 90,000 acres from Grand Canyon to Petrified Forest National Monument. Warning: Once you head down this road, it will be hard to turn back. You can continue even farther to Tuba City's historic trading post and the villages atop the Hopi Mesas.

Echo Cliffs

If you travel U.S. 89 north of Cameron toward Lees Ferry or Page, you'll be driving alongside the colorful Echo Cliffs, a monocline of Triassic and Jurassic rock layers. During the late 1800s, the Honeymoon Trail passed along the base of the cliffs, a wagon route for settlers from St. George, Utah, to Mormon colonies in northeastern Arizona. A trading post was established below a break in the cliffs at **The Gap** (89 miles north of Flagstaff on U.S. 89, 928/283-8932, 7 A.M.–9 P.M. daily) around 1880. This area became known for pictorial rugs showing scenes from reservation life. The present building, erected in 1937 after a fire destroyed an earlier post, is an interesting place to stop and mail a postcard or stretch your legs. The Gap trading post still serves locals, though trading posts no longer play a key role on the reservation. During the late 1800s and early 1900s, trading posts provided necessary supplies, offered a marketplace for crafts, and acted as a social hub. Today, when it's easy to zip along paved roads to Flagstaff's shopping centers, many trading posts have been reduced to convenience marts, and some have faded away altogether.

Navajo Bridge

In order to accommodate growing automobile traffic, construction began on Navajo Bridge (then called Grand Canyon Bridge) in 1927. Four miles upstream, the ferry took cars across the river until it sank in 1928, leaving travelers to drive 800 miles around canyons and cliffs from Utah and the Arizona Strip to the rest of the state. When the bridge opened in June 1929, it was the highest steel arch bridge in the world, drawing nearly 7,000 people to this remote corner of the state for the opening celebration. Because Prohibition was in effect, the bridge was christened with a bottle of ginger ale.

In 1995, a new span was built alongside the narrow historic bridge—its mirror in appearance, though more than twice as wide and designed to carry heavier loads. The historic bridge continues its service as a pedestrian crossing, and from its center you can peer 467 feet to the waters of the Colorado River, watching as river runners float past far below. The bridge is their last view of civilization until they reach Phantom Ranch, 84 miles downriver. Keep your eyes open for the **California condor** that likes to hang out on the steel supports underneath the bridge.

On the Navajo Reservation side of the bridge, vendors sell jewelry and other crafts. On the other side, the **Navajo Bridge Interpretive Center** (928/355-2319, 9 A.M.–5 P.M. daily mid-Apr.–Oct., 10 A.M.–4 P.M. Sat.–Sun. early Apr. and Nov.) has a bookstore, restrooms, and outdoor exhibits honoring early canyon river expeditions.

Lees Ferry

All white-water rafting trips through Grand Canyon put in at Lees Ferry, the former outpost of John D. Lee, a Mormon pioneer who was involved in the Mountain Meadow Massacre of 1857. Brigham Young ordered Lee to this lonely spot, called Lonely Dell, so he could avoid prosecution for his part in the incident. (It worked, but only for awhile—Lee was arrested in 1874 and executed in 1877, though many believe he was merely a scapegoat.) Lee established a ranch on the Paria River, 0.5 miles above its confluence with the Colorado. The 17th of Lee's 19 wives, Emma, operated the ferry after his death. Short hikes lead to historic ranch buildings, ferry workings, and traces of a placer gold-mining operation.

Today, Lees Ferry is a boat launch and popular fly-fishing area, with an adjacent campground and ranger station. The nearest "town" is Marble Canyon (pop. 250), a small scattering of motels and restaurants a few miles west along U.S. 89A. Here you can find gas, limited groceries, and plenty of fishing gear.

Glen Canyon

Most of Glen Canyon, which John Wesley Powell named in 1869, lies under the waters of Lake Powell. If you have your own boat, you can motor up from Lees Ferry to explore the remaining 15-mile stretch of Glen Canyon below the dam. If not, you can take a tour from the bridge downriver. Beautiful cliffs of Navajo sandstone rise up on either side of the Colorado River. Among the highlights is a cliff face on river left, with archaic and Ancestral Puebloan petroglyphs depicting bighorn sheep and rectangular humanlike figures. This peaceful 15-mile float is a great trip for birders in winter months, when there are fewer boaters and migrant waterfowl shelter in the canyon. As many as 19 species have been reported wintering in the area, with a density of 136 ducks per mile.

Marble Platform

The Colorado River cuts sharply through the rock layers of the Marble Platform to create **Marble Canyon,** bounded by the Navajo Reservation on the east and Bureau of Land Management (BLM) and U.S. Forest Service land on the west. Dispersed camping is allowed in most areas managed by the Forest Service or BLM; however, if you hike below the canyon rim, you'll be crossing into Grand Canyon National Park, where permits are required for overnight stays.

Many people consider Marble Canyon, with its colorful Permian Age cliffs, to be the loveliest section of Grand Canyon. Dirt roads stretch across the Marble Platform and **House Rock Valley** to remote Marble Canyon overlooks, including Triple Arches and Buck Farm.

Tributary canyons cut across the Marble Platform to the Colorado River, and several can be explored by canyoneering, including Soap Creek, Rider, and South Canyons. Canyoneering combines climbing, boulder-hopping, hiking, and wading or swimming in order to descend canyon routes. Do your

ROBERT BREWSTER STANTON

© KATHLEEN BRYANT

Point Hansbrough, from the Saddle Mountain Wilderness

We were not exploring the Grand Canyon, nor seeking adventure in it, nor looking for anything except that railroad line. Therefore I think it out of place to speak even of the somewhat startling adventures that we did meet with which resulted in the death, by drowning, of three of my companions, and the maiming of a fourth. . . .

So begins the tale of Grand Canyon's second river expedition, led by railroad engineer Robert Brewster Stanton. Though the very idea seems ridiculous today, Stanton believed that the canyon bottom might prove a suitable rail route, and in 1889, he and 15 others set out to survey the canyon on behalf of the Denver, Colorado, Canyon and Pacific Railroad. Company president Frank Brown, a Denver businessman, led the expedition. What Stanton first thought of as "an ordinary railway survey" became a harrowing ordeal.

They launched from Green River, Utah, in May 1889. To save weight, Brown had equipped the expedition with six lightweight boats and deliberately excluded lifejackets. By the time they reached Lees Ferry, only three boats remained. Brown, Peter Hansbrough, and Henry Richards drowned a few miles downriver from Lees Ferry in Marble Canyon. Stanton and the rest of the crew stashed their gear in a cave in the Redwall and climbed out via South Canyon.

In December, Stanton led a second attempt, this time equipped with life jackets. The expedition ran into bad luck once more in Marble Canyon, when their photographer fell from a cliff and broke his leg. Again, Stanton and his men hiked out of the canyon, carrying the injured man, but this time they returned to complete the journey. Stanton finished photographing the expedition himself, and they reached the Gulf of California in April 1890.

Though he gave up the idea of a railroad, Stanton never gave up on Grand Canyon. He returned to the area at the end of the 19th

century, this time determined to dredge gold from the Colorado River in Glen Canyon. The venture failed dismally. It cost investors of the Hoskaninni Mining Company more than $100,000 to transport the 180-ton dredge to Glen Canyon, and it was abandoned only months after its trial run in 1901. The behemoth still skulks beneath the waters of Lake Powell near Bullfrog Marina.

But Stanton's interest in the canyon went far beyond profit-driven dreams. Although he left canyon country after the failure of the Hoskaninni mining venture, working in Canada, Mexico, Cuba, and the East Indies, he tirelessly researched the canyon, writing a voluminous manuscript that he tried unsuccessfully to publish. His research drew him into the debate over whether prospector James White was the first nonnative to float down Grand Canyon, eight years before Powell's expedition. Stanton argued against White's case in *Colorado River Controversies,* published in 1932, which was 10 years after his death from pneumonia in 1922. The story of his own canyon expedition would wait even longer. *Down the Colorado* was finally published in 1965, more than half a century after Stanton's journey. It remains one of the most gripping accounts of canyon exploration.

research first: Some routes require technical climbs or rappels, many do not have water sources, and all are subject to flash floods.

◖ Vermilion Cliffs

Two of the Southwest's premier canyoneering adventures lie within the 112,500-acre **Paria Canyon-Vermilion Cliffs Wilderness Area,** administered by the BLM (www.blm.gov/az). Those who wish to explore the slot canyons of the Paria River or Buckskin Gulch usually start north of the Vermilion Cliffs, and permits are necessary for these multiday adventures. For more information, contact the Arizona Strip Interpretive Association (www.azstrip. org, 435/688-3246), the BLM's Kanab field office (435/644-4600, www.blm.gov), or the Kanab Visitors Center (435/644-4680, www. blm.gov) for **Grand Staircase-Escalante National Monument.**

Permits aren't necessary to spend a couple of hours exploring the base of the Vermilion Cliffs. Rising 1,000 feet above House Rock Valley, the cliffs are part of the geological Grand Staircase that descends from Zion National Park to Grand Canyon. You can begin a hike almost anywhere off U.S. 89A, walking below the Vermilion Cliffs' gorgeously banded Triassic and Jurassic layers, where springs and seeps nurture small oases. Here and there, large blocks of Shinarump conglomerate have fallen to the valley floor, sometimes supported by small pedestals of mudstone.

As you explore the base of the cliffs, remember to scan the skies above. Six **California condors** were released from the top of the Vermilion Cliffs in 1996, the first time in 72 years that the large birds had flown freely over Northern Arizona. Additional releases since have led to a current population of around 60 birds, and several individuals continue to soar over the Marble Canyon area.

Domínguez-Escalante Historical Marker

Along U.S. 89A near milepost 557, a historical marker commemorates the Domínguez-Escalante expedition of 1776. The two priests

© KATHLEEN BRYANT

The Vermilion Cliffs mark the edge of the Marble Platform.

crossed the Colorado River near Lees Ferry before returning to Santa Fe, New Mexico. They failed in their attempt to establish a trail between Santa Fe and missions in California, but their journals include some of the earliest written descriptions of the Southwest's canyon country. Nearby, a dirt road leads two miles north to springs at the base of the Vermilion Cliffs, where another of John D. Lee's families lived.

Buffalo Ranch

You can watch free-range buffalo at the 60,000-acre House Rock Ranch, 20 miles south of U.S. 89A. Charles Jesse "Buffalo" Jones and "Uncle" Jim Owens brought a herd of buffalo to the Kaibab Plateau after the Grand Canyon Game Preserve was established in 1906. Jones convinced backers to invest in his "cattalo" venture, breeding bison with cattle, an experiment that failed (though you may see cattalo wandering the Kaibab Plateau even today). Jones sold his bison to the State of Arizona in the 1920s, and the herd was relocated to the ranch, where 75–100 offspring graze on shrubby grassland under permit from the Kaibab National Forest. To get to the ranch, go south on Forest Road 8910 for 19 miles. Turn east at Forest Road 632 and take it the last two miles to ranch headquarters.

NORTH OF GCNP
🄲 Kaibab Plateau

John Wesley Powell gave the Kaibab Plateau its name from a Paiute word meaning "mountain lying down." The plateau is 8,000–9,000 feet high, and its rolling meadows and forests end at the faulted, eroded cliffs of the North Rim. High peninsulas of land extend like fingers toward the canyon, and forest roads and trails lead to the tips, where undeveloped viewpoints give visitors a sense of discovery. The plateau has the largest stand of old-growth ponderosas in the southwest and the highest density of the endangered northern goshawk. It's also home to the Kaibab squirrel, an endemic species found nowhere else.

To get to the national park's developed Bright Angel Point, you will cross the heart of the Kaibab Plateau on paved, scenic Highway

67. Though remote, the rest of the plateau is easily accessed by a network of forest roads that range from good gravel roads suitable for passenger cars to rocky two-tracks that can pose challenges for a high-clearance 4WD vehicle. Administered by the Kaibab National Forest, the plateau doesn't have the amenities of the national park—nor the restrictions. Here, you can hike with your dog or camp at large, and you can bike almost anywhere outside of designated wilderness areas.

The **Saddle Mountain Wilderness Area** bridges the east side of the plateau and the lower elevations of House Rock Valley. Though winter snows usually close Highway 67, determined hikers can reach the plateau on foot trails that start in the lower elevations and climb to the plateau's east rim, such as the **Nankoweap** or **North Canyon Trails.** From the East Rim Viewpoint off Forest Road 611, you can access trails and peer into the roadless 40,610-acre Saddle Mountain Wilderness.

The Kaibab Plateau's western reaches border the 68,596-acre **Kanab Creek Wilderness Area,** which straddles Forest Service and Bureau of Land Management land and edges Grand Canyon National Park. The **Jumpup-Nail Trail** leads from the Kaibab Plateau into this wilderness, which protects one of the Southwest's most complex canyon systems.

Crazy Jug Viewpoint has one of the best views of the canyon's vast Tapeats Amphitheater, with Steamboat Mountain, the Powell Plateau, and other landforms as backdrops. The point, about 55 miles south of Fredonia, can be accessed by passenger cars when roads are dry, traveling Forest Roads 22, 425, and 292.

Just east, five scenic viewpoints—Parissawampitts, Fence, Locust, North Timp, and Timp—are linked by the 18-mile-long **Rainbow Rim Trail.** Each offers a different perspective, and they are best accessed in a high-clearance vehicle. Check current road conditions at the Fredonia ranger station (928/643-7395) or Kaibab Plateau Visitors Center (928/643-7298) before setting out on forest roads, and be sure to take a current map, as road access can change.

Recreation

With a few exceptions, trails outside the boundaries of the national park start and end in remote locations. Be sure to pack everything you need for your hike, and let someone know your itinerary. Choices range from strenuous rim-to-river hikes to shady rim or plateau trails to explorations in tributary canyons. Some hikes connect with National Park Service trails. If you are connecting to a trail inside the park and plan to spend the night within park boundaries, you must get a backcountry permit. Permits are also needed to hike on reservation lands and for certain areas within the Paria Canyon–Vermilion Cliffs Wilderness Area.

HIKING WEST OF GCNP

Contact tribe tourism offices for permits if you plan to hike or camp on Hualapai (928/769-2636 or 888/868-9378) or Havasupai (928/448-2121, 928/448-2141, or 928/448-2174) land.

◖ Havasu Canyon Trail

- Distance: 16 miles round-trip to Supai Village
- Duration: 2 days
- Elevation loss: 2,500 feet
- Effort: Strenuous
- Trailhead: Hualapai Hilltop

All visitors must have reservations before entering the canyon. Be aware that a reservation is no guarantee that you'll be able to complete your hike; Havasu Canyon closed to visitors in 2008 and again in 2010 due to flooding. The trailhead is about four hours' drive from Grand Canyon Village or an hour from Peach Springs. Take I-40 west from Williams to Seligman, turning north on Route 66 for 28 miles. Turn right on Indian Highway 18, a paved road leading northeast for 61 miles to the parking area at Hualapai Hilltop. There's a pit toilet here but no water. It may be remote, but this is a busy staging area, with helicopters and mule trains

leaving daily. The hours of advance planning and travel will melt away when you reach the Eden waiting for you at trail's end.

The trail descends steep switchbacks through Toroweap Formation and Coconino sandstone before becoming a more gradual descent through brick-red Hermit Shale. At 1.5 miles, the trail enters Hualapai Wash, prone to flash floods after rains. At six miles, the wash joins Havasu Canyon and the perennial waters of Havasu Creek. You'll shortly come to a fork. Go left for Supai Village. (The right fork leads to Havasu Spring, and the tribe asks that visitors not travel here unless they are with a Havasupai guide.)

Not long after the fork, you'll be able to see the creek. The trail crosses a bridge and enters the village. Proceed to the tourist center to pay the remainder of your fees, unless you are staying at the lodge. The campground is two miles past the village. En route, you'll pass Supai Falls, which is hidden by lush vegetation, though you can hear it. From the campground, it's a short distance to the beautiful Havasu and Mooney waterfalls.

Experienced hikers who've planned an extra night in the canyon can hire a guide to hike the challenging route around Mooney Falls to Beaver Falls (4 miles) or the Colorado River (6 miles).

HIKING EAST OF GCNP

The lands east of the park, especially around the Marble Platform and Vermilion Cliffs, are prone to flash floods. If you're hiking and exploring area canyons, avoid the summer monsoon season, July–mid-September. A storm cell miles away can create flash-flood conditions. No matter what the season, check the forecast before you leave. Always be aware of current conditions: In 2010, several destructive floods ripped through Paria Canyon, damaging campsites and dumping obstacles like trees and boulders in the river channel.

River Trail

- Distance: 1.2 miles round-trip
- Duration: 45 minutes
- Elevation gain: Minimal
- Effort: Easy
- Trailhead: Lees Ferry at launch ramp parking area

This gentle stroll leads upriver a short distance from the parking area, a walk through historic ferry and mining operations. The trail follows an old wagon road that begins at Lees Fort. It was built in 1874, when tensions with the local Navajo increased. The building, still intact, served over the years as a trading post, a residence, a school, and a miners' mess hall. Less than 0.5 miles up the trail, the submerged wreck of the *Charles H. Spencer* lies along the river's north bank, brought here in pieces from San Francisco in 1911 to carry coal from Warm Creek, 28 miles upriver, to a short-lived placer-gold mining operation at Lees Ferry. Unfortunately, the paddlewheel steamer needed as much coal to get to Warm Creek as she could carry back to Lees Ferry, so

she was abandoned after only a few runs. Not far from the wreck, the Spencer Trail leads up the rocky cliffs. The River Trail continues to the ruins of a way station once used by ferry travelers. Look across the river to see cables, the ferry landing, and the old road, built by Robert Brewster Stanton in 1899 after his expedition through Grand Canyon.

Spencer Trail

- Distance: 4.4 miles round-trip
- Duration: 2–3 hours
- Elevation gain: 1,700 feet
- Effort: Difficult
- Trailhead: Lees Ferry at River Trail

Spring and fall are the best times to hike this trail, which leads up an exposed talus slope to the Vermilion Cliffs, for outstanding views of the Colorado River and surrounding desert. The trail is named for Charles Spencer, the head of the short-lived placer-mining operation that attempted to extract gold from the soft gray hills of Chinle shale at Lees Ferry. Spencer built the trail to transport coal from

A hiker pauses on the Spencer Trail to look down at Lees Ferry.

© TOM GRUNDY/123RF.COM

Warm Creek to the mining site, a feat later undertaken by the steamer submerged about 0.7 miles upriver from the parking lot. The final climb to the top of the cliffs is steep but well worth the effort: From the top, you can see north to Page and Lake Powell. Marble Canyon is a shadowy gash across the Marble Platform. If you make the hike in late spring or early fall (it's too hot in summer), you'll have a hawk's-eye view of river runners scrambling to load up before departing from Lees Ferry.

Cathedral Wash

- Distance: 2.5 miles round-trip
- Duration: 1–2 hours
- Elevation gain: 300 feet
- Effort: Moderate
- Trailhead: Along Lees Ferry access road

To reach the trailhead, drive 1.3 miles from the junction of U.S. 89A and the access road leading to Lees Ferry, where there's a large pullout. Park here and descend into the wash, located on the right side of the road. Head for the river, though you may want to explore farther up the wash on your return. Do not attempt this trail if regional rain is a possibility, as the wash is susceptible to flash flooding. The Kaibab limestone walls hold fossils, and water has carved interesting shapes and formations. The hike offers a mild introduction to the sport of canyoneering. The trail follows the bed of the wash, requiring some scrambling around and over chockstones or down pour-overs, and there's even a section of limestone narrows. The wash opens up at Cathedral Wash Rapids, about three miles below Lees Ferry.

Lonely Dell Trail

- Distance: 1 mile round-trip
- Duration: Less than 1 hour
- Elevation gain: Minimal
- Effort: Easy
- Trailhead: Parking lot at Lees Ferry

This easy walk explores the historic buildings,

now in ruins, constructed by John D. Lee and others who worked the ferry, which was used until shortly before Navajo Bridge was completed in 1929. The trail follows an old road that leads to Lonely Dell Ranch, where Lee brought two of his families to live in 1871. Emma (one of Lee's 19 wives) is said to have exclaimed, "Oh, what a lonely dell," when she saw her new home at the mouth of Paria Canyon. A booklet describing the area's historic buildings is available for $1 at the kiosk. Historic remains include a log cabin, a stone house, an orchard, and a cemetery. There are picnic tables and shade but no water, so be sure to bring some with you.

Paria Canyon

- Distance: Up to 47 miles one-way
- Duration: Multiday backpacking trip
- Elevation gain: 1,300 feet
- Effort: Difficult
- Trailhead: Multiple

To hike the length of Paria Canyon, which many consider the finest narrow-canyon hike on the Colorado Plateau, you'll need to plan ahead and get a permit from the Bureau of Land Management. The best times to hike the Paria are spring and fall, before or after the summer monsoon. Most backpackers start upcanyon and hike down to Lees Ferry. Trailhead options include Buckskin Gulch, Wire Pass, and White House (all in Utah). Trailheads are relatively remote, so it's wise to leave your car at Lees Ferry and arrange for a shuttle to reach the trailhead. Booklets describing the hike are available from the **Arizona Strip Interpretive Association** (345 E. Riverside Dr., St. George, UT 84790, 435/688-3246). The association can also provide information on shuttle services. Shuttle arrangements must be made in advance; don't expect to get a cell phone signal in this area.

No permit is required to explore a couple of miles up Paria Canyon on a day hike from Lees Ferry. To get here, take the trail past Lonely Dell Ranch. Once you reach the mouth of the

BEYOND THE BOUNDARIES

Paria, there is no actual trail; you'll be following the bed of the canyon. Depending on how far you hike, you may see the ruins of other ranches, petroglyphs, or even a bighorn sheep.

Saddle Mountain Trail (#31)

- Distance: 12 miles round-trip
- Duration: 4–6 hours
- Elevation gain: 640 feet
- Effort: Moderate
- Trailhead: Intersects with the Nankoweap Trail in House Rock Valley

To reach the trailhead, take U.S. 89A (from Jacob Lake or Marble Canyon) to Buffalo Ranch Road (Forest Rd. 445). Follow the road south 25 miles to Forest Road 445G. Take 445G west (right) to the end of the road, about five miles. Take the Nankoweap Trail (Forest Trail #57) for one mile to the intersection with the Saddle Mountain Trail (Forest Trail #31).

The Saddle Mountain Trail traverses a bench overlooking Marble Canyon, with the gorgeous Vermilion Cliffs and Kaibab Plateau as backdrops. The trail fades before it reaches the rim, but it's easy to walk through the open piñon-juniper woodland, approaching the canyon rim for dramatic views of the Colorado River cutting through steep-walled Marble Canyon.

Nankoweap Trail (#57)

- Distance: 8 miles round-trip
- Duration: 3–6 hours, depending on destination
- Elevation gain: 2,320 feet
- Effort: Difficult
- Trailhead: Forest Road 445 in House Rock Valley or Forest Road 610 on the Kaibab Plateau

Forest Service Trail #57 is usually used as a connector route for backpackers attempting the Nankoweap Trail in Grand Canyon National Park. It can also be used by cross-country skiers who want to access the Kaibab Plateau after winter snows have closed Highway 67. The

higher Kaibab Plateau trailhead, snow-covered and inaccessible November–May, is reached from Highway 67 south of Jacob Lake. The lower elevation trailhead begins at the end of the House Rock Valley's Buffalo Ranch Road. Either trailhead takes about 1.5–2 hours to reach from Jacob Lake, and if the roads are dry, they are suitable for passenger cars.

About a mile up from the House Rock Valley trailhead, the trail intersects with the Saddle Mountain Trail (#31). Continue on the Nankoweap Trail (#57), cutting through the Saddle Mountain Wilderness. Sections of the steep and narrow trail are difficult to follow, especially as you near the Kaibab Plateau, where postfire growth includes shrubby locust and aspen. At about 2.5 miles, you'll come to Nankoweap Saddle, where you can view the network of washes and smaller canyons that drain into Marble Canyon. At the saddle, the Forest Service's Nankoweap Trail intersects with the National Park's Nankoweap Trail, which drops south toward Nankoweap Canyon. If you stay on Trail #57, it's another 1.5 miles to the Kaibab Plateau trailhead.

Triple Alcoves Trail

- Distance: 1 mile round-trip
- Duration: Less than 1 hour
- Elevation gain: 250 feet
- Effort: Easy
- Trailhead: Forest Road 8910 in House Rock Valley

More of an overlook than a trail, this easy walk is accessed by a 30-mile drive on unpaved Forest Road 8910, which heads south from U.S. 89A in House Rock Valley, between the Marble Canyon motels and Jacob Lake. If the road is dry, passenger cars can manage it. Take Forest Road 8910 south 23.5 miles to a fork, turning right and driving another seven miles to the trailhead. The road may be washboardy in places, so allow plenty of time for the drive and to enjoy the awe-inspiring views of the Vermilion Cliffs en route.

The Triple Alcoves Trail leads 0.5 miles

through piñon-juniper woodland to the rim of Marble Canyon. Be sure to bring binoculars to spot Harding Rapids below and the Triple Alcoves near the mouth of Saddle Canyon. Navajo lands rim the canyon's other side. The river loops around Point Hansbrough, an entrenched meander named for the crew member who drowned here while on Stanton's ill-fated 1889 expedition.

HIKING NORTH OF GCNP

On the Kaibab Plateau, heavy snows close roads November–mid-May, and muddy roads can persist into June. Elevation changes can mean sudden shifts in the weather, so be prepared. If you're hiking in the Saddle Mountain or Kanab Creek Wilderness Areas, a good topographical map is a must. Plan backpacking trips carefully, researching water availability and trail conditions in advance. Let someone know your itinerary before you set out, and share your wilderness experience with hiking companions. Always be alert for flash floods when hiking canyon areas, especially during the summer monsoon.

East Rim Trail (#7)

- Distance: 3 miles round-trip
- Duration: 2–3 hours
- Elevation gain: 1,000 feet
- Effort: Difficult
- Trailhead: East Rim Overlook off Forest Road 611 (Kaibab Plateau)

This Saddle Mountain Wilderness trail is used most often to link to the upper section of the North Canyon Trail (#4). The trailhead is about an hour's drive south of Jacob Lake, suitable for passenger cars in dry weather. Take Highway 67 south 26.5 miles to Forest Road 611, turning left (east). Continue on Forest Road 611 for 2.6 miles to the East Rim Viewpoint. There's parking and a restroom here, but no overnight camping is allowed. The trail descends sharply from the rim, passing through thickets of oak and conifer forests, before ending at the North Canyon Trail. Views of House Rock Valley and

Marble Canyon disappear behind a forest of aspen, bigtooth maple, and ponderosa pine. This trail is accessible only late spring–early fall, when Highway 67 is open.

North Canyon Trail (#4)

- Distance: 14 miles round-trip
- Duration: 10 hours
- Elevation gain: 2,670 feet
- Effort: Difficult
- Trailhead: Forest Road 611 (Kaibab Plateau) or Forest Road 631 (House Rock Valley)

The North Canyon Trail cuts across the Saddle Mountain Wilderness from House Rock Valley to the Kaibab Plateau, connecting with the East Rim Trail (#7). The trail can be accessed at either end, but you'll need a high-clearance vehicle to reach the lower trailhead, which is about two hours from Jacob Lake. From the Kaibab Plateau, take Highway 67 south of Jacob Lake to Forest Road 611, an hour's drive suitable for passenger cars in dry weather. The trailhead is near the wilderness boundary. From U.S. 89A, take the House Rock Valley Road (Forest Rd. 8910) south to Forest Road 631, turning right. The trailhead is located where Forest Road 631 begins to climb out of North Canyon Wash. The trail will loop south a short distance before entering the wash and climbing toward the Kaibab Plateau. In the upper canyon, a perennial stream waters conifer and oak as well as flowers and plants seen nowhere else on the plateau. Here and there, the stream has created pools—some large enough to shelter native Apache trout, a protected species in Arizona.

South Canyon Trail (#6)

- Distance: 5 miles round-trip
- Duration: 2–3 hours
- Elevation gain: 2,200 feet
- Effort: Moderate
- Trailhead: Forest Road 610 (Kaibab Plateau) or Forest Road 211 (House Rock Valley)

This Saddle Mountain Wilderness trail can

BEYOND THE BOUNDARIES

be accessed from the Kaibab Plateau or House Rock Valley. When roads are dry, access from the Kaibab Plateau is relatively easy, about 1.5 hours from Jacob Lake on Highway 67 south to Forest Roads 611 and 610. From the House Rock Valley Road (FR 8910), drive south to Forest Road 211. The trailhead is at the end of the road. The trail starts out on an old pipeline access, then climbs sharply to the head of South Canyon, a major canyon tributary, passing along rocky outcroppings offering glimpses of Marble Canyon. The narrow, rocky trail tops out on the Kaibab Plateau at 8,800 feet, passing through a forest of ferns, aspen, and mixed conifers. Because of the elevations, this shady trail is accessible only late spring–early fall.

Rainbow Rim Trail

- Distance: 18 miles one-way
- Duration: 1 day to several days
- Elevation gain: 800 feet
- Effort: Moderate
- Trailhead: Parissawampitts Point

The trail traverses the North Rim, linking five points: Parissawampitts, Fence, Locust, North Timp, and Timp. Most people will hike this trail in sections, starting at one of the trailheads and hiking out and back, but you can arrange to have a second vehicle waiting for you at another of the trailheads. Directions are given from Parissawampitts, the northernmost point. To get to Parissawampitts Point, take Highway 67 south from Jacob Lake for 26.5 miles. Turn right on Forest Road 22 and drive 10.5 miles to Forest Road 206, turning left. Continue on Forest Road 206 for 3.5 miles. Turn right on Forest Road 214 and drive eight miles to Parissawampitts Point. The first 14 miles are good gravel roads. After that, the roads get progressively narrower and rockier, and a high-clearance vehicle is recommended. Because the trail lies entirely within the national forest, you can camp at the trailhead or en route, tackle the trail with a mountain bike or bring your dog, but be aware that equestrians also use the trail and have the right of way.

Mountain bikers can plan loops incorporating forest roads with the trail for long day trips or overnights.

After leaving the parking area at Parissawampitts, the trail turns south, moving in and out of ponderosa pine forest, playing peekaboo with canyon views that change with each point: the basin of the Tapeats Amphitheater with Powell Plateau, Steamboat Mountain, and Great Thumb Mesa rising above. The lightly used trail has a primeval feel, alternating between mixed forests of conifers and aspen, grassy meadows, and rocky draws overgrown with Gambel oak, New Mexico locust, and ferns. The trail rolls up and down drainages, but grades don't exceed 10 percent.

Jumpup-Nail Trail (#8)

- Distance: 12 miles round-trip
- Duration: 7–8 hours
- Elevation gain: 1,970 feet
- Effort: Difficult
- Trailhead: Sowats Point

This trail into the Kanab Creek Wilderness Area is difficult to access, requiring a high-clearance vehicle to negotiate nearly 40 miles of dirt road, but the rewards are solitude, scenery, and beautifully sculpted rocks. To get to the trailhead from Jacob Lake, head south on Highway 67 about 0.25 miles, turning right on Forest Road 461. Forest Road 461 joins Forest Road 462. Continue on Forest Road 462, turning left (south) on Forest Road 22, driving for 11 miles to Forest Road 425. Turn right on Forest Road 425, drive eight miles, and take another right on Forest Road 233. Continue nine miles to the trailhead at Sowats Point. The trail descends from Sowats Point, providing views of Sowats and Jumpup Canyons. Below the point, the trail follows a bench to the edge of Sowats Canyon, crossing the canyon and winding around the point before descending into Jumpup Canyon. The piñon-juniper woodland yields to sculpted sandstone formations and steep canyons for a rugged but scenic hike. The trail intersects tributary canyons and trails leading to Kanab Creek, and experienced wilderness hikers can plan multiday backpacking trips. The Kanab Creek Wilderness Area borders Grand Canyon National Park, and overnight stays across the boundary require a permit.

BIKING

The Kaibab Plateau has miles of single-track, double-track, and forest roads for overnight trips or out-and-backs. However, some of the hiking trails leading down the edge of the plateau are steep and rocky, with dangerous drop-offs, and bikes aren't allowed in wilderness areas or on trails that enter the boundaries of Grand Canyon National Park. A couple of good single-tracks for mountain bikes are the 18-mile **Rainbow Rim Trail,** which skirts the southwest edge of the plateau, and the 70-mile **Arizona Trail** on the plateau's east side. The Kaibab Plateau Visitors Center (928/643-7298, 8 A.M.–5 P.M. daily mid-May–mid-Oct., shorter hours later in the season) has trail maps and suggestions.

HORSEBACK RIDING

For a $20 trail fee, you can take your own horse or mule down Hualapai Hilltop Trail to Havasu Canyon, a ride lasting about three hours. You'll need to bring your own feed. Contact the **Tourism Office** (928/448-2121, 928/448-2141, 928/448-2174, or 928/448-2180, 7 A.M.–7 P.M. daily Mar.–Nov., 7 A.M.–5 P.M. daily Dec.–Feb.) for more information.

The Kaibab Plateau has miles of forest roads and trails open to equestrians, but some trails are too steep, rocky, and narrow to be negotiated safely, and lack of water may limit your choices. A good option is the Arizona Trail, which travels 70 miles near the plateau's east rim. For more information, contact the **Kaibab Plateau Visitors Center** (928/643-7298, www.fs.usda.gov/kaibab, 8 A.M.–5 P.M. daily mid-May–Nov., closed Dec.–mid-May).

BOATING

If you have your own boat or if you rent one in nearby Page, you can motor up Glen Canyon from Lees Ferry to the dam. The trip is only 15 miles, and sand bars and beaches offer several good campsites. This is the only remaining section of Glen Canyon, described so lyrically by John Wesley Powell in his 1875 report to Congress, "Exploration of the Colorado River of the West," which detailed the expeditions he made in 1869 and 1872.

This river is especially popular with anglers because the cold, clear waters below the dam are ideal for trout. Along the route, signs distinguish areas set aside for picnicking and day use from the canyon's six official campsites, which are available on a first-come, first-served basis. For more information, contact the **Glen Canyon National Recreation Area** (P.O. Box 1507, Page, AZ 86040, 928/608-6200, www. nps.gov/glca). You can also charter a trip with local river guides, or take a half-day tour downstream from the dam.

FISHING

Fishing is available 365 days a year at Lees Ferry. The waters below the dam are a constant 47°F, making the area a trophy trout fishery managed by the Arizona Game and Fish Department (www.azgfd.gov). Rainbow trout are common, though brown and cutthroat trout catches have been reported. Fall and winter are less busy, with more open water for casting. Spawning season begins in mid-November and continues through March. Midges may hatch from March through June (the fish like the midges, but the midges *love* you—wear protective clothing or insect repellent). Waters are shallower in the fall, good for walk-and-wade fly-fishing.

Only barbless artificial lures and flies may be used at Lees Ferry; no live bait is allowed. The daily bag limit is four trout per person, with a possession limit of eight trout. Possession of live fish is prohibited.

Local guides offer equipment and boat charters. The people who choose to live and work in this sparsely populated area have a genuine passion for their surroundings. Most local fishing guides have extensive knowledge of the region in addition to angling expertise.

Ambassador Guide Services (800/256-7596, www.ambassadorguides.com) charters trips on the Colorado River and Lake Powell. You can fish the Colorado River elbow-to-elbow with the experienced guides of **Lees Ferry Anglers** (928/355-2261 or 800/962-9755, www.leesferry.com). Their website has detailed fishing reports that can help you decide between zebra midges or pink Glo Bugs. The owner of **Marble Canyon Outfitters** (928/645-2781 or 800/533-7339, www.leesferryflyfishing.com) has been fishing the river since childhood.

HUNTING

The Hualapai Wildlife Conservation Department (P.O. Box 249, Peach Springs, AZ 86434, 928/769-2227) sells permits for hunting big game: desert bighorn sheep, elk, pronghorn antelope, and mountain lions. For information about hunting on Havasupai lands, contact the nation's offices (928/448-2217). The North Kaibab Ranger District has seasons for deer and game birds on the Kaibab Plateau. Contact the Arizona Game and Fish Department (602/942-3000) for details.

Entertainment

Visitors won't find a nightly or weekly entertainment scene in the wide-open spaces surrounding the park, but a number of annual events draw participants from far-flung places. If your timing is right, you may be able to try your hand at weaving fiber sandals, join a powwow circle dance, or follow a parade of vintage vehicles on Historic Route 66.

EVENTS

During **Arizona Archaeology Month,** observed annually in March, the state's rich prehistoric and historic traditions are highlighted. Pipe Spring National Monument (www.nps.gov/pisp, 928/643-7105) hosts a number of events, including beading and rug-making demonstrations and a hike into a canyon with petroglyphs.

The Historic Mother Road inspires a number of festivals and events across northern Arizona, including the annual **Route 66 Fun Run,** held the first weekend in May. Open to all street-legal vehicles from bikes to buses, the run covers 140 miles between Seligman and Topock, passing through Peach Springs and Grand Canyon Caverns. Each community en route welcomes visitors with its own spin on the celebration, including traditional Indian dances, car shows, barbecues, and live music.

In mid–late August, when peaches ripen in Havasu Canyon orchards, Supai Village hosts the annual **Peach Festival.** Peaches were introduced by the Spanish and adopted by many Southwestern Native American communities, who still tend historic orchards watered by nearby creeks. If you hope to visit Havasu Canyon during the Peach Festival, make your plans at least a year in advance. This event is a homecoming for tribe members who live outside Havasu Canyon and also draws many visitors from other Pai tribes.

Kaibab Paiute Heritage Day is held in September, with most events around the band's small reservation near Pipe Spring National Monument.

In October, many Arizona tribes celebrate **Indian Day,** when local communities host events honoring their heritage. Indian Day is not so much a festival for visitors as it is a community celebration, but if your visit happens to coincide with the festivities, most of which focus on schoolchildren, you'll enjoy the lively family-oriented atmosphere. Activities vary from area to area but may include dances, feasts, or art shows.

During autumn months, fairs are held throughout the Navajo Nation. Events often include Miss Navajo pageants, parades, rodeo competitions, art shows, and traditional social music such as two-step and skip dance songs. The closest fair to the Grand Canyon region is the **Western Navajo Nation Fair,** held in Tuba City in mid-October.

SHOPPING

The Hualapai Nation operates a gift shop in Peach Springs and the **Hualapai Market** at Grand Canyon West. Traditionally, Pai tribes are known for basketry, although very few basket makers still practice the craft on the Hualapai and Havasupai Reservations. The Havasupai are also known for beadwork. At the **Havasupai Trading Post and General Store** (928/448-2951) in Supai Village, you'll find a few souvenirs, including postcards, which you can take next door to the post office for the most coveted souvenir in Havasu Canyon: a cancellation stamp that reads "Mule Train Mail, Havasupai Reservation."

If you're interested in Native American art, the **Cameron Trading Post** (60 miles north of Flagstaff on U.S. 89, 800/338-7385, www. camerontradingpost.com, 6 A.M.–10 P.M. daily, shorter hours in winter) has one of the finest selections in northern Arizona. The original post was established in 1916 by the Richardson brothers, and the current trading post is employee-owned. Trading posts once served remote corners of the reservation, and the Cameron trading post continues to sell everything from hanks of dyed wool to groceries. You'll find a huge selection of crafts made by Navajo, Hopi, Paiute, Tohono O'odham, Apache, and Pueblo artisans. Don't miss the gallery, which sells antique and higher-end items in a museum-like setting. The trading post also has a hotel, an RV park, a restaurant, and a convenience market, and there's a gas station and post office nearby.

The **Navajo Arts & Crafts Enterprise** (NACE, 928/679-2244 or 866/871-4095, www.gonavajo.com) operates a small store closer to the junction of U.S. 89 and Highway 64, the junction for those traveling to Grand Canyon's East Entrance.

Simpson's Market (928/679-2340, 6 A.M.–9 P.M. daily summer, 7 A.M.–8 P.M. daily winter), also at the junction of U.S. 89 and Highway 64, is primarily a grocery, but the owners make a point of carrying a few craft items by local artists.

If you're en route to the North Rim, **Marble Canyon Lodge** (928/355-2225), established as a trading post in Marble Canyon during the 1920s, still carries work by Navajo artists, along with a good selection of books and souvenirs.

Navajo artisans and their families sell jewelry and other crafts at roadside stands along several reservation routes, including Highway 64, which leads from Cameron to Grand Canyon's East Entrance at Desert View; and on U.S. 89A at Navajo Bridge Interpretive Center. The specialty at these open-air markets is jewelry, but you may also find Navajo rugs, pottery, sand paintings, baskets, and souvenirs.

The bookstore at **Navajo Bridge Interpretive Center** (928/355-2319, 9 A.M.–5 P.M. daily mid-Apr.–Oct., 10 A.M.–4 P.M. Sat.–Sun. early Apr. and Nov.) sells regional histories and guidebooks as well as maps, posters, videos, and souvenirs.

North of the park, the U.S. Forest Service's **Kaibab Plateau Visitors Center** (928/643-7298, 8 A.M.–5 P.M. daily mid-May–mid-Oct., shorter hours later in the season) has a bookstore with Grand Canyon gifts and maps. Next door, the **Jacob Lake Inn** (928/643-7232) has an excellent selection of Native American arts and crafts, including tapestries, silver and turquoise jewelry, sand paintings, pottery, kachina carvings, baskets. The inn also has a wide selection of books, maps, and gifts. Closer to the park, **Kaibab Lodge** (928/638-2389) has a small selection of gifts and souvenirs, including flint knives and arrowheads knapped by a local artisan.

Accommodations

You're a long, long way from swanky resorts and fine dining when you're traveling in Grand Canyon's hinterlands. If you're accustomed to a particular thread count or a daily cappuccino, you'll need to make some adjustments. Accommodations are basic, from mom-and-pop motels to simple lodges—or a sleeping bag.

WEST OF GCNP
Lodges and Motels
Havasupai Lodge in Supai Village (928/448-2111 or 928/448-2201, $145) has only 24 guest rooms, so make reservations early. All guest rooms are nonsmoking and can accommodate up to four people with two double beds. There are no phones or TVs, but the lodge has air-conditioning.

Hualapai Lodge (900 Rte. 66, Peach Springs, 928/769-2230 or 888/255-9550, $70–100) has 80 guest rooms with coffeemakers, free Wi-Fi, a seasonal saltwater pool and spa, and a fitness center, along with basic amenities. Hualapai Lodge is a popular staging area for trips to the nearby Havasupai Reservation and Grand Canyon West, the Hualapai Nation's tourist center. Try to get a room on the side of the hotel opposite the railroad tracks.

The Caverns Inn (115 Rte. 66, Peach Springs, 928/422-3223 or 877/422-4459, www.grandcanyoncaverns.com, $60–70) has 48 guest rooms with two double beds, TVs, phones, and Wi-Fi access in the motel lobby. If you're feeling brave, you can spend a night in the inn's cavern suite, located underground. Because the inn is just nine miles east of Peach Springs and its busy freight line, many travelers to Havasu Canyon choose to stay here. Indian Road 18, which leads to Hualapai Hilltop, starts a couple of miles farther down Route 66. You can explore nearby Grand Canyon Caverns during your stay, and the inn's staff can also help you with area information, such as touring Grand Canyon West or arranging horseback rides with neighboring ranches. An outdoor pool and coin-operated laundry are on the premises, with a restaurant and bar nearby. Pets are allowed with a deposit.

Guests often fly to **Grand Canyon Ranch** (3750 E. Diamond Bar Ranch Road, Meadview, 800/359-8727, www.grandcanyonranch.com, from $149) from Las Vegas, but you can also drive to this 116,000-acre dude ranch via the Pearce Ferry Road. Accommodations are in log cabins and tepees, and rates include meals and entertainment. Internet discounts are available.

Camping
Havasu Campground (928/448-2141, 928/448-2121, or 928/448-2174, $17 pp, discount for children under age 12), sprawled along Havasu Creek, can hold up to 250 people, but at press time the campground was still undergoing reconstruction after the 2010 flood. There are composting toilets at either end, and the piped spring water must be treated before drinking. There are no showers; bring biodegradable soap for washing in the creek. Most sites have picnic tables, but campfires aren't allowed, so pack a camp stove. All trash must be packed out. You'll pay a $5 pp deposit when you enter, which will be refunded if you carry a bag of trash on your hike out. Sites are selected on a first-come, first-served basis. You must make a reservation in advance and pay a deposit of 50 percent, refundable up to two weeks before your trip (less a 25 percent surcharge). Exceptions are made if the campground closes (due to flooding, for example) during your travel dates, in which case a full refund is made.

A few **primitive campsites** are available at the end of Diamond Creek Road, 20 miles from Peach Springs inside Grand Canyon's Lower Granite Gorge. Campsites lie along the Colorado River, and the beach is exposed and hot during summer months, when the canyon is busy with river runners. There are no facilities other than a toilet, and river water must be treated before drinking. Stop at the tourism desk inside Hualapai Lodge to register, get a permit, and pay driving and camping fees ($16–30). You can also inquire here about backcountry camping on the Hualapai Reservation.

Grand Canyon RV Park (mile marker 115 on Rte. 66, Peach Springs, 928/422-3223, www.grandcanyoncaverns.com, $15–30) has 50 sites with full hookups and another 15 sites without hookups. The campground has restrooms and showers. As a bonus, you can access the pool and other amenities at nearby Grand Canyon Caverns Inn.

EAST OF GCNP
Lodges and Motels

A trip through the Navajo Reservation on U.S. 89 offers panoramas of the Painted Desert's badlands and glimpses of reservation life, including trading posts, hogans, grazing sheep and ponies, roadside markets, and plenty of pickup trucks. A stay at the **C Cameron Trading Post Motel** (60 miles north of Flagstaff on U.S. 89, 928/679-2231 or 800/338-7385, $60–160) or the **Anasazi Inn** (42 miles north of Flagstaff on U.S. 89, 928/679-2214 or 800/678-2214, $60–70) allows quick access to the canyon's East Entrance Station (30 miles west of Cameron), with lots of potential for side trips deeper into the reservation.

If you're continuing on to the North Rim, you'll pass through a vast, seemingly empty desert platform between the Vermilion Cliffs, Marble Canyon, and the Kaibab Plateau. This looks like the land that time forgot, where you'll see bison and condors, with family-run lodges offering simple but good food and comfortable accommodations, just the way they've been doing for half a century. Frequenting the area are river runners, anglers, and travelers headed for the North Rim. From the Marble Platform, it's about 40 miles to Jacob Lake, atop the Kaibab Plateau, and another 45 miles to the developed North Rim.

Marble Canyon Lodge (Marble Canyon, 928/355-2225 or 800/726-1789, www.marblecanyoncompany.com, $45–140), once a trading post operated by Lorenzo Hubbell, was

built in 1929. Guest rooms are comfortable and basic, and some have kitchenettes; condo-style lodging is available for guests using the lodge's guide services. On the premises, you'll find a restaurant, a gift shop, a fly shop, a convenience mart, a coin-operated laundry, a gas station, and a post office, with an airstrip across the highway.

Lees Ferry Lodge (24 miles east of Jacob Lake on U.S. 89, 928/355-2231, www.vermilioncliffs.com, from $50 off-season) has 10 guest rooms without phones or TVs, though some have a Franklin stove for chilly nights. Larger guest rooms can accommodate up to five people.

Cliff Dwellers Lodge (32 miles east of Jacob Lake on U.S. 89, 928/355-2261 or 800/962-9755, www.cliffdwellerslodge.com, $70–80) was built in 1949 by Glen Canyon boatman Art Greene. The 20 guest rooms in the old lodge have satellite TV. A newer guesthouse ($175) has accommodations for groups or families up to six. The nearby "ruins" tucked underneath the huge Shinarump boulders that have fallen from the Vermilion Cliffs were part of a trading post dating to the 1920s. There's a convenience store and gas pumps as well as a restaurant.

Camping

Cameron Trading Post RV Campground (U.S. 89, 1 mile north of Hwy. 64, 800/338-7385, from $15) has full hookups and pull-through spaces for RVs, with weekly and monthly rates. There are no campground restrooms or showers.

C Lees Ferry Campground ($12) has 54 designated sites with no hookups available on a first-come, first-served basis. Sites have grills, and there are toilets and drinking water at the campground, located just above the boat launch. To get to the campground, take the road to Lees Ferry (off Hwy. 89A near Navajo Bridge) for approximately five miles, following the signs. For more information, call Glen Canyon National Recreation Area (928/608-6200).

Dispersed camping is allowed in much of

the backcountry around the Paria Canyon–Vermilion Cliffs Wilderness Area and in the forest and wilderness areas west of Marble Canyon. Restrictions include stays no longer than 14 days, with no camping near archaeological sites or within 200 feet of a water source. Campfires are prohibited in many areas: Check with the appropriate land manager (BLM or Forest Service). Your campsite should look undisturbed when you leave. As the BLM says, "Good campsites are found, not made." Contact the Bureau of Land Management's Arizona Strip Field Office (435/688-3258, www.blm.gov/az) or Kaibab National Forest (928/643-7395, www.fs.usda.gov/kaibab) for more information.

NORTH OF GCNP
Lodges and Motels

About 45 miles north of Bright Angel Point, at the intersection of Highway 67 and U.S. 89A, the historic **Jacob Lake Inn** (928/643-7232, www.jacoblake.com) has 61 beds in cabins ($89–137), a motel ($119), and a hotel ($138). Rates vary according to the season. Cabins have 1–2 rooms and can accommodate 2–6 people. All cabins are nonsmoking, with showers and heaters but no air-conditioning, TVs, telephones, or Internet access. Motel rooms have air-conditioning, and hotel rooms, the inn's newest accommodations, include Internet access, TVs, and phones. Unlike most North Rim spots, the inn is open year-round, making it a center for snowmobilers, cross-country skiers, and snowshoers.

Eighteen miles north of Bright Angel Point and seven miles from the park's Entrance Station, **Kaibab Lodge** (928/638-2389, www.kaibablodge.com, mid-May–Nov., $85–180) offers a collection of cabins, including rustic duplexes with a double bed and a shower, a historic log cabin for up to six people, and a larger cabin with two bedrooms and a loft that can accommodate up to eight. All guest rooms have private baths and heaters but no TVs or phones. The lodge, a former cattle ranch, is open depending on snowfall and road closures.

Farther from the rim, but with easy access to

Grand Circle parks and monuments like Zion, Bryce Canyon, and Arches, the small towns of Fredonia, Arizona, and Kanab, Utah, offer a few dozen lodging choices, including roadside motels, hotel chains, and short-term rental homes.

Camping

Elevations on the Kaibab Plateau and North Rim range 6,300–8,000 feet, so campers should be prepared for cool evenings, even in the summer (during winter months, campgrounds are closed). Campgrounds near the North Rim tend to fill up quickly. **DeMotte Campground** (928/643-7395, www.fs.fed.us/r3/kai/recreation/campgrounds, late May–Oct. 15 depending on snowfall, $17 for up to 6 people) is located on the edge of a meadow just off Highway 67, six miles north of the park's entrance station. Operated by the U.S. Forest Service, the campground has 38 sites with tables and grills, drinking water, and vault toilets. Tents, trailers, and small motor homes are allowed, but there are no hookups.

The Forest Service also operates **⟨ Jacob Lake Campground** (U.S. 89A and Hwy. 67, 928/643-7395, www.fs.fed.us/r3/kai/recreation/campgrounds, May 15–Nov. 1 depending on snowfall, $17 for up to 6 people), 45 miles north of the park's Bright Angel Point. The campground has 53 sites available on a first-come, first-served basis. Sites can accommodate tents, trailers, or small motor homes, but there are no hookups.

Kaibab Camper Village (928/643-7804 or 800/525-0924, 928/526-0924 off-season, http://kaibabcampervillage.com, May 15–Oct. 15) is located just south of Jacob Lake, less than one mile off Highway 67 on Forest Road 461. The campground offers sites with full hookups to RVers ($35), dry or tent sites ($17), and a small cabin with two queen beds ($85), with additional charges of $4–11 per night for extra people.

Indian Hollow Campground (free), a primitive Forest Service campground on the Kaibab Plateau about 50 miles south of Fredonia via Forest Roads 22, 435, and 232, offers nearby access to the North Rim's Thunder River Trail, forest overlooks, and trails leading into the Kanab Creek Wilderness Area. Officially, there are three campsites with tables, grills, and a nearby vault toilet. Unofficially, this little corner of the forest can get busy on summer weekends. A high-clearance vehicle is necessary to negotiate the last few miles.

No-fee dispersed camping is allowed in **Kaibab National Forest** (928/643-7395, www.fs.usda.gov/kaibab). Restrictions include stays no longer than 14 days, and no camping within 100 yards of the highway or near the East Rim Day Use Area along Forest Road 611. Campsites are accessible by dirt roads, many of them suitable for passenger cars. For road

conditions and maps, visit the Kaibab Plateau Visitors Center (928/643-7298, 8 A.M.–5 P.M. daily mid-May–mid-Oct., shorter hours later in the season) in Jacob Lake, or the district ranger's office in Fredonia.

Bordering the Kaibab Plateau on the west, the 1-million-acre **Grand Canyon-Parashant National Monument** is managed jointly by the National Park Service and Bureau of Land Management (BLM). No-fee dispersed camping is allowed unless otherwise posted. There is a 14-day stay limit, and all trash must be packed out. For more information, contact the BLM's Arizona Strip field office (435/688-3258, www.blm.gov/az) in St. George, Utah.

Food

Dining choices are basic in the lightly populated spaces outside Grand Canyon National Park, but menus often feature local specialties such as mutton, ranch-raised beef, or fresh trout. Be sure to try some fry bread, which can be eaten with sugar or honey for a beignet-like confection, or used as the foundation for a savory Navajo taco.

WEST OF GCNP

Supai Village, at the bottom of Havasu Canyon, has a small **café** (928/448-2981, $5–12) that serves breakfast, lunch, and dinner daily to visitors and locals. Cash, debit cards, and credit cards are accepted. The **Diamond Creek Restaurant** at Hualapai Lodge (6 A.M.–9 P.M. daily, $5–18) offers American-style meals and Indian specialties in a casual setting. If you're making arrangements for a tour at the Hualapai Reservation's Grand Canyon West, you'll have additional meal options, including a cowboy-style cookout at Hualapai Ranch or a picnic at Guano Point.

Just outside the reservation, the **Caverns Restaurant** (928/422-3223 or 877/422-4459, www.grandcanyoncaverns.com, $5–20) serves breakfast, lunch, and dinner daily off the menu or buffet-style, although hours may be limited during winter months. The restaurant will also

prepare box lunches for hikers heading into Havasu Canyon. A full bar and patio dining are offered in the summer.

If you're packing a picnic for a day of exploring, Peach Springs has a general store, and there's a convenience mart nine miles east of town at Grand Canyon Caverns. At the bottom of Havasu Canyon, Supai Village has a general store that sells groceries and snacks. Keep in mind that prices will reflect the high cost of transporting goods here.

EAST OF GCNP

Along Grand Canyon's eastern boundaries, between Flagstaff and Page, **Cameron Trading Post Restaurant** (1 mile north of the junction of U.S. 89 and Hwy. 64, 928/679-2231 or 800/338-7385, $6–25) and the **Anasazi Inn** (near milepost 457, 42 miles north of Flagstaff on U.S. 89, 928/679-2214 or 800/678-2214, $5–25) serve breakfast, lunch, and dinner daily. **Simpson's Market** (928/679-2340, 6 A.M.–9 P.M. daily summer, 7 A.M.–8 P.M. daily winter) has a deli counter.

Marble Canyon Lodge restaurant (Marble Canyon, 928/355-2225 or 800/726-1789, 6 A.M.–10 P.M. daily, shorter hours in winter,

$6–25) serves up huge breakfasts off the menu or buffet-style. Fry bread addicts, take note: You can order a circle of crispy goodness here. Next door at the convenience market's **deli counter** (7:30 A.M.–8 P.M. daily, longer hours in summer), you can grab a snack or order takeout from the restaurant.

Next to the Lees Ferry Lodge, the **Vermilion Cliffs Bar and Grill** (928/355-2231, 6:30 A.M.–10 P.M. daily, $6–25) is famous for its exhaustive beer menu, featuring brews from Belgium to Brazil. They serve steaks, chops, ribs, chicken, burgers, and even vegetarian fare.

The restaurant at **Cliff Dwellers Lodge** (32 miles east of Jacob Lake on U.S. 89, 928/355-2261 or 800/962-9755, breakfast 6–11 A.M. daily, dinner 5–9 P.M. daily, $5–25) serves hearty breakfasts and Southwestern specialties, as well as burgers and steaks. The patio is a relaxing place to dine on a summer evening.

If you're traveling the Navajo Reservation on Grand Canyon's east side, Simpson's Market has a good selection of groceries, and Cameron Trading Post sells a few grocery items and snacks in its convenience store.

There's a gas station and convenience mart at Marble Canyon Lodge, a good place to stop if you need more ice for the hot drive across House Rock Valley. Cliff Dwellers Lodge also has gas pumps and a convenience store, your last chance to fuel up before Jacob Lake.

NORTH OF GCNP

Kaibab Lodge (928/638-2389, $4–20), seven miles north of the park entrance, serves breakfast and dinner when the lodge is open, mid-May–mid-October. In 2011 the lodge plans to begin offering daily lunches. If you're planning an early hike or an afternoon picnic, you can order something to go.

Jacob Lake Inn (U.S. 89A and Hwy. 67, 928/643-7232, 6:30 A.M.–9:30 P.M. daily summer–fall, 8 A.M.–8 P.M. daily winter–spring, $6–25) serves breakfast, lunch, and dinner year-round. The inn also has a small deli where you can pick up picnic items, including gigantic home-baked cookies.

INFORMATION AND SERVICES

You'll find the basics (phones, restrooms, and information) at visitors centers, but gas stations are few and far between. Peach Springs, Supai Village (where mail is delivered by mule), Cameron, Marble Canyon, and Jacob Lake all have post offices. Carry plenty of cash or traveler's checks. ATMs will be scarce, and banks even scarcer. If you're traveling to the Hualapai or Havasupai Reservations, gas up first in Kingman, Seligman, or Williams. The nearest garage services are located in Fredonia and Kanab, Williams, Flagstaff, and Page.

Weather and Road Conditions

Grand Canyon National Park's website (www. nps.gov/grca) provides detailed regional forecasts. Recorded information about Arizona road conditions (888/411-7623, www.az511. gov) focuses on major roads. To find out current conditions on forest or reservation roads, contact local visitors centers.

Pets

Pets are OK in *some* areas on *some* reservations, but not everywhere. The Havasupai Nation, for example, asks visitors not to bring pets to Havasu Canyon. Frankly, it's a good idea to make other arrangements for your pets if you'll be doing more than just driving through Indian land and staying in motels or in your RV. Keep in mind that many tribe members have stock animals, such as the sheep and horses that range along Marble Canyon's east rim. Also, in some reservation areas, stray dogs are a nuisance—and not likely to be vaccinated, spayed, or neutered—so Fido would be safer at home. If you like to hike and camp with your dog, head north for the national forest lands on the Kaibab Plateau, where adventure awaits you both.

Emergencies

Cell phone service is sketchy at best on the reservations and public lands surrounding Grand Canyon. West of the national park, Supai Village in Havasu Canyon has an Indian

Health Service clinic and a resident physician. At Havasu Campground, a ranger station is staffed during the day, with security service at night. Peach Springs Health Center, also part of the Indian Health Service, provides urgent care and has after-hours transport services to Kingman.

If you are traveling on the east side of Grand Canyon, including Lees Ferry and Marble Canyon, the nearest hospitals are in Page or Flagstaff. At Lees Ferry, rangers and river guides have first-aid training.

North of Grand Canyon, trails and roads are particularly remote. Phones and first aid are available in Jacob Lake or inside park boundaries at Bright Angel Point, the park's developed area on the North Rim. The nearest hospital is in Kanab, Utah.

Getting There and Around

The remote areas around the park are best explored in your own vehicle or a rental. The exception is Grand Canyon West, the Hualapai Nation's developed area on the rim. A number of tours originate from Las Vegas or nearby Boulder City, Nevada, and you can let someone else do the driving (or flying) if you want to see the Skywalk or go on a whitewater raft expedition with the Hualapai River Runners.

If you're driving from Williams, Arizona, or Las Vegas, you'll have good access to the Hualapai and Havasupai Reservations. If you want to explore the canyon's east side, Page or Flagstaff make good launching points. The Kaibab Plateau and Arizona Strip on the canyon's north side are closest to Page or Flagstaff but can also be reached fairly easily from Las Vegas.

When traveling on reservations or in the national forest, bring everything you need and fill your car up with gas when you can. Gas stations and grocery stores are few and far between. Check current conditions before you leave. It's not just inclement weather that can close roads and trails: Sometimes in June, fire danger shuts down the entire Kaibab National Forest to hiking and camping.

BEYOND THE BOUNDARIES

GATEWAYS TO GRAND CANYON

It's tempting to race to Grand Canyon as quickly as possible, but that old adage about enjoying the journey as much as the destination rings true for the canyon's gateway towns. Flagstaff, Williams, Page, Fredonia, and Kanab all promise convenient access to the canyon, but each of these gateways offers much more than that. The mountain town of Flagstaff combines urban pleasures with a dazzling array of outdoor activities. Williams will delight train buffs and Route 66 fans. At Page, Lake Powell's sandstone canyons lure boaters and backpackers alike. Fredonia and Kanab straddle the Arizona-Utah border and make a convenient jumping-off point not only for the North Rim but also for Zion, Bryce Canyon, and other national parks and monuments on the Grand Circle of the Southwest.

Along with access to Grand Canyon, each of these gateways features its own unique blend of recreation, history, and scenery—forested mountains (Flagstaff or Williams), rocky canyonlands (Page), and colorful plateaus (Kanab and Fredonia). The mountain towns of Flagstaff and Williams are cool havens in summer. While summers in Page are hot, the waters of Lake Powell are a great place to cool off. The sun-drenched plateau country of Fredonia and Kanab can be hot in the summer, but it's a short drive up the Kaibab Plateau to the shady forests of the North Rim.

Page lies along the Utah border, making it an excellent gateway for exploring the sandstone canyons of the Paria and Colorado Rivers. Because it's close to Lees Ferry, Page is a good base if you'll be rafting through the

© KATHLEEN BRYANT

HIGHLIGHTS

◖ Museum of Northern Arizona: For an introduction to the natural and cultural history of the Colorado Plateau and Grand Canyon, head for this splendid museum, tucked among the ponderosa pines north of Flagstaff. Exhibits range from paleontology to prehistoric pottery to paintings. Throughout the summer months, the museum hosts festivals highlighting Native American traditions and art (page 193).

◖ Kachina Trail: The San Francisco Peaks, formed by an extinct volcano, dominate Flagstaff's skyline and offer an unmatched variety of recreational activities, from scenic drives to downhill skiing. The Kachina Trail (10 miles round-trip) meanders through the peaks' aspen-and-pine forests and grassy meadows, with lovely views of surrounding mountains and valleys (page 196).

◖ Route 66: You can get your kicks driving Route 66 through historic downtown

Williams, or explore older sections of the Mother Road by bicycle. Either way, it's a journey back to the golden age of travel, when flickering neon signs beckoned weary cross-country travelers to roadside motels and attractions (page 204).

◖ Glen Canyon: Whether you hike to Horseshoe Bend for a dramatic overlook or float lazily downriver from Glen Canyon Dam on a smooth-water tour, the remaining 15-mile stretch of Glen Canyon will enchant you with its varnished sandstone cliffs and lush hanging gardens (page 209).

◖ Pipe Spring National Monument: This oasis on the Arizona Strip is rich with the history of the Kaibab Paiute Indians and Mormon pioneers. You can tour the old stone fort, learn how to make fiber sandals, or picnic under shady cottonwoods while you imagine what life was like here centuries ago (page 214).

LOOK FOR ◖ TO FIND RECOMMENDED SIGHTS, ACTIVITIES, DINING, AND LODGING.

---

canyon. If you want to ride the Grand Canyon Railway, however, make Williams your gateway. For generations, this small town has been a crossroads for mountain men, wagon trains, railroaders, and Route 66 travelers.

For a greater selection of accommodations, restaurants, and transportation options, choose Flagstaff, where you'll also find an unmatched variety of outdoor activities, from skiing to mountain biking. Like Page, Flagstaff makes a good base if your Grand Canyon adventure includes a river trip.

No matter which gateway you choose, you'll have a scenic journey to the canyon with many opportunities to explore along the way. Rather than rush, pack a picnic and keep your camera ready.

PLANNING YOUR TIME

The simplest way to make the most of your canyon gateway is to plan your itinerary, then add a couple of days to the beginning or end.

Page, Williams, and Flagstaff are destinations with numerous local attractions, from hikes to historic sites. You can easily make a loop of Flagstaff, Williams, and the canyon's South Rim, allowing you to take in more scenery during your Grand Canyon trip. If your Grand Canyon plans include backpacking or camping, you might want to linger in Flagstaff for a few days to adjust to the altitude and stock up on supplies. If you plan to stay in Fredonia or Kanab so that you can visit other Grand Circle national parks, set aside at least two days for the North Rim, or better yet, three.

Besides being a popular Grand Canyon gateway, Flagstaff has cool summers and winter sports activities that make it a destination city for visitors year-round. Williams, Page, Fredonia, and Kanab are busiest during summer months. During the off-season, you may be able to get deep discounts on accommodations, though some establishments may close for weeks or months during winter. (Keep in

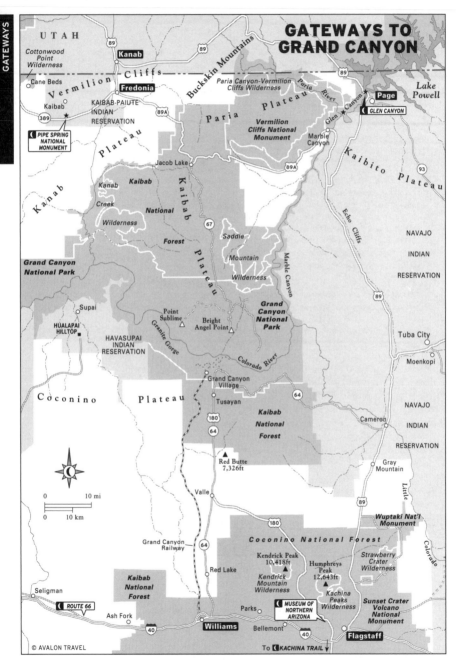

GATEWAYS TO GRAND CANYON

UTAH

Cottonwood Point Wilderness

Cane Beds

Kanab

Vermilion Cliffs

Fredonia

Kaibab

KAIBAB-PAIUTE INDIAN RESERVATION

Paria Canyon-Vermilion Cliffs Wilderness

Buckskin Mountains

Paria Plateau

Paria River

Page

Lake Powell

Glen Canyon

GLEN CANYON

☾ **PIPE SPRING NATIONAL MONUMENT**

Plateau

Vermilion Cliffs National Monument

Marble Canyon

89A

Kaibito Plateau

Kanab

Kaibab

Kanab Creek Wilderness

National

Jacob Lake

Kaibab Plateau

67

Saddle

Mountain

Wilderness

Marble Canyon

Echo Cliffs

89

NAVAJO

INDIAN

RESERVATION

Forest

Grand Canyon National Park

Supai

HUALAPAI HILLTOP

Point Sublime

Bright Angel Point

Granite Gorge

Grand Canyon National Park

Tuba City

HAVASUPAI INDIAN RESERVATION

Colorado River

Grand Canyon Village

Moenkopi

Coconino Plateau

Tusayan

64

NAVAJO

INDIAN

RESERVATION

180

64

Kaibab National Forest

Cameron

Gray Mountain

Red Butte 7,326ft

Little Colorado

0   10 mi

0   10 km

Valle

89

Wuptaki Nat'l Monument

180

Coconino National Forest

Grand Canyon Railway

Kendrick Peak 10,418ft

Humphreys Peak 12,643ft

Strawberry Crater Wilderness

64

Red Lake

Kendrick Mountain Wilderness

Kaibab National Forest

Seligman

☾ **ROUTE 66**

Ash Fork

Parks

Kachina Peaks Wilderness

Sunset Crater Volcano National Monument

☾ **MUSEUM OF NORTHERN ARIZONA**

40

Williams

Bellemont

40

Flagstaff

© AVALON TRAVEL

To ☾ KACHINA TRAIL

mind that the park's North Rim facilities close in the winter, making it a suitable destination only for prepared winter campers and skiers.)

Rooms book quickly during the busy summer season, particularly in Page, a destination for desert dwellers hoping to cool off on Lake Powell. Flagstaff has numerous rooms for every budget, and it's possible to find one at the last minute, even during summer. But why wait? Make reservations well in advance (weeks for Kanab and Fredonia, months for Williams and Page) so that you can spend your time looking at the scenery instead of looking for vacancy signs.

Flagstaff

Less than two hours from Grand Canyon, Flagstaff is surrounded by the world's largest ponderosa pine forest, its northern horizon dominated by the San Francisco Peaks. In winter months, the Peaks provide snowboarding as well as telemark and downhill skiing, with snow-play and cross-country ski areas nearby. Miles of scenic byways and hiking and mountain-biking trails meander through Coconino National Forest. Add nearby national parks, more than half a dozen city and county parks, and an extensive urban trail system, and you'll see why Flagstaff is an outdoor lover's paradise.

About 6 million years ago, the San Francisco Peaks volcanic field rumbled over 2,000 square miles across northern Arizona. Gazing up at the San Francisco Peaks, snowcapped many months out of the year, you might have a hard time picturing a massive volcano that blew its top 10,000 years ago, creating the cluster of peaks seen today. At 12,633 feet, Humphreys Peak is the highest point in Arizona, visible more than 100 miles away.

A historic lumbering, ranching, and rail town in the late 1800s, Flagstaff gained a reputation during the early 1900s as a science center. Pluto was discovered in February 1930 at Lowell Observatory, and Flagstaff was the first to be designated an International Dark Sky City in 2001. Northern Arizona University, founded in 1899, is known today for its science programs, particularly forestry, conservation biology, climatic change research, and engineering.

The university infuses the city with a vibrant, youthful energy. The local live music scene runs the gamut from rock clubs to the Flagstaff Symphony. National acts appear onstage at the Orpheum Theater or at various campus venues. During summer months, it's hard to keep residents indoors, and entertainment shifts to numerous outdoor stages. Heritage Square, the heart of Flagstaff's historic downtown, hosts musical performances and family films, and hardly a week goes by without an alfresco festival at Wheeler Park, Fort Tuthill, or other locations.

A number of river guides, landscape photographers, and dedicated canyon worshippers call Flag home. If you strike up a conversation with the people sitting next to you at the local brewpub, you just might get some valuable inside tips on favorite trails or photo locations.

SIGHTS

You can enjoy Flagstaff's beautiful mountain scenery while exploring the city's scientific and historic attractions.

The Arboretum at Flagstaff

Four miles south of town, the Arboretum (4001 S. Woody Mountain Rd., 928/774-1442, www .thearb.org, 9 A.M.–5 P.M. daily Apr.–Oct., adults $7, tour free with admission) interprets Flagstaff's natural history. Daily guided tours include bird walks, wildflower walks, and garden tours. Musical events and other programs are held throughout summer, and there's a picnic area and a nature-themed gift shop.

Riordan Mansion State Park

On the edge of the Northern Arizona University

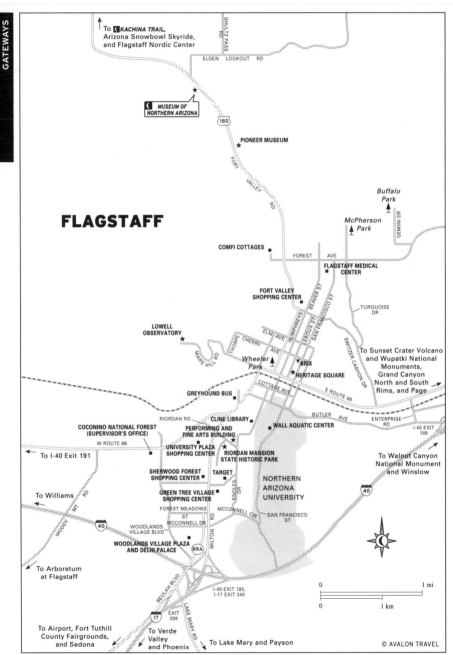

To **KACHINA TRAIL,**
Arizona Snowbowl Skyride,
and Flagstaff Nordic Center

SHULTZ PASS RD

ELDEN LOOKOUT RD

**MUSEUM OF
NORTHERN ARIZONA**

180

★ **PIONEER MUSEUM**

FORT VALLEY RD

*Buffalo
Park*

GEMINI DR

*McPherson
Park*

FLAGSTAFF

COMFI COTTAGES

FOREST AVE

**FLAGSTAFF MEDICAL
CENTER**

BEAVER ST

**FORT VALLEY
SHOPPING CENTER**

HUMPHREYS

BROAD ST

SAN FRANCISCO ST

TURQUOISE DR

**LOWELL
OBSERVATORY**

MARS HILL RD

THORPE

ELM AVE

CHERRY AVE

*Wheeler
Park*

SWITZER CANYON DR

To Sunset Crater Volcano
and Wupatki National
Monuments,
Grand Canyon
North and South
Rims, and Page

▼ **BRIX**
★ **HERITAGE SQUARE**

COTTAGE AVE

E ROUTE 66

GREYHOUND BUS

RIORDAN RD

CLINE LIBRARY

BUTLER AVE

ENTERPRISE RD

**COCONINO NATIONAL FOREST
(SUPERVISOR'S OFFICE)**

**PERFORMING AND
FINE ARTS BUILDING**

WALL AQUATIC CENTER

I-40 EXIT
198

W ROUTE 66

**UNIVERSITY PLAZA
SHOPPING CENTER**

**RIORDAN MANSION
STATE HISTORIC PARK**

To I-40 Exit 191

To Walnut Canyon
National Monument
and Winslow

**SHERWOOD FOREST
SHOPPING CENTER**

TARGET

**NORTHERN
ARIZONA
UNIVERSITY**

40

To Williams

WOODY MT RD

**GREEN TREE VILLAGE
SHOPPING CENTER**

KNOLES DR

FOREST MEADOWS ST

MCCONNELL CIR

WOODY

40

MCCONNELL DR

SAN FRANCISCO ST

WOODLANDS
VILLAGE BLVD

**WOODLANDS VILLAGE PLAZA
AND DELHI PALACE**

89A

MILTON RD

To Arboretum
at Flagstaff

BEULAH BLVD

LAKE MARY RD

I-40 EXIT 195,
I-17 EXIT 340

0 ——— 1 mi

0 ——— 1 km

17 EXIT
339

To Airport, Fort Tuthill
County Fairgrounds,
and Sedona

To Verde
Valley
and Phoenix

To Lake Mary and Payson

© AVALON TRAVEL

campus, Riordan Mansion State Park (409 W. Riordan Rd., 928/779-4395, 10:30 A.M.–5 P.M. Thurs.–Mon., adults $7, tour free with admission) preserves a sprawling craftsman-style duplex designed by Charles Whittlesey, the architect of Grand Canyon's El Tovar. Visitors can learn more about Flagstaff's pioneer past on guided tours of the mansion, once home to the Riordan brothers, who owned a nearby lumber mill.

Lowell Observatory

At Lowell Observatory (928/774-3358, www .lowell.edu, 1400 W. Mars Hill Rd., hours vary by season, adults $10, tours and programs included), atop Mars Hill overlooking historic downtown, daily guided tours are followed by evening telescope viewing, multimedia presentations, and 3-D space tours.

🚺 Museum of Northern Arizona

The Museum of Northern Arizona (3101 N. Fort Valley Rd., 928/774-5213, www .musnaz.org, 9 A.M.–5 P.M. daily, adults $7) provides an excellent introduction to the cultures and landscapes of the Colorado Plateau and Grand Canyon. Exhibits and collections hold everything from prehistoric pottery to contemporary Southwestern art. The museum's summer heritage festivals, including the venerable Hopi Festival in early July, highlight Native American artisans, traditional dances, and demonstrations.

Arizona Historical Society and Pioneer Museum

The Arizona Historical Society and Pioneer Museum (928/774-6272, www.arizonahistorical society.org, 9 A.M.–5 P.M. Mon.–Sat., adults $5) has family-friendly exhibits featuring Arizona's territorial era, including a steam locomotive.

Walnut Canyon National Monument

Walnut Canyon National Monument (7.5 miles east of Flagstaff on I-40, 928/526-3367, www.nps.gov/waca, 8 A.M.–5 P.M. daily May–Oct., 9 A.M.–5 P.M. daily Nov.–Apr., adults $5)

preserves cliff dwellings made by the Sinagua people more than 700 years ago. The shady Rim Trail (0.7 miles round-trip) offers views of the ruins across a pretty limestone canyon. Along the Island Trail (1 mile round-trip), visitors can peer inside masonry rooms.

Elden Pueblo

The Sinaguas also constructed Elden Pueblo (1 mile north of the Flagstaff Mall on U.S. 89, sunrise–sunset year-round, free), now a U.S. Forest Service site. You can take a self-guided tour of this 60–80-room village, situated beneath the slopes of a lava dome and shaded by ponderosa pines. In summer and fall, the Elden Pueblo Project hosts an archaeological field school. Occasional public dig days are offered. For more information about classes and special events, contact the Elden Pueblo Program Manager at the Coconino National Forest Supervisor's office (928/527-3452).

Sunset Crater Volcano and Wupatki National Monuments

Flagstaff is surrounded for 200 square miles by cinder cones, lava domes, and other volcanic features. One place to discover more about the area's volcanic past is at Sunset Crater Volcano National Monument (12 miles north of Flagstaff on U.S. 89, 928/526-0502, www .nps.gov/sucr, 8 A.M.–5 P.M. daily May–Oct., 9 A.M.–5 P.M. daily Nov.–Apr., entry $5/adult, good for both monuments). The crater—actually a 1,000-foot-tall cinder cone—was named by Grand Canyon explorer John Wesley Powell, who noted that its slopes sometimes appeared to glow like a sunset. Sunset Crater's reddish cinders are colored by oxidized iron particles. Gases from steam and evaporated minerals such as limonite, sulfur, and gypsum tinted the crater's rim yellow, orange, and purple. Park visitors can get a closer look at fumaroles (gas vents) and lava tubes or hike to the top of Lenox Crater.

Sunset Crater is believed to have erupted in A.D. 1065. The glow in the sky must have been visible for hundreds of miles, a possible factor in the prehistoric population boom

ruins at Wupatki National Monument

that occurred at Wupatki, 33 miles north of Flagstaff. The Sinaguas were among those who constructed pueblos as the cinder cone was erupting. The ruins are now preserved as Wupatki National Monument (928/679-2365, www.nps.gov/wupa, 9 A.M.–5 P.M. daily year-round). Wupatki and Sunset Crater National Monuments are linked by a 36-mile paved loop off U.S. 89, an interesting and scenic side trip for those heading to Grand Canyon National Park's East Entrance.

RECREATION

Flagstaff is surrounded by 1.8-million-acre Coconino National Forest, offering a bounty of recreation opportunities that include hiking, cycling, camping, and skiing. Summers are deliciously cool (in Arizona terms), with daytime highs around 80°F and nighttime temperatures dipping into the 40s. The crisp, clean air and 7,000-foot altitude have turned Flagstaff into a high-altitude training destination for the Arizona Cardinals football team, Olympic athletes, and elite runners. Maybe

it's from rubbing elbows with world-class athletes, or maybe it's just something in the air, but most Flagstaffians are dedicated outdoor enthusiasts.

Buffalo Park

The main draw for outdoor lovers is the cluster of mountains known collectively as the **San Francisco Peaks.** For great views of the Peaks, head for Buffalo Park (2400 N. Gemini Rd., sunrise–sunset), the brightest gem among Flagstaff's sparkling city parks. Buffalo Park's wide-open expanse is traversed by an interconnecting network of walking and biking trails. Many link to the city's urban trail system, known affectionately as FUTS, which joins neighborhoods and businesses with more than 50 miles of multiuse trails.

Forest Roads

During summer and fall, dirt forest roads are gateways to mountainside trails and meadows. While many forest roads in Flagstaff's high country are closed to vehicles during winter

THE SAN FRANCISCO PEAKS

North of Flagstaff, a cluster of peaks – Mounts Humphrey, Agassiz, Fremont, Abineau, Rees, and Doyle – are actually the remnants of a single extinct volcano estimated to be 16,000 feet high. An eruption about 1 million years ago collapsed the volcano, creating the peaks and their Inner Basin, a beloved local hiking and camping destination. At 12,633 feet, Mount Humphrey is Arizona's tallest mountain.

The first maps to indicate the peaks were drawn by Spanish explorers in the 16th century. The friars who accompanied the expedition likely bestowed the peaks with their name, Sierra Sinagua de San Francisco. *Sierra* denotes jagged ridges; *sin agua,* "without water," acknowledges that the Spanish found no lakes or streams here; and Francisco was their patron saint.

Long before the Spanish arrived, however, Native Americans throughout the Grand Canyon region revered the big mountain and its distinctive jagged silhouette. To the Hopi clans, the peaks were the home of the kachinas, the benevolent supernatural beings who bestow rain and other blessings. The Hopi name for the peaks, Nuva'tuk-iya-ovi, means "Place of High Snows." Tribe members continue to visit shrines on the mountain.

The peaks' Navajo name is Dook'o'oosliid, Abalone Shell Mountain, the westernmost of the four sacred mountains that mark the boundaries of the nation's homeland, Diné Bikéyah. Navajo healers collect plants on the mountainsides.

The Havasupai once roamed the peaks' northern flanks and called it Hvehasahpatch (Big Rock Mountain). Thirteen tribes continue to regard the peaks as sacred, a place for resources, ceremonies, and stories that figure into tribe identity.

When Anglos entered area in the mid-1800s, they valued the peaks for other reasons: as a source of water, minerals, and timber. The peaks were logged intensively, and ranches grazed cattle on lower slopes. Water from springs was shipped to pioneer Grand Canyon village by rail. In the late 1800s, C. H. Merriam developed his concept of life zones on the peaks' slopes. A ski lodge was built in 1930, and in later decades pumice was mined from the mountainside for "stonewashing" denim jeans.

In recent years, Native Americans fought the ski lodge's request to manufacture snow from treated wastewater, a case that reached the Supreme Court in 2009. Though the court ruled against the tribes, controversy continues to rage, with tribe members and environmentalists on one side and skiers and tourism-based businesses on the other.

The San Francisco Peaks dominate Flagstaff's skyline.

© KATHLEEN BRYANT

months (and may be impassable in early spring due to muddy conditions), they can be explored on snowmobile or skis.

Schultz Pass Road (Forest Rd. 420), suitable for passenger cars or bikes, cuts 26 miles through the mountains. The road can be accessed from the west (2 miles north of Flagstaff on Hwy. 180) or the east (11 miles north of Flagstaff on U.S. 89). The 2010 Schultz Fire damaged some sections; check with the Flagstaff Ranger District (5075 N. U.S. 89, 928/526-0866, www.fs.fed.us/r3/coconino, 8 A.M.–4:30 P.M. Mon.–Fri.) for current conditions. **Hart Prairie Road** (Forest Rd. 151), a 10-mile loop beginning 10 miles north of Flagstaff on Highway 180, is spectacular in the fall when aspen groves turn golden.

Arizona Snowbowl

Seven miles north of Flagstaff on Highway 180, paved Snowbowl Road winds up the mountainside to the ski resort. During summer months, the Arizona Snowbowl Skyride (928/779-1951, www.arizonasnowbowl.com, 10 A.M.–4 P.M. daily Memorial Day–Labor Day, skyride, $12 adults, lift tickets $25–60) carries visitors to 11,500 feet for panoramic views that take in the Grand Canyon. During winter, the ski resort (9 A.M.–4 P.M. daily Dec.–mid-Apr.) hosts a ski school and has 32 runs for skiers and snowboarders.

Flagstaff Nordic Center

Cross-country enthusiasts can head for Flagstaff Nordic Center (16 miles north of Flagstaff on Hwy. 180 at mile marker 232, 928/220-0550, www.flagstaffnordiccenter .com, 9 A.M.–4:30 P.M. daily mid-Dec.–Mar. depending on snow conditions, trail passes $12–18, equipment rentals additional) for miles of groomed trails as well as full moon tours, skiing clinics, and equipment rentals.

Hiking

Coconino National Forest contains the largest contiguous stand of ponderosa pines in world along with a variety of terrain, including mountains, meadows, and canyons. The forest's Flagstaff Ranger District (5075 N. U.S. 89, 928/526-0866, www.fs.fed.us/r3/coconino, 8 A.M.–4:30 P.M. Mon.–Fri.) contains more than 30 official trails and dozens more unofficial trails, most of them accessed from forest roads.

◀ KACHINA TRAIL

A popular forest trail near Flagstaff includes the Kachina Trail (10 miles round-trip, strenuous). Although the trail is not particularly steep, most hikers will find any climb at this elevation somewhat demanding. The Kachina Trail begins off paved Snowbowl Road (Forest Rd. 516). Take Highway 180 north of Flagstaff seven miles, then turn on Forest Road 516 and drive another seven miles to the first parking area on the right. The trailhead is at the end of the parking lot. The Kachina Trail meanders through the San Francisco Peaks' aspen-and-pine forests and grassy meadows, offering gorgeous views of the surrounding mountains and valleys.

INNER BASIN TRAIL

The Inner Basin Trail (8 miles round-trip, strenuous) begins in **Lockett Meadow,** a popular hiking and picnicking area during summer when wildflowers are blooming and in fall when aspens shimmer in yellow and gold. To get to Locket Meadow, take U.S. 89 north of Flagstaff 11 miles, turning on Schultz Pass Road (Forest Rd. 420). After 0.5 miles, turn right on Forest Road 522 and follow signs to the trailhead.

MOUNT ELDEN

Several trails climb the basalt-cobbled slopes of 9,299-foot Mount Elden, a petrified lava dome, including **Fat Man's Loop** (2 miles round-trip, easy), which links to the **Elden Lookout Trail** (6 miles round-trip, strenuous). The trailhead is just north of the Flagstaff Ranger District Office (5075 N. U.S. 89).

KENDRICK PEAK AND LAVA RIVER CAVE

North of Flagstaff, hikers can choose between

three challenging wilderness trails to the fire lookout tower at the top of 10,418-foot Kendrick Peak, a lava dome formed by flowing magma. A shorter hike heads into Lava River Cave, a chilly mile-long lava tube. Be prepared with flashlights, warm clothes, and sturdy shoes—the uneven lava floor can be slippery and sharp, and the cave temperature hovers around 40°F, even in summer. To reach the trailhead, drive north of Flagstaff on Highway 180 for nine miles, turning left (west) on Forest Road 245 and continuing 3 miles to Forest Road 171. Turn left and continue another mile to Forest Road 171B, which leads to the cave.

ENTERTAINMENT AND EVENTS

Northern Arizona University (928/523-9011, box office 928/523-5661, http://events.nau.edu, http://nau.ticketforce.com) hosts sporting events, art exhibits, and concerts by touring musicians and comedians. During summer months at downtown's **Heritage Square** (E. Aspen Ave. between N. Leroux St. and N. San Francisco St.), you can listen to live music on Thursday evenings and weekend afternoons, or watch an outdoor family movie on Friday night. On the **first Friday** of every month, downtown galleries stay open late for an art walk. **Wheeler Park** (W. Aspen Ave. and N. Humphrey St.), next to the public library, is a frequent site of weekend festivals.

Though Flagstaff residents know how to make the best of winter, when the high country's sweet and brief summer arrives, it seems like barely a weekend goes by without a festival or party of some kind. Annual events include the **Flagstaff Rodeo** (June), **Summer Pops concerts** (Fourth of July and Labor Day weekends), the **Flagstaff Yoga Festival** (August), **Route 66 Days** (September), and the **Pickin' in the Pines Bluegrass Festival** (September).

For the latest word on events, as well as restaurant reviews, movie schedules, and current entertainment listings, pick up a copy of *Flagstaff Live!*, the free local weekly that hits the streets on Thursday mornings.

SHOPPING

If you're looking for unique gifts, souvenirs, or Native American art, browse though the galleries, trading posts, and shops in historic downtown. **Winter Sun Trading Company** (107 N. San Francisco St., 928/774-2884, www.wintersun.com, 9 A.M.–5 P.M. Mon.–Sat., 11 A.M.–4 P.M. Sun., hours may vary in winter) sells kachina carvings, ethnobotanical remedies, and marvelous natural skin care products.

The **Artists' Gallery** (17 N. San Francisco St., 928/773-0958, www.flagstaffartistsgallery.com, 9:30 A.M.–6:30 P.M. Mon.–Sat., 9:30 A.M.–5:30 P.M. Sun.) is a co-op where you can talk to local artists and photographers about their work.

Flagstaff Mall (4650 N. U.S. 89, 928/526-4827, www.flagstaffmall.com, 10 A.M.–9 P.M. Mon.–Sat., 11 A.M.–6 P.M. Sun.), anchored by Sears, Dillards, and JC Penney, is located on Flagstaff's northeast side. Not far from the university, off Milton Road, you'll find Target (1650 S. Milton Rd., 928/774-3500, 8 A.M.–10 P.M. Mon.–Sat., 8 A.M.–9 P.M. Sun.), WalMart (2750 S. Woodlands Village Blvd., 928/773-1117, 24 hours daily), and other retailers.

Equipment Rental

Per capita, Flagstaff probably has more stores specializing in outdoor gear than any other city in Arizona. (It's also the home of Teva, the sports sandals brainstormed by a Grand Canyon boatman a few decades back.) You can rent equipment at **Babbitt's Backcountry Outfitters** (12 E. Aspen St., 928/774-4775, 9 A.M.–7 P.M. Mon.–Sat., 10 A.M.–5 P.M. Sun.) and **Peace Surplus** (14 W. Rte. 66, 928/774-4521, www.peacesurplus.com, 8 A.M.–9 P.M. Mon.–Fri., 8 A.M.–8 P.M. Sat., 8 A.M.–6 P.M. Sun.) If you're supplying a river trip, several private-trip outfitters have made Flagstaff their base of operations.

ACCOMMODATIONS

From mom-and-pop motels along Route 66 to large national chains to quaint B&Bs, Flagstaff has a wide range of accommodations. Chains include Best Western, Comfort Inn, Days Inn, Holiday Inn, Howard Johnson, Motel 6, Quality Inn, Radisson, Ramada, Rodeway Inn, Super 8, and Travelodge. Hotels at the south end of Milton Road have quick access to I-17 and I-40, plus lots of nearby shops and restaurants.

For historic atmosphere (and perhaps a ghost or two), consider the **Hotel Weatherford** (23 N. Leroux St., 928/779-1919, www.weather fordhotel.com, $89–130) or **Hotel Monte Vista** (100 N. San Francisco St., 928/779-6971 or 800/545-3068, www.hotelmontevista .com, $50–125), downtown mainstays that have stood for roughly a century.

Whether you plan to stay a night or make Flagstaff your base of explorations for awhile, **Comfi Cottages** (3365 N. Antler Crossing, 928/774-0731 or 888/774-0731, www.comfi cottages.com, $140–285) rents comfortably furnished 1–4-bedroom homes, some historic, in various locations.

If you're on a tight budget, Flag has two highly regarded hostels under the same management: **Grand Canyon International Hostel**

© KATHLEEN BRYANT

Hotel Weatherford is located in Flagstaff's historic downtown.

(19½ S. San Francisco St., 928/779-9421 or 888/442-2696, www.grandcanyonhostel .com, year-round), and **Dubeau International Hostel** (19 W. Phoenix Ave., 928/774-6731 or 800/398-7112, www.grandcanyonhostel.com, closed winter). Both offer dorm-style rooms ($18–20) or private doubles ($44–48) between downtown and Northern Arizona University.

Camping

A number of campgrounds surround Flagstaff, and camping at large is permitted in the Coconino National Forest. **KOA** (5803 N. U.S. 89, 928/526-9926 or 800/562-3524, www .koa.com, $30–50) has full hookups and lots of amenities, including free Wi-Fi. Cabins and tent spaces are available, and reservations are recommended.

Coconino National Forest operates first-come, first-served **Bonito Campground** (928/526-0866, www.fs.fed.us/r3/coconino, May–Oct., $18), located just outside Sunset Crater Volcano National Monument, north of Flagstaff near U.S. 89. The campground has no hookups or showers. *Bonito* means "pretty," and it is—a shady haven on the edge of a meadow blooming with sunflowers and paintbrush.

The U.S. Forest Service rents historic cabins through its Rooms With a View program (800/444-6777, www.recreation.gov). Cabins are fairly rustic, and guests need to bring linens and other supplies, but in exchange for doing your own housekeeping, you have privacy and lots of room to roam. **Kendrick Cabin** ($75–125), a retired U.S. Forest Service fire guard station, sits in an open meadow with sweeping views of Arizona's tallest peaks. Grand Canyon's South Rim is a mere 58 miles from the cabin's front porch. Up to 10 people can stay in the cabin's three bedrooms and generous living spaces, available May–early November. Cabin guests can hike, bike, and ride horses against a backdrop of mountains. **Fernow Cabin** ($125/night mid-May–early Oct., $75/night when water is unavailable in early May and late fall, closed Nov. 14–May 4), a log A-frame with two bedrooms, is tucked into the forest about 22 miles south of Flagstaff on Woody Mountain Road (Forest Rd. 231).

FOOD

When Flagstaff's population passed 50,000 (it's now more than 60,000), chain restaurants from Arby's to Olive Garden sprouted up, and if you're looking for a familiar joint, you'll find one. Most chains are located on Flag's south side near the university or en route to the mall in northeast Flag. If you prefer local flavor, you can stroll through historic downtown and choose from a number of interesting eateries.

Brewpubs that serve food include **Beaver Street Brewery** (11 S. Beaver St., 928/779-0079, 11 A.M.–11 P.M. Sun.–Thurs., 11 A.M.–midnight Fri. and Sat., $10–20) in the rapidly gentrifying area south of the train tracks, and **The Lumberyard Brewing Company** (5 S. San Francisco St., 928/779-2739, lunch and dinner daily, $8–20), located in one of Flagstaff's historic lumberyards.

Nearby breakfast and lunch favorites are vegetarian-friendly **La Bellavia** (18 S. Beaver St., 928/774-8301, $5–10) and the beloved bohemian hangout **Macy's** (14 S. Beaver St., 928/774-2243, $5–10). An aside to vegetarians: Savor your stay in Flagstaff, because it will be the last place en route to the canyon where you'll feel truly understood.

Among a growing number of restaurants serving ethnic cuisine, **Swaddee Thai** (115 E. Aspen Ave., 928/773-1122, lunch and dinner daily, $8–16) stands out. **Mountain Oasis** (11 E. Aspen Ave., 928/214-9270, 11 A.M.–9 P.M. daily, $8–20) has a casual but far-ranging menu of global flavors, with many vegetarian options. South of downtown in the Wal-Mart shopping center, ◖ **Delhi Palace** (2700 S. Woodlands Village Blvd., 928/556-0119, lunch and dinner daily, $8–17) serves exquisitely spiced Indian specialties.

If you want to impress your sweetie with a romantic dinner, try **Josephine's** (503 N. Humphreys St., 928/779-3400, lunch Mon.–Fri., brunch weekends, dinner nightly, $10–30), where tables are tucked into the rooms and corners of a craftsman-era bungalow, or ◖ **Brix**

(413 N. San Francisco St., 928/213-1021, lunch and dinner daily, $10–35), whose farm-to-table menu is often hailed as evidence of Flagstaff's increasing culinary sophistication.

If you're planning on stopping for a picnic on the way to the canyon, **Crystal Creek Sandwich Company** (1051 S. Milton St., 928/774-9373, $5–10) builds tasty combinations. For healthful deli selections, head for **New Frontiers Natural Marketplace** (320 S. Cambridge St., 928/774-5747, $5–12), east of campus off Butler Avenue.

INFORMATION AND SERVICES
Visitors Centers

The **Flagstaff Visitors Center** (1 E. Rte. 66, 928/774-9541 or 800/842-7293, www.flag staffarizona.org, 8 A.M.–5 P.M. Mon.–Sat., 9 A.M.–4 P.M. Sun.) shares space with Amtrak in downtown's historic train depot. Stop here for information about shuttles, tours, and local attractions. The local **Chamber of Commerce** (101 W. Rte. 66, 928/744-4505, www.flagstaff chamber.com) is a few steps away.

Visit the **Flagstaff Ranger District** offices (5075 N. U.S. 89, 928/526-0866, www .fs.fed.us/r3/coconino, 8 A.M.–4:30 P.M. Mon.–Fri.) for information about recreation on the Coconino National Forest or to buy maps, passes, or permits. You can pick up an America the Beautiful interagency pass here.

Walnut Canyon National Monument Visitors Center (7.5 miles east of Flagstaff on I-40, 928/526-3367, www.nps.gov/waca, 8 A.M.–5 P.M. daily May–Oct., 9 A.M.–5 P.M. daily Nov.–Apr.) has interpretive displays, a small retail area, and a shady picnic spot.

Sunset Crater Volcano National Monument Visitors Center (12 miles north of Flagstaff on U.S. 89, 928/526-0502, www .nps.gov/sucr, 8 A.M.–5 P.M. daily May–Oct., 9 A.M.–5 P.M. daily Nov.–Apr.) has a nearby campground, hiking trails, and fascinating displays about volcanism.

At **Wupatki National Monument Visitors Center** (33 miles north of Flagstaff on U.S. 89, 928/679-2365, www.nps.gov/wupa,

9 A.M.–5 P.M. daily), you can learn about the area's ancient cultures, take a nature stroll, or sign up for a guided tour of Wupatki Pueblo.

Local Services

Flagstaff Medical Center (FMC, 1200 N. Beaver St., 928/779-3366) is the region's largest hospital. A Level 1 trauma center, FMC has 24-hour emergency services. **Concentra Clinic** (1100 E. Route 66, Suite 100, 928/773-9695) provides walk-in urgent care.

At the main branch of **Flagstaff Public Library** (300 W. Aspen Ave., 928/779-7670, 10 A.M.–9 P.M. Mon.–Thurs., 10 A.M.–7 P.M. Fri., 10 A.M.–6 P.M. Sat.), visitors can use the Internet up to 30 minutes daily at no charge and can purchase additional time.

The **main post office** (2400 Postal Blvd., 928/527-2440) is on Flagstaff's northeast side. There's also a downtown branch (104 N. Agassiz St., 928/779-2371).

GETTING THERE AND AROUND

Flagstaff is located at the intersection of I-40, which runs from Albuquerque to Kingman, and I-17, which leads north from Phoenix and Tucson. From Phoenix, Flagstaff is a two-hour drive up I-17. You'll regret it, however, if you don't spend a few hours (or longer) in Sedona's scenic red rock country en route. U.S. 89A cuts through this small art town and climbs 2,000 feet up to Flagstaff via gorgeous Oak Creek Canyon.

Although it's only 25 miles from Uptown Sedona to downtown Flagstaff, allow an hour for the winding drive, longer if you plan to stop and picnic, wade, or hike in Oak Creek Canyon National Recreation Area. You'll rejoin I-17 near the airport, three miles south of Flagstaff. I-17 ends at its junction with I-40, becoming Milton Road as it travels past the university area, then turning east and becoming Route 66 as it reaches downtown.

The shortest—and arguably the most scenic—route to the canyon from Flagstaff is via Highway 180 (78 miles): From downtown Flagstaff, turn north on Humphreys Street. At Columbus Avenue, turn left. Columbus Avenue becomes Highway 180. Continue west on Highway 180 to Highway 64 (about 55 miles). Turn right (north) on Highway 64 and drive to the South Rim (another 23 miles).

It's a fast 90 miles from Flagstaff to the canyon's South Entrance via I-40: Take I-40 west (about 30 miles) to Highway 64 (Exit 165). Drive north on Highway 64 to the South Rim (about 60 miles).

The canyon's East Entrance is 107 miles from Flagstaff via U.S. 89: Follow Route 66 northeast through Flagstaff. Route 66 becomes U.S. 89 as you leave town. Continue on U.S. 89 north for about 65 miles. Turn left (west) onto Highway 64 and drive 30 miles to the East Entrance and Desert View.

Airport

US Airways (800/235-9292, www.usairways .com) serves Flagstaff's **Pulliam Airport** (FLG), located three miles south of town along I-17. This is a municipal airport that also hosts corporate, charter, and private flights.

Train

Amtrak's (800/872-7245, www.amtrak.com) *Southwest Chief* stops at the Flagstaff depot (1 E. Rte. 66, 4:15 A.M.–11:45 P.M. daily), arriving once daily in each direction from Los Angeles or Albuquerque. There's no train service between Flagstaff and Phoenix or Las Vegas.

Bus and Shuttles

Greyhound (399 S. Malpais Lane, 928/774-4573 or 800/231-2222, www.greyhound .com) has service in Flagstaff with connections nationwide.

Open Road Tours (602/997-6474, 877/226-8060, or 800/766-7117, www.open roadtours.com, 7 A.M.–6 P.M. daily), based in Phoenix and Flagstaff, has daily shuttle service between Flagstaff, Williams, and Grand Canyon. The shuttle to the canyon departs in the morning from the train depot (1 E. Rte. 66) and makes stops at Williams and Tusayan before continuing to Grand Canyon Village. Open Road/Arizona Shuttle also has shuttle service several times daily to the Phoenix airport.

Flagstaff Express Shuttle Services (928/225-2290 or 800/563-1980, www.flagstaff express.com) has twice-daily runs between Flagstaff, Williams, and Grand Canyon Village, and travels three times daily to Phoenix locations, including the airport. Flagstaff Express can also arrange private-car transportation for those whose schedules or needs differ from established shuttle schedules.

A Friendly Cab (928/774-4444, www.a friendlycab.com) has shuttle service between Flagstaff, Phoenix (Fast Track Park, near the airport), and Grand Canyon. **Sun Taxi & Tours** (928/779-1111) has service from Flagstaff to the South Rim. Both companies also offer in-town taxi services.

For getting around town, you can also hop on one of Flagstaff's **Mountain Line buses** (928/779-6624, www.naipta.az.gov), with five different routes operating daily every 30–60 minutes.

Car Rental

Several national car-rental agencies have service counters at Pulliam Airport and/or downtown Flagstaff, including Alamo (928/774-3322 or 800/462-5266), Avis (929/714-0713 or 800/331-1212), Budget (928/779-5235 or 800/527-7000), Enterprise (928/774-9407 or 800/736-8222), Hertz (928/774-4452 or 800/654-3131), and National (928/774-3321 or 888/868-6204). X-Press Rent-A-Car (928/522-0773, www.xpress rentacar.net) has offices in town on Route 66.

RV Rental

Cruise America (824 W. Rte. 66, 928/774-4707 or 800/671-8042) has a rental office in town. **Luxury Travel Service** (3889 Fanning Dr., 928/526-8521 or 800/644-9319, www .luxuryts.com) is a local alternative.

Williams

Sixty miles south of the canyon's South Rim Entrance Station, Williams sits at the foot of forested Bill Williams Mountain, named for the famed trapper and guide. A legendary mountain man and one of the West's trailblazers, it's only fitting that the town named after him sprang up along one of Arizona's most traveled routes.

The first Anglos to enter the territory of Arizona in the early 1800s were rugged types who traveled along rivers trapping beaver and trading with the Indians. Following the Mexican-American War, Army expeditions and government surveys used these older trails to explore lands ceded to the U.S. by Mexico in the 1848 Treaty of Guadalupe Hidalgo. One notable expedition was led by Lieutenant Edward F. Beale, whose 1853 mission was to plot a wagon road along the 35th parallel. Beale was also charged with an Army experiment, leading 25 camels imported from Asia to see if they would fare better than horses in the high desert. The experiment failed. Several camels escaped into the Arizona wilderness, possibly assisted by soldiers who didn't take a shine to the animals.

The Prescott–Santa Fe Stage Line followed part of Beale's route, and later so did the Atlantic and Pacific Railroad. In 1926, part of the National Old Trails Road, once known as Beale's wagon road, became Route 66. The Mother Road led dust bowl refugees west to California. Later, vacationers traveled it as America's Main Street, the downtown thoroughfare of small communities throughout the West. Its bright neon signs beckoned across the dark desert.

The last Route 66 town to be bypassed by a freeway, Williams is dotted with vintage signs and buildings that recall the great American road trip. Though Route 66 has faded to a few crumbling segments of original pavement, its sense of adventure endures.

Most of the open land around Williams is administered by the Kaibab National Forest. Though it is home to fewer than 3,000 people, Williams has a large number of motels

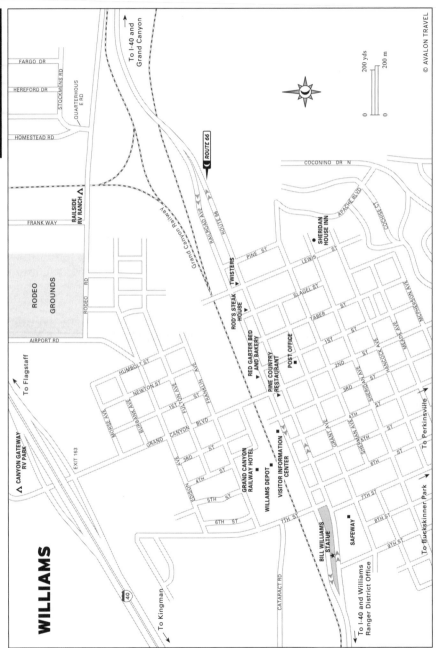

WILLIAMS

To Kingman

To Flagstaff

EXIT 163

CANYON GATEWAY RV PARK

FARGO DR

HEREFORD DR

STOCKMENS RD

QUARTERHOUSE RD

HOMESTEAD RD

FRANK WAY

RAILSIDE RV RANCH

To I-40 and Grand Canyon

RODEO GROUNDS

RODEO RD

AIRPORT RD

Grand Canyon Railway

RAILROAD AVE

ROUTE 66

ROUTE 66

COCONINO DR N

PINE ST

LEWIS ST

SLAGEL ST

TABER

SHERIDAN HOUSE INN

APACHE BLVD

COCHISE DR

MCPHERSON AVE

MELDE AVE

HANCOCK AVE

TWISTERS

ROD'S STEAK HOUSE

RED GARTER BED AND BAKERY

PINE COUNTRY RESTAURANT

POST OFFICE

HUMBOLT ST

NEWTON ST

MORSE AVE

BURBANK AVE

FULTON AVE

FRANKLIN AVE

1ST ST

GRAND CANYON BLVD

EDISON AVE

3RD ST

4TH ST

5TH ST

6TH ST

7TH ST

WILLAMS DEPOT

GRAND CANYON RAILWAY HOTEL

VISITOR INFORMATION CENTER

BILL WILLIAMS STATUE

SAFEWAY

CATARACT RD

1ST ST

2ND ST

3RD ST

4TH ST

5TH ST

6TH ST

7TH ST

8TH ST

GRANT AVE

SHERMAN AVE

SHERIDAN AVE

7TH ST

8TH ST

To Perkinsville

To Buckskinner Park

To I-40 and Williams Ranger District Office

ROUTE 66

200 yds

200 m

0

0

© AVALON TRAVEL

and restaurants that cater to Grand Canyon and Route 66 visitors, and the town calls itself "the Gateway to Grand Canyon." It's also home to the Grand Canyon Railway, and if you're planning to arrive at the South Rim via train, Williams is the gateway for you.

SIGHTS

Don't worry about being on the wrong side of the tracks in Williams. Straddling both sides of the rails are the old freight depot, currently a visitors center and museum, and the historic passenger depot, now home of the **Grand Canyon Railway** (233 N. Grand Canyon Blvd., 800/843-8724, www.thetrain.com). Even if you're not planning to ride a steam locomotive to the canyon, you'll soon discover the train tracks are where the action is. The train bound for Grand Canyon departs at 9:45 A.M. and returns at 5:45 P.M., but if you're visiting midday, you can take a look at the train cars parked along the tracks or browse through the gift shop housed in the historic passenger depot. The depot and adjacent Fray Marcos Hotel (now offices) were once operated by the Fred Harvey Company, and the railway district is on the National Register of Historic Places.

Across the tracks, the old freight depot houses the **Williams Visitors Center and Museum** (200 Railroad Ave., 928/635-4061 or 800/863-0546, www.experiencewilliams.com, www.williamschamber.org, 8 A.M.–6:30 P.M. daily summer, 8 A.M.–5 P.M. daily fall–winter). While you're here, pick up a walking tour map so you can stroll along historic **Saloon Row**, or cruise along Route 66 for a nostalgic trip down **America's Main Street.**

The **Railroad Museum,** currently housed inside the visitors center, is slated to get expansive new digs in 2012, coinciding with Arizona's statehood centennial. Displays will highlight the state's 76 historic railroads and the communities that grew up along the tracks.

RECREATION

Kaibab National Forest offers plenty of backroad drives, hiking and biking trails, fishing lakes, picnic areas, cross-country skiing, and even a small downhill ski resort on Bill Williams Mountain. For more information about recreation in the 550,411-acre **Williams Ranger District** or to pick up maps and learn about current road conditions, contact the district office (742 S. Clover Rd., 928/635-5600,

© KATHLEEN BRYANT

Downtown Williams straddles old Route 66.

www.fs.usda.gov/kaibab, 8 A.M.–4:30 P.M. Mon.–Fri.) or the **Williams Visitors Center** (200 Railroad Ave., 928/635-4061 or 800/863-0546, 8 A.M.–6:30 P.M. daily summer, 8 A.M.–5 P.M. daily fall–winter).

Forest Roads and Hiking

During the 1800s, wagons, stages, and mule trains crossed Garland Prairie, bringing settlers, supplies, and soldiers to Prescott. Today, you can retrace their route via the **Garland Prairie Road** (Forest Rd. 141), which makes a scenic 21-mile loop south of I-40, beginning at exit 167, traveling eastward and rejoining the freeway at exit 178. The gravel road is suitable for passenger cars, and you can complete the loop in 2–3 hours. But give yourself extra time to explore nearby lakes, hiking and biking trails, vistas, and historic sites. The prairie comes alive with wildflowers in late spring, and in autumn, aspens turn gold on the slopes of Bill Williams Mountain and Kendrick Peak. Watch carefully as you travel through the open prairie: Wagon ruts can still be seen near the Overland Trail and Beale Roads.

In 1859 Beale's expedition left an inscription at Laws Spring, where travelers marked the spring's location with petroglyphs centuries earlier. It's possible to access the Beale Road here for an easy stroll. The trailhead is reached by taking the Garland Prairie Road (Forest Rd. 171) to Forest Road 100, continuing approximately four miles to its junction with Forest Road 107, where you can park. From here, the Beale Road heads southwest, marked by rock cairns and wooden posts. You can walk as far as you like, but a good turnaround point is at the edge of the prairie, making a five-mile round-trip.

Hikers, mountain bikers, and equestrians can also follow 25 miles of the **Overland Road,** established by the Army in 1863 to connect to the goldfields near Prescott. There are several trailheads, including one along the Garland Prairie Road, 5.4 miles south of its intersection with I-40 at exit 178.

◖ Route 66

When Route 66 was born in 1926, a new era of travel began. Passenger cars can still drive Route 66 for 22 miles east from downtown Williams, with a short segue on I-40, the freeway that replaced the Mother Road in the 1960s. Two older alignments, dating from the 1920s and 1930s, serve as mountain bike trails, the **Devil Dog** and **Ash Fork Hill** loops.

The easy five-mile Devil Dog loop begins west of Williams on Forest Road 108 (just south of I-40 exit 157). For the intermediate 12-mile Ash Fork Hill loop, go 12 miles west of Williams on I-40 to exit 151. Drive a short way north on Forest Road 6 and park. A high-clearance vehicle is recommended to reach the trailhead. Begin the loop clockwise so that you can tackle the steepest grade going downhill.

Golf

Golfers who want to aim at a few small holes before traveling to the big one (Grand Canyon) can head northwest of Williams to **Elephant Rocks** (2200 Country Club Dr., 928/635-4935, www.elephant-rocks.com), named for the large dark gray basalt boulders at its entrance. At 7,000 feet in elevation, this 18-hole course, designed by Gary Panks, is a cool escape for desert dwellers.

ENTERTAINMENT AND EVENTS

Williams is a party town. Rarely does a summer weekend go by without some kind of festival or event. If you want to continue the celebration into the wee hours, a fitting place to start is the Sultana (301 W. Rte. 66, 928/635-2021), which holds the honor of being Arizona's longest-running liquor purveyor. You can shoot pool or shoot the breeze with locals before ambling off to another downtown establishment.

Route 66, train travel, and Western traditions are feted in Williams spring–fall. Transportation-themed events include fly-ins, car shows, a motorcycle rally, and the annual **Historic Route 66 Fun Run,** when motor enthusiasts from all over the United States drive the fabled Mother Road from Seligman to Topock over the first weekend in May. In June, working cowboys gather for the **Cowpunchers**

Reunion Rodeo, one of several annual events that highlight Western traditions. The town's old-fashioned **Fourth of July celebration** features live entertainment all day long and, of course, a parade.

SHOPPING

It's no surprise that downtown shops carry a wide range of Route 66 memorabilia and Grand Canyon souvenirs, but the variety might intrigue you. Poke around the corners of a shop or two and you may uncover such treasures as a Burma Shave sign, hood ornaments and hubcaps, or even an antique juke box. Most stores vary their hours with the seasons.

For train-themed items, you need look no farther than the **Grand Canyon Railway's gift shop** (235 N. Grand Canyon Blvd., 800/843-8724, www.thetrain.com). **De Berge Western Wear** (213 W. Rte. 66, 928/635-2960) carries hats and boots, and makes custom saddles for your horse—or your Harley. The **Quilters Mercantile** (226 W. Rte. 66, 928/635-5221) sells supplies and handmade quilts, and you might find one with a Grand Canyon scene.

ACCOMMODATIONS

From national chains to charming B&Bs, Williams has about 30 hotels, motels, and inns in various price ranges. Most are located within a few blocks of I-40 along Route 66 or Grand Canyon Boulevard. Chains include Days Inn, Best Western, EconoLodge, Fairfield Inn, Holiday Inn Express, Howard Johnson, Motel 6, and Travelodge. Off-season rates are often significantly lower than summer rates.

If your trip centers on the train, you might want to splurge on the stately and comfortable **C Grand Canyon Railway Hotel** (235 N. Grand Canyon Blvd., 928/635-4010 or 800/843-8724, www.thetrain.com, $169–349, discounts with train travel).

Equally elegant but tucked away from the railroad tracks and Route 66 on two woodsy acres, the **C Sheridan House Inn** (460 E. Sheridan Ave., 928/635-9441 or 888/635-9345, www.grandcanyonbbinn.com, $145–195) is a particularly well-appointed B&B.

The **Red Garter Bed & Bakery** (137 W. Railroad Ave., 928/635-1484 or 800/328-1484, www.redgarter.com, $120–145) is a restored—and perhaps haunted—bordello in historic downtown, close to the visitors center.

If you want local color at moderate prices, the European-style **Grand Canyon Hotel** (145 W. Rte. 66, 928/635-1419 or 877/635-1419, www.thegrandcanyonhotel.com, $60–125), built in 1891, offers historic accommodations downtown. This boutique hotel also has dorm-style hostel rooms ($25).

The **Grand Motel** (234 E. Rte. 66, 928/635-1200 or 800/635-9590, http://thegrandmotel.com, $48–78) harks back to the glory days of Route 66.

You can stay in a railcar at the **Canyon Motel** (1900 E. Rodeo Rd., 928/635-9371 or 800/482-3955, http://thecanyonmotel.com, $60–170), a combination motel and RV park located just east of Williams close to Highway 64.

Camping and RVs

For campers and RVers, Williams is a cool summer haven (although in Arizona, this is relative), with a wide variety of campground choices. Two well-equipped KOAs can be found north and east of town. **Circle Pines KOA** (1000 Circle Pines, 928/635-2626 or 800/562-9379, www.koa.com, $30–50) is just off I-40 at exit 167. **Grand Canyon/ Williams KOA** (5333 Hwy. 64, 928/635-2307 or 800/562-5771, www.koa.com, $30–50) is located on Highway 64, the route to Grand Canyon.

If you're planning to ride the excursion train to Grand Canyon, the **Grand Canyon Railway RV Park** (235 N. Grand Canyon Blvd., 800/843-8724, www.thetrain.com, $42) is convenient and offers full hookups, wireless Internet, and cable TV. Discounts with train travel may apply.

The year-round RV park at the **Canyon Motel** (1900 E. Rodeo Rd., 928/635-9371 or 800/482-3955, www.thecanyonmotel.com) has sites with full hookups ($30–39) and tent sites ($20).

Kaibab National Forest (928/635-5600,

www.fs.usda.gov/kaibab) operates four **lakeside campgrounds** (May–Sept., $18–30) near Williams. With the exception of group sites, campgrounds at **Cataract Lake** (928/699-1239), **Dogtown Lake,** and **Kaibab Lake** are first-come, first-served, are suitable for tents and small RVs, and have no utility hookups. Sites can be reserved at the larger **White Horse Lake** campground (877/444-6777, www.recreation .gov, $18–30), 19 miles southeast of Williams. Dispersed camping is allowed throughout the forest. Certain restrictions apply, including a 14-day stay limit. No camping is allowed within a quarter mile of water, on open meadows, within a mile of a developed campground, within 200 feet of main roadways, or within 20 feet of forest roads. Bury human and pet waste at least six inches deep and pack out all trash. Many forest roads are rugged and—depending on rainfall and winter snow cover—can be quite muddy as well. During the summer, fire restrictions may be active. Check with the Forest Service for current conditions.

The Kaibab National Forest's **Spring Valley Cabin** (877/444-6777, www.recreation.gov, $100–150) was built in 1917 as a guard station. Midway between Flagstaff (30 miles east) and Williams (25 miles west), the cabin has room for eight and is surrounded by wide-open vistas of forests, mountains, and prairies. It's an ideal location for scenic drives, especially in autumn, when aspens turn the mountainsides into a patchwork of green and gold. Pack a pair of binoculars so you can watch for herds of pronghorn or elk.

FOOD

Williams has more than a dozen restaurants, from Route 66–style diners like **Twisters** (417 E. Rte. 66, 928/635-0266, 9 A.M.–9 P.M. Mon.–Sat., 11 A.M.–4 P.M. Sun., $5–20) to steak houses, including the iconic **Rod's Steak House** (301 E. Rte. 66, 928/635-2671, lunch and dinner Mon.–Sat., $15–30). Savor the small-town atmosphere and retro flair, and remember you're here for Grand Canyon, not for grand cuisine. As is often the case in tourist towns, quality and service are inconsistent: You

Look for the big cow on the roof to find Rod's Steak House.

might enjoy a fabulous meal and great service one day, only to return to the same restaurant the next day and be disappointed.

If you prefer spicier fare, a good option is (**Dara Thai** (145 W. Rte. 66, 928/635-2201, lunch and dinner Mon.–Sat., $10–15), located in downtown's historic Grand Canyon Hotel.

The **Pine Country Restaurant** (107 N. Grand Canyon Blvd., 928/635-9718, $5–15) is known for its hearty breakfasts but serves up home-style cooking all day long.

Chains include Dairy Queen, Denny's, Jack-in-the-Box, McDonald's, Pizza Factory, and Pizza Hut.

INFORMATION AND SERVICES
Visitors Centers

The historic Santa Fe Railway freight depot houses the **Williams Visitors Center** (200 Railroad Ave., 928/635-4061 or 800/863-0546, 8 A.M.–6:30 P.M. daily summer, 8 A.M.–5 P.M. daily fall–winter), jointly operated by the town's chamber of commerce and the U.S. Forest Service. Stop in to browse the museum and find out about tours and recreational opportunities. You can even pick up an entrance pass for Grand Canyon, which will help you skip long entry station waits.

Kaibab National Forest has additional offices for the Williams Ranger District (742 S. Clover Rd., 928/635-5600, www.fs.usda .gov/kaibab, 8 A.M.–4:30 P.M. Mon.–Fri.) and the Forest Supervisor (800 S. 6th St., 928/635-8200, 8 A.M.–4:30 P.M. Mon.–Fri.). Rangers are on hand at both locations to help you choose among scenic drives, trails, and campgrounds.

Local Services
North Country HealthCare operates an **urgent care clinic** (301 S. 7th St., 928/635-4441, 8 A.M.–8 P.M. daily) in Williams. The nearest hospital is in Flagstaff.

The **Williams Public Library** (113 S. 1st St., 928/635-2263) and post office (120 S. 1st St., 928/635-4572) are located within walking distance of the downtown historic district.

GETTING THERE AND AROUND
The town of Williams sits along the southern edge of I-40 half an hour's drive west of Flagstaff, four hours east of Las Vegas, and three hours northwest of Phoenix. Three exits lead to Williams from I-40. If you're arriving from the west, use exit 161. A few hotels and motels are located on this side of town. Exit 163 leads to the Grand Canyon Railway depot and the heart of the historic downtown. Exit 165 connects with Highway 64, which heads north to Grand Canyon, about an hour's drive.

Airport
Although the nearest commercial airport is 30 miles away in Flagstaff, Williams has an airfield for small planes, **H. A. Clark Memorial Field** (3501 N. Airport Rd., 928/635-1280).

Train
Amtrak (800/872-7245, www.amtrak.com) has service from Flagstaff. The westbound *Southwest Chief* arrives once daily late at night at the Williams Depot (235 N. Grand Canyon Blvd.), which also serves Grand Canyon Railway, on the edge of historic downtown.

The once-daily eastbound train (from Los Angeles) arrives early in the morning.

Grand Canyon Railway (235 N. Grand Canyon Blvd., 800/843-8724, www.the train.com) provides daily train service from Williams Depot to Grand Canyon Village. The depot, built in 1908, is a former Harvey House and retains a historic flair. The railway offers five classes of passenger service to the canyon on refurbished vintage rail cars. You can arrange a package tour that combines the train ride with lodging and guided rim tours. Trains depart from Williams in the morning and return in the afternoon.

Taxis and Shuttles
Smitty's Transportation (117 S. Slagel St., 928/635-9825 or 888/635-9825) operates taxi services around Williams and the Grand Canyon area until 11 P.M. daily. Smitty's also provides car and van service to the canyon, Las Vegas, Flagstaff, Sedona, Cottonwood, Camp Verde, the Phoenix airport, or anywhere else you want to go. Reservations are strongly recommended.

Open Road Tours (602/997-6474, 877/226-8060, or 800/766-7117, 7 A.M.–6 P.M.), based in Phoenix and Flagstaff, has daily shuttle service between Williams, Flagstaff, and Grand Canyon. The shuttle to the canyon departs in the morning from the Grand Canyon Railway depot (235 N. Grand Canyon Blvd.) and makes stops in Tusayan and inside the park at Maswik Lodge.

Twice-daily shuttle runs between Flagstaff, Williams, and Grand Canyon Village are available from **Flagstaff Express Shuttle Services** (928/225-2290 or 800/563-1980). Flagstaff Express can also arrange private-car transportation for those whose schedules or needs differ from established shuttle schedules.

Car Rental
You can make arrangements to pick up a rental car from Budget (928/635-2248 or 800/527-0700, www.budget.com) at the Grand Canyon Railway depot (235 N. Grand Canyon Blvd.).

Page

Situated on a mesa overlooking Lake Powell, the town of Page (pop. 9,500) sprang up during the construction of Glen Canyon Dam, which began in 1956. Most visitors come here to explore the lake and its canyon-cut shoreline, much of it in Utah, including Rainbow Bridge National Monument. Lake Powell glitters like a sapphire among a setting of reddish sandstone buttes, luring photographers and watersports enthusiasts alike. Equally photogenic are the sinuous curves of Antelope Canyon, east of town on the Navajo Reservation.

Centuries before Glen Canyon was flooded by the waters of Lake Powell, the ancients built pueblos and left other signs of their passage in the canyon's maze of tributaries. Vestiges of Ancestral Puebloan life can still be found in ruins, rock art, or potsherds scattered across sandstone ledges high above the lake.

When John Wesley Powell's expedition floated through Glen Canyon in 1869, he wrote about the canyon's "oak-set glens and fern-decked alcoves...carved walls, royal arches" and decided to name it Glen Canyon. For decades, the isolated area was an idyllic playground for river runners. Among those who protested when the Bureau of Reclamation decided to flood the Glen's lovely canyons for a reservoir was Edward Abbey. He wreaked fictional revenge on the "Bu-Wreck" when he penned *The Monkey Wrench Gang* (1975), the tale of a motley crew of canyon lovers who plotted to dynamite the dam.

The dam continues to be controversial, but the town of Page, born as a construction camp, has grown into a tourist destination centered on the lake and the bounty of water-sports it provides, from houseboating to fishing to Jet Skiing. At 186 miles long, Lake Powell is the second-largest artificial lake in the United States (the largest is Lake Mead, at the other

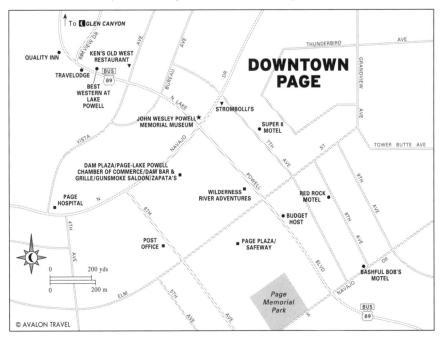

end of Grand Canyon). Lakeside marinas rent boats and offer tours to Rainbow Bridge and other locations. Those who want to turn back the clock to predam time can raft the 15 miles below the dam to Lees Ferry, a lovely stretch of vertical sandstone cliffs that shelters ancient petroglyphs and migrating waterfowl.

SIGHTS

The canyon country surrounding **Lake Powell** is rugged and isolated, with very few access roads. Thus the best way to see the lake and its 2,000-mile shoreline is by boat. Several **boat tours** (928/645-1070, www.lakepowell.com, $32–100) are offered by Aramark, the concessionaire for Glen Canyon National Recreation Area. Lasting 1.5–6 hours, tours depart from Wahweap Marina.

The six-hour excursion travels 50 miles from Wahweap Bay to **Rainbow Bridge National Monument** (928/608-6200, www.nps.gov/rabr). The tiny monument's central attraction is a 275-foot sandstone span carved by water, the largest natural bridge in the world. After docking, visitors can make the short hike (2.5 miles round-trip at current lake levels) to the base of the natural bridge. Sacred to the region's Native Americans for generations, it was "discovered" by nonnatives in 1909. The only way here is by boat or by backpacking from the Navajo Reservation (permit required). Park rangers are on-site May–early October.

◖ Glen Canyon

Another way to explore the area by water is to tour the remaining 15-mile stretch of the Colorado River in Glen Canyon below the dam. **Colorado River Discovery** (130 6th Ave., 888/522-6244, www.raftthecanyon.com, $85–155) leads motorized trips year-round and oar-powered trips during summer months. The peaceful half-day or full-day trips begin at the dam and end at Lees Ferry, floating between the Glen's gorgeous Navajo sandstone cliffs.

The float trip, lake tours, and dinner cruise can also be booked through the visitor services center at the **John Wesley Powell Memorial Museum** (6 N. Lake Powell Blvd., 928/645-

9496, www.powellmuseum.org, 9 A.M.–5 P.M. daily). The museum is a good place to learn more about Major Powell, the one-armed Civil War veteran who ran the Colorado River through Grand Canyon in 1869 and 1872. Displays include a replica of Powell's boat. If you make a tour reservation here, the museum will receive a percentage of the fee.

Whatever you think about **Glen Canyon Dam,** you have to agree that it is impressive. The dam contains nearly 5 million cubic yards of concrete and rises more than 500 feet above the Colorado River. You can get a closer look on a 45-minute tour, departing from **Carl Hayden Visitors Center** (928/608-6404, usually 8:30 A.M.–4:30 P.M. daily, hours vary by season) several times daily. The visitors center is located on U.S. 89, just west of the dam. Reservations for the tours, which are guided by the **Glen Canyon Natural History Association** (928/608-6072, www.glencanyonnha.org), can be made online or by phone up to 24 hours in advance.

Antelope Canyon

Photography buffs flock to Antelope Canyon, a sinuous and colorful slot canyon carved into a sandstone mesa east of Page. It's exquisitely beautiful—and occasionally deadly. In 1997, a flash flood caused by a storm several miles away killed 11 of the 12 people hiking in the canyon at the time. Antelope Canyon is a **Navajo Nation Tribal Park** (928/698-2808, 8 A.M.–5 P.M. daily Apr.–Oct., 9 A.M.–3 P.M. daily Nov.–Mar.), and the only way to get inside is in the company of an authorized guide. Photographers prefer the deeper upper canyon, accessed by climbing down a ladder, although the lower canyon is also lovely. Guides are usually available on-site, but you can also arrange for a tour and transportation to the canyon from Page.

Big Water Visitors Center

If there's a budding paleontologist in your family, you won't want to miss the Bureau of Land Management's Big Water Visitors Center (100 Revolution Way, Big Water, UT, 435/675-3200, www.blm.gov, 8 A.M.–5 P.M. daily Nov.–Mar.,

Horseshoe Bend Trail overlooks the Colorado River near Page.

9 A.M.–6 P.M. daily Apr.–Oct.), 12 miles north of Page. Recent discoveries in the area include the remains of a therizinosaur, a sickle-clawed, big-bellied, feathered dinosaur.

RECREATION

Water is the word at **Glen Canyon National Recreation Area.** You can go on a guided cruise of the lake and its canyons, or rent a boat and explore on your own. You'll find most everything that floats, from kayaks to houseboats, at the lake's marinas. Many boaters pull into Lake Powell's canyon tributaries and tie up for a few hours (or days) to explore twisting sandstone slots and hidden alcoves. Tucked into these winding sandstone passages are a number of historic and prehistoric sites. Three miles up the middle fork of **Defiance Canyon** is an Ancestral Puebloan dwelling with associated pictographs and petroglyphs.

Away from the lake's brilliant blue waters, trails are rocky and sun-baked. Stick to shorter trails until you get a feel for hiking in this high, dry country. **Hanging Garden Trail**

(an easy 1-mile round-trip) begins across the bridge from Carl Hayden Visitors Center (U.S. 89 just west of the dam). **Horseshoe Bend Trail** (moderate, 3 miles round-trip) leads to an iconic panorama of the Colorado River as it makes a 270-degree turn around a neck of sandstone. For the trailhead, take U.S. 89 five miles south of Page to mile marker 545 and turn west into the parking area.

As you hike toward Horseshoe Bend, you'll have views of the Vermilion Cliffs, part of the vast tract of public lands administered by the Bureau of Land Management (www.blm.gov). Remote canyons and mesas can be explored by hiking, backpacking, and canyoneering, but trips into the stony wildernesses of the Paria or Escalante need to be well planned. Even far from the lake, water is still the word.

ENTERTAINMENT AND EVENTS

Check at the visitors centers for daily ranger programs and special events, such as performances or lectures by artists-in-residence. Rangers host programs at Wahweap Campground's outdoor amphitheater on Friday and Saturday evenings during the summer months.

Winter months are relatively quiet in Page, but a few local bars host live music on high-season weekends and during spring break, when the lake is frequented by college students. As you might expect, country music is the theme at **Ken's Old West** (718 Vista Ave., 928/645-6150, until 11 P.M. Sat.–Sun., until 10 P.M. Mon.–Fri.). **The Dam Bar & Grill** (644 N. Navajo Dr., 928/645-2161, until 2 A.M.) has a large dance floor and pool tables.

During the off-season, October–April, the **Lake Powell Concert Association** (928/660-3367, www.lakepowellconcertassociation .com) brings live performances to the 800-seat Cultural Arts auditorium of Page High School (500 S. Navajo Dr.). Lake Powell's premier event, the **Balloon Regatta,** takes place on the first weekend in November, when dozens of hot air balloons float serenely above red sandstone and blue water.

SHOPPING

A number of local shops peddle souvenirs and crafts. Look for art galleries and trading posts, such as **Dinnebito Trading Post** (626 N. Navajo Dr., 928/645-3008 or 800/644-3008, www.blairstradingpost.com), that feature Native American art or photography of the lake and its surrounding canyon lands.

Perhaps no one has captured the area's beauty more expertly than local photographer **Gary Ladd,** whose photos appear in books, magazines, and galleries as well as on his website (www.garyladd.com). He has made dozens of hikes inside Grand Canyon, and his photos convey Grand Canyon's magic.

ACCOMMODATIONS

More than 20 hotels and motels offer lodging in Page, but many visitors who come here choose to stay on a houseboat. At Wahweap Marina's **Lake Powell Resort** (100 Lakeshore Dr., 888/896-3829, www.lakepowell.com, $70–286), you can stay in a hotel room or rent a houseboat. The resort and marina are operated by Aramark, the recreation area's concessionaire.

Courtyard by Marriot (600 Clubhouse Dr., 928/645-5000 or 877/905-4495, www.marriott courtyardpage.com, $89–209) provides resort-style accommodations near the golf course.

About 30 minutes' drive from Page in Utah, you'll find the area's newest—and the most luxurious—resort, ◖ Amangiri (1 Kayenta Rd., Canyon Point, UT, 435/675-3999 or 877/695-3999, www.amanresorts.com, from $850). Simply designed with an international flair, it offers suite accommodations surrounded by sandstone mesas and anchored by a 25,000-square-foot spa.

For less expensive options, look to numerous local mom-and-pop operations, such as **Bashful Bob's** (750 S. Navajo Dr., 928/645-3919, www.bashfulbobsmotel.com, $40) and the **Red Rock Motel** (114 8th Ave., 928/645-0062, www.redrockmotel.com, $49–80), or the national chains: Best Western, Budget Host, Days Inn, Holiday Inn Express, Motel 6, Quality Inn, Rodeway Inn, Super 8, and Travelodge are represented here. Lower rates may be available during winter months. Book well in advance for summer months, when Arizonans beat the desert heat by escaping to the lake.

Camping and RVs

The marinas (888/896-3829, www.lake powell.com) at **Wahweap** (928/645-2433), **Bullfrog** (435/684-3000) and **Halls Crossing** (435/684-7000) have developed campgrounds with tent sites and RV hookups ($20–40). **Glen Canyon National Recreation Area** (928/608-9200, www.nps.gov/glca) operates the developed campground at Lees Ferry as well as several primitive campgrounds around the lake. Backcountry camping is allowed in the national recreation area, with some restrictions. Restrictions vary, depending on whether you are camping along the lakeshore or in a wilderness area. All shoreline campsites are required to have a portable toilet, unless toilets are available within 200 yards. Burying waste of any kind on beaches is prohibited. Waste must be contained in an NPS-approved waste containment system. Houseboats must be anchored at least 100 feet apart. Ground fires (wood only) must be below the high-water line. If you are camping away from the lake, dispose of human waste in a "cat hole" six to eight inches deep, at least a quarter-mile from the lake and 100 feet from any water source. Choose campsites on dunes or sandstone; avoid vegetation or organic soil. Pack out all trash, including toilet paper. Leave the campsite looking the same as—or better than—it did when you found it.

FOOD

Page offers a wide range of eateries, from fast-food joints to the tablecloths-and-a-view seating at the **Rainbow Room** (100 Lakeshore Dr., 928/645-1162 or 928/645-1040, breakfast, lunch, and dinner daily spring–fall, reservations recommended, $8–30), one of several dining options at Wahweap Marina's Lake Powell Lodge. If you want to get even closer to the lake, you can join Aramark's two-hour dinner cruise (928/645-1070, www.lakepowell.com, departing 6 P.M. June 1–Aug. 15, 5 P.M. Apr. 1–May 31, 5 P.M. Aug. 16–Oct. 31, $75) from Wahweap Marina.

Strombolli's (711 N. Navajo Dr., 928/645-2605, lunch and dinner, hours vary seasonally, $7–20), a popular pasta-and-pizza joint with sister restaurants in Flagstaff and Cottonwood, is a great place to carbo-load before a day of hiking and water-play. If you're looking for nightlife, the **Dam Bar & Grill** (928/645-2161 or 644 N. Navajo Dr., 7 P.M.–2 A.M. Tues.–Sun., $8–25) serves up dance music, pool tables, and video games along with their burgers and brews.

Several national chains can be found in Page, including Denny's, KFC, McDonald's, Pizza Hut, Subway, and Taco Bell. If you're packing a picnic to take on the lake or trail, the deli at Safeway (650 Elm St., 928/645-8155, $5–10) has sandwiches and salads to go.

INFORMATION AND SERVICES
Visitors Centers

Stop by the local **Page Chamber of Commerce**

(34 S. Lake Powell Blvd., 928/645-2741, www.pagechamber.com, 9 A.M.–5 P.M. Mon.–Fri.) for more information about guided tours and current attractions.

Sharing space with the John Wesley Powell Museum is a **visitors information center** (6 N. Lake Powell Blvd., 928/645-9496, www.powellmuseum.org, 9 A.M.–5 P.M. daily) that can assist with selecting and booking local tours.

Boat rentals can be arranged at Wahweap Marina through Lake Powell Resorts (100 Lakeshore Dr., 888/896-3829, www.lakepowell.com, 8 A.M.–5 P.M. daily, shorter hours in winter) or at the lake's newest marina, Antelope Point (22 S. Navajo Dr., 928/645-5900, 8 A.M.–5 P.M. daily).

Glen Canyon National Recreation Area operates two year-round visitors centers: **Carl Hayden Visitors Center** (928/608-6404, usually 8:30 A.M.–4:30 P.M. daily, hours vary by season) near the dam, and the **Glen Canyon National Recreation Area Headquarters** (928/608-6200, 7 A.M.–4 P.M. Mon.–Fri.) in the town of Page.

The visitors center at **Bullfrog Marina** (435/684-7423) is open intermittently during summer months, as are the ranger stations at Halls Crossing and Dangling Rope.

Navajo Bridge Interpretive Center (928/355-2319, 9 A.M.–5 P.M. daily Apr.–Oct.) is located on U.S. 89 near Lees Ferry, the boundary between the national recreation area and Grand Canyon National Park.

Local Services

The 25-bed **Page Hospital** (501 N. Navajo Dr., 928/645-2424) has 24-hour emergency services and helicopter transport. Urgent care is available nearby at **Canyonlands Community Health Care** (440 N. Navajo Dr., 928/645-1700).

The **main post office** (44 6th Ave., 928/645-2571) is located a couple of blocks from the hospital near downtown Page. There's also a post office branch inside Lake Powell Mart (101 W. Glenn St., 928/353-4821).

The local **public library** (479 S. Lake Powell Blvd., 928/645-4270) is located in the same complex as Coconino Community College, and there are several computers available for Internet users.

GETTING THERE AND AROUND

Page is a little more than two hours' drive north of Flagstaff on U.S. 89. The most practical way to explore the area is by driving your own vehicle or a rental, although you could fly into Page and arrange for air or ground transportation to Grand Canyon.

Five marinas offer lake access: Antelope Point, Bullfrog, Dangling Rope (open March–late Nov.), Halls Crossing, and Wahweap. The largest, Wahweap, and the newest, Antelope Point, are in Arizona near Page. Boat tours and rentals are available at both Wahweap and Antelope Point Marinas. The Utah marinas are more than 200 miles uplake from Page.

From Page, head south on U.S. 89 to get to the Grand Canyon's North Rim (120 miles) or South Rim (130 miles). For the North Rim, turn west on U.S. 89A and continue to Jacob Lake, then turn south on Highway 67 and drive the remaining 45 miles to the rim.

To get to the South Rim, stay on U.S. 89, turning west at Highway 64. You'll reach the park's East Entrance Station in 30 miles. It's about the same distance to continue from the East Entrance to Grand Canyon Village.

Airports

The **Page Municipal Airport** (238 10th Ave., 928/645-4337) is served by Great Lakes Airlines (928/645-1355 or 800/554-5111, www.greatlakesav.com) with flights to Phoenix and Denver. Classic Aviation (928/645-5357 or 800/444-9220) offers charter flights. Tour companies flying out of Page include Westwind Air Tours (928/645-2494 or 800/245-8668) and Papillon (702/736-7243 or 888/635-7272). Smaller airstrips are located near Lake Powell marinas.

Cars and Shuttles

A number of local hotels offer shuttles to and from the airport and around town. Avis (928/645-2024 or 800/331-1212) rents cars at the Page airport. Locally owned **Buggy Rent a Car** (928/645-9347) can hook you up with a midsize sedan or, if you're feeling adventurous, an ATV or 4WD. Taxi service is available from **Grand Circle Shuttle** (928/645-6806).

Fredonia and Kanab

Does your Grand Canyon itinerary include visiting Toroweap, one of the canyon's most isolated and beautiful overlooks? Are you interested in a canyoneering adventure in Kanab Creek wilderness or the slot canyons along the Paria River? Are you thinking about extending your trip to the Grand Canyon to include the Grand Circle? If the answer to any of these questions is yes, then Fredonia or Kanab will make a convenient and pleasant base for your explorations.

Fredonia, Arizona, is seven miles south of Kanab, Utah, and about 75 miles from the North Rim. For years, the expanses of Grand Canyon isolated the Arizona Strip from the rest of the state, and towns like Fredonia, along U.S. 89A, aligned more closely with neighboring

Utah than with Arizona. Both Fredonia and Kanab are tidy and historic, with a small-town atmosphere. Kanab is a bit larger, and you'll find more lodging and dining choices.

Although their combined population is small (7,000), Fredonia and Kanab make an ideal launching point for those traveling the Arizona and Utah parklands long known as the Grand Circle—the largest concentration of scenic national parks and monuments in the United States. Grand Canyon, Zion, Bryce Canyon, Arches, Cedar Breaks, Capitol Reef, and Canyonlands are linked together by scenic and historic byways, most less than two hours from Kanab. The towns are situated between the White Cliffs and Vermilion Cliffs of the

Grand Staircase, and colorful horizons mark the edges of high, dry plateaus.

It's hot here in summer and cold in winter. Big sagebrush *(Artemisia tridentata)* dominates the wide-open landscape around Fredonia, bracingly aromatic after a summer rainstorm. In early fall, yellow-blooming rabbitbrush lines two-lane roads and forest tracks, and you might feel like you're driving through time to a more primal era.

Centuries ago, this stark environment was home to the Ancestral Puebloans, who left behind ruins and rock art like footprints across the land. Few Anglos visited this region until the mid-1800s, when Mormon colonists established ranches and farms. This was the last area of the continental United States to be mapped, and even today it holds a sense of discovery for intrepid travelers.

SIGHTS
◖ Pipe Spring National Monument

Pipe Spring National Monument (14 miles west of Fredonia on Hwy. 389, 928/643-7105, www.nps.gov/pisp, 7 A.M.–5 P.M. daily), operated jointly by the National Park Service and the Kaibab Paiute tribe, is a good place to learn more about the people who called the plateau landscape home. Mormon leader Brigham Young purchased this oasis on the Arizona Strip for the church's cattle herds. The stone house was built for self-sufficiency, featuring a walled courtyard complete with gun ports, a dairy, and gardens, and it became a stop along the famed Honeymoon Trail. The trail was named for the newlywed couples traveling between the temple in St. George, Utah, and colonies in Arizona.

Best Friends Animal Society

If you love animals, your heartstrings will be tugged during a tour of the Best Friends Animal Society (5001 Angel Canyon Rd., Kanab, 435/644-2001, www.bestfriends.org, 8 A.M.–5 P.M. daily, free). The sanctuary, typically home to 1,700 cats, dogs, birds, horses, and other critters, is nestled within the sandstone walls of Angel Canyon about five miles north of Kanab.

wooden buggy at Pipe Spring National Monument

Coral Pink Sand Dunes State Park

If the gorgeously colored landscape of Coral Pink Sand Dunes State Park (12 miles southwest of Kanab on U.S. 89A, 435/648-2800, http://stateparks.utah.gov) gives you a sense of déjà vu, you may be remembering scenes from *The Greatest Story Ever Told,* filmed here in 1965. The 3,730-acre park has nature trails, a small campground, and a very large play area for off-road vehicles.

Other movies and TV episodes filmed near Kanab include *The Lone Ranger* (1950), *Gunsmoke* (1960), *The Outlaw Josey Wales* (1976), and, fittingly, *Brighty of the Grand Canyon* (1967). At the **Little Hollywood Museum** (297 W. Center St., 435/644-5337, www.frontiermovietown.com, 8 A.M.–5 P.M. daily Mar.–Dec.) in the heart of Kanab, you can walk through movie sets and view stills and props from familiar shows.

RECREATION

Besides being the hub for the Grand Circle of national parks, Kanab and Fredonia are also gateways to the Paria Canyon–Vermilion Cliffs Wilderness, Grand Staircase–Escalante National Monument, and Grand Canyon–Parashant National Monument, all administered by the Bureau of Land Management (www.blm.gov), and the Kanab Creek and Saddle Mountain wilderness areas, which lie within the Kaibab National Forest's North Kaibab district (430 S. Main St., Fredonia, 928/643-7395, www.fs.usda .gov/kaibab, 8 A.M.–4:30 P.M. Mon.–Fri.). These wild lands offer recreation experiences that range from peaceful back-road drives to challenging canyoneering adventures. Backpackers need to prepare carefully for rugged terrain, poorly marked trails, and infrequent water sources.

You can bike to the edge of **Grand Staircase-Escalante National Monument** via the paved **Johnson Canyon Road,** which begins 10 miles east of Kanab on U.S. 89, passing ranch land, an old movie set, a sandstone arch, gnarled juniper trees, and beautifully eroded cliffs. Be respectful of private property. The pavement ends at 15 miles, but you can continue for another five—or even more, if you have the legs for it.

For a moderate in-town hike, the three-mile

© NATALIA BRATSLAVSKY/123RF.COM

The Grand Staircase, a series of colorful plateaus, rises above Kanab.

(round-trip) **Squaw Trail** climbs to great views of the series of colorful plateaus making up the Grand Staircase. The trailhead is located near Kanab's Jacob Hamblin Park (531 N. 100 E., Kanab).

South of Fredonia, a network of forest roads links to Jacob Lake and the North Rim. Although U.S. 89A is a paved and scenic route to the park—especially if you stop to enjoy views of the Grand Staircase from **LeFevre Overlook**—you can add some new vistas by making a loop with **scenic back roads** to Jacob Lake. Paved Forest Road 22, lined with golden-blooming chamiso (rabbitbrush) in early autumn, cuts 21 miles through ranch country before joining Forest Road 462 and Forest Road 461, good dirt roads that climb the Kaibab Plateau for the final nine miles to Jacob Lake. The route, which begins a mile east of Fredonia on U.S. 89, is suitable for passenger cars in dry conditions.

The nine holes at **Coral Cliffs Golf Course** (755 E. Fairway Dr., Kanab, 435/644-5005, www.coralcliffsgolfcourse.com) are edged on three sides by the foothills of the Vermillion Cliffs.

ENTERTAINMENT AND EVENTS

These tidy twin towns roll up their sidewalks fairly early, though you can always catch a movie at the **Kanab Theater** (29 W. Center St., Kanab, 435/644-2334). If you prefer classics, the **Old Barn Theater** (89 E. Center St., Kanab, 435/644-2601) at Parry Lodge screens old movies filmed in the Kanab area.

Western-themed stage shows pop up for awhile before riding off into the sunset, but the **Crescent Moon Theater** (150 S. 100 E., Kanab, 435/644-2350) generally has something clever up its sleeve, from cowboy poetry to old Westerns or live music.

Throughout the month of March, prehistoric and historic traditions are highlighted at **Pipe Spring National Monument** (14 miles west of Fredonia on Hwy. 389, 928/643-7105, www.nps.gov/pisp) as part of **Arizona Archaeology Month.**

The Amazing Earthfest, held the third week in May in Kanab, celebrates the nature and science of the Colorado Plateau region. The festival combines education with fun during photography workshops, interpretive hikes, green-building lessons, and other events.

Summer months in Kanab and Fredonia are punctuated by classic small-town celebrations. **Jacob Hamblin Days,** held each June, honors Kanab's founder. The **Western Legends Roundup** in August includes a parade, a street fair, a fiddling contest, a film festival, and other attractions.

SHOPPING

You'll find an assortment of gift shops, Western-wear stores, and rock shops in Kanab. The **Gift Shop at Best Friends Animal Society** (5001 Angel Canyon Rd., Kanab, 435/644-2001, www.bestfriends.org, 8 A.M.–5 P.M. daily) has toys and necessities for your pet friends and some pretty cool stuff for humans too.

ACCOMMODATIONS

Lodging choices in Fredonia, 75 miles from the North Rim, are mostly inexpensive motels along U.S. 89A, the town's Main Street. Continue another 7 miles to Kanab, Utah, and you'll also find home rentals, chain motels, and local inns. You'll have about 30 lodging options, including Best Western, Holiday Inn Express, Rodeway Inn, and Quality Inn. Many motels and lodges offer off-season rates during winter months; a few close for the season.

The two towns are tidy, charming, and historic, with local lodges to match, including the retro **Quail Park Lodge** (125 N. 300 W., Kanab, 435/215-1447 or 866/702-8099, $90–110) and **Kanab Garden Cottages** (435/644-2020, www.kanabcottages.com, $130–160), which are historic homes in various Kanab locations.

Moderately priced **◖ Parry Lodge** (89 E. Center St., Kanab, 435/644-2601 or 888/286-1722, www.parrylodge.com, $80–136) hosted movie stars during Kanab's heyday of Western filmmaking. The hotel is listed on the National Register of Historic Places, and the owners play up the old-time feel. Rooms and amenities vary; inquire about recent renovations.

Kanab has several commercial RV campgrounds, including the **Kanab RV Corral** (483 S. 100 E., Kanab, 435/644-5330, www.kanabrvcorral.com, $30), located on the east edge of town near the golf course. Public campgrounds include lovely **Coral Pink Sand Dunes State Park** (12 miles southwest of Kanab on U.S. 89A, 435/648-2800, http://stateparks.utah.gov/parks/coral-pink, $16), a favorite of off-roaders and photographers.

FOOD

If you like home-style cooking, you'll find a number of restaurants in Kanab and Fredonia offering Western fare, including the **Three Bears Creamery Cottage** (210 S. 100 E., Kanab, 435/644-3300, lunch and dinner Mon.–Sat., $5–10) and **Nedra's Too** (310 S. 100 E., Kanab, 435/644-2030, breakfast, lunch, and dinner daily, $10–15), which features Southwestern favorites served by three generations of family cooks.

Located in a historic mercantile-turned-art gallery, the ◖ **Rocking V Café** (97 W. Center St., Kanab, 435/644-8001, hours vary, spring–fall, $10–40) dishes art and music along with fresh, hip meals. Reservations are recommended during the busy summer season, when diners can sit outdoors on the patio.

INFORMATION AND SERVICES
Visitors Centers

For more information about tours and recreation, contact the City of Kanab (76 N. Main St., Kanab, 435/644-2534, www.visitkanabinfo.com, 9 A.M.–5 P.M. Mon.–Fri.) or the **Fredonia Chamber of Commerce** (130 N. Main St., Fredonia, 928/643-7684).

Pipe Spring National Monument (14 miles west of Fredonia on Hwy. 389, 928/643-7105, www.nps.gov/pisp, 7 A.M.–5 P.M. daily) has morning ranger programs and tours throughout the day. If you're planning a backpacking trip to remote areas of Grand Canyon National Park, such as Kanab Creek Canyon, you can

pick up a backcountry pass here within six days of your trip date.

North Kaibab National Forest district headquarters (430 S. Main St., Fredonia, 928/643-7395, www.fs.usda.gov/kaibab, 8 A.M.–4:30 P.M. Mon.–Fri.) has maps and information about local trails and forest roads to Toroweap and Jacob Lake.

In Kanab, the **Bureau of Land Management** (BLM) operates a district field office (435/644-4600) and the Kanab Visitors Center (318 N. 1st E., Kanab, 435/644-4680, www.blm.gov, 8 A.M.–4:30 P.M. Mon.–Fri. summer) for Grand Staircase–Escalante National Monument.

Local Services

Kane County Hospital (355 N. Main St., Kanab, 435/644-5811) has emergency services. The attached clinic (435/644-4100, 8 A.M.–6 P.M. Mon.–Thurs., 8 A.M.–5 P.M. Fri.) provides walk-in urgent care 5–6 P.M. Mon.–Thurs. The **Fredonia Community Health Center** (100 E. Wood Hill Rd., Fredonia, 928/643-6215, 7 A.M.–12:30 P.M. and 1:30–5 P.M. Mon.–Wed., 7–11 A.M. Thurs.) provides urgent care.

The **Kanab City Library** (374 N. Main St., Kanab, 435/644-2394, 10 A.M.–5 P.M. Mon. and Fri., 10 A.M.–7 P.M. Tues.–Thurs., 10 A.M.–2 P.M. Sat.) has computers for public use as well as free Wi-Fi. The **Fredonia Public Library** (130 N. Main St., Fredonia, 928/643-7137, 8 A.M.–6 P.M. Mon.–Thurs., 10 A.M.–2 P.M. Fri.) has a bank of computers with Internet access.

Post offices are located along Main Street in Fredonia (84 N. Main St., Fredonia, 928/643-7122) and Kanab (39 S. Main St., Kanab, 435/644-2760).

GETTING THERE AND AROUND

Though only a skip away from several national parks, Fredonia and Kanab are splendidly isolated from major urban areas, about 200 miles east of Las Vegas and 70 miles east of St. George, Utah. The best way to explore the wide-open spaces of the Arizona Strip is in your own vehicle or a rental.

To get to the North Rim from Kanab, take U.S. 89A south. The highway swings east after passing through Fredonia and begins to climb the Kaibab Plateau, turning south again as it nears Jacob Lake, about 30 miles. At Jacob Lake, turn south on Highway 67 and proceed another 43 miles to the North Rim's Bright Angel Point.

If you are heading for the South Rim, stay on U.S. 89A until it joins U.S. 89. Take U.S. 89 south to Highway 64 and the South Rim's East Entrance Station. Grand Canyon Village is approximately 220 miles from Fredonia.

To get to Grand Canyon National Park's remote Toroweap overlook via the Sunshine Route, take Highway 389 west from Fredonia about seven miles. Turn south on the Mount Trumbull Road and travel 60 miles, following signs for Toroweap. Do not attempt this trip unless you have planned carefully, checked current road conditions, and adequately prepared yourself and your vehicle with maps, food, water, and at least one good spare tire.

Airport

The nearest commercial airport is in St. George, Utah, about 70 miles west. The **Kanab Municipal Airport** (2378 S. U.S. 89A, Kanab, 435/644-2299) is located two miles south of Kanab. Based at the airport, Kanab Air Service offers scenic and charter flights.

Cars and Shuttles

Xpress RentACar (435/644-3408, www.xpress rentalcarofkanab.com) can arrange for a rental at Kanab's airport or local hotels. You can rent a jeep at **Canyon Country Jeep Rental** (285 S. 100 E., Kanab, 435/644-8250). You'll find national car-rental companies in St. George, about 70 miles west.

A number of taxi and shuttle services based in St. George or Cedar City, Utah, cover the Kanab area, including **Hail Harry** (800/966-4245) and Quality Cab (435/656-5222).

BACKGROUND

The Land

GEOGRAPHY

Grand Canyon slices roughly east–west through the southwestern edge of the Colorado Plateau, an uplifted platform with an average elevation of 6,000 feet centering on the Southwest's Four Corners area and covering about 130,000 square miles. Ninety percent of this vast semi-arid plateau is drained by the Colorado River and its tributaries. The Colorado Plateau's colorful sedimentary rock layers, broken by faults and carved by streams, are dramatically revealed in cliffs and canyons.

Within the major physiographic province of the Colorado Plateau, shifts along fault lines have created several distinct smaller plateaus.

The canyon's north side is dominated by the Kaibab and Kanab Plateaus. On the south is the Coconino Plateau. The eastern section of Grand Canyon, known as Marble Canyon, runs roughly north–south through the lower elevations of the Marble Platform.

From the heights of the Kaibab Plateau (9,200 feet) to the Marble Canyon Airport (3,603 feet), the Grand Canyon region encompasses a number of environments. Inside the boundaries of Grand Canyon National Park (1.2 million acres), the North Rim's Grand Canyon Lodge sits 1,180 feet higher than Grand Canyon Village on the South Rim, with 10 air miles (220 road miles) between.

Grand Canyon ends at the Grand Wash Cliffs, which form the edge of present-day Lake Mead, impounded by Hoover Dam. Here begins another major physiographic province, the alternating valleys and escarpments of the Great Basin.

The Colorado River, the canyon's main artery, flows from north-central Colorado to the Gulf of Mexico. Glen Canyon Dam impounds the river northeast of Grand Canyon, restricting flows and changing the river's muddy, red-brown water to cold, clear green. The distance from rim to river varies but averages 4,000 feet. The river averages about 35 feet deep and varies in width from 76 feet to more than 300 feet.

The 277-mile stretch from Lees Ferry to the Grand Wash Cliffs drops 1,900 feet in elevation and crosses countless tributary canyons. Debris from these side canyons creates the most common type of rapids, constriction rapids, where water tumbles over boulders swept into the main channel by floods. River runners encounter more than 160 rapids on the journey through the canyon, and the Colorado River drops in gradient about eight feet per mile. Most of Grand Canyon's tributaries flow only intermittently after rainstorms or during spring melt. About a dozen have year-round water, including the Little Colorado River, Bright Angel Creek, and Havasu Creek.

The Colorado River and Grand Canyon create a barrier between Arizona's northwest corner and the rest of the state. Until the Navajo Bridge was completed in 1929, the Arizona Strip was relatively isolated. Even today, the corner of Grand Canyon known as Tuweep or Toroweap requires a long drive through ranch country and Bureau of Land Management (BLM) land.

GEOLOGY

The rock layers of Grand Canyon record more than one-third of the earth's history, beginning with the Precambrian period. The oldest, deepest rock found in Grand Canyon's Inner Gorge is Vishnu schist, a hard, fine-grained rock formed under heat and pressure nearly 2 billion years ago. The source of the schist lay at the bottom of an early Precambrian sea, where deposits of mud, silt, clay, and sand buried far below the earth's surface consolidated under pressure.

Then, 1.7 billion years ago, the continent buckled and folded as it collided with a chain of volcanic islands. The heat and pressure metamorphosed layers of sediment and ash into schist, and volcanic intrusions solidified to form granite. The gray-to-black Vishnu schist and pinkish Zoroaster granite interweave to form the hard cliffs of the Inner Gorge. These rocks are part of the Precambrian Basement Complex on which the North American continent rests.

The high mountain range formed by the collision eventually eroded away as the continent continued to shift. About 1.2 billion years ago, the schist and granite were exposed as a coastal plain that became engulfed by the Bass Sea. Over the next 430 million years, late in the Precambrian period, 14,000 feet of marine sediments formed the nine strata collectively known as the Grand Canyon Supergroup.

Single-celled bacteria formed clumps, preserved in the Bass limestone as stromatolites, the oldest fossils in Grand Canyon. Gray or reddish Bass limestone, 120–340 feet thick, is interbedded with sandstone and siltstone, indicating a shifting coastal environment. In areas, Bass limestone has been partly metamorphosed, resulting in asbestos, which was mined by Grand Canyon pioneers like William Bass and John Hance.

Subsequent layers, primarily sandstone and shale, are cross-bedded, cracked, and rippled, some even bearing raindrop impressions, as the land alternated between marine and dry coastal environments. Overlying the Bass limestone is bright orange-red Hakatai shale, 430–830 feet thick. Above it, Shinumo quartzite varies 1,060–1,500 feet thick, with marbled patterns suggesting earthquakes or tremors. Reddish Dox sandstone, deposited about 1.2–1.1 billion years ago, is soft and easily eroded.

Volcanic activity occurring just over 1 billion years ago is recorded by Cardenas lava, forming intrusions and basalt cliffs nearly 1,000 feet

© SCOTT GRIESSEL/123RF.COM

A multitude of layers are visible from the North Rim.

during the **Great Unconformity,** a period that lasted 250 million years and left only colorful remnants of the Supergroup layers in wedges and folds near Unkar Delta, Phantom Ranch, Bass Camp, and downriver between miles 130 and 138. In most of the canyon, the Supergroup has completely eroded away, and the contact line between schist and Tapeats sandstone—the edge of the Tonto Platform—represents 1 billion years of missing geology.

Following the period of rifting and erosion, the Grand Canyon region lay along a relatively tranquil coastline. Over the next 325 million years, throughout the Paleozoic era, sediments 3,500–6,500 feet deep formed 15 rock layers. These horizontal strata are the canyon's most visible layers, recording a proliferation of life forms in fossils—the most complete record of the Paleozoic era on the planet.

The Cambrian period began with beaches and tidal flats, preserved as coarse-grained Tapeats sandstone, a dark-brown, stratified, 150–250-foot-thick cliff that lies directly on top of the basement rocks in many areas of the canyon. Above and intermingling with the Tapeats are the green and purple mud, silt, and sand of the Bright Angel shale, up to 450 feet thick, formed in a shallow marine environment. Both the Tapeats sandstone and Bright Angel shale are riddled with worm burrows and trilobite fossils. Deeper waters deposited the Muav limestone 535 million years ago. These three layers, known collectively as the Tonto Group, represent a shifting coastline.

The next 130 million years, the Ordovician and Silurian periods, are completely missing from Grand Canyon. The Devonian period is only partially represented by Temple Butte limestone, more predominant in the western canyon. In the eastern canyon, Redwall limestone lies directly on top of the Cambrian rocks of the Tonto Group.

The Redwall formation dates to the Mississippian period, 360–320 million years ago, when ocean covered all of western North America. Redwall cliffs rise 500–800 feet above the Tonto Platform in the central

thick in places. The volcanic activity was part of a greater collision and uplift, the Grenville Orogeny, which formed mountain ranges along a supercontinent.

At the center of this supercontinent, the Grand Canyon region was a low area of trapped seawater. Deep sediments from this time are represented by the Nankoweap, Galeros, Kwagunt, and Sixtymile Formations. The Nankoweap Formation, 1 billion years old, is a purplish sandstone 370 feet thick, visible primarily in Nankoweap Canyon in the eastern canyon, as are the Galeros and Kwagunt Formations, shale and siltstone deposited 900 million years ago. The Sixtymile Formation, exposed on top of Nankoweap Butte and in Sixtymile Canyon, is sandstone and conglomerate deposited 820 million years ago as widespread geologic unrest began to break the supercontinent apart.

During this period, 820–770 million years ago, the Grand Canyon Supergroup layers were tilted and uplifted along fault lines. The exposed layers eroded as much as 15,000 feet canyon. Redwall limestone is naturally grayish, but has been stained red by overlying rock. The limestone is often pocked with caves and alcoves where softer deposits have been dissolved by seeps. Sheer Redwall cliffs are often draped with tapestries of desert varnish, dark mineralized stains. Nodules of chert (fossilized sponge), along with nautiloids, brachiopods, crinoids, and other fossils indicate a rich marine life.

The Supai Group of shale, limestone, and sandstone was laid down in a coastal environment during the late Pennsylvanian and early Permian periods, 310–285 million years ago. The topmost member, Esplanade sandstone, forms a hard shelf in western Grand Canyon, and the sculpted reddish bedrock of eastern tributaries like North and South Canyons. Reptile tracks can be seen in the upper members of the Supai Group, which forms a band of alternating cliffs and slopes 950–1,350 feet thick.

The transition from the Pennsylvania to Permian periods was marked by a continental collision that formed steep mountain ranges. During the Permian period, drainage from the ancestral Rockies reached the Grand Canyon region, depositing muddy sediments in a delta-like environment, rich with plant life. In Grand Canyon, 35 types of ferns and other plants were fossilized in Hermit Shale, laid down 286–245 million years ago. It's easy to spot the 250–1,000-foot-thick Hermit Shale, which forms dark red slopes.

When the ancient rivers ceased flowing, the mud left behind began to crack and dry out, and by 270 million years ago, the canyon region was a desert environment. Windblown sand dunes reached up to 1,000 feet high and covered a vast area, all the way to present-day Montana. Buff-colored Coconino sandstone forms eolian (wind-deposited) cross-bedded cliffs 350 feet high in the eastern canyon, pinching out to the west.

Some 265 million years ago, seawater returned, evaporating quickly in the tidal flats of an arid environment. The Toroweap Formation, silty limestone 250–450 feet thick,

left steep slopes of pale yellow, usually vegetated by trees and shrubs.

Over the next 5 million years, seawater continued to engulf the canyon, laying down the Kaibab Formation, limestone rich with marine invertebrate fossils and even fish. This layer, 290–500 feet thick, forms the canyon's rims. By this time, the Grand Canyon area was just north of the equator, part of the supercontinent Pangaea formed as the planet's landmasses collided and slowly coalesced.

At the end of the Permian period, 245 million years ago, the rocks that make up Grand Canyon's gorgeous walls had been laid down, with the Kaibab formation at sea level. The canyon itself had yet to be formed. The canyon's predominant Paleozoic layers can be memorized, top to bottom, by the acronym formed from the first letters of the phrase "Know The Canyon's History, Study Rocks Made By Time": Kaibab, Toroweap, Coconino, Hermit, Supai, Redwall, Muav, Bright Angel, Tapeats.

Mesozoic geology is visible in areas outside the park's boundaries. On the drive to Lees Ferry, you can see Mesozoic rocks: the Chinle Formation of the Painted Desert, the Moenave and Kayenta Formations at the base of the Echo and Vermilion Cliffs, and the Navajo sandstone upstream in Glen Canyon. During the Mesozoic Era, Pangaea broke up during uplifts, earthquakes, and volcanoes. About 65 million years ago, at the beginning of the Cenozoic era, a mountain-building period known as the Laramide orogeny raised the Colorado Plateau region, creating the series of monoclines known as the Grand Staircase. Mesozoic rocks eroded away from the heights of the Kaibab Plateau, stripping Grand Canyon back to its Permian layers and setting the stage for canyon cutting.

Several forces have combined to create Grand Canyon, and many geological theories about the canyon's formation have been advanced during the hundred-plus years that geologists have studied the region. Most agree that although its rocks are very old, the canyon itself is relatively young. But exactly when and how the canyon was formed is still under debate.

Many geologists believe that sometime between 5 and 6 million years ago, the ancestral Colorado River began cutting through rock layers that had been laid down over billions of years. Recent research suggests that canyon formation may have begun as long as 16 million years ago. Although canyon-cutting theories conflict in regard to timing, scientists agree that the ancestral Colorado River was a powerful erosional force.

We know that before the completion of Glen Canyon Dam in 1963, the Colorado River carried 380,000 tons of sediment daily through Grand Canyon, giving it a tremendous cutting power that probably pales in comparison to that of the ancestral river. During a volcanic period 1 million years ago, the river was powerful enough to grind through several lava dams formed in western Grand Canyon. And as ice age glaciers advanced and retreated, the ancient river carried debris-laden floods from the Rockies.

Erosion continues, although today most sediments are trapped behind Glen Canyon Dam, and the 30,000–40,000 tons of sediment that flow through the canyon daily are from tributaries such as the Little Colorado or Paria Rivers. Yet the canyon continues to change. Though its glowing cliffs and temples may appear to be frozen in time, the canyon continues to be shaped by water and wind at a pace humans are barely able to comprehend.

CLIMATE

The Grand Canyon region is semiarid, with great variation in temperature and rainfall due to elevation. Average annual precipitation is less than 10 inches at Phantom Ranch, 15 inches on the South Rim, and more than 20 inches on the North Rim. Most of the moisture arrives during the late summer monsoon season or during the winter. Temperatures vary from below 0°F to higher than 100°F in the inner canyon. Rims are often windy, and the inner canyon "breathes," with upstream winds during daylight and downstream winds

at night. The seasonal descriptions below are general and hardly a guarantee. Expect the unexpected: snowstorms in June, 90°F temperatures in October, dry winters when the North Rim is accessible for stretches at a time, and long, cool springs when wildflowers seem to be in constant bloom.

In late March, when the calendar says it's spring, the North Rim will still be tucked under a blanket of snow. On the South Rim it may be cold and windy, but if you find a sunny, sheltered spot, you can already feel the power of the sun's rays. During the next couple of months, spring creeps up from the inner canyon as wildflowers bloom along trails and birds go about the business of establishing territories and nests. Lingering Pacific storm patterns may dump inches of snow on the South Rim into April, but the snow melts quickly as the sun gains strength. By May, inner canyon temperatures are already reaching into the 90s, and winter loses its grip on the North Rim.

May and June are dry and cloudless. While the North Rim begins to experience spring, inner canyon temperatures edge toward the 100°F mark as the dry desert foresummer tightens its grip. The South Rim is pleasant, with highs in the 70s and 80s, perfect for hiking. The intense sun quickly dries the forests surrounding the rims, and by the end of June, fire danger may trigger camping and hiking restrictions in the national forest lands surrounding the park.

As southern Arizona deserts heat up and weather patterns shift, pulling in moisture from the Gulf of Mexico, clouds begin to build, heralding the arrival of the annual monsoon. Hot, dry air may evaporate moisture before it reaches the earth, creating dry storms that spawn dangerous lightning. By mid-July, the rains arrive at last in the form of brief, powerful thundershowers that sweep across the canyon, usually in the afternoon. The monsoon pattern lasts through August, the month when the inner canyon receives the most rain. A second bloom of wildflowers begins with the rains.

By mid-September the monsoon retreats and cloudless skies return. Inner canyon

GRAND CANYON WEATHER

Arizona's higher elevations, including the rims of the canyon, receive more precipitation than the state's deserts and valleys. Though much of Arizona (including the inner canyon) is desert, the state has two rainy seasons. The seasonal rains are different in character, and the Navajo have long referred to them as male or female rains.

The winter rainy season, beginning in December, brings snow to the high country and rain to the desert. These relatively gentle "female" rains can linger for days. Locals listen to weather reports for snow levels (the elevations at which rain changes to snow). At this time of year, clouds occasionally fill the inner canyon, a rare and beautiful sight.

More dramatic and dangerous "male" rains characterize the Arizona monsoon. In summer, prevailing winds shift and humidity rises. By mid-July, the rains arrive, often as brief but fierce afternoon storms. These squalls are usually localized, moving quickly across the canyon and producing thunder and lightning. Flash flooding is possible as water sweeps down tributary canyons, sometimes from storms occurring miles away. Still, the rains are a welcome respite from the intense summer heat, scenting the air and bringing rainbows in their wake. The monsoon pattern usually ends in mid-September.

Month	South Rim		Inner Canyon		North Rim	
	Low/ High (°F)	Precip. (inches)	Low/ High (°F)	Precip. (inches)	Low/ High (°F)	Precip. (inches)
January	18/41	1.32	36/56	0.68	16/37	3.17
February	21/45	1.55	42/62	0.75	18/39	3.22
March	25/51	1.38	48/71	0.79	21/44	2.63
April	32/60	0.93	56/82	0.47	29/53	1.73
May	39/70	0.66	63/92	0.36	34/62	1.17
June	47/81	0.42	72/101	0.30	40/73	0.86
July	54/84	1.81	78/106	0.84	46/77	1.93
August	53/82	2.25	75/103	1.40	45/75	2.85
September	47/76	1.56	69/97	0.97	39/69	1.99
October	36/65	1.10	58/84	0.65	31/59	1.38
November	27/52	0.94	46/68	0.43	24/46	1.48
December	20/43	1.62	37/57	0.87	20/40	2.83

temperatures moderate. Birds begin to migrate south, and on the North Rim the aspens turn gold as October approaches. Sometime in November, the first heavy snowfall may close the road to the North Rim.

In December, Pacific storms again march their way west, bringing winter moisture to the canyon in the form of rain or snow. The North Rim can receive as much as 120 inches of snow; the South Rim, 65 inches. Ground squirrels hibernate, while deer and elk sink into winter sluggishness, conserving energy by browsing the piñon-juniper woodlands near the village and West Rim. Snowpack is important in the West, providing a slow release of moisture as the weather warms, recharging springs and maximizing Colorado River flows. Glimpses of spring begin as early as February in the inner canyon, when brittlebush sends up its golden blooms and the cycle of seasons turns again.

Flora and Fauna

FLORA

The scientist who developed the concept of life zones, C. H. Merriam, based his theory on research he did in the Grand Canyon region in 1889 as head of the U.S. Biological Survey. He proposed that plant and animal communities change not only with latitude but also with elevation. The life zones, or biomes, identified by Merriam are the Lower Sonoran, Upper Sonoran, Transition, Canadian, Hudsonian, and Arctic-Alpine. Grand Canyon encompasses five of the six life zones Merriam identified, often likened to traveling from Mexico to Canada.

Merriam's system is still used in the western United States, although most scientists today think in terms of biologic communities rather than zones. Even so, plants and animals aren't aware of the neat scientific boundaries assigned to them. The canyon acts as a barrier to some species and a corridor to others. Orientation to the sun, rainfall amounts, differences in terrain and soils—these factors create a range of microclimates within biologic communities. Desert species extend higher on sunny ridges and slopes, while deep, shady draws allow higher elevation species to move downward. The intermixture between neighboring biologic communities is referred to as an ecotone, where flora and fauna mingle in amazing variety. Approximately 1,800 species of plants grow in Grand Canyon, nearly half of the flora found in Arizona, which is considered one of the most botanically diverse states in the country. A dozen plants are endemic, found only in the Grand Canyon area. One is the endangered sentry milk vetch *(Astragalus cremnophylax* var. *cremnophylax)*. Its Latin species name means "gorge watchman."

Deserts

The Lower Sonoran life zone, found below 3,500 feet, primarily within the Inner Gorge, includes plants from the Sonoran and Mojave Deserts. Species vary east to west, with some Great Basin desert plants growing in Marble Canyon, and Mojave Desert species appearing as the canyon approaches Lake Mead. Temperatures rise above 100°F on summer afternoons, and little rain falls. Saltbush and creosote are common. On talus slopes, Mormon tea, brittlebush, ocotillo, and crucifixion thorn join prickly pear, hedgehog, fishhook, and barrel cacti.

In sharp contrast, along the river and its tributary creeks or nearby springs, riparian communities nourish moisture-loving species. Tributaries may be cooler and more sheltered than the main canyon, nurturing redbuds, cottonwoods, willows, ferns, and monkey-flower. Along the river, Apache plume, mesquite, catclaw, and saltbush grow above the old predam high-water line. Above the new high-water line, mesquite, coyote willow, arrowweed, and the common reed compete with thickets of tamarisk, an introduced species that has aggressively overtaken Colorado River beaches.

The Upper Sonoran life zone, at 3,500–7,000 feet, includes the yucca, agave, and cacti of the Tonto Platform and the piñon-juniper woodland of the South Rim. Within this zone are desert grassland, chaparral, sagebrush, and other plant communities, often intermixed. Blackbrush predominates the Tonto Platform, giving it a gray-green appearance. In the canyon's western reaches, Joshua trees make an appearance. Cliffrose, New Mexico locust, barberry, and other spring-blooming shrubs grow on and below the South Rim, appearing in sunny pockets below the North Rim. Along trails and roadsides, fleabane, asters, phlox, globe mallow, Indian paintbrush, snakeweed, goldeneye, and other wildflowers put on changing displays from spring to fall.

Forests

At 7,000–8,000 feet, the ponderosa forests of the Transition zone yield to thickets of Gambel oak near the rims. On the North Rim, lupine and butterweed make purple and yellow carpets below the ponderosas during the summer. Above 8,000 feet the North Rim Canadian zone is home to white fir, while the moister and cooler Hudsonian zone is typified by spruce-fir forests. These two zones do not have distinct boundaries but interweave with each other according to topography, so they are often referred to in combination as the Boreal life zone. The Boreal life zone receives 25–30 inches of precipitation annually, supporting forests of spruce and fir, with open meadows edged by aspen, shimmering yellow and gold in fall. The first major snowfall often arrives in November. Temperatures sometimes plummet below 0°F, and snows can last into May or even June. High-meadow lakes form from snowmelt in the spring, attracting coyotes, wild turkeys, deer, elk, and other wildlife.

FAUNA

Grand Canyon's elevations vary from 1,200 feet at river level to 9,200 feet on the North Rim, creating myriad wildlife habitats that are mostly unbroken within the park's 1,217,403 acres. The varied environments support

Ponderosa pines grow on both rims of Grand Canyon.

© KATHLEEN BRYANT

thousands of invertebrates, 17 fish species, 9 amphibian species, 17 reptile species, 355 bird species, and 89 mammal species.

Insects

Along the river, you may encounter caddis flies, numerous beetles, moths, and butterflies, such as the lovely yellow-and-black swallowtails. The showy sphinx moth is an important pollinator, often mistaken for a hummingbird. There are blessedly few mosquitoes, but other biters include midges, fire ants, centipedes, millipedes, and the dreaded cedar gnats that plague piñon-juniper woodlands in late spring. Several scorpion species inhabit the desert areas along the river, including the tiny bark scorpion. Higher up the canyon walls and along the rims are secretive black widow spiders and tarantulas, often venturing across roads and trails around the time of the summer monsoon. Preying on the harmless giant spiders are tarantula hawks, low-flying blue-black wasps.

Fish

The completion of Glen Canyon Dam changed the Colorado River from a sediment-laden river with widely fluctuating flows to a cold, clear river. Since then, several native fish species have become endangered, extirpated, or threatened, including the humpback chub, razorback sucker, and flannelmouth sucker. Native species are more often spotted near the confluence with the warmer waters of the Little Colorado River. Introduced species include rainbow trout, present in such large numbers that in certain areas they attract bald eagles during spawning season.

Reptiles and Amphibians

Along the river and its tributaries, tree frogs and red-spotted toads serenade campers. Numerous lizard species live in the inner canyon and on the rims, including the chuckwalla, gecko, skink, yellow-backed spiny lizard, tree lizard, jewel-colored collared lizard, and short-horned lizard, colloquially but incorrectly referred to as a "horny toad." On a hot summer afternoon, when many animals retreat, lizards continue to scramble around rocks and rims.

Snakes do not tolerate extreme heat or cold, spending winter months hibernating underground and reappearing in the spring to sun themselves on rocks. In midsummer, snakes are most active in early morning and at dusk. Six rattlesnake species inhabit the inner canyon and its rims, including a couple not usually seen outside the area, the Grand Canyon pink rattlesnake and the speckled rattlesnake. Two rattlesnake predators are also present, with gopher snakes (also known as bull snakes) more common on the rim and king snakes seen more often in the river corridor.

Birds

From tiny black-chinned hummingbirds to enormous condors, birds are numerous throughout the canyon and its surrounding forests and woodlands. The diverse environments are a birder's paradise, with more than 200 species on the North Rim alone. Willow flycatchers, phoebes, and kingfishers catch insects along the river while mallards, mergansers, teals, goldeneyes, and other waterfowl swim its waters. Great blue herons and spotted sandpipers ply the river's edges. Canyon wrens sing from the canyon's rocky walls, a descending, flutelike trill that delights hikers and river runners. Peregrine falcons nest in cliffs, and red-tailed hawks and kestrels are fairly common. In the fall, the canyon becomes a flyway for other hawk species. Through the month of October, members of HawkWatch International station themselves at East Rim overlooks and count migrating raptors, usually 10,000–12,000 each season. (Public participation is welcome.) Ponderosa forests are lively with scrub jays, Steller's jays, woodpeckers, chickadees, towhees, wild turkeys, and other species. The most ubiquitous canyon avian is the common raven, exceptionally clever and equally at home raiding a river campsite, soaring across the canyon, or entertaining visitors at rim overlooks.

Mammals

Mule deer often wander around the North Rim's Bright Angel Point and the South Rim's Grand Canyon Village. Elk graze the

CRITTER ALERT

Many visitors to the Southwest are unnecessarily obsessed with spiders and snakes. Yes, several poisonous critters inhabit Grand Canyon, including rattlesnakes, Gila monsters, and scorpions. But for the most part, avoiding harm is commonsense: Look before you step, and never put your hands somewhere you can't see.

The most common bite is from scorpions, usually found in the inner canyon. Always shake out your boots, clothes, and bedding in case a scorpion, spider, millipede, centipede, or tick has decided to make camp along with you. Though scorpion bites can be excruciatingly painful, they are rarely life-threatening, except to children, the elderly, and immune-compromised individuals.

If you are bitten by a scorpion, apply a cool compress to the area, and take an antihistamine if the swelling is severe. For any insect bite: Monitor the bite area for infection (redness, swelling, heat, streaking), and see a doctor as soon as you can.

Though they look plenty scary, tarantulas, seen most often in higher elevations, are harmless unless harassed. When provoked, they'll bite or launch irritating hairs from their abdomens.

The park counts six rattlesnake species, including the relatively common Grand Canyon pink rattlesnake. Rattlers are most active at snake-friendly temperatures, around 80°F. This means in the shade or at twilight in the summer, so be especially careful hiking after sunset. Unlike in certain television commercials, rattlesnakes do not pursue humans. They'd much rather reserve their venom for prey that's easier to swallow. Most snakebites are a result of provocation, and most victims are young men, usually under the influence (which seems to indicate that excess testosterone and alcohol are as dangerous as most things Mother Nature can throw our way). If you're bitten by a rattlesnake, send someone for help. If you'd feel safer, carry an extractor kit, which works for snake venom and insect bites.

Mountain lions, though notoriously reclusive, have been spotted in areas of the park frequented by humans. It's unlikely you'll encounter a mountain lion, but it's safest to hike with companions. A mountain lion's chase instinct may be triggered if you run, so it's best to face a lion, making yourself appear bigger by flapping a jacket and backing away slowly. Rangers are currently monitoring the park's mountain lion population, so if you see a lion, inform a ranger of the date and location.

With a wingspan of nine feet, condors are formidable birds. Don't approach them. If you plan to day hike from base camp, be aware that curious condors can destroy a campsite, shredding tents and sleeping bags, and even making away with shoes or gear. Report condor sightings to a ranger, making a note of the bird's tag number if you can.

high-country meadows between Jacob Lake and the North Rim in the mornings and evenings. Though they do occasionally wander the rim, desert bighorn sheep are seen more often scrambling inner canyon cliffs. These large prey animals attract the canyon's largest predator, the mountain lion. Coyotes are more likely heard than seen, and black bears, bobcats, and gray foxes are reclusive.

Many mammals are nocturnal or crepuscular, active around dawn and dusk. Hike the North Rim's Transept Trail early in the morning to see Kaibab squirrels in their native ponderosa pine forest. Found only on the Kaibab Plateau, the squirrels have been designated a National Natural Landmark. Their more common South Rim cousins, Abert squirrels, are often spotted near Grandview Point. Trails along the rim and into the canyon are busy with chipmunks, golden-mantled ground squirrels, and rock squirrels. Unfortunately, accustomed to handouts, rodents and ringtails raid backpackers' food stores. Deer mice, kangaroo rats, packrats, and, in riparian areas, raccoons and skunks can make unwelcome nighttime campsite visits.

History

Humans have been present at Grand Canyon continuously for 12,000 years. Scientists have recorded nearly 5,000 archeological sites, and only 3 percent of the park's area has been fully surveyed. The canyon's rims and travel corridors are a rich repository of human history, from prehistoric occupation through Euro-American exploration, mining, and early tourism.

NATIVE AMERICANS

The first humans to see Grand Canyon were Paleo-Indians who traveled large distances in pursuit of megafauna, such as bison and mammoths, around 10,000 years ago. These hunters used large stone points on thrusting spears, moving with game herds and leaving little evidence of their passage. Only one Paleo-Indian site has been located at Grand Canyon.

As the last ice age receded and the megafauna died out, hunters began to rely more on smaller game and plants. During this period 2,000–9,000 years ago, the **Desert Archaic** culture roamed the Grand Canyon Region. Archaic hunter-gatherers traveled in groups, moving with the seasons as plants ripened or game animals migrated. They used atlatls (throwing tools) with darts. Remains from this period include flakes from dart points or other stone tools, grinding stones, hearths, basketry, rock shelters, and perhaps the most intriguing archaeological remains in the canyon, rock art and split-twig figurines.

One rock-art site on the western end of Grand Canyon bears a number of large anthropomorphs (humanlike figures) painted with reddish pigment, perhaps representing shamans. Split-twig figurines may also have a shamanic element. Often in the shape of deer or bighorn sheep, the figurines have been found in caves in the inner canyon's Redwall Formation. The figurines were made 2,000–4,000 years ago from a single long piece of wood, usually willow, split down the middle and folded into shape. Some are quite refined,

with details that include smaller twigs representing antlers or spears piercing the body of the figurine. Sometimes dung was stuffed inside. Carefully placed in dry caves that have helped preserve them over the millennia, these are not toys but may be totems used to ensure or reenact a successful hunt. Several examples are on display at Tusayan Museum on the South Rim.

Around 3,500 years ago, corn agriculture arrived in the Southwest. Archaic people began experimenting with cultivation to supplement hunting and gathering. They seeded flood plains, which hold moisture longer than other areas. Storage cists were used to protect surplus corn or beans, introduced later. Beans require longer cooking, leading to another innovation, pottery, dating to A.D. 500.

As people began to rely more on agriculture, they became more sedentary, at first building pit-houses, partially underground circular structures. Later, they built aboveground pueblos, structures with multiple rooms, including Tusayan Ruins along the South Rim's Desert View Drive and Walhalla Glades on the North Rim. Both villages were occupied during the summer, linked to the Colorado River via trails leading to the Unkar Delta area, where a broad floodplain and lower elevation offered a longer growing season and comfortable winter temperatures.

By A.D. 1000, the Puebloans were building kivas and outdoor plazas. Pottery types indicate trade relationships with people living in the Virgin River area north of the Grand Canyon. Archaeologists identify these and other farmers, potters, and pueblo dwellers in the Four Corners area as a single cultural group, known as **Ancestral Puebloan** or **Anasazi** (though not all archaeologists include the Cohonina in this group). Some archaeologists speculate that a combination of internal conflict, drought, and other environmental pressures pushed the Ancestral Puebloans from their homes, beginning around A.D. 1200. Others suggest that

The kiva at Tusayan Ruins was built 800 years ago.

new cultural developments centered around the Hopi Mesas pulled the Puebloans east. In any case, today's Hopi people are the descendants of the Ancestral Puebloans.

Sometime around A.D. 1300, seminomadic hunter-gatherers moved into the Grand Canyon area from farther west. The Kaibab Paiutes foraged along the North Rim. The Pai, or Cerbat, used the river corridor, supplementing hunting and gathering with agriculture and trade, and living in seasonal camps evidenced by rock shelters and stone rings where they constructed brush shelters known as wickiups. They roasted agave, a staple food, in stone-lined roasting pits. Cactus buds and blooms, piñon pine nuts, and berries added to a varied diet. Their descendants, the **Havasupai** and **Hualapai** of western Grand Canyon, continued a long trading relationship with the Hopi, while the Paiutes established ties with the Mormon colonists who entered their territories.

The Navajo Reservation bordering Grand Canyon to the east is home to the largest American Indian nation in the United States.

Ancestors of the Navajo, Athabascan hunter-gatherers, entered the area from the north around A.D. 1400. Highly adaptable, the Navajo learned agriculture from their pueblo neighbors and stock-raising from Spanish colonists.

THE ENTRADA

In 1540, Francisco Vásquez de Coronado led an expedition of 300 soldiers, several hundred Indians, and thousands of horses, cattle, sheep, and other livestock northward from New Spain. Coronado sought cities of gold described by shipwrecked Spanish sailors who had wandered from Florida to Mexico City. The expedition crossed present-day Arizona, and Coronado sent detachments westward to the Hopi villages and the vast river they had described.

Hopi guides led García López de Cárdenas and his men to the edge of Grand Canyon somewhere between Lipan Point and Desert View, the South Rim's highest reaches. Expedition journals describe the soldiers' futile struggle to get to the river, which the Spanish judged to be around six feet wide. (This says a great deal about the unprepared mind's ability to grasp the canyon's vast size, as well as the Hopi guides' cleverness at keeping their rim-to-river trails a secret.) The Spaniards returned to Mexico City in 1542, their expedition deemed a failure.

Later explorations led to colonization farther east in present-day New Mexico and farther west in California. In 1776, Silvestre Vélez de Escalante and Francisco Atanasio Domínguez left the colony of Santa Fe to find a northern route to settlements near Monterey, California. On their return journey, winter forced them southward, and they crossed the Colorado River in historic Glen Canyon (now flooded by the waters of Lake Powell). A year earlier, Friar Francisco Garcés, scouting a southern route, had named the river "Colorado" for its reddish waters. Garcés, Domínguez, and Escalante were the last Spanish explorers to venture near the canyon.

EARLY EXPLORATION

After Mexico gained independence from Spain in 1821, hunters and fur trappers explored the Colorado River and its tributaries at either end of the canyon. One, James O. Pattie, described his 1827 venture as a horrid ordeal. Trappers and traders created new routes west, and after 1848, gold hunters followed. Next came the Army and government surveyors interested in identifying transportation routes and resources.

At Fort Yuma, steamboats plied the Lower Colorado, transporting settlers, soldiers, and supplies to California. In 1857 the Army sent Lieutenant Joseph Christmas Ives upriver via a stern-wheel steamer, which ran aground far downriver from the Grand Wash Cliffs. Ives continued his explorations on foot with the

BUYING NATIVE AMERICAN ART

Whether you're a serious collector or simply want something to remember your visit, you'll discover an impressive variety of Indian arts and crafts at Hopi House, Hermits Rest, and other Grand Canyon shops, from tiny Zuni fetishes and Apache horsehair baskets to room-size Navajo rugs.

Many artists learned their skills from a grandmother, uncle, or other family member, and traditions reach back through time for generations. Though modern tools and materials have inspired exquisite craftsmanship and experimentation, handwork is still the hallmark of Indian art.

Look for signs of careful craftsmanship, such as fineness of line in designs, pleasing proportions, and symmetry. Keep in mind that some "imperfections" are actually desirable: Hopi potters use dung fires, believing the resulting smoky "fire clouds" make each piece unique. Many kachina carvers use simple tools like dremels in their work, while others – particularly carvers of old-style dolls – use only a knife

and rasp to create a more primitive look. Prices will reflect the skill and reputation of the artist, as well as his or her investment of time.

The high value of Indian art has tempted unscrupulous companies to produce counterfeits. The Indian Arts and Crafts Act of 1990 makes it illegal to market any non-Indian product as an Indian-made item. Be aware, however, that not everything marked "Indian-made" is handcrafted by an individual artist. Indian-owned factories and co-ops produce lovely jewelry and pottery, for example, but items are created assembly-line style, reflected in lower prices.

If possible, inquire about the artist and his or her work. This will not only help you make an informed purchase, but also add to your Grand Canyon memories. And remember, the wisest purchase is one you'll feel good wearing, giving, or displaying in your home. Much more than a good investment, authentic handmade Indian art is a link between you, the artist, and traditions that extend back through time.

help of Havasupai guides, abandoning eastward progress after a couple of weeks and heading south for the Army's Beale Road (present-day I-40). He summed up the region as "uninhabitable," "impassable," and "altogether valueless."

While exploration and settlement continued north, south, west, and east of Grand Canyon, the canyon itself remained one of the last blank spots on the U.S. map. The man who would change that, John Wesley Powell, was a 35-year-old Civil War veteran turned college professor. Powell's expedition was remarkable in many ways, including the fact that he didn't receive government funding for it. He undertook the trip mostly out of a desire for knowledge.

After Powell's first and second runs through the canyon in 1869 and 1871–1872, only a handful of expeditions followed over the next half century. One of the most dramatic was led by Robert Brewster Stanton, an engineer surveying the inner canyon for a possible rail line. Although that scheme sounds preposterous today, Stanton made two attempts at running the canyon. He aborted his first run in 1889 after three of his crew drowned in Marble Canyon, then successfully navigated the canyon the following year, becoming only the second person to do so.

PIONEERS

As the Mormon communities of St. George and Kanab, Utah, expanded north of the canyon, pioneers began settling the region. Timbermen logged Mt. Trumbull and the Kaibab Plateau to supply St. George and Kanab with building materials. Ranchers raised cattle west of the Kaibab Plateau, and colonists settled towns west and east of the canyon.

Prospectors began exploring the inner canyon, mining lead, zinc, silver, copper, and asbestos. Seth Tanner, a Mormon scout and guide, settled along the Colorado River in 1876 and established the Little Colorado Mining District in eastern Grand Canyon, mining copper. Dozens of prospectors followed, though few found mineral deposits rich enough to make the effort and expense of mining worthwhile.

The Atlantic and Pacific Railroad completed tracks across northern Arizona in 1882, and communities sprang up in Flagstaff and Williams, attracting settlers from the East and Midwest. Miners who had scratched out only a meager living saw potential in guiding others to the canyon for sightseeing. One, William Wallace Bass, became the first to raise a family at the canyon. He arrived in Williams, established a base camp near Havasupai Point, constructed a wagon road, and improved Indian trails to the river, combining prospecting with guiding tourists. Bass built the canyon's first rim-to-rim trail, crossing the river by cable, and constructed two frame houses that doubled as hotels.

On the other end of the canyon, the sheepherding Hull brothers and prospector John Hance built a wagon road to the Grandview area. Hance guided tourists and erected a tent camp near his cabin on the rim, serving meals and offering accommodations. James Thurber bought out Hance's interests and established a regular stage route from Flagstaff, a two-day trip that cost $20. Pete Berry began mining copper at Horseshoe Mesa in 1892, building the Grandview Trail to his mines. He and his wife owned and operated the Grand View Hotel until 1901. Martin Buggeln, who bought out James Thurber, shifted his attention farther west along the rim, where a Santa Fe Railway spur was nearing completion.

The first to settle at the future Grand Canyon Village was Sanford Rowe, who filed mining claims three miles south of the rim at Rowe Well as early as 1890. Here he established a small tourist camp, building a road to Hopi Point. Not far away, Pete Berry and Ralph Cameron improved a Havasupai trail to Indian Garden in order to prospect their claims in this area. Cameron registered the trail as a toll road with Coconino County. Thurber extended his stage line from Grandview to this part of the rim, building another hotel. He and Rowe guided tourists on Cameron's toll road.

When the Santa Fe Railway completed its spur line in 1901, travelers could choose between a $15–20 bumpy, two-day-long stage trip

JOHN HANCE AND TOURIST, ARIZONA

Known as the canyon's "most talented prevaricator," the miner, pioneer, trail builder, hotelier, postmaster, and mendicant John "Cap" Hance is a beloved figure in Grand Canyon lore. Even so, Hance's actual background has become as questionable as some of his tales. One of the first nonnatives to settle at Grand Canyon, Hance built a cabin on the rim near Grandview Point and worked an asbestos mine near the river. Some say he came to escape a less than savory past. Regardless of what brought Hance to Grand Canyon, his love affair with the region lasted throughout his life. Buckey O'Neill once said, "God made the Canyon, John Hance the trails. Without the other, neither would be complete."

One of the first to realize there was more profit in guiding tourists than in prospecting, Hance advertised his services in the Flagstaff newspaper. A few dozen visitors a year paid $20 each for a bumpy and hot two-day stage journey, and another $1 for food and lodging at Hance's tent camp or Pete Berry's Grand View Hotel. Hance led tourists down the trail to his mine, and some made a note of the experience in his visitors book: A guest from San Francisco wrote, "Our pleasures here have been enhanced by chivalrous, daring, entertaining, and ever obliging Captain Hance." Another noted, "Splendid guide, in spite of his economy of the truth."

Some say John Hance cut quite a fine figure. Despite his fondness for pie and sweets of all kinds, he was lean and trim and kept himself neat, even though it must have been hard, dirty work mining asbestos and guiding tourists down the trail. He sported a dignified, flowing mustache, and most photographs show him dressed in a suit jacket.

Hance also became the postmaster of Tourist, Arizona, the small settlement that sprang up on the rim near Grandview Point. In addition to his tent camp, the log Grand View Hotel, and the mining operations on Horseshoe Mesa below the rim, Martin Buggeln ranched nearby, and the Hull brothers supplemented their sheepherding by guiding tourists. But when the Santa Fe Railway built a spur line to the rim 12 miles west, it was the beginning of the end for Tourist.

Hance's stories had become so much a fixture of the Grand Canyon experience that the Fred Harvey Company gave him room and board at the Bright Angel Lodge in exchange for telling his whoppers to tourists. Some 100 of Hance's tall tales have been recorded in interviews with those who remember him. Many involved Darby, his faithful mare (or mule, depending on the story). In one tale, Darby attempted to leap across the canyon with a band of desperados in hot pursuit. Halfway across, Hance realized she wasn't going to make it. When astonished tourists begged to know what happened next, it was Hance's cue to say, "Why, we turned around and jumped back, of course."

In one of his most famous confabulations, Hance told visitors how he strapped on snowshoes to cross the canyon when it filled up with fog. Unfortunately, when the fog lifted, he found himself stranded on the top of Zoroaster Temple, spending three days without food or water, until the fog was thick enough to cross again.

When Hance's health declined, Harvey employees kept him at the canyon as long as possible, then moved him to the Weatherford Hotel in Flagstaff. The hotel staff kept him comfortable until his death in 1919. Hance's body was returned to his beloved canyon, and funeral services were held under the shed on the railroad platform. He is buried in Grand Canyon's pioneer cemetery.

and a comfortable three-hour train ride from Williams for $3. Most chose the train, and the canyon's pioneer enterprises faded away, with one exception: Over the years, Ralph Cameron acted as sheriff, county supervisor, and U.S. senator, a man with powerful friends and the resources to take a stand against the railroad. Cameron had moved the Red Horse stage station to the head of his toll trail and remodeled it into the Cameron Hotel. The Santa Fe Railway partnered with Martin Buggeln and his Bright Angel Hotel and camp, a few hundred feet east, until the railroad could complete its own hotel, El Tovar. A bitter competition ensued.

PRESERVATION

In the meantime, interest in conservation was growing on a national level. The Forest Reserve Act passed in 1891. While a senator, Benjamin Harrison had unsuccessfully tried to preserve Grand Canyon as a public park. In 1893, as president, Harrison was able to establish the Grand Canyon Forest Reserve. Theodore Roosevelt visited the canyon in 1903, making his famous speech urging its protection for future generations.

After becoming president, Roosevelt signed the 1906 Act for the Preservation of American Antiquities, which led to the establishment of several national monuments, including Grand Canyon National Monument in 1908. With this act, the canyon was protected from further private development. The Santa Fe Railway was content to lease rather than own land, partnering with the Fred Harvey Company to negotiate contracts with the government to build and maintain attractions and lodging. They hired Mary Colter and other professional architects to design tourist facilities that were interesting and attractive. In 1913 they built the Hermit Trail and camp to compete with Bright Angel Trail, still a county toll road surrounded by Ralph Cameron's mining claims.

Focused on rail travel, the Santa Fe did little to improve roads or accommodate the growing number of tourists arriving by automobile. Nor was the Forest Service, with its mandate of resource management, equipped to manage rising levels of tourism. In 1916, growing public sentiment and congressional support led to the establishment of the National Park Service. Its first director, Stephen Mather, supported transferring Grand Canyon to the Park Service, and three years later, on February 26, 1919, President Woodrow Wilson signed the bill proclaiming Grand Canyon the nation's 17th park.

GOOD TIMES AND BAD

With the National Park Service came improved roads and trails, administrative sites, campgrounds, sanitation, and much-needed utilities. By 1919 the Santa Fe Railway was hauling 60,000–100,000 gallons of water daily to the South Rim from Flagstaff via rail car. The septic system installed with the construction of El Tovar, unable to meet increasing demand, had overflowed into an open ditch along the railroad tracks. Employees were housed in a ramshackle collection of boxcars, tents, and shanties literally on the other side of the tracks. The less visited North Rim was virtually ignored. One or two rangers assigned to that area of the park fended for themselves, often staying in vacated Forest Service cabins or bunking with game manager Jimmy Owens.

In order to fund infrastructure, the fledgling Park Service clearly needed the large capital investment provided by the Santa Fe Railway and Fred Harvey Company on the South Rim, and the Union Pacific Railroad and Utah Parks Company on the North Rim. Only a few family businesses were awarded concessionaire contracts, among them the McKee family on the North Rim, and the Babbitts, Verkamps, and Kolbs on the South Rim. Some, like the Bass family, were bought out. Ralph Cameron's reign ended not long after his unsuccessful re-election bid for the U.S. Senate in 1926. In 1928, Cameron's holdings transferred to the National Park Service.

By 1929, with capital provided by concessionaires, the park developed housing, utilities, and basic services to meet the needs of employees and visitors, who numbered 184,000 that year. The park weathered the Great Depression, relying on Civilian Conservation Corps labor for needed improvements. But World War II brought a loss in funding, drops in visitation, and a scarcity of materials. Nearly half the park's staff left for war-related jobs, and many lodges and attractions closed. During the last year of the war, only 74,000 people visited the park.

Yet it wasn't the bust but rather the boom that threatened the park most. The year after war's end, 334,000 people visited the park, and the steadily rising number of visitors outstripped the Park Service's ability to manage. Vandalism, littering, theft, traffic accidents, and frequent rescues burdened ranger services. Adding to the burden was a bed shortage: 15–30 percent of visitors seeking overnight lodging had to be turned away by 1949.

In 1956 the Park Service's hopes for government funding materialized with Mission 66, a 10-year program intended to add infrastructure to national parks. Efforts focused on the South Rim, and many park additions, including the Yavapai, Kachina, and Thunderbird Lodges, date to this program, which extended into the early 1980s at Grand Canyon.

In 1965 the Union Pacific Railroad donated the North Rim's water system, and the Park Service launched plans to pipe water from Roaring Springs to the South Rim. Seven footbridges and the cross-river Silver Bridge carried more than 12 miles of pipeline to Indian Garden. Just before its completion, the pipeline was virtually destroyed by a record-breaking flood that swept down Bright Angel Canyon. The transcanyon pipeline was finally completed in 1970. With improvements, the pipeline continues to serve the South Rim today, although there is growing concern about its adequacy and the burden on groundwater in the canyon region.

ENVIRONMENTAL ISSUES

During the 1950s and 1960s, momentum was building among environmental groups and canyon lovers to protect the Colorado River within the canyon. Congress approved the construction of Glen Canyon Dam in 1956, but President Lyndon B. Johnson created Marble Canyon National Monument in 1969, preventing two other proposed dams that would have flooded Marble Canyon.

The effects of Glen Canyon Dam remain under debate. On the one hand, a tamed river with predictable flows from the timed releases from the dam makes commercial river running possible. On the other hand, native warm-water fish have become endangered and extirpated, and aggressive nonnative plants, such as tamarisk, have overtaken beaches.

The beaches themselves are in danger: The river continues to erode the canyon's sandy beaches without the periodic flooding needed to replenish them. An environmental impact statement, completed in 1995 after a lengthy scoping period involving several public hearings from Los Angeles to Washington, D.C., concluded that controlled flooding might benefit the canyon. The first controlled flood was staged in 1996, and several have followed.

Controlled flooding is one of the latest attempts to manage or correct species distribution in Grand Canyon. During the early 1900s, hundreds of mountain lions and wolves were killed in order to "protect" deer herds in the Grand Canyon game reserve. This contributed to a tragic overpopulation of mule deer, with a huge die-off from overgrazing, weakening, and disease. Miners introduced burros to the canyon in the late 1800s, and by the mid-1900s, a feral burro population was impacting desert bighorn sheep. The Park Service's plan for control included shooting burros from small planes. The Humane Society intervened, leading to federal protection for burros and the ambitious plan to remove burros from the canyon via helicopter. By 1981, nearly 600 burros had been airlifted from the canyon's depths.

Dam building and other issues spurred discussions among Native American groups, federal land managers, and environmental groups over how best to protect the canyon's resources. These discussions resulted in the Grand Canyon National Park Enlargement Act of 1975, which doubled the park's size to

1.2 million acres and established its present boundaries.

Yet despite physical boundaries, national parks and wilderness areas have little control over airspace or underground resources. The Enlargement Act of 1975 recognized the importance of natural quiet, but the number of tourist flights over Grand Canyon continued to increase after the construction of the airport in Tusayan in 1967. In 1987, Arizona senator John McCain and others won the fight to establish a no-fly zone over the central canyon, setting a precedent for other national parks. However, nearly 100,000 air tours continue to buzz the east and west two-thirds of the canyon every year. On the river, the use of motorized boats continues to be debated between those who believe the inner canyon's wilderness should include natural quiet, and those who say limiting tours to nonmotorized boats would impact business and limit visitors' ability to access the inner canyon.

For most visitors, air quality is perhaps the most noticeable environmental concern at the park, especially during the summer, when prevailing winds blow haze northeast from the Los Angeles basin, limiting canyon views. On a clear day, it's possible to see 200 miles or farther. On some days, haze from a number of sources cuts visibility to less than half that distance.

Grand Canyon Trust, formed in 1985 to lobby Congress about overflights, began negotiating with the Navajo Generating Station regarding the use of scrubbers to reduce sulfur dioxide emissions. Studies conducted by the National Park Service showed that the power plant was responsible for as much as 70 percent of the canyon's visible air pollution. In 1991 the plant agreed to reduce emissions by 90 percent. Another contributor to haze, the Mohave Generating Station near Laughlin, Nevada, closed in 2005 due to noncompliance with pollution controls. Over the years, the Trust's focus has expanded to include sustainable grazing, groundwater protection, species diversity, forest health, and other issues in the Grand Canyon region.

Another very noticeable issue is traffic on the canyon's busy South Rim. It seemed like a solution was near in 1999, with plans for a light-rail system to cut vehicle traffic by 80 percent. Opposed by private tour operators and scuttled in Congress just as the plan went out for bids, the light-rail system stalled. Today, the canyon has a station (Canyon View Information Plaza) without a train, and the summer influx of cars continues to create congestion, noise, clouds of exhaust, and downright peevishness among frustrated drivers.

Grand Canyon National Park is still car-centric, although park administrators continue to make strides to reduce traffic, making the South Rim more bike friendly, improving the shuttle system, and moving parking away from Mather point so that visitors' first experience of the canyon is as it should be: a grand theater where Nature takes center stage.

People and Culture

Paleo-Indians and hunter-gatherers roamed Grand Canyon thousands of years before Columbus stumbled onto the New World. These indigenous peoples lived lightly on the land, hunting game and gathering wild plants, leaving behind few clues to their passage. Then, some time after the beginning of the first millennium A.D., people in the Grand Canyon region began experimenting with agriculture.

Other cultures moved into the region: Trade relationships and subsistence strategies shifted. Canyon farmers moved or returned to hunting and gathering. Although they left their masonry villages behind, including the ruined pueblos at Tusayan and Walhalla Glades, their descendants continue to live in the region today.

Many contemporary Native American

cultures continue the traditions of their ancestors, farming and herding inside the canyon or along its rims, gathering plants for medicines or basketry, weaving rugs from sheep's wool, or making silver and turquoise jewelry. Some may live far away, but their histories are part of the canyon's history, and for them, the landscape has deep cultural significance.

HOPI, THE PEACEFUL PEOPLE

Thirteen villages lie east of Grand Canyon on the Hopi Reservation, 1.5 million acres completely surrounded by the larger Navajo Nation. Most villages sit at the foot or top of three rocky peninsulas known individually as First, Second, and Third Mesa, or collectively as the Hopi Mesas. Settlement increased after A.D. 1100 as people migrated from Homolovi, Chavez Pass, and other ancient sites. The Third Mesa village of Oraibi, established in 1150, is considered to be one of the oldest continuously inhabited settlements in the United States.

According to Hopi stories, their ancestors climbed up to this world, the fourth, on a reed. They were met by Masaaw, who told them to leave their footprints as they journeyed through this world in search of its center. On arriving at the mesas, each group contributed a duty or ceremony to the community, creating cohesiveness among clans. Collectively, the clans became known as *Hopituh Shi-nu-mu,* the peaceful or well-mannered people.

But life wasn't always peaceful. In 1540 members of Francisco Vásquez de Coronado's expedition ventured north from New Spain in search of fabled cities of gold. Hopi men drew a line of sacred cornmeal on the ground, but the Spanish crossed it. Hopi guides led the Spanish to the South Rim of the Grand Canyon. Unable to find a way across the Colorado River, the Spanish expedition left, disappointed by the value of the lands they had claimed.

Later, New Spain sent colonists and priests, who established missions at all the Southwestern pueblos, from the Hopi Mesas to the Rio Grande villages. Priests entered kivas, destroying ceremonial items and forcing villagers to build churches. In 1680, nearly 100 years before English colonists in the East would rebel against British rule, the pueblos revolted against Spain. When the Spanish returned in 1692, many people from the Rio Grande pueblos took shelter at the Hopi Mesas, and villages grew. One Hopi village allowed the Spanish to reestablish a mission, sparking strife among the clans. In 1700 the village was destroyed and burned. Nearly 200 years would pass before any missionaries would return to Hopi lands.

By this time, Anglo photographers, artists, and anthropologists had "discovered" the Hopi Mesas. Ceremonies grew crowded with curious onlookers, many of them toting bulky box cameras on tripods. The U.S. government started sending agents in 1870, and a boarding school opened in Keams Canyon in 1887 with the goal of "reeducating" Hopi children. Hopi farms were plotted into allotments. Traders arrived with manufactured goods and food staples. The government mandated missionaries to go to the pueblos, parceling them out among different faiths.

Hopi villagers split between those who were hostile or friendly to government interference, with Oraibi village at the center of the storm. Oraibi splintered, and factions moved to Hotevilla, Bacavi, Kykotsmovi, and Moenkopi. Many ceremonies became closed to outsiders. Over time, some ceremonies were lost as the number of clans dwindled. Even so, Hopi remains the most traditional of all the Southwest's pueblos.

The Hopi calendar is divided between social and kachina ceremonials, the latter held late December–July. If you are fortunate enough to visit during an open ceremony, keep in mind that these are spiritual events, not entertainment. The basket dances held by women's societies in September and October are often open to the public and highlight one of the oldest art forms on the mesas. Basketry, weaving, and pottery are ancient crafts with forms, symbols, and techniques going back to prehistoric times.

Pottery began to be used by Ancestral Puebloans when they settled in villages and raised food crops that required long simmering, such as beans. The first pottery was utilitarian and simple in design. As villages grew and skills became more specialized, pottery designs evolved and flourished. Today, Hopi potters still make pottery the way their ancestors did: by coiling and scraping to shape the pot, then firing it over open embers.

The Hopis' ancestors left Grand Canyon centuries ago, but clans continued to journey to the canyon to mine salt and trade with the Havasupai. The Hopi name for the Grand Canyon means "salt canyon." Although the Hopi didn't live at Grand Canyon during its pioneer period, several individual tribe members lived and worked in Grand Canyon Village. One was famed Tewa potter Nampeyo, who demonstrated her artistry at Hopi House. Another was painter Fred Kabotie, who assisted architect Mary Colter with Desert View Watchtower and other projects. His mural on the Watchtower's first floor tells the story of Tiyo, who, according to Hopi oral history, navigated the Colorado River through Grand Canyon.

ZUNI, THE CITIES OF GOLD

By the time the pilgrims stepped off the *Mayflower,* Spain had already explored and colonized the Southwest. The first nonnative to "discover" the region was not Spanish but was a former slave named Esteban. He and three others were survivors of an expedition that landed off the coast of Florida in 1528, following the gulf and wandering west on foot. Eight years later they met a group of Spanish slavers, who delivered them to the viceroy of New Spain.

They had a fabulous story to tell of golden cities they'd heard about in the north. The viceroy assembled an exploring party led by Friar Marcos de Niza, with Esteban as an advance scout, to locate these cities. At the Zuni pueblos, Esteban's luck ran out. Some say he offended the men with his overly familiar behavior toward the village women. Others say it was the women's curiosity and interest in Esteban that offended Zuni's warriors. In any case,

Esteban was killed, and Marcos de Niza wisely decided not to approach the hilltop pueblos any closer. He claimed the land for Spain and returned to Mexico City, confirming that fabulous cities of gold did indeed exist.

Months later, in 1540, the viceroy dispatched an expedition led by gentleman Francisco Vásquez de Coronado. At Zuni, Coronado discovered not seven cities of gold but six villages of mud adobe. (Marcos de Niza had observed the hilltop pueblos from a distance, and perhaps the sun's angle turned the adobe walls to a golden hue.) Nevertheless, Coronado moved in for the winter, commandeering several rooms, displacing the residents, and appropriating stores of food while sending scouting parties to the Hopi Mesas and other areas.

Coronado and his soldiers eventually returned to New Spain without the riches they'd sought, but in 1598 Juan de Oñate arrived with farmers, priests, livestock, and a soldier escort. Colonists settled along the Rio Grande River, and priests moved into the pueblos. During the years of revolt and reconquest, the Zuni left their villages and took refuge on Dowa Yalanne, Corn Mountain, before returning to the village of Halona, where Zuni Pueblo stands today.

The 450,000-acre Zuni Reservation is home to about 10,000 people, most of them residing in Zuni Pueblo, making it the largest of New Mexico's 19 pueblos. The Zuni people, who call themselves A:shiwi, observe an annual ceremonial cycle that includes the winter Shalako activities. The Shalako are 10-foot-tall beings who visit selected Zuni households in December, ensuring continued blessings.

Many Zunis are artisans, creating fetishes, jewelry, basketry, and pottery. Modern Zuni silverwork includes a variety of styles and techniques but is best known for delicate needlepoint and petit point turquoise designs, as well as exquisite inlay depicting birds, Shalako, and other designs.

Fetishes have been carried by Zunis since prehistoric times for use in prayers and ceremonies and also for protection. Modern fetishes (more accurately known as carvings because

CORN

Spend any time in the Southwest at all, and you begin to appreciate how much of the local cuisine is based on corn: tortillas, tamales, cornbread, fry bread, parched corn, roasted corn, stewed corn. Traditional Navajos still carry corn pollen. Corn designs adorn jewelry and pottery. Sculpted kachinas depict the Red, Yellow, White, or Blue Corn Maiden.

In the Zuni language, the word for corn, *dowa*, also means "ancient." Thousands of years ago, a New World grass called teosinte began to evolve, with human help, into *Zea mays*. By selecting seeds, humans influenced genetic change, and resulting strains of maize varied according to soil type and climate. In the lower deserts, corn plants with long tap roots reached precious moisture. In the north, corn with a short growing season ripened before frost. Corn agriculture changed the ancients' way of life from hunting and gathering to settled villages and farms.

Corn became the main sustenance of the Ancestral Puebloans. For their Hopi descendants, corn's growing cycle is inextricably connected to the human cycle of life. Hopi brides once ground corn for three days at their in-laws home to prove their wifely skills. Corn is sacred also to the Navajo, who use corn pollen or cornmeal in many ceremonies, including the traditional wedding. The bride and groom each take pinches of cornmeal from a basket, which is then passed to guests.

Feast days feature corn food, such as Hopi piki bread made from delicate layers of blue corn, and posole, a rich stew made with hominy. The many colors of corn are also sig-

Artist Fred Kabotie depicted corn plants in this Watchtower mural.

© KATHLEEN BRYANT

nificant. Corn symbols adorn silver jewelry and are woven into rugs. Even the landscape honors the Southwest's most important plant: Dowa Yalanne, Corn Mountain, rises east of Zuni Pueblo. At Hopi, the Corn Twins stand like sentinels on Second Mesa.

Francisco Vásquez de Coronado, perhaps the Southwest's first tourist, didn't impress easily. Yet he noted in his journal how efficiently pueblo women ground corn, swearing that they made "the best tortillas that I have ever seen anywhere."

---

they haven't been ritually blessed) may depict snakes, foxes, bears, or other animals. It is likely that Zuni individuals carried fetishes during the Zunis' migrations eastward.

The Zunis consider Grand Canyon to be the place where their ancestors emerged into this world. From this place of emergence (which some say is the inner canyon's Ribbon Falls), they traveled for generations. Their migrations roughly trace the path of the Little Colorado

River. The people left behind rock art, potsherds, and villages until they reached the middle place, Zuni Pueblo.

HAVASUPAI, PEOPLE OF THE BLUE-GREEN WATERS

The Havasupai have called the rims and waterways of Grand Canyon home for at least 800 years. Their oral tradition links past events and village life to features in the landscape. One of the many stories Havasupai people associate with their canyon home refers to the twin pillars of reddish stone they call the Wigleeva. According to most versions of the story, if the stone pillars should ever crumble and fall, the walls of the canyon will close in and destroy the tribe.

Traditionally, the Havasupai hunted in the forests and plains along the rim and farmed within the canyon during summer months, raising corn, beans, squash, sunflowers, and later, peaches. Many of the inner canyon trails used by hikers today were established by the Havasupai. Indian Garden, the popular resting point along Bright Angel Trail, was once a Havasupai community.

In the 1880s, the tribe was restricted to a 500-acre reservation at the bottom of Havasu Canyon, a mere fraction of their traditional lands. The limited agricultural land, bounded by the canyon's stony cliffs, barely supported the tribe, and many Havasupai sought work outside Supai Village. Grand Canyon pioneer William Wallace Bass relied on Havasupai guides to establish his mining and tourism activities. Other Havasupai found work with the Santa Fe Railway and Fred Harvey Company at Grand Canyon Village. Many worked for the National Park Service, helping construct the Kaibab Suspension Bridge across the Colorado River.

In 1975, an act of Congress restored 185,000 acres on the plateau to the Havasupai. The present 188,077-acre reservation encompasses Havasu Canyon and plateaus along the South Rim west of Grand Canyon Village. The village of Supai, reachable only on foot or by horseback or helicopter, lies within the walls of Havasu Canyon (also known as Cataract Canyon). The village is home to 450 people, more than half the tribe's total population.

For decades the Havasupai have welcomed visitors to their edenic canyon home, where pools lined with deposits of travertine limestone reflect cerulean blue skies and gorgeous waterfalls tumble from rocky cliff sides. Tourism has become the tribe's main source of income, and the Havasupai have struggled to maintain the delicate balance between tradition, ethnic identity, and economic reality.

In recent years, floods have damaged the village and canyon several times. The residents of Supai Village had barely recovered from the 2008 flood that destroyed Navajo Falls when disaster struck again. In October 2010, heavy rains flooded Havasu Creek, damaging homes, bridges, campground, trails, and causing the evacuation of visitors. The tribal council declared Havasu Canyon a disaster area. The U.S. government granted the tribe's declaration, estimating $1.63 million in damages. Obviously, the loss of tourist facilities has had a devastating economic impact on the Havasupai, but imagine the emotional and spiritual costs of such devastation to a landscape alive with cultural meaning.

HUALAPAI, PEOPLE OF THE TALL PINES

Traditionally seminomadic hunter-gatherers, the Hualapai once roamed over 5 million acres from the canyon south to Bill Williams Mountain, west to the lower Colorado River, and east to the Little Colorado River. Like the neighboring Havasupai, they migrated seasonally, occupying upland plateaus in the winter, returning to inner canyon springs and tributaries in the summer. They participated in a vast trade network with other tribes in the region, trading beads, shells, mineral pigments, and buckskins for salt, wool or cotton blankets, and horses.

When gold was discovered near Prescott, Arizona, in 1863, miners, settlers, and soldiers poured into Hualapai lands. The Hualapai responded fiercely to the incursion. They signed a peace treaty in 1868, and afterward many Hualapai warriors assisted General Crook's Army as scouts. In 1874 the U.S. Army was ordered to relocate the Hualapai to a reservation 150 miles south. The removal sparked a deep sense of betrayal among the Hualapai. On the reservation, starvation and disease ran rampant, and the Hualapai petitioned the government to return their lands.

In 1883 the Hualapai tribe was granted a

small reservation along western Grand Canyon. They adopted ranching, lumbering, and wage labor. In 1947, lands that had been given to the railroad were returned to the tribe. Today, the Hualapai Reservation includes 1 million acres along 108 miles of Grand Canyon's rim, south of the Colorado River and west of the national park boundaries. The Hualapai call it Hakataya, or "the backbone of the river."

The Hualapai are closely related to the neighboring Havasupai, and also to the Yavapai, Paipai, Maricopa, and Mohave tribes, all Yuman-speakers with common ancestors from the lower Colorado River. (The word *pai* means "people.") The Pai tribes are linked by the river, reflected in many of their traditions and histories.

According to the Hualapai creation story, the earth was once covered by floodwaters. Only one old man escaped, and a dove brought him instructions from the Creator. Following the instructions, he used the horn from a mountain sheep to dig a hole (some say this became Grand Canyon), and the water drained away. Later, the Creator made two brothers who took the canes growing beside the river and breathed life into them so that they became human. The older brother guided the people to Grand Canyon and taught them what plants to gather and where to find water and game— all that they needed to know to survive in this rugged landscape.

Today, the Hualapai population is approximately 2,100, about half of them based in Peach Springs. The small town along Route 66 acts as gateway to neighboring Havasu Canyon as well as to Grand Canyon West, the tourist center the Hualapai opened in 1988. The tribe has continued to find the means to survive and adapt—enterprises include timber and ranching, hunting permits, river running, helicopter tours, and most famously, the Skywalk. The Skywalk's construction was controversial, even among tribe members. Some believe that it is an affront to nature, and that those who benefit from it the most are the Las Vegas businessmen who developed it. Others see the Skywalk as an investment in the tribe's economic future, another way to draw visitors to Grand Canyon West, where they can share the tribe's legends and lifeways with others.

KAIBAB PAIUTE, THE LAST HUNTERS AND GATHERERS

Many of the names on the canyon's landscape—Kaibab, Kaiparowits, Shivits, Tuweep, and others—are derived from Paiute (Nuwuvi) words. Paiute ancestors migrated east from the Great Basin deserts to the Colorado Plateau about eight hundred years ago. Seminomadic Southern Paiute bands lived along the North Rim of the Grand Canyon, where a wide range of environments, from desert to forest to meadow, provided diverse resources throughout the year. They cultivated garden plots, hunted game, and gathered wild plants on some of the most isolated land in North America.

Like many of the region's native people, generations of Southern Paiutes saw their territory reduced in size over time. Their traditional lands once extended as far west as California and east to the San Juan River. One Paiute story hints at a migrating population as it describes the creation of Grand Canyon:

A Paiute chief mourned his dead wife until the god Tavwoats told him that she was living in a land far away and that he would take the chief to see her if he would cease to mourn. The chief agreed, and Tavwoats blazed a deep trail westward through the mountains. The chief followed, and he saw his wife living happily in a warm desert. Tavwoats ordered the chief to keep the land a secret, and after they returned, he poured water into the deeply furrowed trail, creating the Colorado River to guard the land to the west.

Many Southern Paiutes were captured by Navajo and Ute raiders and sold as slaves to the Spanish. To avoid capture, Southern Paiute bands moved away from traveled areas along the Old Spanish Trail, a move that furthered their dependence on hunting and gathering. As Mormon pioneers began arriving in the Arizona Strip country in the mid-1800s, they claimed water sources at Pipe Spring and other locations, water that once support game and crops.

When John Wesley Powell, head of the newly formed Bureau of Ethnology, returned to document the region's native peoples, the Kaibab Paiute (Kaivavwits) band, the last of the canyon's hunters and gatherers, was still practicing a foraging culture. He recommended that the remaining Paiutes be removed to reservations.

During the latter half of the century, ranching, mining, and timbering continued to impact the tribe's resources. Diseases flourished. Game vanished, crops withered, and the people starved. By 1913, when the Kaibab Paiute Reservation was at last established, the band's population was decimated. Today, the Kaibab Paiute's 250 members are spread among five villages on a 121,000-acre reservation about 50 miles north of Grand Canyon. The reservation encompasses Pipe Spring National Monument, where the tribe operates a visitors center with the National Park Service. Tourism is their major source of revenue.

NAVAJO, LORDS OF THE EARTH

From the powerful spires and buttes of Monument Valley to the sweeping sandstone walls of Canyon de Chelly, the landscape of the Navajo people is a rich repository of oral history. Navajo creation stories tell of a great flood. To drain the waters, Humpback God used his cane to draw the Colorado River, forming Grand Canyon. Other Holy People, including Salt Woman and Talking God, are said to dwell in Glen Canyon and Grand Canyon.

The Navajo Nation borders Grand Canyon National Park on the east, where sheep pastures extend to the very rim of Marble Canyon. The reservation is the largest in the United States, sprawling 25,000 square miles across northeastern Arizona, western New Mexico, and into Utah. Even so, the reservation is far smaller than the territory the Navajo once controlled.

Navajo ancestors, Athabascan speakers, migrated to the New World and settled in what is now Alaska and Northwestern Canada. About a millennium ago, they ventured south, carrying little with them but the bows they used for hunting. When the Diné ("the people") arrived to the Four Corners area sometime before A.D. 1500, they encountered the pueblo tribes, whose settled lifestyle included corn agriculture. As the Diné adapted to their new homeland, they too incorporated corn into to their repertoire of survival. Life was relatively peaceful, but for all Southwestern peoples, this was the eve of change.

In 1540 Spanish explorer Francisco Vásquez de Coronado led an expedition to the Southwest in search of the fabled seven golden cities of Cibola. Coronado left without the riches he sought, but in 1598 Spanish colonists came to stay. Don Juan de Oñate arrived with farmers, priests, servants, and an army escort, trailed by oxcarts and thousands of cattle, sheep, and goats. The Spanish introduced peaches, livestock, metalwork, and horses. They gave, but they also took away.

New Spain's mines and ranches spurred an extensive slave trade, especially among the Navajo, who were difficult to convert and difficult to control, since they did not live in large, easily targeted villages like their Pueblo neighbors. Fierce raiding and shifting alliances ensued between colonists and Native Americans. One colonist estimated 5,000–6,000 Navajo slaves lived in New Mexican households, but hundreds of thousands of colonists' cattle, sheep, and horses lived in Navajo herds. The Navajo became such accomplished horsemen they were known as the Lords of the Earth.

Indian lands once claimed by Spain were won by Mexico and later ceded to the United States. Treaties were signed and broken, and raiding continued, followed by harsh punitive expeditions. The Civil War left settlers vulnerable, and frontiersman Kit Carson was appointed to defend them. Carson's campaign against the Navajos focused on destroying their herds, fields, and orchards. They sought refuge in places like Canyon de Chelly, Wupatki, and Grand Canyon.

Within a matter of months, in January 1864, Navajo leaders agreed to go to Fort

Sumner, New Mexico, a treeless plain with alkaline water, land traditionally claimed by the Comanche. The hardships of the campaign and the grueling 400-mile winter march to Bosque Redondo are known as the Long Walk. Those who didn't die or escape suffered four years of poor food, smallpox, Comanche raids, and crop-destroying hail and floods.

Navajo leaders argued eloquently for return to their homeland. In 1868 the Navajo went home, although tightened boundaries excluded much of their original lands. In exchange for agreeing to stop raiding settlers, the Navajo received rations, and later, sheep and goats. Herding became the foundation of the Navajo economy, and Anglo traders were awarded contracts to supply goods such as coffee and flour.

As tourism to the Southwest increased, trading posts offered a ready market for traditional crafts, another economic opportunity for the Navajo and other tribes. A few trading posts still dot the reservation. Cameron Trading Post, now owned by tribe members, is the nearest to Grand Canyon. The post stocks many items for locals but specializes in Navajo weavings and silver as well as work from other regional artisans.

The political center of the Navajo Nation lies southeast of Grand Canyon in Window Rock, Arizona. The population of the "Big Rez" is 250,000, making the Navajos the largest Native American nation in the country. Although ranching and herding continue to be important, the nation's revenues also stem from mineral resources and tourism. The journey along the edge of the reservation to Grand Canyon involves incredible scenery: the Little Colorado River gorge and Painted Desert near Cameron, the colorful Echo Cliffs en route to the Gap, and long views of the San Francisco Peaks, one of four sacred mountains that mark the traditional boundaries of the Navajo homeland.

ESSENTIALS

Getting There

ORIENTATION

Grand Canyon National Park is in Arizona's northwest corner, close to the Utah and Nevada borders. The nearest major cities are Las Vegas, 278 miles west, and Phoenix, about 230 miles south.

Geography divides Grand Canyon National Park into three areas: the South Rim, the North Rim, and the river corridor that bisects the park east to west. The North Rim is accessible only by Highway 67, and heavy snows usually close the road mid-November–mid-May. The inner canyon is accessible on foot from either rim, but the most feasible way to travel its length is by boat.

River trips put in at Lees Ferry, east of the park's boundaries.

Most visitors head for the canyon's South Rim, further delineated as the East and West Rims. The South Rim is accessible via two entrance stations. The South Entrance Station is close to Grand Canyon Village and the West Rim. The East Entrance Station is at Desert View, about 25 miles east of the village.

TIME

If you're traveling to Grand Canyon from another state, be aware that Arizona does not observe daylight saving time. Arizona stays on mountain standard time year-round, except for

the Navajo Reservation. That means if you're arriving from New Mexico for a summer vacation at Grand Canyon and stopping to visit the Hopi and Navajo Reservations en route, you'll be changing your watch four times. (Newer residents consider it confusing, but after an appropriate period of adjustment, most Arizonans are grateful to have the sun set an hour earlier on summer days.)

SUGGESTED ROUTES
Williams to South Entrance

This is the simplest route to the canyon, a 60-mile straight shot north from Williams, which lies along I-40. To get to the South Entrance Station, take I-40 exit 165, turning north on Highway 64. The road cuts through open prairie scattered with one-seed junipers, where you might glimpse a herd of elk or pronghorn. After passing through Valle (about 40 miles) look for Red Butte to the northeast. Straight ahead, the canyon is barely recognizable, a dark line on the horizon where the North Rim juts above. This is a good route if you neglected to make reservations: You'll be passing several campgrounds around Williams, Valle, and Tusayan, and Valle's two motels may have vacancies even during busy summer months. Most visitors experience their first canyon panorama four miles past the South Entrance station at Mather Point. A couple of miles farther along, historic Grand Canyon Village is tucked in a forest of ponderosa pine along the rim.

Flagstaff to South Entrance

Travelers bound for the canyon from Flagstaff have three options. They can head for Williams (about 30 miles west on I-40) or the East Entrance, or take Highway 180 northwest, connecting to Highway 64 at Valle. At 78 miles, Highway 180 is the shortest route from Flagstaff to the canyon, and it's also very scenic, skirting just west of the San Francisco Peaks through a forest of ponderosa pine and aspen before cutting across an open juniper woodland. Coconino National Forest offers several possibilities for side trips, including a back-road drive through Hart Prairie's aspen groves, a

---

GRAND CANYON BY THE NUMBERS

How old?
- Oldest rocks: 1,840 million years
- Canyon formed: 5-6 million years
- Park established: 1919

How deep?
- 1 mile average, 6,000 feet at its deepest

How long?
- 277 river miles

How wide?
- 10 miles average (narrowest point, 600 feet; widest point, 15 miles)

How big?
- 5.45 trillion cubic yards volume
- 1,218,375 acres in the park

How many?
- 5 life zones
- 1,500 plant species
- 355 bird, 89 mammal, 47 reptile, 9 amphibian, and 17 fish species
- 160-plus named rapids
- 5 million visitors annually

---

ride up the chairlift to the Arizona Snowbowl, or hikes around and up Kendrick Peak. As Highway 180 swings west toward Valle, the road passes close to Red Mountain, an extinct volcano and fascinating geology hike. At Valle, turn north (right) on Highway 64 for the remaining 20 miles to Grand Canyon.

East Entrance

The East Entrance Station, less trafficked, is reached by driving 89 miles north from Flagstaff (or 106 miles south from Page), a scenic route with options for side trips, especially if you're interested in archaeology, geology, or

Indian art. As you leave Flagstaff on U.S. 89, Elden Mountain and the San Francisco Peaks rise on the left. Cinder cones east of the road indicate the region's volcanic past, which you can explore by taking a right at Sunset Crater Volcano National Monument, 11 miles north of Flag. The park's main road loops back toward the highway, passing through Wupatki National Monument, which preserves several major prehistoric ruins. U.S. 89 continues north through the Coconino National Forest and the Navajo Reservation, skirting the edge of the Painted Desert, marked by softly rounded low hills of the colorful Chinle Formation. (If you're driving south from Page on U.S. 89, you'll pass alongside the reddish Echo Cliffs, which rise above reservation farms and ranches. You'll see several traditional Navajo dwellings, circular or octagonal hogans. The old stone building at the Gap is one of the region's historic trading posts. Continue toward Cameron and the junction with Highway 64.)

Highway 64 leads west 30 miles to the Grand Canyon's East Entrance, but a mile north of the junction, you can visit historic and contemporary trading posts at Cameron, a worthy side trip. Along Highway 64, stop for views of the Little Colorado River Gorge at the scenic overlook, where Navajo artisans sell jewelry, pottery, and other items. Desert View, one of the South Rim's highest overlooks, is just beyond the East Entrance. Here you'll find a seasonal campground, Desert View Market, a bookstore, a trading post and deli, restrooms, and, best of all, the intriguing Watchtower, a Mary Colter landmark.

Highway 67 to North Entrance

Only 1 in 10 canyon visitors makes it to the North Rim, usually inaccessible in winter due to heavy snows. Jacob Lake is the nearest town, 30 miles from the park's North Entrance Station on Highway 67. If you're arriving from the west, you'll pass through Fredonia, Arizona, before climbing the high Kaibab Plateau on U.S. 89A. Stop at the LeFevre Overlook for a dramatic view of the pink, gray, white,

vermilion, and chocolate cliffs of the Grand Staircase to the north.

If you're arriving from Flagstaff or Page, turn west on U.S. 89A, crossing the Colorado River over the Navajo Bridge and continuing through House Rock Valley. (Lees Ferry is a short but scenic side trip to the launching point for most white-water rafting trips.) In 1996, six condors were reintroduced to the wild from atop the Vermilion Cliffs, rising to the north above the low Marble Platform. Dirt roads lead south to Marble Canyon overlooks and north to the Bureau of Land Management's Paria Canyon–Vermilion Cliffs Wilderness. The highway quickly climbs the Kaibab Plateau toward Jacob Lake, where you can stop at the Kaibab Plateau Visitors Center, operated by the U.S. Forest Service, or grab a bite to eat at the Jacob Lake Inn.

From Jacob Lake, turn south on Highway 67 (usually closed by snow during the winter). The 45 miles from Jacob Lake to the North Rim are one of the loveliest drives in Arizona, through grassy meadows edged by hills with ponderosa pine, fir, spruce, and aspen.

FROM PHOENIX

The Valley of the Sun includes Phoenix and its surrounding communities, about 230 miles south of Grand Canyon in Arizona's central desert. The sun shines more than 300 days a year above Arizona's largest city. Popular with winter visitors, the Valley of the Sun is known for year-round golf, Cactus League baseball in the spring, and blistering temperatures during the summer.

To get to the canyon, about 4–5 hours away, take I-17 north to Flagstaff. From Flag, drivers can choose between I-40 west to Williams, Highway 180 northwest to Valle, or U.S. 89 to the park's East Entrance.

Airport

Phoenix Sky Harbor International Airport (PHX) is served by more than a dozen commercial carriers, including Aeroméxico, Air Canada, Alaska Airlines, American, British Airways, United, Continental, Delta,

Southwest, and US Airways, with connections to Flagstaff's Pulliam Airport (FLG) via US Airways. Sky Harbor has three separate terminals for commercial flights, and getting around the airport is a bit tricky. If you need to make a connection on an airline located in another terminal, you can use the interterminal shuttle. Ground transportation, including hotel vans, taxis, light rail, and intercity shuttles, is located in each terminal's baggage claim area. Here you'll also be able be to catch the rental-car shuttle, which will transport you to the Rental Car Center.

Train
Amtrak (800/872-7245, www.amtrak.com) is connected to Sky Harbor Airport, the Greyhound Station, and the Metro Center Transit Station via Amtrak's Thruway connecting bus system. Both Amtrak's southernmost route, the *Sunset Limited,* and its *Texas Eagle* line stop at Maricopa, a town on the Gila Indian reservation about 20 miles south of Phoenix. You'll need to arrange another form of transportation to get the rest of the way to Phoenix.

Bus and Shuttles
Greyhound (2115 E. Buckeye Rd., Phoenix, 602/389-4200 or 800/231-2222, www.greyhound.com) makes daily trips from Phoenix to Flagstaff, where you can make connections to Williams or Grand Canyon. The Greyhound station, open 24 hours daily, is near the Phoenix airport.

Arizona Shuttle (877/226-8060, www.arizonashuttle.com) makes several trips a day from Sky Harbor Airport or the Metro Transit Center to Flagstaff. From Flagstaff, they provide twice-daily service to Williams and Grand Canyon Village.

Tours
Open Road Tours (602/997-6474 or 800/766-7117, www.openroadtours.com) is based in Phoenix, with a second office in Flagstaff. They offer a single-day tour to Grand Canyon and Sedona as well as several multiday canyon tours with options for adding a smooth-water float or a ride on the Grand Canyon Railway. **Canyon Tours** (800/301-7152, www.canyontours.net) handles reservations for several companies that offer single-day and multiday tours to the Grand Canyon and surrounding areas. **Grayline** (800/276-1527, www.grayline.com) no longer offers tours originating in Phoenix, but they do book Grand Canyon tours from the company's Tucson location, about 120 miles south.

Car Rental
Most national car-rental agencies have service desks at the **Sky Harbor's Rental Car Center** (1805 E. Sky Harbor Circle S., 602/683-3741), including Alamo (602/244-0897 or 800/462-5266), Avis (602/261-5900 or 800/331-1212), Budget (602/261-5950 or 800/527-7000), Enterprise (602/225-0588 or 800/736-8222), Hertz (602/267-8822 or 800/654-3131), National (602/275-4771 or 800/227-7368), and Thrifty (602/244-0311 or 800/847-4389). To get to the Rental Car Center, look for the rental-car shuttle outside your terminal's baggage claim area. All rental-car agencies use the same shuttle system. A handful of rental agencies don't have service desks in the Rental Car Center; they offer van service to their off-site locations from the center.

RV Rental
If you expected the Valley of the Sun, Arizona's snowbird capital, to have numerous RV rental agencies, you'd be right. **Cruise America** (480/464-7300 or 800/671-8042, www.cruiseamerica.com) has offices in nearby Mesa. Other rental agencies include **Arizona Sunshine Coaches** (602/482-0835), **Arizona Travel Center** (602/208-6121), and **Ultimate RV Rentals** (800/622-2201, www.ultimatervrentals.com).

Equipment Rental
REI has two stores in the Phoenix area, in Paradise Valley (Paradise Valley Mall, 12634 N. Paradise Village Pkwy., Phoenix, 602/996-5400, 10 A.M.–9 P.M. Mon.–Fri., 9 A.M.–8 P.M.

Sat., 10 A.M.–7 P.M. Sun.) and Tempe (1405 W. Southern Ave., Tempe, 480/967-5494, 9 A.M.–9 P.M. Mon.–Fri., 9 A.M.–7 P.M. Sat., 10 A.M.–6 P.M. Sun.). Both rent camp stoves, tents, backpacks, and sleeping bags. The Tempe store also rents mountaineering gear and snowshoes.

Accommodations and Food

You'll probably want to get closer to the canyon before finding a place to hit the rack, but if you're planning to spend some time in the Phoenix area, you'll have a dizzying number of accommodations choices. Most major chains are represented here, and rates are usually cheaper May–mid-September, when Phoenix is sizzling hot and most everyone in the Valley of the Sun escapes northward. If you're planning to catch a Diamondbacks or a Suns game, get a place to stay in Phoenix's renewed downtown, which has risen from urban decay like, well, the proverbial phoenix. For Southwestern resort-style accommodations, neighboring Scottsdale is home to dude ranches, spas, and golf kingdoms like the Phoenician and Westin Kierland.

Before heading north, where most adventures take place outdoors and not on your palate, you might want to fortify yourself with some ethnic food. The Phoenix area has Cuban, Indian, Middle Eastern, Thai, and other global cuisines, but the local specialty is Mexican food, from taco stands to trendy cafés. **Macayo's** is a dependable local chain, but if you like it hotter, try **Los Dos Molinos**, which offers fiery New Mexico–style dishes. At **Via de los Santos** you'll find the classic neighborhood restaurant experience (and outrageously inexpensive margaritas).

FROM LAS VEGAS

At first glance, Las Vegas and Grand Canyon seem worlds apart—at least in spirit, if not in mileage. (It's only four hours from Vegas to the North Rim, and a little longer to the South Rim.) But in a strange sort of way, Vegas and the canyon are soul sisters: Both exemplify extremes, and both are best experienced by immersion. Las Vegas is a convenient launching point for a Grand Canyon trip, easily reached by air from most U.S. cities, with a number of tour and travel options for getting to the canyon.

If you're driving, it's about 270 miles from Vegas to the North Rim: Take I-15 north for 128 miles to St. George, Utah. Just past St. George, take Highway 9 east 10 miles to Highway 59. Continue east on Highway 59 for 32 miles. The highway number changes at the Utah-Arizona border, becoming Highway 389. Continue east another 33 miles to Fredonia and turn east on U.S. 89A for 30 miles to Jacob Lake. Turn south on Highway 67 for 43 miles to the North Rim.

From Las Vegas to the South Rim is 280 miles: Take U.S. 93 south to I-40. Take I-40 east to Williams, Arizona. Turn north on Highway 64 and drive 60 miles to the South Rim.

Airports

McCarran International Airport (LAS), the primary commercial airport for Las Vegas, is located a few miles outside city limits in Clark County. More than 20 commercial carriers land here, including Aeroméxico, Air Canada, Alaska Airlines, American, British Airways, Continental, Delta, JetBlue, Southwest, United, US Airways, and Virgin Atlantic. The airport uses two terminals. If you're looking for a taxi or shuttles to downtown hotels, you'll find them outside the baggage claim area of Terminal 1.

North Las Vegas Airport (701/261-3801) serves general aviation pilots as well as many of the scenic airlines that fly tours to Grand Canyon.

Bus

Greyhound (200 S. Main St., Las Vegas, 702/383-9792 or 800/231-2222, www.greyhound.com) has connections to Las Vegas from locations nationwide. The bus station is open 24 hours daily.

Tours

It seems a bit odd to wander down the Strip, surrounded by flashing neon and porn peddlers, and see advertisements for Grand Canyon tours. But almost everything in Vegas is a commodity, and the canyon is no exception. Tour choices are plentiful and competitively priced.

Papillon Helicopters (702/736-7243 or 888/635-7272, www.papillon.com) has tour options with or without flights, as does **Sightseeing Tours Unlimited** (702/471-7155 or 800/377-2003, www.sightseeingtourslv.com). **Coach America/Grayline** (702/384-1234 or 800/634-6579, www.graylinelasvegas.com) has ground tours to the South Rim and Grand Canyon West.

Making reservations through a tour broker can save you some time sorting through the various options: **Grand Canyon Today** (800/957-6329, www.grandcanyontoday.com) and **Best Tours** (702/851-8436 or 866/828-1608, www.besttourslv.com) represent a wide selection of operators and tours.

Car Rental

McCarran International Airport's **Rent-A-Car Center** (702/261-6001) hosts several national car-rental agencies, including Alamo (800/462-5266), Avis (800/331-1212), Budget (800/922-2899), Enterprise (800/736-8222), Hertz (800/654-3131), and Thrifty (800/367-2277). To get to the Rent-A-Car Center, find door 10 or 11 inside Terminal 1 and wait for the shuttle, which arrives every 5–10 minutes. If you're in Terminal 2, the Rent-A-Car Center is across the road from the baggage claim area.

For travelers using North Las Vegas Airport, Hertz and Enterprise rent cars here.

RV Rental

Bates International (702/737-9050 or 800/732-2283, www.batesintl.com) is headquartered in Las Vegas. **Cruise America** (702/456-6666 or 800/671-8042, www.cruiseamerica.com), **Sahara RV Center** (702/384-8818 or 800/748-6494, www.sahararv.com), and several other RV rental agencies have offices here.

Equipment Rental

If you need to rent camping gear, **REI** has two locations in the Las Vegas area, on the west side of town in Boca Park (710 S. Rampart Blvd., Las Vegas, 702/951-4488, 10 A.M.–9 P.M. Mon.–Fri., 10 A.M.–8 P.M. Sat., 11 A.M.–7 P.M. Sun.) and in Henderson (2220 Village Walk Dr., Henderson, 702/896-7509, 10 A.M.–9 P.M. Mon.–Sat., 11 A.M.–6 P.M. Sun.).

Accommodations and Food

You can choose among major hotel chains and accommodations convenient to the airport or the interstate, but if you want the full Vegas experience, head for the Strip and its casino hotels. The Stratosphere rises above the northern strip, where the Sahara and Riviera have held court for more than half a century, and Circus Circus has become a family favorite. At the heart of the Strip you'll find the classic Flamingo, the restructured Caesars Palace, and the luxurious Bellagio. On the South Strip, hotels like New York New York and Excalibur offer entertaining themes at midrange prices.

Dining can be equally adventurous. You'll find a few bargain buffets like the ones your grandpa raved about, but Vegas dining has evolved to include sushi, nouvelle Chinese, upscale Italian, and creole cuisine. If you're hoping to spot a celebrity (or a celebrity chef), slip into Harrah's for **KGB,** home of Kerry Simon's Iron Chef–winning burgers. Simon, dubbed the "Rock-n-Roll Chef" by *Rolling Stone* magazine, is also behind the menu at **Simon at Palms Place,** where you'll find comfort food with a twist and great views.

Getting Around

DRIVING

For the most part, driving in Grand Canyon National Park is relatively easy—so easy that it can lead to a false sense of security. The park's semiarid climate and high elevations mean that both desert and mountain driving conditions apply. And because of Grand Canyon's remote location, if your car breaks down, help is sometimes a long way away.

Prepare for your trip with a maintenance check. Be sure your tires, including the spare, are in good condition. Check to see that your tool kit is complete, and that your motor-oil grade is appropriate for the season. Pack jumper cables, plenty of water, and a flashlight. If you're traveling in winter, pack a shovel and warm clothing with your roadside emergency kit. (You do have one, don't you?) The **Arizona Emergency Information Network** (www.azein.gov) has driving tips, suggested emergency items, bulletins about weather and fire conditions, and real-time updates about emergency conditions.

You might notice that a disproportionately large number of Arizonans drive white cars and trucks, but you'll soon stop wondering why. During the summer, a window shade can help keep your car's interior temperatures from reaching volcanic heights. If your car has leather or vinyl seats, drape them with towels or blankets to keep them from getting uncomfortably sticky. And if you wouldn't put it in an oven, don't leave it on the car seat: This includes your favorite CD, a chocolate bar, or the family dog.

Gas Stations and Garages

It's a good idea to keep your gas tank at least half full, even if you intend to stick to the park's developed roads and sites. If you plan on backcountry driving, fill up before you start out, and top off the tank whenever you get a chance. There won't be many opportunities; gas stations are few and far between in the region.

Inside the park, you'll find only two gas stations. The **North Rim's gas station** (7 A.M.–7 P.M. daily mid-May–mid-Oct.) is on the road leading to the campground and store. Pumps have 24-hour credit-card service. You can also get minor repairs done here. You can buy gas and basic automotive supplies at the North Rim Country Store, about 18 miles from the North Rim. The service station next to Jacob Lake Inn, about 45 miles north of the rim, sells fuel and provides some emergency repairs such as tires, belts, and batteries.

On the South Rim, the only gas station inside park boundaries is at Desert View, 25 miles from Grand Canyon Village. **Desert View Chevron** (9 A.M.–5 P.M. daily) has pumps with 24-hour credit-card service. There's no gas station in Grand Canyon Village, although you'll find limited garage services at the **Public Garage** (926/638-2631, 8 A.M.–noon and 1–5 P.M. daily) just east of the train depot. The nearest gas station is in Tusayan, about two miles south of the park entrance.

There's a 24-hour emergency towing service (928/638-2631) at the South Rim. The nearest garage services from the North Rim are in Fredonia, Arizona, or Kanab, Utah.

Road Conditions

Check road conditions before you drive to the canyon, especially if you are traveling during the winter. Conditions can change quickly at high altitude and vary dramatically, even within a relatively short distance. For example, on a June trip to the North Rim, you can be driving through desert temperatures in House Rock Valley only to climb the Kaibab Plateau and find it snowing in Jacob Lake, 30 miles up the road. Late-summer thunderstorms are also highly localized, and flash-flood conditions can arise miles away from a storm cell.

Road conditions for your route and destination are available from the Arizona Department of Transportation (dial 511 or 888/411-7623, www.az511.gov), Grand Canyon National

Park's information line (928/638-7888), the Nevada Department of Transportation (dial 511 or 877/687-6237, www.nevadadot.com), and the Utah Department of Transportation (dial 511 or 866/511-8824, www.udot.utah. gov).

Current weather forecasts and bulletins for the Grand Canyon Region are available from the National Weather Service (www.wrh.noaa. gov), Grand Canyon National Park (928/638-7888, www.nps.gov/grca), North Rim Visitors Center (928/638-9875), and Kaibab Plateau Visitors Center (928/643-7298).

Backcountry Driving

If you plan to visit the canyon's more remote overlooks, such as Point Sublime or Toroweap, fill your gas tank, pack plenty of water, double-check your spare, and inquire about road conditions before setting out. It's also a good idea to let someone know your itinerary. You'll need a high-clearance 4WD vehicle to negotiate the rough road to Point Sublime. For Toroweap, you'll need high-clearance for the last seven

miles and the campground. The National Park Service warns that 25 percent of visitors driving to Toroweap get a flat tire (sometimes more than one), and that towing services to this remote area can cost as much as $2,000. Cell-phone service here is spotty, and there are few residents or travelers in this area.

Good maps are essential for backcountry travel. Many forest roads are suitable for passenger vehicles, but surfaces vary. If you are driving on forest roads on the Kaibab Plateau, keep in mind that road conditions usually downgrade as you approach the canyon rim. A wide gravel road, suitable for passenger cars, might end up as a two-track with rocks, ruts, and a high center, so narrow that it's difficult to turn around. Forest Service maps indicate surface types and help you make sense of what can be a confusing maze of fire roads.

On forest and Bureau of Land Management roads, muddy conditions can last into late spring, especially on the North Rim's Kaibab Plateau. Think twice before continuing down a soggy two-track. Even a 4WD vehicle can

© KATHLEEN BRYANT

A high-clearance vehicle is needed for some backroad drives.

get hopelessly mired. Besides, "mudding" damages roads, creating ruts that harden and persist until the next rain, and causing erosion along roadsides when vehicles skirt wet spots by driving around them. Muddy conditions also occur after summer thunderstorms. Be wary of stream crossings in lower areas, such as on the Marble Platform. Flash flooding can turn a dry wash into a dangerous stream.

SHUTTLE BUSES AND TOURS
Shuttles and Taxi

The South Rim's free shuttle system covers the Grand Canyon Village area year-round and Hermit Road from March through November. Shuttle buses stop at parking lots, lodges, visitors centers, and overlooks from Yaki Point west to Hermits Rest. See *The Guide,* the park's seasonal newspaper, for a map showing routes and schedules, which vary seasonally.

The Hikers' Express is a morning shuttle that picks up passengers at Bright Angel Lodge and the Backcountry Information Center before traveling to the visitors center and the South Kaibab Trailhead. It makes three departures daily during the high season, and two during the winter.

The **Trans Canyon Shuttle** (928/638-2820) provides daily round-trip van service between the South Rim and North Rim May 15–October 15. You can also take the shuttle to the Marble Canyon area near Lees Ferry. The shuttle leaves the South Rim at 1:30 P.M., arriving at the North Rim at 6 P.M. Reservations are required.

You can also get around the South Rim's Grand Canyon Village and Tusayan by taxi (928/638-2822 or 928/638-2631, ext. 6573). Services are available every day, 24 hours a day, and drivers can deliver hikers and backpackers to trailheads.

Bus Tours

Xanterra Parks & Resorts offers year-round guided motor coach tours along the South Rim. Call or visit one of the transportation desks (928/638-2631) in Bright Angel Lodge, Maswik Lodge, or Yavapai Lodge for more information, or read about them online (www.grandcanyonlodges.com). Times vary according to the season, but options include sunrise or sunset tours as well as scenic drives along Hermit Road and Desert View Drive.

Train Tours

Grand Canyon Railway (800/843-8724, www.thetrain.com) offers five classes of passenger service from Williams to Grand Canyon's South Rim. The route passes through ponderosa pine forest, piñon-juniper woodland, and open prairie. Although you won't get canyon views from the train, you can sign up for a package tour that combines the train ride with lodging and guided rim tours.

River Trips

For the most complete inner canyon experience, reserve a white-water rafting trip lasting 3–18 days. More than a dozen concessionaires and guides lead commercial rafting tours in Grand Canyon. Outside the park, smooth-water floats from Glen Canyon Dam to Lees Ferry make a pleasant 15-mile, half-day tour. Contact Canyon Discovery (888/522-6244, www.raftthecanyon.com) or visit one of the lodge transportation desks to make arrangements.

Horse and Mule Tours

On the South Rim, **Xanterra Parks & Resorts** (303/297-2757 or 888/297-2757) offers two options for mule rides into the canyon: a day ride along the rim to the Abyss overlook, and overnight rides with a stay at Phantom Ranch. Reservations can be made up to 13 months in advance, although last-minute cancellations are possible, particularly during the winter.

On the North Rim, **Grand Canyon Trail Rides** (435/679-8665, www.canyonrides.com) offers one-hour rides along the rim, half-day trips along the rim or partway down the North Kaibab Trail, and full-day trips into the canyon to Roaring Springs.

Horseback tours in Kaibab National Forest are available from concessionaires. These rides stick to forest roads and trails outside the park. **Apache Stables** (928/638-2891, www .apachestables.com) offers horseback tours and wagon rides near the South Rim, while **Allen's Guided Tours** (435/644-8150 or 435/689-1370) leads horseback trips near Jacob Lake.

BY RV

The roads in historic Grand Canyon Village were made for horses and stagecoaches, not RVs and modern traffic, so you may find it challenging to negotiate the narrow Village Loop. If you're not camping in your RV, park it, and rely instead on the park's free shuttle system. You'll find parking spaces large enough for RVs at Grand Canyon Visitors Center near the park's South Entrance Station. The paved lot at the Backcountry Information Center (Lot E, south of Maswik Lodge) also has RV-sized spaces.

If you're camping, make reservations well in advance. Inside the park, only the South Rim's **Trailer Village** (928/638-2631 or 888/297-2757, www.grandcanyonlodges.com) has RV sites with full hookups for vehicles up to 50 feet long. Showers and laundry are available at the Camper Services building near Mather Campground. You can camp at Mather Campground, although there are no hookups, and vehicle length is limited to 30 feet. Very few sites at first-come, first-served Desert View Campground can accommodate RVs, and there are no hookups. The South Rim's disposal station is located next to Mather Campground.

Outside the park in Tusayan, **Grand Canyon Camper Village** (928/638-2887, Mar.–Oct.) has 250 RV sites with hookups. The campground also has coin-operated showers and laundry, a store, a playground, restrooms, and a dump site. Several restaurants and a grocery store are within walking distance.

A couple of miles south of Tusayan, **Ten X Campground** (877/444-6777, www.recreation .gov, May–Sept.) has pull-through sites. RVs up to 30 feet long can be accommodated, although there are no hookups. The campground often sells out in the summer.

Farther south in Valle, **Bedrock City** (928/635-2600, Feb.–Nov.) has RV sites with hookups and a grocery, a diner, a gift shop, a game room, laundry, and showers nearby.

Thirty miles east of the park's East Entrance, **Cameron Trading Post RV Park** (928/679-2231 or 800/338-7385) has RV sites with full hookups. The RV park is adjacent to historic and modern trading posts, a convenience store, and a restaurant.

The North Rim Campground, inside the park, can accommodate RVs. There are no hookups, but there's a dump station within the campground. Outside the park, 17 miles north of the rim, **DeMotte Campground** (928/643-7395, www.fs.fed.us/r3/kai/recreation/campgrounds, late May–Oct. 15, depending on snowfall) allows small motor homes, but there are no hookups. This Forest Service campground doesn't take reservations, and it does fill up, so arrive early.

The forest service also operates **Jacob Lake Campground** (928/643-7395, www.fs.fed.us/r3/kai/recreation/campgrounds, May 15–Nov. 1, depending on snowfall) at the intersection of U.S. 89A and Highway 67, which is 45 miles north of the rim. The no-reservations campground has sites that can accommodate small motor homes, but there are no hookups.

If you want hookups, make reservations for **Kaibab Camper Village** (928/643-7804 or 800/525-0924, off-season 928/526-0924, http://kaibabcampervillage.com, May 15–Oct. 15). Just south of Jacob Lake, this commercial campground has 62 RV sites with full hookups.

For RV repairs, you'll need to drive to Williams, Flagstaff, or if you're on the North Rim, Kanab, Utah. Automotive repairs are limited at the North Rim and Jacob Lake service stations.

BY BICYCLE

Bicycles are allowed on all paved and dirt roads on the South Rim and North Rim. However, many park roads are narrow and curving, and traffic is heavy, especially on summer weekends. Wear a helmet and bright colors, use hand signals, and ride single-file in the same direction as traffic. In Arizona, bikes are subject to the same traffic rules as automobiles. The South Rim's free shuttle buses will accommodate bikes.

All hiking trails inside the park are off-limits to bicycles, with two exceptions. On the North Rim, cyclists can use **The Bridle Path.** On the South Rim, **The Greenway** is open to bicycles. The Greenway is a walking and cycling path that connects the historic village area with the Grand Canyon Visitors Center and plaza. Another Greenway segment begins at the Abyss overlook on Hermit Road.

Outside park boundaries in Kaibab National Forest, traffic is much lighter. Dirt and gravel forest roads offer miles of shady rides on the canyon's north and south sides, some with canyon views. In the North Kaibab, Forest Roads 610 and 611 take you to the edge of the Kaibab Plateau for views of the eastern canyon and Marble Platform, with links to a 22-mile section of the Arizona Trail. Just a few miles from the park boundaries near Grandview Point, forest roads travel to historic Hull Cabin, the Grandview Lookout tower, and the Moqui Stage Station, with distant canyon views from the Coconino Rim.

For more information about bike touring in Kaibab National Forest near the South Rim, contact the Tusayan Ranger District (928/638-2443). If you're interested in rides near the North Rim, contact the Kaibab Plateau Visitors Center (928/643-7298) in Jacob Lake.

BY MOTORCYCLE

Spring and autumn, between winter snowstorms and the blazing summer sun, are the best times for motorcycle touring in the Grand Canyon area. Watch out for late-summer thunderstorms, which can spout hail and lightning July–mid-September, mostly during the afternoon. Arizona law requires helmets for riders younger than 18 and eye protection for drivers of motorcycles without windshields.

Be visible: Traffic around Grand Canyon Village is heavy, with lots of distractions, and the long, open, straight stretch on Highway 64 from Williams to Grand Canyon is notorious for inattentive drivers. Stick to walking and shuttle buses in the South Rim's congested village area, and save the bike for Desert View Drive. If you prefer open road, head for the North Rim.

If you like to keep a close watch on your ride, note that Maswik and Yavapai Lodges are most likely to have parking spaces near your room. Mather, Desert View, and the North Rim Campgrounds all allow motorcycles.

Route 66 towns near Grand Canyon, including Williams, Flagstaff, and Kingman, are popular with bikers, and if you need repairs or gear, these are your best bet.

Recreation

The majority of Grand Canyon visitors stay for only a few hours, rarely getting closer to the canyon than peering over its rim. But the best way to experience the canyon's vast reaches is to venture within them. Exploration has its risks: sheer cliff edges, hyperthermia or hypothermia (depending on the season), dehydration, rock falls, lightning strikes, flash floods, drowning, and unpleasant critter encounters. Park rangers rescue an average of 400 people in the canyon's backcountry each year. Most have failed to prepare adequately or have overestimated their abilities. But if you've done your homework, the canyon will reward you with inspiring views that change at every turn in the trail, and up-close encounters with geology, history, and desert life.

DAY HIKING

If you've never hiked before, don't let that stop you from hiking at Grand Canyon. Yes, the canyon is intimidating, but a guided ranger walk or a rim hike is a great way to get your feet dusty. If you're a hiker but you've never hiked

Grand Canyon before, start with one of the popular, maintained, and patrolled trails in the central corridor of the canyon: Bright Angel, South Kaibab, or North Kaibab Trails.

Sufficient water and sun protection are critical. So is determining the "point of must return." Hiking guides, rangers, and even the kiosks in the plaza outside the South Rim's Grand Canyon Visitors Center can help you choose an appropriate day-hike destination. Keep in mind that it will take you roughly twice as long to hike back up to the rim as it did to hike down.

You don't need a permit for a day hike, but your preparations might include dropping a quarter into one of the metal trailside containers for an informative brochure. The brochures are available for the North Rim's Bright Angel Point, Walhalla Glades, and Widforss Trail, and the Rim Trail on the South Rim. The Grand Canyon Association (GCA) publishes inexpensive booklets for a number of trails, including the Bright Angel, South Kaibab, and Hermit Trails, available at visitors centers and GCA bookstores. Learning a little bit about geology, plants, animals, and history before or during your hike will add to your experience.

Trail Etiquette

Be respectful of other hikers by doing your part to maintain natural quiet. Don't throw rocks into the canyon, a highly dangerous impulse. The traditional rule of the trail is to yield to hikers going uphill, but use common sense. Sometimes uphill hikers welcome a break, and sometimes they'll want you just to get out of their way. Always yield to mules by stepping off the trail on the inside.

Many Grand Canyon trails are historic and even prehistoric, used by pioneers and ancients. Structures, rock art, artifacts like pottery shards and lithic scatters, and less obvious evidence like roasting pits are fascinating reminders that humans have traveled the canyon for millennia. Treat these reminders as though you were in an outdoor museum—feel free to look, but leave them in place. Even the thin layer of oils on your fingertips can damage rock

© KATHLEEN BRYANT

Hikers must yield to mules on canyon trails.

art. Federal and state laws protect all archaeological and historic sites, including artifacts, on federal lands. Violators are subject to fines and imprisonment. If you witness theft or vandalism, contact the park's Silent Witness Program (928/638-7767).

Help prevent erosion by staying on trails. Don't shortcut switchbacks. Watch for **cryptobiotic soils**—lumpy, grayish-black crusts that protect soil by retaining moisture and preventing wind erosion. "Crypto" is a symbiotic community of bacteria, lichens, and mosses. It takes decades to form and only a footstep to destroy.

For your own safety and for the health of the animals, do not disturb or feed wildlife. Pack out all trash, including food scraps. If you see a condor, mountain lion, or feral burro, report the sighting to a ranger.

BACKPACKING

Hiking to the river or a scenic tributary and spending the night inside the canyon are magical experiences. If you're lucky, you may feel completely in sync with nature, as though you've stumbled across your very own private Eden. But chances are, you won't be alone. Nearly 40,000 people camp in Grand Canyon's backcountry each year. In an effort to keep this wilderness as wild as possible, the park has instituted a permit system limiting the number and location of campsites.

If you want to spend the night in the canyon, you'll need to apply for a backcountry permit. Keep your permit in a visible location, such as attached to the outside of your trip leader's pack. In camp, the permit must be in plain view, such as attached to a tent, so that patrolling backcountry rangers can check it.

The same safety issues that concern day hikers are magnified for backpackers, and careful preparation is a must. Most canyon backpackers train for a trip, acclimating to elevation, distance, terrain, and load with aerobic conditioning, strength training, and endurance work. Attitude is as important as physical condition: being able to focus and concentrate, setting and achieving goals, and keeping a positive outlook.

Planning requires attention to detail, from packing enough of the right kind of food to researching water availability along your route. Good maps and trail guides can help you locate routes and water sources. The online bulletin board managed by **Grand Canyon Hikers and Backpackers Association** (www.gchba.org) is another helpful resource.

Aside from clothing, personal items, a tent (optional in summer), and a sleeping bag and pad, things to pack include: water, a filtration system, iodine tablets, electrolyte replacement, a backpacking stove (though in the summer, you may wish to pack foods that don't require cooking), hand sanitizer, animal-proof food storage containers, matches, a pocketknife, a flashlight or headlamp, sun protection, a first aid kit (including blister treatment), extra socks, a signaling device (a mirror and/or whistle), a repair kit (duct tape, safety pins, needle and thread), and 20–30 feet of nylon rope. You'll also need to deal with sanitation: Bring a trowel for digging a cat hole and ziplock bags for carrying out used toilet paper.

Leave No Trace Principles

To protect the canyon and respect other backcountry users, all backpackers should practice "leave no trace" ethics:

- Stay on trails and camp in designated areas. Don't trench, dig, or rearrange Mother Nature to build a tent site—use an established site.

- Open fires are not allowed in the backcountry. Use a backpacking stove or bring food that doesn't require cooking.

- Pack out all trash. Leave campsites in the same condition as you found them (or better). Even the tiniest crumbs can attract rodents and ants. Discard dishwater at least 200 feet from small water sources, and strain food particles from the dishwater.

- Use biodegradable soap. Do not contaminate water pockets or small streams, which may be needed by wildlife or other backpackers. If you are camped at the Colorado River, discard strained dishwater or urinate into the water, as the river's volume is adequate for dilution.

- Bury solid human waste 200 feet from all water sources (including dry washes), camps, and trails. Dig a cat hole at least 4–6 inches deep. Look for organic soil; do not use sand or dunes. Pack out used toilet paper. The park is studying the use of "wag bags" in some backcountry areas, and waste disposal guidelines will likely be updated in the future.

FISHING

To fish inside the park, you'll need an Arizona fishing license and a trout stamp. At the South Rim, you can buy a license at the General Store. If you're traveling to the North Rim, you'll need to stop and pick up a license at Jacob Lake Inn or Marble Canyon Lodge, not far from Lees Ferry, a popular fly-fishing area. For more information, contact the **Arizona Game & Fish Department** (602/942-3000, www.azgfd.gov) before your trip.

Tips for Travelers

INTERNATIONAL TRAVELERS
Visas and Passports

Most international visitors need a passport and a visa to enter the United States. A nonimmigrant visa allows you to travel to a U.S. port of entry for the purpose stated on the visa and request permission to enter the country from the immigration inspector on duty. If the officer grants permission, a passport is required to enter the United States. Visas are waived for 27 countries, including France, Italy, Germany, and Japan. If you enter the States without a visa, an individual machine-readable passport is required. Check with your home country's foreign ministry about obtaining a passport or visa, or to learn more about visa and passport requirements, visit the U.S. Department of State's website (http://travel.state.gov).

Air Travel

If you will be traveling within the U.S. on a commercial airline, be aware that carry-on regulations are subject to change. Generally, you can carry on personal toiletries in containers of three ounces or less, grouped together in a clear, quart-size, ziplock plastic bag. Some items, such as mace or pepper spray, are prohibited. Bottled water, beverages, snacks, and other items can be carried on if they are purchased in the airport's secure boarding area. For more information about current travel regulations on domestic airlines, visit the Transportation Security Administration website (www.tsa.gov). Security checkpoint wait times vary by location, time of day, and day of the week. Contact your airline and airport for recommended arrival times.

Money and Currency Exchange

U.S. currency recently underwent a design change, and both new and old bills are in circulation. The newly designed bills include additional security features to prevent counterfeiting, including colors and microprint. Be aware that if you return home with U.S. currency, your bank may be unwilling to exchange the older-style bills.

Many U.S. coins have also been redesigned. For example, the quarter (25-cent coin) has changed five times each year during the last 10 years, and at least 50 different quarter designs are in circulation. If that sounds confusing to you, you're not alone; it can be confusing for U.S. residents also. If you need to ask the local behind you in line whether you're holding a quarter or a nickel, you'll probably get a sympathetic smile. If you'd like a primer on coins, visit the U.S. Mint's website (www.us-mint.gov).

Major credit cards and traveler's checks are accepted almost everywhere. Before you leave on your trip, be sure your credit card and bank card have PINs (personal identification numbers) that will work overseas. Also check with your bank and credit-card companies about transaction fees or foreign exchange fees. (Some credit-card companies offer lower fees than others, and you may be able to avoid ATM fees by using your debit card to obtain cash at banks and grocery stores.)

At the South Rim, you'll find ATMs at Maswik Lodge and **Chase Bank** (928/638-2437, 9 A.M.–5 P.M. Mon.–Thurs., 9 A.M.–6 P.M. Fri.). The bank's lobby, where the ATM is located, is open 24 hours daily. There's also an ATM in Tusayan at the IMAX Theater. At the North Rim, you'll find ATM machines in the general store near the campground and at the Roughrider Saloon next to Grand Canyon Lodge.

Tipping

At restaurants, it's standard to tip 15–20 percent, before taxes, depending on the quality of service. If you are dining in a group of six or more, a gratuity may be automatically added to the bill. (If so, this must be clearly stated on the menu or on the bill.) A minimum tip should be $1, even if you've ordered something less than $5. If you are ordering counter service (such as at a coffee bar or deli), you may see a tip jar near the cash register. In this case, tips are appreciated (especially if you've made a special request or substitution) but not required. Tipping at a bar is customarily $1–2 per drink or 5–20 percent of the total bill. (People often tip ahead on the first drink to encourage attentive service.) For baggage handling, tip $1–2 per bag. Leave $2–3 per day in your hotel room for housekeeping service. A room-service bill may or may not include a gratuity. Check to see if the gratuity has been included; if not, tip the waiter. If you sign up for a commercial tour, tip your guide 15–20 percent.

TRAVELING WITH CHILDREN
Junior Ranger Program

The park's Junior Ranger Program is free, and it's a good way to keep kids focused as they participate in hikes or activities to earn a certificate and badge. Five different awards and program levels target age groups from 4–14. Required activities include at least one ranger program. On the South Rim, you can pick up a *Junior Ranger Activity Booklet* at the Visitors Center at Canyon View Information Plaza, Yavapai Observation Station, Park Headquarters, or Tusayan Museum. On the North Rim, Junior Ranger booklets are available at the visitors center. There's also a Junior Ranger program specifically for Phantom Ranch.

Hikes

Many canyon trails have fine day-hike destinations suitable for kids, but if trails leading into the canyon are too steep for your parental peace of mind, stick to gentler trails above the rim. On the South Rim, some paved portions of the Rim Trail are manageable for strollers. On the North Rim, the Uncle Jim, Transept, Cliff Springs, and Widforss Trails follow the rim or head through the forest, especially good choices for hiking with kids age four and older. Along park trails, you'll find many opportunities to introduce your kids to nature: wildlife-viewing, fire ecology, and identifying birds or wildflowers. (Remember: It's illegal to pick plants or collect seeds within the park.) If you'd rather turn the nature talk over to an expert, rangers guide short hikes several times a day on both rims. Look for family-friendly walks in the ranger program schedule, usually listed in the first few pages of *The Guide,* the park's newspaper.

Ranger and Naturalist Programs

Most of the park's free ranger programs are suitable for kids, and any ranger program fulfills the activity requirement for the Junior Ranger Program. Some programs are specifically family oriented, including fossil walks, story times, and games. Look for the Family Fun symbol on the program schedule in *The Guide.* Children must be supervised and accompanied by a parent.

Naturalists with the **Grand Canyon Field Institute** (GCFI, 866/471-4435, www.grand-canyon.org/fieldinstitute) hold single-day family classes called "Meet the Canyon." You can pick a date by calling the GCFI. Private, customized outings may also be available.

Xanterra Parks & Resorts (928/638-2525 or 928/638-2485) and the GCFI team up for twice-weekly Learning & Lodging programs that combine accommodations, meals, and naturalist-led walks. Children must be 10 or older and accompanied by an adult.

Trains, Planes, Mules, and Boats
The **Grand Canyon Railway** (928/635-2461, 928/773-0147, or 800/843-8724) has daily departures between Williams and Grand Canyon Depot. Most air-tour companies offer discounts for children on scenic flights and on tour packages combining flights with land tours or boat trips. Mule trips (888/297-2757) to Phantom Ranch or the Abyss don't have an age limit but require that all riders be at least 4 feet, 7 inches tall. Children 15 and younger must be accompanied by an adult on mule trips.

On the North Rim, hour-long mule tours (435/679-8665) are suitable for kids as young as seven years. Wagon rides and horseback tours are offered by concessionaires in neighboring Kaibab National Forest (near North Rim, 435/644-8150; near South Rim, 928/638-2891 or 928/638-3105). Colorado River Discovery (928/645-9175 or 888/522-6644, www.rafttheecanyon.com) leads half-day motorized, smooth-water floats from Glen Canyon Dam to Lees Ferry, suitable for children as young as four.

Day Care
On the South Rim, the **Kaibab Learning Center** (928/638-6333, 7:30 A.M.–5:30 P.M. Mon.–Fri.) offers day care services for infants and children up to 12 years old, when spaces are available. Immunization records must be provided.

TRAVELING WITH PETS
Pets are not permitted in lodges, on shuttle buses, or on hiking trails below the rim. The only exceptions are service animals. (If you want to take a service animal below the rim, you must first check with the Backcountry Information Center.) At the South Rim, you can walk your pet on a leash on paved sections of the Rim Trail. On the North Rim, leashed pets are allowed on the Bridle Path. Pets are permitted in developed areas of the park, including campgrounds, but must be leashed at all times and cannot be left unattended. A violation can cost you $500.

When visiting the South Rim, you can board your dog or cat for the day or overnight at the **kennel** (928/638-0534, 7:30 A.M.–5 P.M. daily), located off Rowe Well Road west of Maswik Lodge. Reservations are recommended, and proof of vaccination is required. You can make arrangements to pick up your pet later than 5 P.M. by calling 928/638-2631. There are no kennel services on the North Rim.

An alternative is to board your pet outside the canyon in Williams, 60 miles south of the South Rim, or in Flagstaff, 90 miles away. **Canyon Pet Resort** (928/214-9324, www.canyonpetresort.com) in Flagstaff offers day care and overnight boarding, with optional extras such as walks, treats, or an executive doggy suite. In Williams, Grand Canyon Railway's air-conditioned **Pet Resort** (800/843-8724) is available to the general public as well as visitors staying at the adjacent RV park or riding the Grand Canyon Railway.

Never leave an animal alone inside a vehicle, even with the windows rolled down a few inches. During much of the year, Arizona's intense sunshine can heat up the interior of a car to 130–180°F in a matter of minutes. Like you, your pet will need extra water to stay hydrated at Grand Canyon.

SENIORS
The America the Beautiful Senior Pass ($10 lifetime fee) replaces the Golden Age Passport, which may be exchanged at no charge. The Senior Pass is a lifetime interagency pass for U.S. citizens age 62 and older, providing access at no charge to all federal recreation fee sites. It must be obtained in person at the park with proof of age, such as a driver's license. The pass admits up to three accompanying adult passengers in a noncommercial vehicle.

In addition, pass holders receive a 50 percent discount on other park fees, such as for campsites in national park campgrounds. Senior discounts may or may not be offered by park concessionaires. (But it never hurts to ask, does it?)

TRAVELERS WITH DISABILITIES

Many of the park's facilities were designed before ADA standards were established. Because of steps and narrow doorways, some of the park's historic buildings are only partly accessible, but most lodges have a number of accessible rooms, and several overlooks have wheelchair access. Restrooms vary in ease of use, but many are accessible. Wheelchairs are available for short-term loan at the North Rim Visitors Center, the South Rim's Grand Canyon Visitors Center, Yavapai Observation Station, and the bookstore at Desert View. For specific information about entryways, parking, grade, restrooms, and other details for attractions and facilities on the North and South Rims, refer to the park's *Accessibility Guide*. It's available online (www.nps.gov/grca), at the park entrance stations, and at Grand Canyon Visitors Center.

Fees

The America the Beautiful Access Pass is a free interagency pass for legally blind or permanently disabled U.S. citizens, good at all fee-based federal recreation sites. The Access Pass replaces the Golden Access Passport, which may be exchanged at no charge. The pass must be obtained in person at the park, with accompanying documentation such as a physician's statement, a document issued by a federal agency (such as the Veterans Administration or Social Security Administration), or by a state agency such as a vocational rehabilitation center. The pass admits the pass holder and up to three adult passengers in a noncommercial vehicle. The pass also provides a 50 percent discount on many park-based fees, such as for Mather Campground or the North Rim Campground.

ENTRANCE FEES

The entrance fee for Grand Canyon National Park is $25 per vehicle, which includes all passengers in the vehicle. If you are entering on foot, bicycle, or motorcycle, the fee is $12 per person. (There's no charge for kids 15 and younger.) A $12-pp fee also applies to those entering as part of an organized noncommercial group, such as church groups, scouting troops, and so on. Admission fees are good for seven days and include all areas of the national park, even if you exit to go from one rim to the other.

If you're planning more than a couple of visits to the canyon in a single year, you can purchase an annual Grand Canyon pass for $50. An annual interagency pass (good for all national parks, monuments, and recreation areas) is $80 annually. Discounted or free passes are available for seniors, people with disabilities, and federal lands volunteers with more than 500 hours of service.

There are no entry fees for the areas bordering the park that are managed by the U.S. Forest Service or the Bureau of Land Management. Fees for hiking, camping, or photographing on neighboring Indian reservation lands vary; contact tribal governments for information.

If you plan on backpacking or camping during your visit to the canyon, be sure to get a backcountry permit and make campground reservations well in advance. Additional fees apply for these and other special uses.

Parking and Shuttles

If you are traveling at the South Rim in your own vehicle, you can ask for an Accessibility Pass at the entrance stations or visitors centers. The pass, placed on the dashboard of your vehicle, allows access to some areas that are closed to general traffic. The transportation desks, Kolb Studio, and Tusayan Museum also issue Accessibility Passes (though, ironically, Kolb Studio itself is inaccessible).

All park shuttle buses are accessible to wheelchairs. Trained service animals are allowed on shuttles.

Accommodations

Most park lodges on the South Rim have a number of accessible guest rooms, with the exception of El Tovar and Bright Angel Lodge. Shower chairs and TDD phones are available on request. Contact Xanterra Parks & Resorts (303/297-2757 or 888/297-2757) for information and reservations. The South Rim's **Mather Campground** (800/365-2267) has accessible campsites. Request an accessible site when making your reservation and confirm accessibility when you register at the campground. The South Rim's Camper Services building has a combination shower and restroom accessible to wheelchairs. The onsite attendant has the key. The North Rim Campground (800/365-2267) has designated sites with accessible picnic tables. These are linked to the showers and restrooms by a level paved trail, and roll-in showers are available. The North Rim's **Grand Canyon Lodge** (888/386-4383) has a few cabins that are minimally accessible. Cabins are scattered through the forest, with steep, narrow, rough sidewalks and stairways.

Tours, Trails, and Programs

Many ranger programs are accessible, as noted in *The Guide*. Some are adapted for the visually impaired. With advance notice, bus tours offered by Xanterra Parks & Resorts can accommodate wheelchairs. Even mule tours may be accessible under some circumstances. Call the Bright Angel Lodge transportation desk (928/638-2631) for advance tour reservations. For white-water river trips, contact individual outfitters and guides about accessibility. **Colorado River Discovery** (928/645-9175 or 888/522-6644, www.raftthecanyon.com) offers half-day smooth-water floats from Glen Canyon Dam to Lees Ferry, appropriate for passengers with mobility or sensory disabilities.

Gentle trails are available on either rim of the canyon. Along the South Rim, portions of the Rim Trail are paved and fairly level, particularly the two-mile section between Bright Angel Lodge and Mather Point. The North Rim's Bridle Path has a hard surface and is fairly level between Grand Canyon Lodge and the campground entrance (1 mile). Trails below either rim are steep, with uneven surfaces and dangerous drop-offs. If you wish to take a service animal on hiking trails, arrangements can be made at the Backcountry Information Center (928/638-7875) in Grand Canyon Village near Maswik Lodge, or the North Rim's Backcountry Office (928/638-7868), located along the service road north of the campground entrance.

Health and Safety

Hospitals and Clinics

For emergencies, call 911 (or 9-911 if you are calling from a room in one of the park lodges). Emergency phones at ranger stations connect directly to the park switchboard and do not require coins. Your cell phone isn't likely to get a signal inside the canyon or on the North Rim. River guides carry satellite phones and are trained to assist in emergencies. Rangers and clinic staff handle emergencies on the South Rim, where a walk-in clinic (928/638-2551) is open all year. You can fill prescriptions here, but only with a handwritten order from your doctor. Flagstaff Medical Center is about 90 minutes from the South Rim by car. The North Rim is more remote, and park rangers have first-aid certification or EMT training. The nearest small hospitals are in Page (125 miles) or Kanab, Utah (82 miles). Air transport to Flagstaff Medical Center is possible from either rim.

Altitude

Elevations range 6,600–7,400 along the South Rim and 8,200–8,800 on the North Rim, high enough to affect many flatlanders, especially the elderly or those with existing health problems. Signs of altitude sickness are headache, weakness, fatigue, shortness of breath, and dizziness. Dehydration is often a factor, so drink plenty of water. Taking a day or two to acclimate before hiking helps, as does slowing your pace and taking rest breaks.

Falls

A family trip to Grand Canyon turned into tragedy in 2007 when a four-year-old girl fell 450 feet to her death, and her father was injured trying to reach her. Every year, falls at Grand Canyon result in injuries and 1–3 deaths. Many of the victims were trying to get a photograph or scrambling around on rocks outside guardrails. Keep a close watch on kids (and a closer watch on your husband or boyfriend—most victims are young men). Stay behind fences and barriers and be cautious near the rim: Even large rocks can break loose, icy patches are common in the winter, and sand or small rocks make surfaces slippery any time of year. If you're hiking, don't cut switchbacks or go off-trail, and step to the inside of the trail and wait for mules to pass. The canyon's terrain is rugged, and it's a long way down.

Heat-Related Illnesses

High altitude, dry air, and hot summer temperatures multiply the effects of the sun. Below the rim, the canyon's rocky walls hold heat and reflect the sun's rays. Extreme inner canyon heat catches many people unprepared, and heat-related conditions are common. Protect yourself from sunburn by wearing a wide-brimmed hat, UV lenses, sunscreen or long sleeves, and lip balm. Above all, drink plenty of water.

Because the hot, dry air quickly dries perspiration, hikers may not realize how much moisture they are losing from sweat—up to two quarts of water every hour. Rangers along the Bright Angel Trail treat as many as 20 cases of heat exhaustion daily during summer months. Symptoms are pallor, nausea, headache, cramps, and cool, moist skin.

Left untreated, heat exhaustion can lead to heatstroke, a life-threatening emergency. The face becomes flushed and the skin dry. The pulse is weak and rapid. The body's ability to regulate temperature is overwhelmed, and body temperature goes up, leading to mental confusion and eventual unconsciousness.

Hyponatremia (water intoxication) can look like heat exhaustion, with cramping, clamminess, headache, and nausea. But this serious condition is the result of drinking too much water without replacing electrolytes, leading to low concentrations of sodium in the blood. Like heatstroke, hyponatremia can lead to altered mental states and rapid pulse, and it too can be deadly.

To prevent heat-related illnesses, drink plenty of water and balance water intake by eating salty snacks and/or using electrolyte-replacement powders, gels, or drinks. Keep cool, resting in the shade and hiking within your abilities. If your hiking companion's mental state becomes altered, get immediate help. If you suspect heatstroke, cool the victim immediately by pouring water on his or her skin, clothing, and hair.

Hypothermia

With so many dire warnings about dehydration and heat, it's easy to forget that hypothermia is also a danger. Exposure to cold and wet conditions can lead to the point where the body can't warm itself. Symptoms are the "umbles": mumbling, grumbling, stumbling, fumbling. If you're hiking during the winter, wear fleece rather than denim or heavy cotton, and pack a Thermos with a hot drink. Treat hypothermia with dry clothing, warm liquids, and protection from the elements.

Drowning

Do not hike in tributary canyons when flash floods are a possibility, particularly during the late-summer thunderstorm season. Boaters should always wear a personal flotation device (PFD) or life jacket. Colorado River currents are swift, with bone-chillingly cold water and dangerous rocks and rapids. To protect beaches from ammonia buildup, campers and river runners urinate in the river or in the wet sand at

Painful bites are one of many reasons not to feed animals.

the water's edge. This can be a tricky proposition in the middle of the night when it's dark and you're sleepy. Carry a flashlight or headlamp, and be cautious on wet rocks.

Bites and Stings

The canyon is home to several biting insects, including scorpions and bees, as well as several species of rodents and rattlesnakes. If you are allergic to beestings or insect bites, carry an EpiPen and be sure your hiking companions know how to use it. Prevent bites by watching where you place your hands and feet. Shake out clothing and bedding. Don't feed or pester wildlife. Although snakebites are rare, they are almost always the result of people trying to handle snakes. Deer, bighorn sheep, coyotes, and rock squirrels have bitten people offering them handouts.

Rabies and plague aren't uncommon in Arizona. Never handle a bat; if you see one during the day, it is quite likely infected with rabies. Keep your food supply secured when you are in camp: Ringtails, rodents, and ravens can get into packs even when they are hanging, so consider using animal-proof containers. Hantavirus, a deadly respiratory illness, can be transmitted by inhaling dust from rodent waste. If you discover that your ziplock bag of GORP has been chewed into, pack it out with the rest of your trash.

Some hikers feel safer carrying a bite extractor, which works for removing poison or stingers from insect bites as well as for snakebite venom. Any animal bite should be checked by a physician and monitored for signs of infection.

RESOURCES

Suggested Reading

Thousands of books have been written about Grand Canyon, from field guides to adventure stories. The Grand Canyon Association maintains a bibliography (http://grandcanyon biblio.org) of canyon books, maps, periodicals, and other resources more than 40,000 items long. The titles listed below are a mere sampling of helpful, fascinating, and entertaining canyon lore.

HUMAN HISTORY AND ARCHAEOLOGY

Anderson, Michael F. *Along the Rim*. Grand Canyon, AZ: Grand Canyon Association, 2001. A 72-page booklet that provides a concise history of Grand Canyon Village and 22 overlooks along Hermit Road and Desert View Drive, making it an excellent take-along resource for a driving tour.

Anderson, Michael F. *Living at the Edge: Explorers, Exploiters, and Settlers of the Grand Canyon Region*. Grand Canyon, AZ: Grand Canyon, Association, 1998. This thorough history begins with Paleo-Indian use of the canyon and extends to the rise of tourism in the 1930s. River runners, miners, Harvey Girls, Mary Colter, and other pioneer figures are emphasized. Illustrations include maps and archival photographs, several of them taken by the Kolb Brothers.

Coder, Christopher M. *An Introduction to Grand Canyon Prehistory*. Grand Canyon, AZ: Grand Canyon, Association, 2000. The author provides a concise but comprehensive description of 12,000 years of human life in Grand Canyon. Coder, a tribe archaeologist, has studied Grand Canyon sites and links his perspective to contemporary Native American cultures.

Grattan, Virginia L. *Mary Colter: Builder Upon the Red Earth*. Grand Canyon, AZ: Grand Canyon Association, 1992. An excellent biography of eccentric and talented Mary Elizabeth Jane Colter, who designed the South Rim's most spectacular buildings.

GEOLOGY AND NATURAL HISTORY

Alden, Peter, et al. *National Audubon Society Field Guide to the Southwestern States*. New York: Alfred A. Knopf, 1999. Plants, animals, geology, weather, and more are covered in this field guide, a good companion for a trip around the region. Color photos and star charts aid identifications of plants, animals, constellations, and landforms. Details include travel information for Grand Canyon, Coconino National Forest, and other Arizona parks and recreation areas.

Blakely, Ron, and Wayne Ranney. *Ancient Landscapes of the Colorado Plateau*. Grand Canyon, AZ: Grand Canyon Association, 2008. If you've ever wished you could travel back in time to see what the Grand Canyon area looked like millions of years ago, this book will take you there through paleogeographic maps and illustrations.

Kavanaugh, James, and Raymond Leung. *Field Guide to the Grand Canyon*. Phoenix: Waterford Press, 2001. A laminated and folded brochure that is a pocket-sized introduction to the canyon's most common plants and animals.

Lamb, Susan. *Grand Canyon: The Vault of Heaven*. Grand Canyon, AZ: Grand Canyon Association, 1995. If you're looking for an all-around book about Grand Canyon's human and natural history that doubles as a souvenir, this gorgeously photographed, oversize book fits the bill.

Ranney, Wayne. *Carving Grand Canyon*. Grand Canyon, AZ: Grand Canyon Association, 2005. The author outlines historic theories about how the Colorado River carved Grand Canyon, then details his own ideas, reminding us that even with all the evidence, some elements remain enigmatic. Excellent illustrations and clear writing make this geological history easy for laypeople to understand.

Whitney, Stephen R. *A Field Guide to the Grand Canyon*. Seattle: The Mountaineers, 1996. The guide describes many plants and animals of the canyon's rims and gorge, with black-and-white and color illustrations for identification. The natural history introduction covers geology and the environment.

HIKING AND RECREATION

Abbot, Lon, and Terri Cook. *Hiking the Grand Canyon's Geology*. Seattle: The Mountaineers, 2004. Introductory chapters explain canyon geology, followed by step-by-step geologic information for 18 hikes. Illustrations include helpful geologic diagrams and excellent black-and-white photography. Suggested day-hike destinations are offered, along with backpacking information.

Adkison, Ron. *Hiking Grand Canyon National Park*. Guilford, CT: Globe Pequot Press, 2011. A thorough hiking guide that includes detailed trail information, maps, trail profiles, and black-and-white photography. Day-hike destinations are suggested for most trails, but this 260-page guide is especially useful for backpackers, with information about campsites and water sources. Geology, natural history, and trail highlights make it a rich resource.

Annerino, John. *Hiking the Grand Canyon*. San Francisco: Sierra Club Books, 2006. Thousands of canyon hikers have consulted this small but mighty guide to the canyon's maintained trails, unmaintained trails, and unofficial routes. Natural history information, safety tips, trail details, and other essentials help backpackers plan multiday trips.

Belknap, Buzz. *Grand Canyon River Guide*. Boulder City, NV: Westwater Books, 2007. This book's 95 pages include a sequence of river maps showing rapids, topography detail, and sights. Details about history, geology, anthropology, plants, and animals are also included.

Lane, Brian. *Hikernut's Grand Canyon Companion*. Sedona, AZ: A Sense of Nature, 2007. For anyone planning to day hike or backpack the canyon's corridor trails—Bright Angel, South Kaibab, or North Kaibab—this 90-page book is an excellent resource. Detailed trail descriptions, maps, color photographs, and a gear list are particularly helpful for first-time backpackers or those new to the canyon. Trail profiles include not only distance and elevation but also a key to the canyon's geologic layers.

Lankford, Andrea. *Biking the Grand Canyon Area*. Boulder, CO: Westcliff, 2003. A former park ranger has written this guide to biking in and around the park, featuring everything from sedate paved roads to mountain bike adventures. She includes maps and trip-planning tips.

Martin, Tom. *Day Hikes from the River*. Flagstaff, AZ: Vishnu Temple Press, 2010. A hiking guide written from the perspective of the river, this book is indispensable for those on private boat trips. Information includes tips on where and how to tie in, campsites, topographic map sections, and detailed descriptions of 100 hikes.

Martin, Tom, and Duwain Whitis. *Guide to the Colorado River in Grand Canyon.* Flagstaff, AZ: Vishnu Temple Press, 2007. Campsites, rapids, natural history, and points of interest are included in this waterproof, mile-by-mile river guide. Maps include topographical detail, making this an excellent resource for river runners.

Thybony, Scott. *The Official Guide to Hiking Grand Canyon.* Grand Canyon, AZ: Grand Canyon Association, 2005. This easy-to-use and concise guide includes trail descriptions, topographic sections, and trail profiles for the park's most popular trails. Cultural and natural history information and color photographs round out the 68-page book.

Various authors. *Grand Canyon Trail Guides.* Grand Canyon, AZ: Grand Canyon Association, 1996–2006. These 26–46-page, pocket-size booklets cover individual trails, including Grandview, Hermit, North Kaibab, North and South Bass, and South Kaibab. The guides include cultural and natural history information along with trail descriptions and maps—real bargains for less than three bucks. A few are available as electronic downloads.

Williams, Tyler. *Canyoneering Arizona.* Flagstaff, AZ: Funhog Press, 2005. A guide to hiking, scrambling, climbing, and swimming canyons, coverage includes several Grand Canyon tributaries, including Paria Canyon, Soap Creek, Rider Canyon, Tanner Wash, and Diamond Creek.

GOOD READS

Dimock, Brad. *Sunk Without a Sound: The Tragic Colorado River Honeymoon of Glen and Bessie Hyde.* Flagstaff, AZ: Fretwater Press, 2001. This fascinating book recounts one of the Grand Canyon's most enigmatic river expeditions, the honeymoon voyage of the Hydes, who entered the canyon in 1928 and never returned.

Dutton, Clarence. *Tertiary History of the Grand Cañon District.* Tucson: University of Arizona Press, 2001. The U of A has reprinted this classic, first published in 1882. Dutton, who named many of Grand Canyon's temples, makes poetry of geology, and the illustrations by William Henry Holmes and Thomas Moran are breathtaking.

Fletcher, Colin. *The Man Who Walked Through Time.* New York: Vintage, 1989. A classic adventure narrative that describes Fletcher's trek through the length of Grand Canyon. Inspiring and evocative, his account remains as fresh today as when it was written.

Ghiglieri, Michael, and Tom Martin. *Over the Edge: Death in Grand Canyon.* Puma Press, 2001. These accounts of people who've met their deaths in Grand Canyon are not only fascinating but also useful in helping would-be canyoneers develop humility and preparedness.

Powell, John Wesley. *The Exploration of the Colorado River and Its Canyons.* New York: Penguin, 2003. A reprint of John Wesley's classic report, first published in 1872, that combines adventure, geology, and anthropology with stirring accounts of canyon scenes.

Stegner, Wallace. *Beyond the Hundredth Meridian: John Wesley Powell and the Second Opening of the West.* New York: Penguin, 1992. One of the West's most influential authors outlines John Wesley Powell's life and sets the stage for contemporary environmental issues.

MAPS

Black, Bronze. *Grand Canyon Map and Guide.* Flagstaff, AZ: Dragon Creek Publishing, 2008. An artistic map by a Colorado River guide and geologist chock-full of cultural and natural history, trail information, fun facts, and geologic details.

Kaibab National Forest. *North Kaibab Ranger District.* U.S. Department of Agriculture, U.S. Forest Service, 2003. For those who plan on back-roads touring in the aspen and pine forests of the Kaibab Plateau, this map is essential, showing forest roads, road type, distances, trails, and wilderness boundaries.

Kaibab National Forest. *Williams and Tusayan Ranger Districts.* U.S. Department of Agriculture, U.S. Forest Service, 2003. A helpful map for those planning on camping or touring in the forest south of the canyon. However, if your travels will be limited to multiuse trails close to the rim, you can probably make do with less detailed trail-specific maps available at the Tusayan Ranger Station.

Sky Terrain Trail Maps. *Grand Canyon National Park.* Boulder, CO: Sky Terrain, 2007.

An easy-to-read 1:40,000 topographic map that includes trails and backcountry use areas from Desert View to Point Sublime. Trail descriptions and profiles are also included. It's an excellent map for backpackers and hikers, although Bass and Thunder River Trails are off the map.

Trails Illustrated. *Grand Canyon National Park #261.* Evergreen, CO: National Geographic Society, 2010. A 1:35,000 topographic map that details central Grand Canyon, including trails, roads, and the most developed areas of the park.

USGS Quadrangles. *United States Geological Survey.* For an extended backcountry trip, the most detailed map (or maps) is the 7.5-minute 1:24,000 quadrangle matching your route. You can buy USGS quads in Flagstaff's numerous outdoors stores, or order them directly from USGS (888/275-8747, http://store.usgs.gov).

Internet Resources

GRAND CANYON
Grand Canyon National Park
www.nps.gov/grca
The park's official website is an excellent and ever-improving resource for anyone planning a canyon trip. Information includes downloads, maps, permit applications, and details about hiking, sightseeing, campgrounds, the latest weather, and much, much more.

Campground Reservations
www.recreation.gov
You can make campground reservations here, but this site also offers travel-planning tips and helpful links for the region and the rest of the nation.

Grand Canyon Association (GCA)
www.grandcanyon.org
The GCA, a nonprofit organization founded in 1932, uses money from sales to support Grand

Canyon National Park programs and publications. The GCA's stores at Grand Canyon do double-duty as information centers, and its online bookstore has a fine selection of books and maps. Joining the GCA helps support the park, and members receive discounts on classes and purchases.

Grand Canyon Field Institute
www.grandcanyon.org/fieldinstitute
Grand Canyon Field Institute (GCFI) offers programs that incorporate day-hiking, backpacking, and camping, with expert guides who focus on geology, archaeology, photography, and cultural or natural history.

Grand Canyon
National Park Foundation
www.grandcanyonfoundation.org
The foundation works to preserve and protect

the park by fostering stewardship and sponsoring such programs and projects as trail building and wildlife protection.

Grand Canyon Trust
www.grandcanyontrust.org

The trust advocates collaborative, practical solutions to challenges facing the Colorado Plateau and Grand Canyon, focusing on air quality, energy, forest health, water, Native American issues, and other topics.

Grand Canyon Volunteers
www.gcvolunteers.org

This group organizes single-day and multiday trips, from habitat restoration to trail maintenance, in the Grand Canyon area for volunteer conservationists. Grand Canyon Volunteers works with individuals and organizations to plan trips that give something back to the canyon.

Grand Canyon Hikers and Backpackers Association
www.gchba.org

The association promotes and advocates low-impact hiking and backpacking in Grand Canyon. Its website has useful information for trip planning, including status reports about water sources.

Grand Canyon Private Boaters Association
www.gcpba.org

Experienced river runners share information in this Web community, focusing on issues affecting Grand Canyon boating and posting announcements about permits, trips, and schedules.

Leave No Trace
www.lnt.org

This national organization explains and promotes low-impact ethics for responsible use and active stewardship of the outdoors.

SURROUNDING AREAS
Kaibab National Forest
www.fs.usda.gov/kaibab

Start here for current conditions, camping, hiking, and sightseeing in the North Kaibab, Tusayan, and Williams districts of the forest.

Coconino National Forest
www.fs.fed.us/r3/coconino

If you want to explore the Flagstaff Ranger District, or other areas on the Coconino, this website has the latest info about conditions, camping, hiking, and sightseeing.

Southwest Deserts
www.desertusa.com

Desert USA celebrates the people, places, and natural history of the Southwest's deserts. Though the site features a lot more advertising than in the past, it provides up-to-the-minute posts about events and conditions, such as which wildflowers are in bloom or current water levels at Lake Powell.

Glen Canyon National Recreation Area
www.nps.gov/glca

Learn more about boating, fishing, hiking, canyoneering, and sightseeing opportunities on Lake Powell and the canyon country from Lees Ferry to southern Utah.

Glen Canyon Natural History Association
www.glencanyonnha.org

This nonprofit organization supports programs and publications for Glen Canyon National Recreation Area, Glen Canyon Dam, Rainbow Bridge National Monument, and Grand Staircase–Escalante National Monument. The site includes information about visitors centers, museums, events, and hiking trails.

Bureau of Land Management (BLM)
www.blm.gov/az

Unpaved BLM roads travel 4,000 miles through rugged country in the Arizona Strip for remote camping, hiking, canyoneering, and sightseeing. For more information about the Paria Canyon–Vermilion Cliffs Wilderness Area or Grand Canyon–Parashant National Monument, start with the BLM's Arizona page.

Havasupai Tribe
www.havasupaitribe.com

This commercial site offers helpful information for planning a trip to Supai Village and Havasu Canyon, including maps, enticing photos, and information about helicopter and horseback tours as well as lodging. The tribe's official website (www.havasupai-nsn .gov) features information about the history, economy, and government of the Havasupai people.

Hopi Tribe
www.experiencehopi.com

The tribe's recently completed hotel in Moenkopi is the main focus here, but those planning to visit the Hopi Mesas will find helpful information about villages, heritage sites, and guide services. The tribe's official website (www.hopi-nsn.gov) has recent news releases and information about tribe government.

Hualapai Tribe
www.grandcanyonwest.com

Learn more about the Hualapai Nation and their Grand Canyon West attractions, including the Skywalk. The site describes lodging and tour options, such as white-water rafting with the Hualapai River Runners. The tribe's official website (www.hualapai-nsn.gov) includes information about Hualapai history, government, and economy.

Navajo Tribe
www.navajonationparks.org

Learn more about visiting the Navajo Nation's parks, including Antelope Canyon and the Little Colorado River Gorge. The site has information about hunting and fishing permits and fee schedules for camping and hiking on tribe lands. For information on the Navajo, visit the Navajo Nation's official website (www .navajo-nsn.gov).

www.discovernavajo.com

This site offers helpful information about lodging, attractions, events, and tours on the Navajo Reservation. Traditional stories and cultural history are included.

Arizona Trail Association
www.aztrail.org

The almost-completed nonmotorized Arizona Trail, more than 800 miles long, crosses the state from Utah to Mexico. Hikers, bicyclists, and equestrians can access sections of the trail on Grand Canyon's North and South Rims. The website provides directions and descriptions.

Museum of Northern Arizona (MNA)
www.musnaz.org

The MNA has been interpreting and preserving the cultural and natural history of the Colorado Plateau since 1928. Visit the website to find out more about current exhibitions, events, and programs.

GATEWAY TOWNS
Flagstaff
www.flagstaffarizona.org

Attractions, accommodations, and self-guided tours are highlighted on this site, focusing on northern Arizona's largest mountain town.

Kanab, Utah
www.visitkanab.info

Kanab makes a convenient base for exploring national parks and monuments in southern Utah and northern Arizona. You'll find lodging, dining, tours, recreation, and other travel information on this site.

Page
www.pagelakepowelltourism.com

With descriptions of lodging, tours, recreation, and sightseeing, this site will help you plan a stay in Page, on the edge of Lake Powell.

Williams
www.williamschamber.com

Williams bills itself as the Gateway to Grand Canyon, and the local chamber's website has information on canyon tours as well as local attractions, events, and history.

ARIZONA TRAVEL
Arizona Office of Tourism
www.arizonaguide.com

This site includes region-by-region information about visiting Arizona, including tour packages, lodging, events, and itineraries.

Arizona Highways Magazine
www.arizonahighways.com

Arizona's Department of Transportation publishes a monthly magazine with lavish photos of the state's attractions. This website highlights hiking trails, back-road drives, and events, and it also offers photography tips.

Arizona Travel Parks Association
www.azrvparks.com

This helpful site lists member RV parks and provides links to Arizona weather and attractions.

Index

List of Maps

www.moon.com

DESTINATIONS | ACTIVITIES | BLOGS | MAPS | BOOKS

MOON.COM is ready to help plan your next trip! Filled with fresh trip ideas and strategies, author interviews, informative travel blogs, a detailed map library, and descriptions of all the Moon guidebooks, Moon.com is all you need to get out and explore the world—or even places in your own backyard. While at Moon.com, sign up for our monthly e-newsletter for updates on new releases, travel tips, and expert advice from our on-the-go Moon authors. As always, when you travel with Moon, expect an experience that is uncommon and truly unique.

MOON IS ON FACEBOOK—BECOME A FAN!
JOIN THE MOON PHOTO GROUP ON FLICKR